Public Power, Private Dams

THE HELLS CANYON HIGH DAM CONTROVERSY

Karl Boyd Brooks

FOREWORD BY WILLIAM CRONON

In the years following World War II, the world's biggest dam was almost built in Hells Canyon on the Snake River in Idaho. Karl Boyd Brooks tells the story of the dam controversy, which became a referendum not only on public-power expansion but also on the environmental implications of New Deal natural-resources and economic policy.

Private-power critics of the Hells Canyon High Dam posed difficult questions about the implications of damming rivers to create power and to grow crops. Activists, attorneys, and scientists pioneered legal tactics and political rhetoric that would help to define the environmental movement in the 1960s. The debate, however, was less about endangered salmon or threatened wild country and more about who would control land and water and whether state enterprise or private capital would oversee the supply of electricity.

By thwarting the dam's construction, Snake Basin irrigators retained control over water as well as economic and political power in Idaho, putting the state on a postwar path that diverged markedly from that of bordering states. In the end, the opponents of the dam were responsible for the preservation of high deserts and mountain rivers from radical change.

University of Kansas.

WEYERHAEUSER ENVIRONMENTAL BOOKS

William Cronon, Editor

Weyerhaeuser Environmental Books explore human
relationships with natural environments in all their
variety and complexity. They seek to cast new light on
the ways that natural systems affect human communities,
the ways that people affect the environments of which
they are a part, and the ways that different cultural conceptions
of nature profoundly shape our sense of the world around us.
A complete listing of the books in the series appears at the end
of this book.

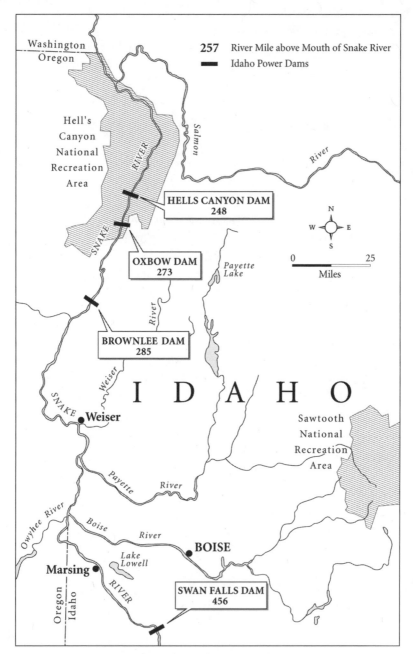

MAP 1. HELLS CANYON COUNTRY: The Salmon River, below Hells Canyon, still nurses the Northwest's principal salmon runs. Idaho Power's dams extinguished migratory fish runs from all rivers upstream. Map by Barry Levely.

Public Power, Private Dams

THE HELLS CANYON HIGH DAM CONTROVERSY

Karl Boyd Brooks

FOREWORD BY WILLIAM CRONON

UNIVERSITY OF WASHINGTON PRESS   Seattle and London

*Public Power, Private Dams: The Hells Canyon High Dam
Controversy* has been published with the assistance of
a grant from the Weyerhaeuser Environmental Books
Endowment, established by the Weyerhaeuser Company
Foundation, members of the Weyerhaeuser family,
and Janet and Jack Creighton.

© 2006 by the University of Washington Press
Printed in the United States of America
12 11 10 09 08 07 06   5 4 3 2 1
Designed by Pamela Canell

University of Washington Press
PO Box 50096, Seattle, WA 98145
www.washington.edu/uwpress

Library of Congress Cataloging-in-Publication Data
Brooks, Karl Boyd.
Public power, private dams : the Hells Canyon High Dam controversy /
Karl Boyd Brooks ; foreword by William Cronon.
p. cm.—(Weyerhaeuser environmental books)
Includes bibliographical references and index.
ISBN 0-295-98597-6 (hardback : alk. paper)
1. Dams—Snake River (Wyo.–Wash.)—Public opinion—History—
20th century.   2. Dams—Hells Canyon (Idaho and Or.)—Public
opinion—History—20th century.   3. Hydroelectric power plants—
Hells Canyon (Idaho and Or.)—Political aspects—History—20th
century.   4. Environmental policy—United States—History—20th
century.   5. Private companies—United States—Privileges and
immunities—History—20th century.   6. Idaho Power Company—
History—20th century.   7. Nature conservation—United States—
History—20th century.   I. Title.   II. Weyerhaeuser environmental book.
TC557.3.S63B76 2006   333.91'4097957—dc22   2005034678

TO MY MOTHER AND MY FATHER

CONTENTS

FOREWORD

Why So Important a Story Is So Little Known

WILLIAM CRONON

In the decade following the Second World War, the government of the United States proposed to build the world's highest dam in the nation's deepest gorge, a place called Hells Canyon on the Snake River between Idaho and Oregon. Deeper by more than a quarter mile than the Grand Canyon of Arizona, Hells Canyon was—and is—virtually unknown to most Americans. Unlike the Colorado River's far more celebrated chasm, it has never been a destination for tourists from all over the world.

When the Bureau of Reclamation proposed for Hells Canyon the greatest hydroelectric structure that any nation had yet constructed, few argued that such a dam would violate the sublime beauty or pristine wilderness of the Snake River gorge. At a time when dams were almost universally acclaimed as among the most benign and heroic technological achievements that humanity had ever conceived, there seemed little reason to doubt that the Hells Canyon High Dam would join other great engineering triumphs like Boulder and Bonneville and Grand Coulee as evidence of how an enlightened government could benefit its citizens by harnessing nature's gifts to advance the goal of human progress. Farms would flourish in the desert, factories would yield a cornucopia of goods and jobs, cities would grow to ever greater prosperity, and ordinary Americans would gain the countless benefits of cheap electricity—lights, motors, phones, radios, televisions, appliances—that made the American standard of living the envy of the world. Here, surely, was a project that would fulfill the longstanding dream of progressive conservation: the greatest good for the greatest number for the longest time. Who could doubt its countless benefits?

Despite all these advantages, the Hells Canyon High Dam was never built. Moreover, the failure of the project was so complete that most Americans have never heard of it. Even historians, engineers, and environmental activists who make it their business to keep track of such things rarely mention the fate of Hells Canyon in the stories they tell about rivers and dams in the American West. Unlike the famously unbuilt Echo Park Dam that the Bureau of Reclamation proposed to construct within the boundaries of Dinosaur National Monument at about the same time, the Hells Canyon High Dam has basically been forgotten. Not much better known are the three much smaller dams that were built instead, not by the federal government but, crucially, by a private power company that against all odds succeeded in defeating the enormous governmental forces arrayed against it. This historical neglect is both curious and unfortunate, since the controversy surrounding Hells Canyon in the 1950s arguably foreshadowed many of the debates that would emerge by the end of the twentieth century as unresolved questions for American environmental politics in the twenty-first century. If ever there were a history worth remembering as we seek to understand our present environmental circumstances, surely this is it.

How the Hells Canyon High Dam came to be forgotten, and why our failure to remember it is unfortunate, turn out to be far more interesting historical questions than our neglect of them would suggest. We can therefore be grateful that this little-known never-built dam has finally been chronicled in *Public Power, Private Dams: The Hells Canyon High Dam Controversy*, written by an author ideally suited for the task. Karl Brooks, an environmental historian at the University of Kansas, is a native Idahoan who grew up in Boise, less than a hundred miles from Hells Canyon. Trained as an attorney, he first learned of the dam controversy while working on a legal case during the 1990s. Having served three terms in the Idaho State Senate, he was intimately familiar with the state's politics, and instantly recognized the significance of the Idaho Power Company's success in defeating the federal government's proposed dam in the 1950s. When Brooks eventually decided to trade his legal and political career for that of an academic environmental historian, he seized upon the Hells Canyon High Dam for his first major research project. The result, happily, is a subtly argued and gracefully written book that finally gives this undeservedly forgotten story the treatment it deserves.

To understand why the defeat of the Hells Canyon High Dam remains important today, one must temporarily set aside a much more familiar historical narrative that portrays an emerging opposition to western dam construction as a first beachhead in the rise of a new political movement called environmentalism. The defeat of the proposed dam at Echo Park in

Dinosaur National Monument in 1956 is typically presented as a classic turning point in which advocates for wilderness, led most prominently by the Sierra Club's flamboyant David Brower, succeeded in defending a national park against the forces of development that half a century earlier had built an infamous dam in the Hetch Hetchy Valley of Yosemite National Park. (The best account of this controversy is that of Mark Harvey in *A Symbol of Wilderness: Echo Park and the American Conservation Movement*, reprinted by the University of Washington Press as a Weyerhaeuser Environmental Classic.)

Important though it undoubtedly was, Echo Park can mislead us into thinking that wilderness advocacy and defense of national parklands were the sole sources of resistance to federal dam construction in the 1950s. At Hells Canyon, almost all parties to the controversy agreed that one or more dams should be built to produce electricity on the Snake River. Protecting a wild river was far from their main concern. Instead, their disagreements centered on the appropriate role of the federal government in developing western resources—a question that could hardly be more relevant to American politics today.

Echo Park can easily mislead in another important way as well. Brower cuts such a dashing figure as the eloquent and brilliantly skillful lone hero standing up to the engineers and policymakers of the Bureau of Reclamation that it is almost impossible not to cast the story in the familiar terms of David and Goliath. It's a kind of tale in which we love to root for the underdog and instinctively identify with the colorful main character. But precisely because Echo Park can so easily be converted into a story of Brower's personal charisma and heroism, it just as easily obscures the complex organizations and processes that would increasingly come to characterize environmental law and policymaking in the second half of the twentieth century. As Max Weber long ago observed, one of the most defining features of modernity is the rise of bureaucracies led by professionals whose expert knowledge enables them to manage the complex organizations and technologies without which modern life would be impossible. Although we most commonly associate this Weberian insight with the rise of the modern state, in fact large-scale organizations have come to dominate virtually every aspect of our lives, from government to the corporate economy to education to medicine to law to . . . you name it. Even nonprofit organizations like the Sierra Club exhibit these same bureaucratic tendencies, and it would not be at all difficult to devise a Weberian interpretation of David Brower as a new kind of manager leading a new kind of institution to give organized voice to a new political movement.

The trouble, of course, is that "faceless bureaucracies" rarely make for compelling reading, so we are drawn to a limited number of stories about them that too often caricature how they actually do their work. David vs. Goliath is one such story, tempting us to focus on an individual with whom we can readily identify as opposed to an organization that challenges both our empathy and our understanding. Other familiar stories about modern organizations include what we could call corruption narratives, in which an otherwise benign institution becomes malignant through the evil actions of its leaders, and stories of Kafkaesque paranoia, in which an individual becomes entangled in a web of bureaucratic intrigue so irrational and inscrutable that it offers no hope of either understanding or escape. Few indeed are the narratives of large organizations that succeed in engaging readers without falling into one or another of these simplifying plot lines— plot lines which, however compelling, surely do inadequate justice to the complexity or importance of such institutions for our world.

Among the greatest virtues of *Public Power, Private Dams* is that Karl Brooks does not shy away from the challenge of exploring the many roles of large organizations in the debate over Hells Canyon during the 1950s. The question at the center of that debate seems simple enough: who should be responsible for damming the Snake River to produce electricity, the federal government or a private power company? But in fact, neither of the two antagonists that seem so clear in this question can be so simply described. The Idaho Power Company was a large organization representing a host of different interests, tied to local agents and advocates in Idaho whose concerns and actions evolved over time. To say that the federal government was hardly monolithic is to understate the obvious, but in the case of the Hells Canyon High Dam, even the agencies directly responsible for the would-be dam were multiple, confused, and conflicting. The Bureau of Reclamation, the Army Corps of Engineers, and the Bonneville Power Administration were all involved, each with different agendas that made their cooperation challenging. The state governments of Idaho, Oregon, and Washington all had interests in the hydroelectric project, with different state agencies inevitably expressing different views about the goals of development. Upriver interests on the Snake were in stark conflict with downriver interests on the Columbia, the federal government implicitly siding with downriver interests while the Idaho Power Company mobilized upriver interests on its own behalf. And so on and on.

What enables Brooks to make sense of all these organizational conflicts without resorting to a too-easy plot line of bureaucratic corruption or paranoia or David vs. Goliath is his core insight that the Hells Canyon debate about public vs. private ownership straddles a defining fault line of twentieth-century American politics. This fault line has only deepened with time. The many individuals and agencies that argued for federal construction of the Hells Canyon High Dam saw themselves continuing the heroic achievements of a triumphant modern state that in the 1940s was associated in the minds of all Americans with Franklin Roosevelt's New Deal. Conversely, those who believed that the Idaho Power Company should instead build its much smaller dams were very much opposed to the New Deal's extension of federal power, casting the debate as a conflict between big government on the one hand and private enterprise on the other. Sound familiar? Because Hells Canyon came to a head just as Dwight Eisenhower's Republican administration was seeking to roll back what it saw as excesses of the New Deal, the power company gained key political allies in a campaign that in an earlier era would have seemed quixotic. In the end, private dams triumphed over public power.

Brooks masterfully conveys the complex organizational maneuvering that ultimately led to this unexpected result, but what makes his book so compelling is his ability to keep the core ideological question—what should be the limits of state power and action?—at the center of the narrative. Brooks offers no simple answer to this question, preferring instead to explore its myriad subtleties and contradictions, so that readers of all political persuasions will find much in this book both to challenge and support their views. Reading about the Hells Canyon controversy half a century later, it is impossible not to see in it an early example of the conservative reaction against New Deal liberalism that would finally reach full flower during the administration of President Ronald Reagan in the 1980s. In the intervening years, many western states, Idaho not least among them, have become increasingly suspicious of federal power and ever more resistant to environmental policies that limit private action through government intervention.

For all the apparent obscurity of its topic, then, *Public Power, Private Dams* offers numerous insights with surprisingly wide-ranging implications. Those who imagine that conservative resistance to state power emerged as a new feature of American environmental politics in the last quarter of the twentieth century would do well to reflect on the parallel forms of resistance that this book portrays in a much earlier period. Those drawn to histories focusing on the colorful doings of heroic individuals will be reminded by this book that environmental change in the modern era has been the product of collective debate and action realized through the agency of organizations both public and private—and that these too can yield compelling stories for those with the patience to discover them. And finally, those who seek to understand the changing nature of environmental politics in our own time could do a lot worse than to ponder the implications of this little-known story about a long-forgotten dam that was never built in a deep Idaho canyon that, to do this day, still sits atop one of the great ideological fault lines of American life.

PREFACE

The morning's *Kansas City Star* flew a banner headline about the collapse of a proposed merger between the region's two great electric utility companies. The business of making and selling electricity was changing fast. The two corporations would probably have to find new partners or other power companies would snap them up. My seatmate on the mid-evening flight to Chicago noticed me reading the story avidly, scrawling notes in the margins. He casually asked what I did for a living. "I'm a historian," I replied. I had the perfect opening to explain how my history of electricity choices in another place illuminated today's energy prospects in our home area. But when I said the words "anadromous fish" and proudly told him I was writing about a place called "Hells Canyon, out west, on the Idaho-Oregon border," he glazed over.

What I should have said to my disappointed acquaintance that January night goes like this: "This is a hell of a tale about a hell of a place. It's even called Hell, . . . Hells Canyon, that is. And I know it's one hell of a place because I've been there." To my midwestern businessman seatmate on that winter-night flight I should have then said, "This place and time matter a lot to me, and if I tell their story right, they should matter to you."

Hells Canyon matters to me. I have inched down its single dirt road, brakes hot, driver intent. I have watched a golden eagle lever ponderously into the cold spring morning air, gorged with roadkill lamb. I have sunk into my seat as our two-place prop plane dipped onto final approach to the canyon's only airstrip, a graveled bench that teeters above the river below Brownlee Dam. I have peered over its eastern rim from Dry Diggins lookout, high up in the Seven Devils Mountains on the Idaho side, to see the Snake twisting silver-blue far below in the warm fall dust-haze. I have scanned Wild Sheep Rapids from an overlook, rafts tied up along the bank below us, hearing its ceaseless roar as sixty thousand cubic feet per second of early May snowmelt pounded downstream toward Pittsburg Landing, Lewiston, and the Columbia confluence. I have seen the Snake literally grab a raft like a coyote grabs a mouse, shake it and flip it up, and over, and out into the white rollers, as its pilot, our party's ablest boatman, arced through the air and disappeared, without a splash, into Wild Sheep's crest. Five long minutes later, our own raft safely through, I hit the water myself, on purpose this time, bobbing along frantically as we struggled to right the overturned raft, six months of winter along the Continental Divide seeping through my wetsuit ("Cold, Jesus, I can't believe it's *this* cold").

I should have then told my seatmate, as we raced high above the cultivated prairie blackness toward Chicago, that the Snake's power planted Hells Canyon in my own postwar history. As a boy growing up in the middle 1960s in Boise, Idaho, I played in tan grass foothills beneath gigantic steel towers. They marched in a long, swooping arc clear across the Boise Front, carrying six strands of high-tension cable up from Hells Canyon, down into the Treasure Valley. The towers ended where the city began, at an Idaho Power Company substation next to where the Oregon Trail dipped down into the valley off the high, dry Mountain Home Desert. Humming perceptibly over the car sounds along Amity Road, the Idaho Power transformers intrigued us. Then we went back to testing soapbox racers along Amity's narrow shoulder.

A dozen vehicles an hour in the late-evening summer shine barely disturbed our test track then. Today, fifteen thousand people live, and another ten thousand work, within a mile of Amity Road. Many design, assemble, and test semiconductors. It is a business that could have sprung up only in a place where electricity and land were cheap—wages, too.

Just seventy-five miles northwest of my Boise birthplace, those electric towers began their march up out of Hells Canyon in 1956, the year I was born. They carried their humming cargo, Idaho Power Company's hard-won bounty, up from the Snake, across the mountains, and out onto southern Idaho's Snake River Plain. Though I thought the towers were cool, a space-age sign that my little corner of the West was worth bragging about, none of their history mattered to me then.

Now my seatmate would be there with me, under the towers, listening to the wind off eastern Oregon's Blue Mountains whine through their cables, seeing my hometown spread out across the Boise River valley, powered by their precious electrical cargo-current. Then I would tell him how I first came to think about, and to question, the tale of those towers.

My Hells Canyon history would jump forward nearly thirty years. As a busy litigating attorney with the Boise office of a big western law firm, I had little time to spare in summer 1992. I was coming off three terms in the Idaho State Senate, plotting my continuing rise toward statewide office, billing as many chargeable hours as I could to the firm's clients. I had been politically active since high school, when I enthusiastically backed Senator Frank Church's and Governor Cecil Andrus's efforts to defend my home state's natural beauty against heedless waste. For the next twenty years, I had wondered why Idahoans seemed harsher about nature's purposes, less interested in my kind of environmental politics. Legislative service convinced me that Idahoans' experiences after World War II somehow explained so much hostility toward the federal government. Somewhere in that history lay the roots of resistance to national authority, the skepticism that impeded environmentalism's spread after its exciting emergence in the early 1970s. A lawsuit encouraged me to see how the Northwest's postwar past explained why Idaho seemed so different from its northwestern neighbors, Oregon and Washington.

My law firm was gearing up to sue the U.S. government on behalf of a young, crippled truck driver. His neck had been broken when a Forest Service logging road collapsed beneath his water tanker. But his trial was still a ways off, and as we attorneys sparred with the U.S. Attorney's office, my firm was pursuing different quarry. Typically, we represented big and successful businesses, but my supervising partner's practice focused on helping victims, and he had agreed to help the Nez Perce Tribe for free.

The Nez Perce Indians felt aggrieved. Their reservation two hundred miles north of Boise occupied a remnant of the Snake Basin homeland that their people had inhabited for more than a thousand years. To confine the Nez Perce to this triangular redoubt, along the Salmon and Snake rivers, the United States had negotiated a treaty in 1855. The treaty preserved to the Nez Perce their usual and accustomed salmon-fishing grounds, but by the early 1990s the migratory fish were disappearing. The Nez Perce were feeling betrayed: by the federal government certainly, but especially by dams that transformed Snake River current into hydroelectricity and, as a by-product, barred migrating adult fish from reaching their upriver spawning beds and down-running juvenile smolts from reaching the ocean.

What the Indians wanted from my firm was nothing less than a legal assault on the dams that thwarted the Snake River's migratory fish runs. However, the Nez Perce did not intend to take on all the dams—eleven of them, eight built by the United States—between central Idaho and the mouth of the Columbia. Instead, they wanted to challenge only three Idaho Power Company dams deep within Hells Canyon. Silver tendrils from those dams had reached out of the mountains, across my native foothills, and through my remembered Idaho.

Tasked to help build the tribe's case on an emergency basis, I walked five blocks west from my law office to Idaho Power's new general offices. There, I joined a small squad of lawyers and legal assistants hurriedly examining and loosely organizing documents supplied by Idaho Power. Trial lawyers call this phase of trying a case "discovery." No truer term described the effect this work would have on me.

That was my first time in the new headquarters building. On my only other visit to the company's executive nerve center, I had gone to its older, art deco building across Idaho Street. During that visit, in fall 1988, Idaho Power's chief lobbyist had presented me, or rather my legislative reelection campaign, with a sizable contribution. I had not sought the contribution, but I did not reject it either. I was proud of my emerging record as the timber-company lawyer with the best pro-environmental voting record among Boise's eight-member delegation in the state senate.

Although I spent only a couple of days helping my colleagues, and left the law firm (and political campaigning and, ultimately, the practice of law altogether) before the Indians' case against Idaho Power advanced much further, I discovered something for myself. The process of sifting through cardboard boxes in that windowless conference room, boxes stuffed with yellowing onionskin copies, tattered newspaper cuttings, and blue-faded mimeographs, threw my switch. Electric current arced through my own western environmental history. The more I sorted, the more I paused to read. The more I read, the more I murmured, "Damn, I didn't know that."

While I now know far more than I did in 1992, I still know far less about Idaho Power's Hells Canyon hydroelectric complex than I should. The company's general counsel barred me from using the corporation's archives in early 1999, as I wrote this book. I told him Idaho Power would benefit from a thorough, independent history about the company's moment in the national spotlight. I still believe that. Moreover, I suspect that a publicly regulated utility, whose principal asset is a public license to dam a public waterway, cannot long maintain the legal fiction that records connected with obtaining that license are somehow "private." However, that test is a ways down the road.

By the time my discovery work ended in *Nez Perce Tribe v. Idaho Power Company*, I had found the trail to a tale, a hell of a tale about a hell of a place in a remarkable time: Hells Canyon of the Snake River, on the Idaho-Oregon border, in the decade or so between the end of World War II and my appearance on history's stage in 1956.

The Nez Perce people ultimately lost their case at the pretrial stage. A federal judge in Boise decided that the United States had properly sacrificed the tribe's treaty fishing rights by licensing Idaho Power to build its three hydropower dams in Hells Canyon. Before the litigants could test his decision on appeal, they settled their dispute. We will probably never know whether, as a matter of federal law, Idaho Power improperly seized the Nez Perce Tribe's treaty rights by planting three dams in Hells Canyon. We should know, as a matter of historical fact, how important Hells Canyon was, not just to Indians and utility managers in Idaho, but to farmers and laborers, politicians and lawyers, federal planners and ordinary electricity customers throughout the nation.

The Pacific Northwest, that corner of the United States framed by the Columbia and Snake rivers falling down the Continental Divide into the ocean, cradles the world's most hydroelectrified society. While the salmon's ancestral waters trace the Northwest's boundaries, the electricity drawn from those same waters made the modern Northwest after World War II.

To make the modern Northwest took a lot of hydroelectricity. To generate that much electricity took many dams. Nearly all of those dams appeared in barely twenty-five years, from the end of the Second World War through 1970. Hydroelectric histories there are aplenty. Most of the Northwest's major power dams were built by the United States, so most of the region's hydroelectric history details how various federal dams rose against the rivers' currents to spin out their humming cargo across webs of steel. Another study of the postwar dam-building era, when the modern Northwest emerged, needs hardly any defense.

However, my hydroelectric history is different. It is a tale of the dam-that-never-was, Hells Canyon High Dam. The High Dam deserves close study. It would have been not only the biggest federal power dam in the hydroelectric homeland of the northwestern United States but also the biggest dam in the world. So instead of explaining why a federal dam was built in the Northwest, I ask: Why *didn't* a federal dam appear in the post-war era in that region of the country most dependent on hydroelectricity generated by the United States? And rather than ask, as so many fine hydroelectric historians do, how the United States decided to locate a new dam in a particular place, I ask: How did the United States fail to dam the premier waterpower site during the most intensive phase of dam building in the nation's most hydro-dependent region? The decision not to build Hells Canyon High Dam seems unexpected, almost shocking, given the time and place. Yet even in an era when the federal government was racing to construct dams throughout the Pacific Northwest, public dams encountered economic limits, incited political opponents, and faced natural obstacles too great to overcome.

This book also asks a slightly different, but equally important, question: Why, in the same time and place, did a private power company succeed in building three small dams and the United States fail to build one stupendous dam? This is another "dam history," but not about a mighty federal dam. Rather, it explains how High Hells Canyon, the biggest dam ever planned, died on the drawing board. It illuminates how American law operated to decide that an obscure private electric utility company should build three small dams that, taken together, generated less hydroelectricity than the single, large federal dam would have spun out.

Knowing more about the Hells Canyon controversy helps us wonder constructively about America's energy future. We use fantastic quantities of electricity. The computers that define our postindustrial information age run on electricity. Our electrical system undergirds our way of living, its organization and management as important to capitalism and community as any feature of the technological and economic landscape. We have dammed rivers and overturned mountains to reach the fuel that makes power. Control over that power shifts daily, coalescing into multinational energy businesses, fracturing into new corporate and social forms that seem to change weekly in response to investment opportunities and legal opinions. To decide how to use power we need guidance desperately.

We should care about a place far off to the west and about a time now hazily remembered for Ike's broad grin and Korea's frozen hell. During the ten years of the Hells Canyon controversy, Americans engaged in a passionate, profound discussion about how to supply their demands for energy. Had the federal government built Hells Canyon High Dam, publicly owned electricity would have captured the nation's greatest untapped hydroelectric resource. Instead, a small private power company received a limited license to manage a small portion of the Snake's total potential power.

Idaho Power's federal license to build its three Hells Canyon dams expires soon. The company is scrambling to secure another license because the unpredictable economics and politics of electricity expose its principal asset to unprecedented challenges. Another utility could buy the company lock, stock, and dam. Or the United States could relicense the Hells Canyon complex only if its owner agrees to use more water to aid migrating fish, leaving less to make power. Alternatively, some combination of the Federal Energy Regulatory Commission, Congress, and the federal courts could decide that Idaho Power's dams have so damaged endangered salmon and steelhead trout in the Snake Basin that their owner, whoever that might be, must recompense the nation.

The American people continually decide the fate of the Snake, the Columbia, and the Northwest's other power-producing rivers. We face hard choices in Hells Canyon. Some understanding of the last big controversy over the Snake's fate should help us choose better, wiser ways of living along the water with its other inhabitants.

ACKNOWLEDGMENTS

Any work of historical scholarship owes debts too vast and numerous to be catalogued fully and accurately. This book is no exception. Its dedication salutes the two people who, more than any others, got me thinking about living in the Northwest. From my mother I learned to read. Her passion for the written word still nourishes me. My father taught me how to live outside, in the fullest sense of both words. Each time I hike, fish, hunt, ski, or help my own children do so, I pass some of his accumulated knowledge to the future.

As the book's introduction will describe, this account of the Hells Canyon controversy originated during my active practice of law in the 1980s and early 1990s in Boise, Idaho. To legal colleagues Brian King, Walter Bithell, John Clute, and Steven Andersen, I offer thanks for their inspiration and indulgence as I tried to balance the lawyer/politician/scholar calculus. Later, at the Idaho Conservation League, my bosses Glen Stewart and Rick Johnson enabled me to start making sense of the political and legal world I had just left. Kathy Perkins played an important part in encouraging me to pursue the thread I first grasped in those days and in helping me to get started down the road that became this book.

Yet, in a real sense, this work of history saw its genesis during my graduate study at the University of Kansas in the late 1990s under the direction of Donald Worster. I owe him debts nearly as large as those I owe my parents. He believed in my potential as a historian. He took a chance on me. Moreover, he bore magnificently the many burdens that I brought into his office as a middle-aged nontraditional student of unorthodox pedigree for historical study. As his colleague at the University of Kansas, I treasure our opportunity to work together. Don's many close, thoughtful readings of this manuscript have improved it immeasurably.

Others who have read and commented on it deserve my hearty thanks, beginning with my University of Kansas graduate-school colleagues Kip Curtis, John Egan, Dale Nimz, and Lisa Brady. Members of my dissertation committee—Ted Wilson, Peter Mancall, Rob Glicksman, and Dietrich Earnhart—gave me the benefit of their enormous collective wisdom and patience. During a very difficult two-year period, both in my and this book's lives, series editor Bill Cronon and the University of Washington's Lita Tarver demonstrated both the virtues of decency and the crafts of editorship. Along the way, conference panelists and commentators, including Arthur McEvoy and Paul Hirt, spotted the book-to-be's flaws and helped me unlock its potential. Mary Ribesky, of the University of Washington Press, shepherded me professionally through the editing odyssey. And at the end, Mary Brooks contributed her confidence and passion, along with invaluable indexing help.

During the book's lengthy gestation, archivists' and librarians' courtesies and hard work uncovered invaluable resources, some buried in dusty back rooms under fishing gear and others neatly arranged and promptly delivered to my writing table. I thank kindly the professional staffs at the Eisenhower Presidential Library in Abilene, Kansas, and the Truman Presidential Library in Independence, Missouri, who make our section of the Missouri Basin such a gold mine for postwar environmental history. Archivists at two government agencies central to this story—at the Federal Energy Regulatory Commission in Washington, D.C., and at the Oregon Department of Fish and Wildlife in Clackamas and Portland, Oregon— devoted many hours to locating records indispensable to explaining the Hells Canyon controversy. In the state archives of Idaho and Oregon, in Boise and in Salem, capable professionals directed me to holdings that revealed secrets long kept. In particular, Steven King, of the Oregon Department of Fish and Wildlife, took special care to make sure I understood his agency's viewpoint and handled the science of fish as well as a lawyer/ historian can.

During my doctoral study at the University of Kansas, the Madison and Lila Self Graduate Fellowship supplied generous and crucial support.

Hundreds of other friends, colleagues, teachers, and students have each contributed to my fulfilling the objective I set fifteen years ago: to explain what happened in Hells Canyon during the first fifteen years after World War II. Their humor, their food and drink, and their simple confidence in my capacity to achieve my goal mattered so much. Somewhere between draft and accepted manuscript, my two children, Jenni and Dylan, celebrated my birthday by baking a cake in the shape of Hells Canyon. In the late spring of 2004, to celebrate our lives together, we floated the Snake River through Hells Canyon for three thrilling, satisfying days. This book has changed my children's lives as much as it has changed my own, and for their love and inspiration, I can never thank them enough.

ABBREVIATIONS

APA	Administrative Procedure Act
APPA	American Public Power Association
BPA	Bonneville Power Administration
CBIAC	Columbia Basin Inter-Agency Committee
CVA	Columbia Valley Administration
DEPA	Defense Electric Power Agency
EEI	Edison Electric Institute
FCO	Fish Commission of Oregon
FERC	Federal Energy Regulatory Commission
FPC	Federal Power Commission
FWS	U.S. Fish and Wildlife Service
IDFG	Idaho Department of Fish and Game
ISHS	Idaho State Historical Society
ISRA	Idaho State Reclamation Association
LCRFDP	Lower Columbia River Fishery Development Program
NFU	National Farmers Union
NHCA	National Hells Canyon Association
NRECA	National Rural Electric Cooperative Association
NWPPA	Northwest Public Power Association
ODFW	Oregon Department of Fish and Wildlife
PGE	Portland General Electric Company
PNDA	Pacific Northwest Development Association
PUFN	*Public Utilities Fortnightly*
TVA	Tennessee Valley Authority
WRPC	Water Resources Policy Commission

PUBLIC POWER, PRIVATE DAMS

1 INTRODUCTION

Hells Canyon High Dam and the Postwar Northwest

Both nature and people made Hells Canyon's postwar history. Fish swimming from sea to mountains and drifting back again weave two diverse watersheds, the Snake and Columbia, into the Pacific Northwest. Water flowing through Hells Canyon links the Snake Basin to the Columbia. Yet, as the twentieth century unfolded, Snake and Columbia Basin people came to value water differently. In the Columbia Basin, people used water principally as a tool to make hydroelectricity. By contrast, water stored amid the Snake Basin's distinctive topography, soil, and climate made irrigated agriculture the predominant relationship between humans and nature.

Environmental predicates to the human history of the postwar Hells Canyon controversy deserve study in their own right. Landforms and waterways do not merely reflect cultural impressions from humans who have successively occupied the Northwest. Rather, the Snake Basin's natural features and forces have continuously influenced human behavior. Though varied peoples have adapted nature to serve their material needs, the Snake Basin's land and water, its snowfall and fish runs, exercise the prerogative of sovereignty: they make their own history.

The Snake Basin's arable soil, the river's kinetic energy in Hells Canyon, and the rich anadromous fishery in its chief tributary, the Salmon River, exercised power over the controversy about electrifying Hells Canyon. They were historical actors before they became natural resources, and they remained so even after dams began to rise in the canyon. Northwest histories have begun blurring intellectual boundaries that separate culture from nature. Yet any solid understanding of why Hells Canyon became "a controversy" must be grounded firmly both in the water that sustains life in this place and in its human inhabitants' actions. Together, they made Hells

Canyon worth fighting for during the postwar years. One human era's dispute about the Northwest's natural elements recast land, water, and non-human creatures into new relationships. Thus rearranged, nature in the Northwest still shapes succeeding histories.

The New Deal after 1932 set the stage for the Hells Canyon controversy by making the Columbia Basin depend more on public hydroelectricity than did the Snake Basin. New Deal hydropower strategy subordinated regional biology to national economy and state sovereignty to federal primacy. A decisive moment in the Columbia Basin's hydroelectric transformation came when Grand Coulee Dam transferred power over the region's salmon from state to federal hands. New Deal legal innovations erected an administrative state to govern this new public power domain. Industrial production in World War II consolidated federal control over water and fish after 1941.

Ambitious and self-confident after easing economic depression and helping win the war, federal hydroelectric managers after 1945 tried to extend their authority upriver from the Columbia Basin. Their postwar offensive targeted the Snake Basin for annexation into the hydroelectric domain. High Hells Canyon Dam's hydropower would fuel their push to the Continental Divide. To reach the Snake Basin, federal power agencies first had to claim economic primacy for power supply in the Columbia Basin. Downriver private utility businesses after 1946 conceded to federal agencies the initiative for meeting their future power needs. Then, between 1947 and 1948, federal managers overcame downriver political resistance to new upstream power dams. Federal managers negotiated with Oregon and Washington a fishery-conservation plan that effectively sacrificed Snake River salmon and steelhead trout to the upriver offensive. Administrative and technological precedents established at Grand Coulee during the New Deal would limit postwar fish-conservation efforts to the lower Columbia River.

Federal and corporate rivals clashed for hydroelectric authority over the Snake in Hells Canyon. Hells Canyon provoked a fierce ideological and economic contest between public and corporate electricity. Idaho Power Company's victory came after what amounted to a national referendum against New Deal hydroelectric strategy. Each contestant invested Hells Canyon with symbolic status. Each worked hard and successfully to nationalize the politics of its hydroelectrification. After 1948, Hells Canyon's fate became a national political issue. Power policy shaped postwar politics when Dwight Eisenhower's 1952 presidential campaign dramatized opposition not only to Hells Canyon High Dam but also to the Democratic Party's entire

New Deal hydroelectric strategy. President Eisenhower's promise to build dams in "partnership" with private business recast the Hells Canyon controversy. Idaho Power and High Dam advocates argued their claims before the Federal Power Commission for eight years. This epic legal case about power and primacy culminated in the FPC's 1955 decision to license Idaho Power's three-dam project and the Supreme Court's and Congress' ratification of this choice in 1957.

Idaho Power's political and legal victory unplugged New Deal hydropower expansion in the Northwest. Hells Canyon High Dam perfectly expressed the New Deal credo of using cheap hydropower to exploit river basins' maximum economic potential. The campaign over High Hells Canyon energized new contestants. After 1957, they struggled to define not only the public interest in the Snake River flowing through Hells Canyon but also the scope of the public interest in all forms of nature. This Hells Canyon history explains how and why these things happened.

In the postwar era, in the decade or so following World War II, Americans argued as passionately about electricity as they do today about education. Upwardly mobile politicians won elections, and downwardly mobile ones lost them, because of their stand on power dams. The nation's courts made front-page news, and new law, by adjudicating rival claims to water and the life it sustained.

In Hells Canyon of the Snake River, along the Idaho-Oregon border, in the Pacific Northwest, the postwar controversy about hydropower united midwestern labor unions and southern cotton farmers. General Dwight Eisenhower made Hells Canyon the keynote of the first speech in his victorious campaign for president. Home to more mountain goats than voters, Hells Canyon's uncertain fate nevertheless captivated the nation's citizens.

Hells Canyon ignited such an intense controversy following World War II because powerful popular ideas promised such different futures for the Snake Basin. The Hells Canyon controversy did not demand a national verdict on the question of preserving wildness. Its combatants assumed power dams there would replace a wild river with a managed waterway. So the Hells Canyon controversy was not like the better-known struggle over Echo Canyon, though the issue of dams in both wild places engaged Americans during the postwar era. Both Hells Canyon and Echo Canyon encouraged citizens to consider new values about nature transformed, but each posed different questions about the old ways of living with water.

In the struggle over Echo Canyon on the Colorado Plateau, opponents of dams rallied to the cause of nature untrammeled. A federally designated monument encompassed dam builders' target. Conservationists seized this strategic advantage to articulate the outlines of a new philosophy about natural values in an industrial, urban society. These values—scenic beauty, open space, solitude, vigorous recreation—would inspire far-reaching dislocations in Americans' attitudes and actions as the postwar years waned. Out of this shift grew a political movement, environmentalism, that gives Echo Canyon its special historic significance.[1]

The Hells Canyon controversy simultaneously engaged many of Echo Park's principals—Dwight Eisenhower and Wayne Morse, Oscar Chapman and Douglas McKay. However, they did not define their differences in terms of protecting wilderness. Instead, the protagonists passionately disagreed for more than a decade about how to dam the Snake River flowing through Hells Canyon. Out of their struggle emerged, unsteadily at first but with growing momentum after 1957, new legal definitions of "the public interest" in flowing water. Legal change raised novel questions about the ecological consequences of industrializing undammed rivers. The Hells Canyon controversy between public and private power stimulated new doubts about the wisdom of wringing maximum economic gain from waters. Appearing in the aggressive, creative legal advocacy against the federal government's Hells Canyon High Dam, these doubts triggered destabilizing shifts in legal thought and practice.

At the Hells Canyon controversy's heart were two deceptively simple choices. Would the U.S. government or Idaho Power Company, a corporate utility, command the river's hydroelectric potential? And how much power would the victor send into humming high-tension lines? Hells Canyon, linking the two great watersheds of the Pacific Northwest, cradled the biggest untapped dam site in the heart of the world's most hydro-electrified region (map 3). Whichever rival won the contest to dam the Snake would direct an energy source capable, if exploited fully, of generating enough new electricity to light every existing factory, farm, and home the length and breadth of the Snake River Basin.[2]

If it controlled this power, the federal government would become the dominant electricity provider in the Pacific Northwest, from the mouth of the Columbia River to the Continental Divide. To this cause rallied public-power advocates and beneficiaries nationwide: labor unions fearful of corporate mastery, rural people in the Midwest and South who resented utility companies' control over the most basic form of energy, and urban liberals

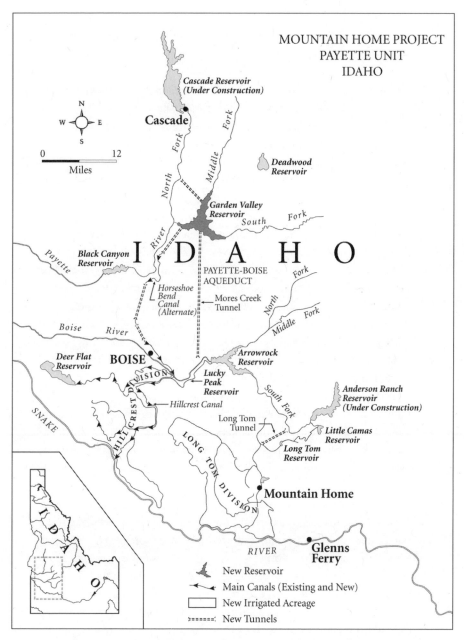

MOUNTAIN HOME PROJECT
PAYETTE UNIT
IDAHO

*Cascade Reservoir
(Under Construction)*

Cascade

N
W   E
S

0   12
Miles

*Deadwood
Reservoir*

North Fork

Middle Fork

River

*Garden Valley
Reservoir*

South Fork

Payette

**Black Canyon
Reservoir**

I D A H O

PAYETTE-BOISE
AQUEDUCT

North Fork

Middle Fork

*Horseshoe
Bend
Canal
(Alternate)*

*Mores Creek
Tunnel*

Boise River

**Deer Flat
Reservoir**

BOISE

*Arrowrock
Reservoir*

*Lucky
Peak
Reservoir*

HILLCREST DIVISION

Hillcrest Canal

South Fork

*Anderson Ranch
Reservoir
(Under Construction)*

SNAKE

LONG TOM DIVISION

*Long Tom
Tunnel*

*Little Camas
Reservoir*

*Long Tom
Reservoir*

Mountain Home

IDAHO

**Glenns
Ferry**

RIVER

New Reservoir

Main Canals (Existing and New)

New Irrigated Acreage

New Tunnels

MAP 2. RECLAMATION'S SNAKE BASIN PLAN, 1947: Hells Canyon High Dam's power
revenues would have paid for the massive construction needed to bring Payette and
Boise river waters south, under the mountains, to irrigate the high desert between
Boise and Mountain Home. This grandiose project accounted for the High Dam's
massive size. Map by Barry Levely.

determined to refit the New Deal for postwar social reform. Hells Canyon became their fighting symbol, a testament to their faith in the New Deal campaign against corporate ownership of the nation's most ubiquitous energy source.

Interior secretary Julius A. "Cap" Krug, a veteran New Deal energy regulator, staked public power's claim to the Snake in 1947. "High Hells Canyon Dam is required to be undertaken as a Federal project," he told the Federal Power Commission, "in order to permit this Department to achieve the goal of the fullest economic development of the land and water resources of the Pacific Northwest." Any smaller private dam "would be inadequate within just a few years . . . [and] would deny to the people of the Pacific Northwest the maximum use of a great natural resource at a time when it is greatly needed." Idaho Democratic senator Glen H. Taylor, who was elected in 1944 as a dedicated proponent of New Deal liberalism, blasted private plans to build a small dam in Hells Canyon. "Our natural resources," he argued, "particularly those resources which belong to all of the people of the United States, . . . should be developed in conformity with the principle of the greatest good for the greatest number, and not for the benefit of any single private individual or corporation." The federal government had to exploit Hells Canyon's "vast quantity of low-cost hydroelectric power . . . if the people themselves are to receive the benefits to which they are rightfully entitled."[3]

Public-power opponents matched their adversaries' passion. For them, the Hells Canyon controversy presented a decisive opportunity at the postwar's outset to trim federal government influence over the economy. Implacably hostile to the New Deal's legacy, private-power supporters made Hells Canyon's fate a national referendum on the New Deal's preference for public control over private initiative. Retired Army Engineers general Thomas M. Robins sounded the charge against federalizing the Snake at the 1951 dedication of a private dam in northern Idaho. "You have an opportunity here," he told the shivering crowd of four thousand gathered beneath the snow-clad Clark Fork canyon walls, "to make the last stand for state's rights . . . if you will stand firm and back up private initiative, private enterprise, and democratic ways of determining what your region will develop into." A federal Hells Canyon High Dam, Idaho Power Company general counsel A. C. Inman claimed in 1949, "was essentially a $3 billion subsidized public power development program and should be recognized as such."[4]

Government hydroelectric planners sought to annex the Snake Basin into public power's northwestern domain by federalizing Hells Canyon. From Hells Canyon High Dam, cheap public electricity would flow upriver, making the federal government the basin's principal power utility. Federal policy also envisioned selling Hells Canyon power downriver, into the Columbia Basin. There, by the late 1940s, cut-rate New Deal public hydropower had encouraged the nation's most profligate consumption of electricity. Escalating demand for public power, priced at one-third the national average, was outstripping Bonneville Power Administration's supply generated at Bonneville and Grand Coulee, the great New Deal dams on the Columbia River. Together with the Army Corps of Engineers and Interior Department's Bureau of Reclamation, BPA envisioned the High Dam as the solution to both the power shortage they had helped cause and the power domain they sought to expand.[5]

Reclamation, the Army Engineers, and BPA—builders and operators of the Federal Columbia River Power System—provoked the Hells Canyon controversy. Acting in concert through their new Columbia Basin Inter-Agency Committee (CBIAC) after 1945, these federal agencies sought to direct the postwar trajectory of the Snake River Basin by controlling its electric system. Below Hells Canyon, in the Columbia River Basin, federal primacy had been a fact since the New Deal. Bonneville Power administrator Paul Raver told Congress in spring 1946:

> The Bonneville Power Administration as I see it today is a public utility. . . . And when a public utility enters on the responsibility of serving the people of a given area with an essential service it undertakes large responsibilities. . . . We are now in that position for the large part of the Northwest. The government, as I see it, is now in the position of having undertaken a responsibility of supplying the distributing agencies in the Northwest and therefore the people of the Northwest, through those distributing agencies, whether they are public or private, with an essential service, and we can't withdraw.[6]

Bonneville Power published a manifesto in 1950 for geographically expanding this new hydroelectric society in the postwar years. Large posters, bearing the title "*Our Objectives*" above Administrator Raver's signature, declared BPA's "*fundamental objective* is to encourage the use of power from Federal multi-purpose projects as a tool for conservation and development of resources." The intent of BPA was "*to encourage the widest possible use of such power.*" To secure this objective, "the Administrator *shall build trans-*

mission lines, . . . make such power available for sale to existing and potential markets, [and] in disposing of electric energy give *preference & priority to public bodies & cooperatives."*[7]

New Deal transformation of the Columbia Basin shaped the legal, political, and ecological contours of the Hells Canyon controversy. Desperate decisions, made by anxious politicians and aggressive administrators in the depths of the Great Depression, became central to the fate of Hells Canyon and the Snake Basin. Federal policy choices, made during construction of Bonneville and Grand Coulee dams, became precedents justifying postwar expansion of public power into the Snake Basin. By building these two massive hydropower dams on the Columbia River, the New Deal transformed the Columbia Basin between the middle 1930s and the end of the Second World War. Cheap, publicly owned hydroelectricity from Bonneville and Grand Coulee dams industrialized and urbanized a region previously defined by its dependence on farming, fishing, and logging.[8] New Deal strategists enforced the sacrifice of rich salmon and steelhead fisheries to intertwined federal goals: cheap public hydroelectricity for urban consumers to finance extensive irrigated reclamation of arid sagebrush steppes. The United States' "permanent program for control" of Columbia River anadromous fish menaced by Coulee Dam in 1939 ultimately determined the demise of salmon and steelhead that ascended the Snake to spawn above Hells Canyon.

After war erupted around the world in 1941, the New Deal's concrete legacy in the Columbia River poured cheap federal power into a transmission grid managed by the U.S. government. World War II accelerated the New Deal's mission of fashioning a distinctive new relationship between people and water in the Columbia Basin. Wartime control of hydropower accustomed federal planners to envision a postwar public-power domain stretching from the Pacific to the mountainous gates of Hells Canyon.[9] Even after the war dispelled the Depression in the Columbia Basin, New Deal planners studied how to use cut-rate public hydroelectricity to industrialize and irrigate the Snake Basin.[10]

Pushing the Federal Columbia River Power System's frontiers upriver, into the Snake Basin, to the crest of the Continental Divide, presented a logical rationale for redeploying the massed forces of capital, expertise, and technology. Bonneville Power's Raver advised his federal colleagues in spring 1946 that BPA anticipated "the extension of its physical facilities and the formulation of governing policies to develop and tie-in multiple-purpose projects in all parts of the Columbia Basin." The entire Pacific Northwest, in BPA's vision, was "a well-defined and closely-knit region" with "a common interest in water resources." Therefore, federal power planners should seek to realize BPA's goal of becoming "the Northwest's public utility."[11]

Although the Reclamation Bureau and Army Engineers favored different mixes of northwestern dams and water projects, these construction agencies agreed on a common strategic objective with Bonneville Power, which sold the hydroelectricity generated at federal dams. Federal dam builders decided to unleash an upriver hydroelectric offensive, with the Snake River in Hells Canyon as its key target.

The upriver offensive, outlined by CBIAC's November 1948 *Long-Range Objectives for Development of the Economic Potential of the Northwest*, announced that "any resource conservation and development program must be directed, simply stated, to meeting the needs of the Nation [for] better living, greater opportunities for economic and social advancement, and more security, individual and group." The "general objective [of the] coordinated Basin program is the full use of resources through economically sound, comprehensive, integrated development of material wealth." As "the Pacific Northwest's resources are not being used to the Nation's best advantage," CBIAC aimed to boost total hydroelectric capacity from 3,500 megawatts to 8,500 megawatts by 1960. With revenues from selling this public power, the Reclamation Bureau proposed doubling the region's irrigated acreage by building water projects to service 4 million new acres and to deliver more water to 1.5 million acres.[12]

The upriver offensive's prime objectives required annexing the Snake Basin, thereby pushing the eastern boundary of the federal hydroelectric domain out from the Columbia Basin to the Continental Divide, the source of the Snake. Its planners intended to drive the New Deal's strategy for industrial development and reclamation agriculture into the Snake Basin, fueling its advance with cheap hydroelectricity from a mammoth new dam, High Hells Canyon. Agencies united in the Columbia Basin Inter-Agency Committee planned to deploy power from Hells Canyon High Dam, distributed across publicly owned transmission lines, to develop the basin's mineral resources, farmland, and irrigation water for maximum economic return under federal leadership.

Government plans for Hells Canyon projected the world's biggest dam because hydroelectric administrators intended to use it as a mighty engine, changing nature to remodel society. Revenues earned by Hells Canyon power sales were dedicated to re-creating in the Snake Basin an upriver version of the New Deal Columbia Basin. Federal hydroelectric plans would rearrange nature—irrigate deserts, tunnel under mountains, carve canals, mine phosphate rock—to push public power's domain to the Continental Divide. Hells Canyon High Dam would have become not only the nation's premier hydro dam but also a gigantic social and ecological dynamo, the New Deal writ large across the postwar Northwest.[13]

Hells Canyon High Dam functioned as the pivot for CBIAC's ambitious expansion strategy. Rooted in Depression-fighting policies pioneered in the Columbia Basin, the postwar New Deal envisioned using the High Dam's cheap hydroelectricity to jolt the Snake Basin's economy into a new course. On a late-summer 1950 "listening tour" in the Northwest, Reclamation Bureau commissioner Michael Straus told a Portland audience, "Hells Canyon will be a very large dam, larger than Boulder Dam. Its generators are to be larger than those at Grand Coulee for cheaper power." A chamber of commerce lunch in Boise a week later heard Straus extol Hells Canyon as "the last great natural dam site of that scope on the continent. . . . There are 93 miles of river behind it that are nothing but a reservoir site— no roads or railroads to move, no towns or farms to be flooded."[14] Hells Canyon High Dam, in other words, would bestow on Snake Basin people the same bounty New Deal dams had poured into the Columbia Basin between 1939 and 1945.[15]

Power generated at Hells Canyon, sold at cut-rate prices by public-power authorities and transmitted throughout southern Idaho over public high-voltage lines, would build a new industrial economy, anchored by phosphate fertilizer production and food-processing. "Continued strong westward migration and rapidly growing population in Western regions impose an expanding demand on the department of the interior to assist in an accelerated development of the region's resources of land, water, energy, and raw materials," Reclamation's 1947 Snake Basin Plan declared. Phosphate rock was "the most valuable nonmetallic mineral resource, and probably the single most important of all the mineral resources in the Upper Snake River Basin," Reclamation Region 1 director R. J. Newell informed Straus in 1949. Southeast Idaho's rolling foothills held more than five billion tons, 60 percent of the nation's known reserves. "A further expansion of great magnitude in the phosphate industry of the Upper Snake River Basin . . . to meet requirements of the Region and Nation will be possible only when the large amounts of low cost electrical energy which are required for efficient, large-scale production by electrical methods can be made available."[16]

Revenue from selling High Dam electricity would also enable the Reclamation Bureau to expand its influence over Snake Basin irrigators. Collected in a new "Columbia Basin Account," power revenues would fund Reclamation's Snake Basin Plan. Interior secretary Krug explained in 1947 that "revenues from power installations at the Hell's Canyon Dam would materially assist in the financing of irrigation developments. . . . Surplus revenues from that project will be required in the near future to permit the authorization and construction of needed irrigation developments."[17] Written by Reclamation's Region 1 planners in Boise, the Snake Basin Plan aimed at nothing less than reshaping nature's disposition of the basin's granite peaks, arid sagebrush plains, and mountain rivers.[18]

Inspired by Grand Coulee Dam's Columbia Basin Project in eastern Washington State, Region 1 chief Newell and his boss, Reclamation commissioner Straus, aimed to plant thousands of new farms amid nearly one million acres of publicly owned sagebrush plain on the Mountain Home Desert southeast of Boise (map 2). To break the desert into irrigated farms, Reclamation's Snake Plan proposed moving water 150 miles, through tunnels beneath mountains and along huge new canals. "Almost all of the water for irrigation," Newell told Straus, "would be supplied by transmountain diversions from the Payette River. . . . The remainder would be supplied from the portion of the water resources of the Boise River not now utilized." In short, the United States would create twenty-five hundred new farms on four hundred thousand acres of high desert southeast of Boise by rearranging nature's own organization of the Middle Snake Basin. Newell had to redesign the Snake Basin's waterways because nature's disposition of basin topography caused the Snake itself to run through southern Idaho in a deep canyon. Too far below the Mountain Home Desert to water its new farms, the Snake's power would command other waters to flow onto the land.[19]

Howard R. Stinson, longtime Reclamation Region 1 legal counsel, testified that the High Dam was "one of the essential and key elements" of the United States' postwar power and reclamation strategy for the Snake Basin. Stinson characterized High Hells Canyon as indispensable to coordinated federal direction of the postwar Snake Basin's economy. In summer 1952, the Federal Power Commission asked Reclamation to explain how damming the Snake in Hells Canyon would affect land, water, and people living throughout southern Idaho. Stinson testified that the federal government deemed Snake

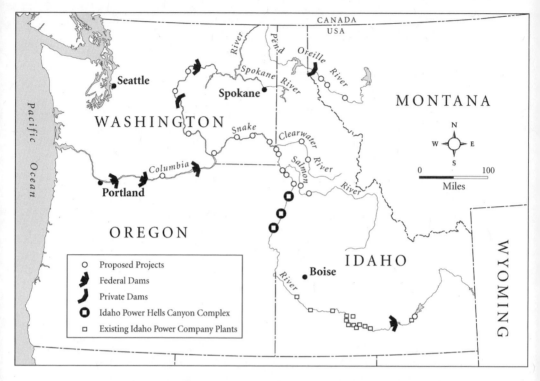

MAP 3. DAMS IN THE NORTHWEST, 1955: Idaho Power's service territory in southern Idaho met Bonneville Power's domain at Hells Canyon, on the Oregon-Idaho border. Federal plans projected many more dams throughout the Snake Basin, four on the lower Snake in Washington alone. Despite projections for more dams below Hells Canyon, only Idaho Power's three-dam complex was built. Map by Barry Levely.

Basin people citizens of a greater Northwest. National policy impressed the water running through their lives with a duty to build a bigger, more diverse economy in the Snake Basin to complement the New Deal's transformation of the Columbia Basin. To build that kind of region required comprehensive exploitation of the Snake, Stinson testified. Spinning power from the High Dam would enable federal dam-building, power-marketing, and reclamation agencies to coordinate their plans "in order to achieve the fullest use of the water resources of the Snake River . . . [so as] to achieve a full development of the land and water resources of the Pacific Northwest."[20]

Both federal and private plans for electrifying Hells Canyon also promised abrupt changes in the lifeways of salmon and steelhead trout, which had coursed throughout the Northwest for ten millennia. The New Deal had already torn the watery web supporting this incomparable anadromous fishery. In the late 1930s, Bonneville and Grand Coulee, gigantic new federal hydroelectric dams rooted in the Columbia River, began impeding adults' upstream migration to spawn. Their slack-water reservoirs delayed smolts' downstream race to salt water. Increased travel times, upstream and down, jeopardized the fishes' very survival as distinctive species.

Wild fish embodied not just the "old" Northwest of Indians and salmon capitalists. Not quaint relics of a bygone age, they still supported a commercial fishing industry in Oregon and Washington valued in 1950 at $15 billion. A vibrant sport fishery in the Snake Basin still thrived on the strength of fish migrating five hundred miles into the western slopes of the Continental Divide. Even the most ardent hydroelectric boosters and reclamationists acknowledged the centrality of sea-run fish to the postwar Northwest. How Snake Basin anadromous fish fared in the Hells Canyon controversy illuminated an irony too often lost in contemporary histories about private capital, public policy, and biological imperatives. Private pursuit of profits in the postwar Snake Basin at least promised a more sustainable relationship between power dams and migratory fish. However, any conservation strategy premised on engineering purely technical solutions to ecological challenges exposed Snake Basin fish to grave risks of extinction.[21]

Both Idaho Power and the Reclamation Bureau conceded any new Snake River dams would do some harm to fish. To minimize that risk, Idaho Power initially proposed, in 1947, building only the first of several low dams. By supplying only as much new power as its service area in the Snake Basin then needed, low Oxbow Dam appeared to mesh company profits with fish survival. Federal and state conservation agencies deemed Idaho Power's cautious approach a more promising strategy to generate hydroelectricity while perpetuating the fishery. Hells Canyon High Dam, by contrast, would have been to the Snake River fishery what Grand Coulee had been to the upper Columbia's: an impassable barrier that extinguished all wild fish runs behind the dam.[22]

Northwestern state fish managers backed Idaho Power's project, albeit reluctantly. The Oregon Fish Commission's chairman, John C. Veatch, told the Federal Power Commission that any Hells Canyon dam posed obvious fish passage problems. Oregon was not yet prepared to bless Idaho Power's single low dam. Still Veatch advised the FPC in spring 1951, "We wish to reiterate that there is a better chance to maintain the upper Snake River salmon runs at a low dam such as Oxbow than at some of the high dams planned for this portion of the Snake River." T. B. Murray, Idaho's Fish and Game director, praised Oxbow's run-of-river design. A low power dam that spun turbines using the river's current instead of a storage reservoir's massed energy both simplified fish passage and kept the Snake's flow reasonably constant, a significant plus for both upstream migrants and down-running juveniles.[23]

High Dam proponents, however, demonstrated how New Deal public-power policies constrained options for postwar fish conservation. The New Deal's Grand Coulee Dam made cheap hydroelectricity an article of faith in the Northwest. Public-power supporters, such as Washington's Democratic senator Warren Magnuson, dismissed Idaho Power's modest proposal as "little dams for a big river." Even Oregon and Idaho conservation-agency support of the company's low-dam strategy mattered little. At Grand Coulee in 1939, the federal government had forced Columbia–Snake Basin states to surrender their legal responsibility for managing anadromous fish to the federal government. Federal planners knew Hells Canyon High Dam would doom the Snake River's anadromous fishery, at least that portion that spawned in the main Snake and its tributaries upstream from Hells Canyon—the Weiser, Burnt, Powder, and Payette rivers. Sacrificing the Snake's fishery to benefit electric customers flowed smoothly from national policy choices made by President Roosevelt and his Interior secretary, Harold Ickes, to embed the New Deal's public-power program in the Northwest. As Paul Pitzer justly observes of Interior's policy at Grand Coulee, "Although the Bureau [of Reclamation] took steps to preserve the salmon, had its measures failed, it was ready to see the salmon disappear, deeming the economic contribution of the dam as far more important than the fish."[24]

President Harry Truman and his postwar Interior secretaries, Julius Krug and Oscar Chapman, considered this New Deal choice both right and dispositive. In summer 1947, Interior's Northwest Field Committee concluded that, even though building big new federal dams in the Snake Basin menaced migratory fish, "all concerned within the Department are agreed that they are the foundation of the ultimate development of the Pacific Northwest and that they considerably outweigh the resulting cost to the commercial fisheries, the Indians and the sportsmen."[25]

Stung by unflattering comparisons of mighty Grand Coulee and modest Oxbow, Idaho Power neutralized public-power criticism of its 1947 low-dam plan by courting ecological catastrophe. Abruptly, in late 1952, the utility announced it would seek an FPC license for a new Hells Canyon Complex, now featuring two low dams—Oxbow and low Hells Canyon—buttressed by a far larger storage facility—Brownlee—on the uppermost reach of the project. The Hells Canyon Complex's robust new design reflected political expediency more than biological sensitivity or economic need.[26]

With the new complex's stepped-up generating capacity and Brownlee's flood-control potential, Idaho Power would successfully undercut the High Dam's principal rationales. However, triumph for Idaho Power at Hells Canyon ultimately meant tragedy for the Snake's fishery. The company's effort to pass fish around its new dams, using untried technology super-intended by indifferent human operators, would cause the infamous 1958 "Oxbow Incident." That autumn, nearly an entire generation of adult chinook salmon died in stagnant pools when the trapping and passage system failed. By 1960, Idaho Power conceded that engineering a solution to the ecological challenge of anadromous fish passage at dams had failed.[27]

Dismal as Idaho Power's salmon-conservation record would prove to be, the company's single-minded focus on Hells Canyon ultimately spared Snake Basin anadromous fish an even more catastrophic fate. High Hells Canyon Dam would have cast a concrete precedent for spreading federal multipurpose dams into the Snake's principal tributary, the Salmon River. The Army Corps of Engineers and Bonneville Power Administration intended to use the High Dam as a launchpad, pushing public-power dams into the Salmon Basin as well. Destructive floods along the lower Columbia in spring 1948 encouraged the Army Engineers to propose a massive "Main Control Plan" for the Northwest. The Main Control Plan projected building eight big new federal dams across what the corps perceived to be the Columbia's main flood source: the Snake and its principal tributary, the Salmon. Federal dam-building plans for just the Salmon and Clearwater basins outlined six new dams.[28]

Hells Canyon High Dam symbolized the postwar New Deal's commitment to "maximum comprehensive development" of the entire Snake Basin. Maximum development, as BPA and the Army Engineers defined the concept in operational terms, compelled construction of more federal dams throughout the watershed. Federal river-basin planning, in other words, treated the Salmon and the Snake as two causes of the same perceived problems: uncontrolled spring runoff and downstream floods in the populous heart of the Columbia Basin (map 2). Had the Hells Canyon controversy been ultimately refereed by Congress, adherents of comprehensive river-basin planning and maximum water-resources development would have gained invaluable momentum in their bid to manage the entire Snake watershed, including the Salmon River, as intensively as the Columbia.[29]

By preempting the Snake Basin for private power in the postwar era, Idaho Power not only blocked future public dams on the Snake itself, below Hells Canyon, but also earned an electric generating source vast enough to supply the Snake Basin's expanding power appetite for decades. Despite their strenuous efforts, between 1956 and 1967, neither the United States nor the Columbia Basin public-power districts could earn congressional authorization or FPC licenses for new Hells Canyon dams. As a matter of economics, Idaho Power's three-dam Hells Canyon Complex delivered just enough electricity to the Snake Basin to sate the demand for further dams in the pulsing heart of the Northwest's anadromous fish nursery, the Salmon River watershed.[30]

The Hells Canyon controversy tested the federal and corporate combatants' competing plans to electrify the Snake River Basin in administrative agencies, courts, legislative halls, election campaigns, and every type of mass media. In 1955, the FPC finally licensed Idaho Power Company to build three hydroelectric dams in Hells Canyon.[31] By national standards, Idaho Power was small potatoes, ranking about thirtieth in most measurements of utility capacity and financial heft. By northwestern standards, Idaho Power's Hells Canyon Complex would be modest. Together, its three low dams could generate less electricity than either Bonneville or Grand Coulee Dam.[32] The FPC rejected the U.S. Bureau of Reclamation's competing plan to build a far larger Hells Canyon High Dam (map 2). The Supreme Court and the Congress ratified Idaho Power's triumph and the High Dam's demise in 1957.[33] Hells Canyon High Dam became the dam-that-never-was.

Making the choice that closed the Hells Canyon controversy required new legal definitions of "the public interest" in the Snake River.[34] In licensing Idaho Power's low dams, the FPC decided it was not in the public interest for the federal government to build the world's largest dam. By rejecting High Hells Canyon, the FPC—as well as Congress and the federal courts—decided it was not in the public interest for the federal government to use hydroelectricity to remodel nature in the Snake Basin. By unplugging the High Dam's cheap public power, the legal system found the public interest to be inimical to federal plans to change society by remodeling rivers.

In the postwar era, genuine fears of foreign war and paranoid delusions of domestic subversion imposed a rigid political consensus. The Hells

Canyon controversy, working in tandem with that in Echo Park, became cold war icebreakers. They unleashed passionate disagreements as ordinary citizens defied government experts' plans to remodel natural systems. Idaho Power's allies, in the region and nationally, engaged in conservative dissent by exploiting deep-running western resentment over federal management of land and water. Shrewdly, the company's political strategy in the Hells Canyon controversy mobilized westerners' historic proclivity to damn federal actions that impeded private efforts to transform nature into capital. Ironically, Idaho Power's own profit-making impulses conserved natural resources—flowing water, migrating fish, flourishing high deserts—that public policy aimed to convert into capital.[35]

Idaho Power's tactics tapped deep veins of resistance against the New Deal nationwide. Chorusing attacks from an array of business and local interests, the company's champions called their public-power opponents socialists and tyrants. They recklessly accused the company's federal rivals of plotting to seize political liberty but correctly perceived the federal hydroelectric agencies' bid for power over water. Idaho Power's ferocious campaign against Hells Canyon High Dam deepened the uncertainty poisoning American public life. However, by protesting the New Deal legacy, writ large in Hells Canyon High Dam's plan for social and ecological transformation on a massive scale, Idaho Power and its conservative allies destabilized a consensus that had inflicted incalculable damage to the Northwest's environmental health.[36]

By favoring corporate capital over public power after a vigorous national controversy, the nation's political system and legal process rewarded dissenters for challenging the New Deal consensus about Hells Canyon's fate. By halting the Federal Columbia River Power System's postwar offensive before it annexed the Snake Basin, Idaho Power's victory encouraged other opponents to begin questioning the economic and ecological consequences of pell-mell hydroelectrification in the Northwest. By discerning a distinctive, new public interest in the Snake River, the Hells Canyon controversy pushed Americans to begin reconsidering the purposes and meanings of rivers. The Hells Canyon controversy—which was really about the kind of postwar Northwest people wanted—triggered a new American debate over the fate of all lands and waters. Its outcome yielded consequences not just for the Snake River Basin, and not only in the postwar era.

We need to know why Americans cared so long about what happened to Hells Canyon. We must better understand the choices they faced about its fate. Moreover, we should carefully study the consequences of their verdict. Little of the historiography to date helps us achieve these goals.

Historians of postwar America have customarily relegated the Hells Canyon controversy between 1945 and 1957 to the hydroelectric history of the Northwest: It was just a nasty, little, local dispute about a dam.[37] Even the best recent scholarship about the American West during the cold war ignores Hells Canyon.[38] An otherwise invaluable collection of recent environmental histories about the Pacific Northwest confines discussion of the controversy to one brief mention in one article.[39] That is the usual place of Hells Canyon, a footnote to the main body of postwar American history, about as interesting and important as Dixon-Yates and Sherman Adams's vicuña coat.

Our ability to understand and assess the meaning of the Hells Canyon controversy has advanced little in more than a quarter-century. After all our rich and burgeoning environmental historiography of North America, Elmo Richardson's *Dams, Parks and Politics*, published in 1973, still offers the most useful analysis. He recognized the controversy over Hells Canyon as central to postwar public policy, but dismissed it as one more tawdry struggle for spoils between corporate monopolists and their pork-barreling rivals in Congress and the executive branch.[40] Though its natural and human histories during the postwar decade illustrate some of their central themes, even masters of western America's environmental history, such as Richard White and Donald Worster, spend too little time in Hells Canyon.[41]

The Hells Canyon controversy transcends hydroelectric history, important as it is to that field. Its distinctive passions and remarkable durability cut an important passageway not just into the history of the postwar Northwest but into our broader national history. Hells Canyon offers a passageway not only to a river but to an epoch: that turbulent decade, between 1946 and 1956, linking victory abroad to new struggles at home about the meaning of citizenship in a democracy and the place of nature in our national culture. By choosing modest corporate hydropower over grandiose public power at Hells Canyon, Americans rejected ambitious federal river-basin planning, the New Deal's environmental legacy in the Northwest. By rejecting federalization of the Snake River's waterpower, Americans registered their dissent from a consensus, rooted in the New Deal's Progressive heritage, that reserved great rivers for national control. By defeating the Federal Columbia River Power System's bid to use cheap public power to remodel the Snake Basin along New Deal lines, Americans tentatively advanced a new and different definition of "the public interest" in natural waters.

Histories of the postwar United States have begun to recast our understanding of that long decade linking the end of World War II to the Birmingham bus boycott and Sputnik. In place of bland consensus, we now behold a nation struggling to make sense of its global responsibilities, a people divided about the promise of victory over fascism and militarism. Where once we depicted a sunny society bathed in the warm glow of material prosperity, we now better understand that prosperity for some accentuated others' misery and inspired many to question the very bases of that consumer cavalcade. Historians seeking to understand what was new in America's postwar, and what endured after nearly two decades of economic depression and world war, have looked closely at relations of production and consumption. As those relations depended, in a fundamental sense, on the ways Americans perceived and organized nonhuman nature, we should expect to find postwar society generating both new demands on nature and novel estimates of its meaning to their lives.[42]

Samuel Hays has maintained that the vast majority of Americans living in the postwar encountered for the first time a level of material comfort qualitatively different from their heritage of scarcity. Many Americans, in the decade after the war, came to believe that they had permanently banished material want. Consequently, they began to act as consumers able to enjoy conditions of plenty rather than as producers compelled to overcome the demands of necessity. In a society seemingly capable of generating more than enough goods and services to satisfy basic needs for food, clothing, and shelter, the new challenge was to distribute production to consumers in ways that enhanced their appreciation of life itself. Hays has argued, in his seminal *Beauty, Health, and Permanence,* that in the 1950s a decisive corps of Americans reevaluated their relationship as humans to nature. No longer acting as desperate producers compelled to transform nature into goods to meet basic needs, they began to explore nature's nonmaterial aspects: as a source of pleasure to the eye and body, as a landscape capable of inspiring healthy thoughts, and as integral to human life itself, deserving as much solicitude as humanity could afford.[43]

We still need to know much more about the ways in which postwar America came to terms with global duties, national prosperity, and nature's meaning. I contend that we should use Hells Canyon as a guidepost on the way to understanding postwar America. This place not only stood as a rampart dividing two basins but also operated as a historical pivot around which contrasting visions of nature swung for a decade. At stake in the fierce national controversy between 1945 and 1957 over Hells Canyon's fate was a deceptively simple question: Should the national state, embodied in federal statutes administered by expert administrators, or private capital, regulated principally by market forces for power, electrify the Snake Basin? However, embedded in that question were large political, social, and cultural issues. Resolution of these issues vitally interested people of the Pacific Northwest, as they had worked out one distinctive mode of addressing them in the Columbia during the Depression and World War II and another contrasting solution in the Snake. Yet northwesterners were not the only contestants struggling to define the Snake Basin's future in the postwar. Only by appreciating how Hells Canyon marked a passageway through the postwar Northwest can we explain the contest's durability, ferocity, and ultimate significance as an environmental historical problem of the first order.

Hells Canyon became a national symbol to postwar Americans. Because it presented such fabulous power possibilities, it made them decide whether the New Deal's vision of comprehensively reorganizing nature and people into a hydroelectric society under federal leadership should dominate all of the Northwest. Hells Canyon's electrification thus presented a national referendum on the New Deal's environmental heritage. The Hells Canyon controversy rendered a verdict against a twenty-year-old strategy of using cheap public electricity to create another version of the Columbia Basin's distinctive hydroelectric society in the higher-elevation Snake Basin.

The Snake River forges a passageway through Hells Canyon to its rendezvous with the Columbia River. The Hells Canyon controversy offers historians a passageway as well. Although energy—to irrigate agriculture, power factories, and halt floods—defined the political and legal terms of the national referendum at Hells Canyon, biology would be its lasting legacy to the Northwest, and to the nation.

2   AT HELL'S GATES

I daho's Seven Devils Mountains overlook Hells Canyon. Seven thousand feet below their granite ridges the Snake River rushes toward the Columbia River, 140 miles northwestward. Seen from the Seven Devils on a crisp autumn afternoon, the Snake glints silver-bright, a thin blade slicing stacks of leather-colored rock. Scattered pines and sagebrush fringe the canyon's terraced walls. Hells Canyon, from a raft on the river, resembles a mad giant's titanic garden, unplumbed shelves lined with untended planters.

The Columbia's largest tributary, the Snake River drains the western slope of the northern Rocky Mountains. The Snake watershed embraces both damp high-altitude forests fringing the Continental Divide and arid sagebrush steppes spreading north from the Great Basin.[1] The Snake and its tributaries, at the end of World War II, nursed the Northwest's second-largest anadromous fishery. Only the main Columbia watershed supported more salmon and steelhead trout.[2]

Hells Canyon divides political sovereignties but compels them to cooperate in the Snake River's management. The river in the canyon defines Oregon and Idaho's common boundary: each jurisdiction shares substantial legal authority over its water flows and biotic communities.[3] As an interstate river, the Snake is also subject to the United States' sovereign power pursuant to the Constitution's commerce, navigation, and federal property provisions.[4]

Hells Canyon divides Idaho from Oregon on a map. Yet the Snake River stitches together the Northwest's two distinctive natural realms. It unites arid uplands, falling west down the Continental Divide, with the wetter Columbia Basin rising east from the Pacific Ocean. Hells Canyon stands between these two watersheds, bridging divergent northwestern topography, climate, vegetation, and biological lifeways. Look eastward from the Seven Devils at

23

the Canyon's brink and the Snake Basin rises toward the Rockies. Turn westward, and the Columbia Basin tips into the sea.[5]

Northwestern geography pivots around the Snake in Hells Canyon, roughly halfway between the Continental Divide and Pacific Ocean. Farewell Bend, at the Canyon's upper or southern end, lies about 285 miles west of the Continental Divide. Graham's Landing, where Idaho, Oregon, and Washington meet at the Canyon's northern foot, is about 310 miles east of the Pacific. The Snake bisects the Columbia as well. At Wallula, Washington, the Columbia has flowed 260 river miles through the United States when it encounters the Snake. About 260 river miles below their confluence lies Astoria, Oregon, where the Columbia roars across the sandy bar between fresh water and salt ocean.[6]

Gus Norwood thought nature and geography providently placed Hells Canyon and the Snake River in the path of postwar federal hydroelectric expansion. The executive secretary of the Northwest Public Power Association portrayed public power's annexation of the Snake Basin as a logical consequence of the New Deal's transformation of the Columbia Basin. "In 1948 BPA won the right to serve in northern Idaho," he wrote in 1950. "In 1949 it won the right to serve in western Montana and in 1950 the southern Oregon 230,000 volt loop was approved. There lacks now only southern Idaho to round out the logical boundaries for Bonneville Power Administration." Federalizing Hells Canyon's waterpower, he contended, simply ratified nature's own hydroelectric logic: "Applications of the Idaho Power Co. to construct a dam on the Middle Snake . . . are further evidence of a private power company scheme to isolate the Snake River Basin from the Columbia River Basin and maintain it as a private power company preserve."[7]

Idaho Power Company also thought history and geography stimulated conflict about Hells Canyon's postwar fate. "It is impossible," the company argued, "to evaluate power production in the Hells Canyon stretch of the river without a study of the irrigation development of the Snake River above it. . . . The Snake River, above Hells Canyon, has characteristics different from any other major river in the Columbia Basin. It is essentially an irrigation stream."[8] The Army Corps of Engineers, though it sought to build Hells Canyon High Dam, nevertheless conceded Snake Basin people were using water differently from their downstream neighbors in the postwar Columbia Basin. "The economy of the Central Snake River sub-basin is dependent on agricultural development," the corps reported to Congress, "which in turn is dependent on ample water for irrigation. Storage or diversion of water for agricultural uses is detrimental to present or future downstream power development because of the resultant reduction in downstream flows."[9]

Hells Canyon's geographic and ecologic centrality to the Northwest shaped human history. Because Hells Canyon and the Snake, as well as the Columbia and Salmon rivers, are where and what they are, people who live in their basins have acted differently. This was as true in the mid-twentieth century as it had been before European Americans came to stay in the second quarter of the nineteenth century. If these rivers and the lands across which they flow lay elsewhere, the postwar controversy about Hells Canyon water and power would not have broken out when and where it did. The controversy would not have raised the issues it did. Its resolution would not have reshaped the Northwest as it did.

At Hells Canyon, in the postwar years, two different ways of using water collided. Each mode of relating to water reflected a distinctive product of the encounter between people and the places where they lived. Since the New Deal, Columbia Basin people had become dependent on cheap public hydroelectricity. Since the 1902 Reclamation Act, people living in the Snake Basin had become dependent on irrigation potential. People in both basins relied on distinctive forms of controlling water to sustain their characteristic modes of adapting to nature. They used politics, laws, and economic power to sustain their methods of control. During World War II, national crisis reinforced prevailing patterns of production. The Columbia Basin used cheap power to industrialize. Snake Basin irrigators grew food to feed the nation and its allies. Each basin's particular contribution to American war-production strategy between 1941 and 1945 further embedded its predominant water use.

Hydropower supplied both the Columbia and Snake basins' basic energy demands at the war's end. Yet each basin's characteristic hydroelectric system reflected its predominant way of valuing water. Columbia Basin people had used law during the New Deal to build mammoth dams to squeeze the maximum attainable number of kilowatts from flowing water. In the Snake Basin, by contrast, people had used law to build modest power dams that subordinated electricity production from stored water to the irrigation imperative.

Idaho Power's dams within Hells Canyon demarcate a cultural, as well as a legal, boundary dividing the Snake Basin of southern Idaho and southeastern Oregon from the Columbia Basin's hydroelectric society. Because of the Hells Canyon controversy's outcome, a society dependent on irrigation still masters water to serve its unique demands. The Snake does spin turbines encased deep in the powerhouses of dams in Hells Canyon, but its principal human use remains what it has been since 1902: the production of crops and the perpetuation of irrigators' political and legal power.

The Seven Devils above Hells Canyon offer a vantage point to see how nature and human history fused to ignite the postwar Hells Canyon controversy. From this perspective, three great issues stand out as landmarks in the northwestern landscape. How would Snake Basin irrigators cement their legal control of water by enlisting Idaho Power to help repel the federal government's offensive to expand its hydroelectric domain? Could that public-power domain, secure in its Columbia Basin hydroelectric homeland, annex the Snake Basin by using postwar New Deal strategies? And what would the confrontation at Hells Canyon mean to the Northwest's signature species, the salmon and steelhead trout?

SNAKE BASIN IRRIGATION SOCIETY

Look from the Seven Devils east and south: sharp granitic ridges, speckled with alpine fir, fold into green waves of Ponderosa pines. The land falls quickly away into the Weiser and Payette river drainages. On the far southern horizon, heat haze rises from the Snake River Plain. Harvest is beginning on the plain's irrigated croplands. The Boise River curls out of the mountains at the very southern limit of our prospect. Within less than forty river miles, the Boise, Payette, and Weiser rivers all meet the Snake on its eastern bank. In that same brief interval, just where the Snake angles abruptly northward, accelerating on its run down into Hells Canyon, the Owyhee and Malheur rivers enter from the west. Their Idaho counterparts plummet westward toward the Snake down steep forested mountains. But the Owyhee and Malheur have twisted eastward through deep volcanic basalt flows in southeastern Oregon. Across what used to be gently rolling sagebrush floodplain at the mouths of these five rivers, thermal updrafts now lift harvest dust to blur the cobalt rim of blue where autumn sky touches brown earth.[10]

When the five rivers met the Snake in 1950, a steady flow of water rushed into Hells Canyon's 600-foot drop. At Weiser, Idaho, the last substantial settlement before the canyon begins, enough water to cover 12.5 million acres a foot deep ran by in a typical year. Despite carrying this volume, the Snake fluctuated less over the course of a year than did any of the Columbia's main tributaries. Even in May 1948, at the onset of the most prodigious flood season in the twentieth century in the Northwest, the Snake entering Hells Canyon carried only about 50,000 cubic feet of water per second. Downstream, below Hells Canyon, the Salmon River discharged twice as much flow, while at Lewiston, Idaho, where the Snake turns west into Washington, the Clearwater River poured 177,000 cubic feet of water per second into the bigger river. Together, the Snake Basin's principal rivers swelled the Columbia by about one-third of its flood-stage flow.[11]

Upstream irrigation diversions in the Snake Basin maintained the Snake's comparatively predictable flow. They restrained the river even in 1948, when spring snowmelt drowned scores of northwesterners and flooded nearly a half-billion dollars worth of riverside property along the Columbia. A half century of irrigation farming had embedded dams, reservoirs, and canal systems throughout southern Idaho. They impounded two-thirds of the Snake's annual average flow. Had all the pooled water been spread across the Snake Basin in 1948, it would have submerged approximately 8.8 million acres one foot deep.[12]

Running out of Wyoming east to west in a wide arc 450 miles long, the Snake churns across a broad, flat plain. More than 50 miles wide through most of its length across southern Idaho, the Snake Plain resembles a great level grin. The smile starts at the foot of the Teton Mountains, which tower 5,000 feet above the plain's eastern edge. The grin fades after the five rivers meet the Snake, at the mouth of Hells Canyon.[13]

For millennia, the Snake Plain functioned as a concourse for Indian peoples. In the second quarter of the nineteenth century, westering white Americans used it as a one-way through route to Oregon Country. The Oregon Trail, dropping out of the Continental Divide in Wyoming's Red Desert, paralleled the Snake across southern Idaho. Union Pacific built its Oregon Short Line along the trail's route in the 1880s to connect Salt Lake City, Utah, with Portland, Oregon. After 1900, farmers began to colonize the Snake Plain, drawn onto its sagebrush flats by natural conjunctions that fitted it for irrigated agriculture: broad and fairly level topography, relatively mild winters compared with the seven months of snow that rendered the mountains north and south barely habitable, rich volcanic soil deposited in alluvial floods where mountain rivers flattened abruptly as they met the Snake, and, crucially, abundant water from the Snake as well as its tributaries.[14]

Abundant water, flowing through a relatively level valley covered with rich volcanic soils, encouraged Snake Basin people to fashion a distinctive relationship between their society and the natural systems within which they lived. Its spring flow swollen with snowmelt running down from Wyoming's Teton Range, the Snake nourished an intensively irrigated agricultural economy along the Snake Plain. Snake Basin irrigators spread the river throughout their fields in a network of canals, lateral ditches, and headgates. Prosperous irrigation farmers depended on federal money and governmental expertise to control the life-giving waters.[15]

People living in the Snake Basin of southern Idaho and eastern Oregon commanded water to work by growing crops. Private desire married to public money enabled irrigators to undertake the extensive construction projects essential to diverting Snake River water for agriculture. Since the first decade of the twentieth century, when the Newlands Reclamation Act inaugurated federally subsidized reclamation, irrigation had dominated the Snake Basin economy, defining its human communities and permeating its polity. Two-thirds of Idaho's population lived outside urban boundaries in 1950. Exactly the same proportion lived in the Snake Basin. As close as any actual place to the archetypal hydraulic society described by Donald Worster, Snake Basin life depended on persuading the United States to spend public money to store and divert water according to the state-law doctrine of prior appropriation.[16]

When World War II ended, irrigated agriculture in the Snake Basin encompassed nearly three million acres. Ambitious boosters foresaw expanding that domain to four million acres by the end of the twentieth century. Potentially, given the mix of level ground and arable soils, another million acres lay within feasible reach of irrigation farming. These farms consumed sizable quantities of water, both to spread on crops and to produce electricity. Idaho Power, the basin's dominant electric utility, estimated that 99 percent of the basin's farms were electrified. Power demands peaked in synchronicity with irrigation demands. In midsummer, electric pumps quietly whined away, lifting water from canals into lateral ditches. So intertwined were water and power in the Snake Plain that one-fifth of all Idaho Power customers were farmers, one of the nation's highest rates of farm-to-urban service.[17]

Each acre of the Snake Plain under cultivation required a lot of water. The volcanic soils were porous; much irrigation water trickled past the root zone into bedrock. Summer temperatures often exceeded 100 degrees Fahrenheit from early July to mid-August. Evapotranspiration withdrew much water before plants absorbed it in the high-desert climate. The crops of choice—especially Russet Burbank potatoes and alfalfa hay—required substantial watering during precisely the hottest, most evaporation-prone, late-summer days. Consequently, "there was general agreement that the average annual consumptive use of water diverted for agriculture was 1.75 to 2.0 acre-feet per acre."

Diverting this much water out of the Snake and its tributaries had not exhausted the basin's irrigation prospects at the outset of the postwar era. Reclamation Bureau projects since 1902 had expanded irrigated acreage about 41,000 acres per year. Of course, the easiest projects had been exploited first: those closest to water, with the best access to transportation routes and the most productive soils. But even as irrigators looked uphill, farther away from the Snake and its tributaries, they beheld expansive possibilities. Agronomists and economists from the University of Idaho and the U.S. Department of Agriculture estimated that postwar irrigation agriculture could overspread another 600,000 acres by 1965, and that was just on lands serviced by existing canal companies using waterworks in place. Three ambitious federal reclamation projects in the Snake Basin aimed to add another 200,000 acres.[18]

Irrigation in the Snake Basin shaped the use of water to favor raising crops over making hydropower. Idaho Power had grown alongside agriculture but had accepted a legal system for apportioning water between farms and power dams that permanently subordinated hydroelectricity to irrigation. In 1954, the company acknowledged that any further Snake Basin electrification, even downstream in Hells Canyon, far below the fields and canals of the Snake Plain, "must be such as will be consistent with present and future upstream irrigation needs, and such as will in no way be in conflict therewith, nor become a potential threat thereto." "The future growth of the area is directly dependent upon the use of the Snake River water for the reclamation of additional lands," the company insisted, "and future hydroelectric developments cannot be evaluated without taking future irrigation (and resulting stream-flow depletion) into account." Its plans to produce more electricity in the postwar all bore "a specific provision which preserves for irrigation, now and in the future, a prior claim upon the use of the water, the claim for power production being secondary to that of the irrigator and farmer." So predominant was the irrigation society's control of water that the Federal Power Commission, which claimed constitutional authority over the Snake's interstate flow, conceded that its licensing power "cannot affect or in any way interfere with the laws of the respective states relating to the control, appropriation, use or distribution of water used in irrigation."[19]

Snake Basin irrigators used their legal power over water and land to amass considerable political influence in Idaho. Successful irrigation farmers formed the Snake Basin's political hub, their aspirations and fears shaping the region's characteristic outlook on all matters touching the life-giving water. Around themselves they steadily arrayed dependent spokes: private bankers, who underwrote their operations with credit for planting and recovered their loans at harvesttime; food processors, who bought their grain and vegetable harvests; construction entrepreneurs, who built and serviced the irrigation works; minions in state government and the legal profession, who administered the prior appropriation system; and federal administrators and politicians, who secured the public money and expertise essential to storing and delivering water.[20]

The first generation of irrigation farmers gained a toehold on the Snake Plain between 1900 and 1925. Their successors nearly lost their grip on the water, and with it, their hold on the society they had created from natural features and forces they controlled. Even before the Great Depression paralyzed the national economy, agricultural prices collapsed in the Snake Basin in the middle 1920s. Deflation struck hard, and the consequences of a countrywide agricultural depression lasted a very long time in southern Idaho. Poverty and migrancy endured stubbornly. Rudimentary federal relief programs after 1930 left some new sidewalks in towns and a few school and civic buildings in rural areas. However, because the Snake Basin lacked political value to the New Deal Democratic coalition, the U.S. government initiated no major public-works projects in the Snake Basin between 1933 and 1940.

World War II did bring national relief. Defense mobilization constructed a string of military air bases in cities along the Snake. The federal government still managed much of the land in the Snake Basin, so War Department planners encountered little difficulty cordoning off vast stretches of sagebrush around Pocatello, Mountain Home, and Boise for the runways and bombing ranges necessary to training heavy-bomber crews. Ample supplies of both flat public lands and clear high-desert skies lent themselves to long-distance gunnery as well as high-altitude bombing: the Navy Department requisitioned four hundred square miles of sagebrush near Arco for testing heavy guns and high-explosive naval ordnance.[21]

Abundant space and desperate dependency on federal investment also made the Snake Basin part of the War Department's strategy for interning Japanese-Americans. On sixty thousand acres of sagebrush, controlled by the Bureau of Land Management, sixteen thousand Nisei from Oregon and Washington lived in the Minidoka Relocation Center between 1942 and 1945. The name of the nearest community was Eden, but federal authorities preferred to identify the internment camp as the Hunt site. That was the Union Pacific siding, northeast of Twin Falls, where the War Department detrained Japanese Americans for their short ride on the bed of army trucks to their tarpaper barracks. Filling the labor gap left by military service and industrial migration, Nisei laborers in irrigators' beet and spud fields enabled Snake Basin agriculture to profit from global war. Higher prices for rationed food, especially sugar from beets, and voracious military demands for caloric foodstuffs, especially dried potatoes, rescued the more resilient reclamation farmers.[22]

Yet Snake Basin society resisted mobilization prosperity that dispelled the Depression nationwide. Idaho's population sank during World War II, from 524,000 to 509,000. An estimated 30,000 Idahoans simply left the state, deepening an exile's channel that had already carried away nearly 75,000 people since 1920.[23] Without nearby coal or oil, the Snake Basin depended on water for its energy, as well as for its life. However, whereas 40 percent of all electric power consumed in the Columbia Basin came from mammoth federal dams built during the New Deal—Bonneville and Grand Coulee—the Snake Basin was still a private-power stronghold at war's end. Idaho Power Company owned sixteen small run-of-river dams that generated nearly all hydropower originating from the Snake.[24]

By 1945, Snake Basin people's dependence on irrigated agriculture had pointed the region along a different economic and political trajectory than that propelling the Columbia Basin. Water still did the work farmers commanded. The federal government had made only slight adjustments in the basin's fundamental relationship to the river. Idaho Power, allied with the irrigators who controlled the water, had grown up with agriculture. Farmers, and the elected officials who represented them in Boise and Washington, D.C., would enter the postwar years convinced that the company's needs served their own. If their control over water were threatened, they would rally behind any champion who promised to safeguard what they viewed as their birthright and proper inheritance. Downstream, in the Columbia Basin, the New Deal and World War II had generated a far different prospect for the future of power over water.

Climb again to the ramparts of the Northwest, above Hells Canyon in the Seven Devils Mountains. West and north, the prospect reveals sinuous ranges of lower, forested mountains rolling away toward the Columbia River. Their sheath of pines and fir rent by geometric gray-green blocks of underbrush left by industrial logging, crisscrossed by tan roads that carried the trees toward sawmills, the Wallowa Mountains tumble toward the Blue Mountains of eastern Oregon.[25]

The Blues mark the outer works of the Columbia Basin, the Northwest's other, damper half. Westering along the Oregon Trail 150 years ago, emigrants rightly felt they had at last penetrated the farther reaches of Oregon Country once they tipped their wagons down the crest of the Blue Mountains. The Blues cradle the Umatilla River Basin, and the Umatilla flows north, into the Columbia River. Just above the mouth of the Umatilla, McNary Dam now looms across the Columbia. Just above McNary's reservoir, the Snake River meets the Columbia.[26]

Begun in 1946, McNary was the first hydroelectric dam on the Columbia built after World War II. It demarcated the eastern frontier of the hydroelectric homeland at the postwar's outset. In that pulsing, vibrant region, embracing the Columbia Basin of Washington and Oregon, cheap publicly generated electricity from federal dams reworked human society and natural systems during the New Deal and wartime. The Hells Canyon controversy that engulfed the Snake Basin in the postwar marched upriver, west to east, from its source in the Columbia Basin. From its bustling cities, flourishing amid fir-carpeted mountains, the federal search for new hydroelectric power pushed east, uphill toward the Snake Basin and Continental Divide.

New Deal public-power policy in the Northwest transformed the Columbia Basin. Abundant, cheap hydroelectricity, the region's basic energy resource, gave federal administrators vast authority over the public-power domain. In less than a decade after their completion, in 1938 and 1940, respectively, Bonneville and Grand Coulee Dams tripled total electric generating capacity in the region, from 1,200 megawatts to 3,700 megawatts. In 1930 a mere 600 megawatts had satisfied total northwestern demand.

Nowhere else on earth did more people depend more intimately on hydroelectricity as their principal energy source. By 1948, industrial and residential customers served by Bonneville Power Administration consumed nearly 300 percent more electricity than the national per capita average. Nationwide, fossil fuels still delivered 96 percent of total energy and, burned in thermal generating plants, 71 percent of electricity. That proportion had remained constant for twenty-five years. By contrast, in the Northwest, home to 40 percent of all national hydropower potential, water generated more than 80 percent of the region's total electric output. As the U.S. government built the dams that produced the power and the high-voltage transmission lines that carried it from the dams to the load centers, nowhere else in America did people depend more fully on federal power policy to satisfy their needs for food, clothing, and shelter.[27]

Looking back on twenty years of public-power growth in the Columbia Basin, the Federal Power Commission appreciated how cheap hydroelectricity had transformed the basin's economy. "It must be kept in mind," FPC judge William Costello wrote in 1955, "that many of the great public undertakings which have taken place in the past several decades have had as a prime purpose the furnishing of large amounts of electric power to consumers at low rates." Since 1937, when Congress enacted the Bonneville Project Act, the federal government in the Columbia Basin had "provided for rate structures which would be based upon a policy of 'encouraging the widest possible diversified use of electric energy.'"[28] Writing shortly after Grand Coulee power surged into Bonneville Power Administration lines, FPC commissioner John W. Scott saw this as a dream of cheap power realized. "The public has invested millions of dollars in these great projects," he ruled, "not for the purpose of increasing the profits of the private utilities, but to provide cheap electric energy for consumers generally."[29]

Bonneville Power Administration, encouraged by New Deal Congresses and President Roosevelt, became the Columbia Basin's indispensable guardian by selling hydropower well below prevailing private-utility rates. "Most of the industrial growth of the Northwest," Costello found during the Hells Canyon controversy, "has been based upon the cheapness of water power which has been relied upon to offset the higher transportation costs of materials and transportation of the processed raw materials to markets which, for the most part, are long distant from the Northwest."[30] Even in a postwar political climate less enthusiastic about New Deal power dams— "less worshipful," Idaho Power's counsel dryly observed—Costello urged northwesterners to "face up to the economic facts of life. One of those is that the Northwest area is a remarkably low-priced power area and is famous therefore, and efforts on the part of anyone—whether it is a public agency or a private agency—to influence the cost of power by bringing higher cost power to the area will have a real battle on his hands."[31]

For more than a decade following 1935, when construction of the gigantic New Deal federal dams began in earnest, no private electric utility in the Columbia Basin added a single kilowatt of new generating capacity. During that same span, total northwestern electric consumption soared 250 percent. Bonneville Power administrator Paul J. Raver's aggressive execution of New Deal hydroelectric philosophy, dedicated to encouraging electricity's maximum use over the broadest possible service area, kept northwestern power costs one-third the national average. By 1946, federal hydropower, distributed across the Columbia Basin on federal transmission lines, had boosted its capacity 500 percent. With every kilowatt-hour of this torrent sold by BPA at $17.50 per kilowatt-year, federal electricity controlled 40 percent of the Northwest's power market. Before 1935, the federal contribution had been zero. By late 1946, private power companies that served the Columbia Basin and Puget Sound conceded permanent federal primacy: they formally asked the United States to assume full responsibility for the Pacific Northwest's power future by building nearly all new hydroelectric capacity, more than 300 megawatts a year, for the next decade.[32]

Mobilizing to fight World War II, the United States learned the value of electrifying the Columbia Basin's rivers under federal leadership. Abundant hydroelectricity became a military asset. Generated chiefly from Bonneville and Grand Coulee dams and transmitted across the Columbia Basin along BPA lines, cheap power went to war.[33] Immediately after Pearl Harbor, the U.S. Office of Defense Mobilization ordered public-power agencies and private electrical companies to interconnect with BPA, federalizing the entire Northwest electrical grid for war production. The Northwest Power Pool linked transmission systems owned by corporate utilities, federal agencies, municipal electric departments, and county-level public utility districts. Across this regional grid, hydropower surged throughout the Columbia and Snake basins, regardless of its source at public or private dams.[34]

By creating a federally controlled electricity distribution network amid patriotic fervor, the federal government accomplished a cherished New Deal aim without costly litigation, controversial legislation, or regional resistance.[35] Power companies retained their assets. Corporate managers, answerable to private shareholders and lenders, still superintended their investments. The Northwest Power Pool nonetheless began redeploying private power to serve national policies. The Power Pool enabled federal hydroelectric managers to market and transmit hydroelectricity generated outside the Columbia Basin. Now BPA began managing Snake River Basin hydropower, heretofore the exclusive province of Idaho Power Company. Idaho Power's sixteen small run-of-river power dams became tributaries of the federal government's total electric supply in the Pacific Northwest.[36]

The postwar, dawning electric blue over the Northwest's green hills and tawny plains, revealed a landscape more urban, industrial, and dependent on federal leadership. Under Northwest Power Pool stewardship, cheap public hydropower had quickly equipped coastal metropolitan areas around Seattle-Tacoma and Portland with world-class shipyards and aircraft factories. Bonneville Power electricity had made Spokane, Washington, into the world's leading aluminum producer. Public hydropower, distributed by rural electric cooperatives and public utility districts, had stimulated major changes in northwestern farming: 95 percent of farms and ranches in the Columbia Basin were electrified by 1945; by contrast, barely half were in Montana and Wyoming.[37]

War around the world steadily consolidated the national government's New Deal primacy over Columbia Basin hydroelectricity. Power supply both led and followed internal migration.[38] Wherever 230-kilovolt BPA trunk lines transmitted cut-rate federal power, industrialization and urbanization followed, beckoned by the fabulous prospect of the world's cheapest electricity. Defense workers swelled payrolls at contracting firms, concentrated around Seattle-Everett-Tacoma in the Puget Sound, and Portland-Vanport in the Willamette Valley. Population in Washington and Oregon soared from 2.8 million in 1940 to 3.9 million by the end of the Second World War. Nearly everyone was clustering in metropolitan areas. Oregon and Washington customers living west of the Cascade Range, served by the West Region of the Northwest Power Pool, consumed three-quarters of the electricity generated in the entire Northwest. By contrast, that part of eastern Oregon in the Snake River Basin, abutting Hells Canyon, actually lost 10 percent of its population during the 1940s.[39]

LAND OF THE SALMON

Take a last view from the Seven Devils, above Hells Canyon, across a different prospect of the Snake Basin. East and north, up there in the mild breeze that blows steadily in the fall, serried lines of gray ridges march away across central Idaho. In numberless rank, they climb toward the Continental

Divide, lost in the blue eastern distance. Lewis and Clark's Corps of Discovery wandered these alpine back alleys two hundred autumns ago, in 1805. Fruitlessly, they sought the Snake and, desperately, the Columbia and Pacific Ocean. Only generous assistance from curious, amused Nez Perce Indians—horses, food, canoes, advice—saved the sagging adventurers from starvation.[40]

Among the Indians' greatest gifts to the exhausted band was salmon. Fall-run chinook swarmed up the Columbia into the Snake Basin in September and October, as many as a half million by later estimates. Unnumbered millions of juvenile smolts, hatched in the basin's gravelly streams, rode fresh spring snowmelt currents back down the Snake and Columbia into the sea. For ten thousand years, at least since the last of the glaciers had receded up the Columbia Basin into what is now Canada, these two life-currents— flowing water and moving fish—had tied together the Columbia Basin and Snake Basin. If rivers were the umbilical, then anadromous fish were the lifeblood of the Northwest. Water and fish, both in perpetual motion uphill and down, unified the humid and arid halves of the Northwest as powerfully and seamlessly as the rain-heavy clouds that streamed inland from the North Pacific.[41]

A careful gaze from the Seven Devils, assisted by map and binoculars, into Nez Perce and Lewis-Clark country reveals Chair Point. A mound of caramel-colored basalt, Chair Point rises where the Salmon River suddenly twists northward after rushing west for 125 miles, unable to punch through the Seven Devils. Rolling past the little riverside hamlet of Riggins, Idaho, the lower Salmon arcs around the range's northern buttress to meet the Snake, some sixty river miles below Chair Point, near White Bird, Idaho.

If nature had given the Salmon more energy, or more time, the meeting of the waters might have come far sooner. At Chair Point, the Snake in Hells Canyon lies barely twenty miles west of the Salmon. If the Salmon had piled head-on into the Snake, had obliterated that sixty-mile bend past White Bird, the history of Hells Canyon would have been far different in the postwar era. Those sixty miles of the lower Salmon, separated from the Snake by the Seven Devils' mile-high ramparts, have enabled Snake Basin migratory fish to survive all the dam building since 1935. Many postwar dam plans, proposed by federal agencies and private utilities other than Idaho Power, contemplated closing the Salmon along with Snake. Ultimately, private dams arose in Hells Canyon only. The lower Salmon freely pours into the Snake below Hells Canyon. Such are the ways that nature makes history, for humans and for fish.[42]

At Chair Point, the Little Salmon River tumbles into the Salmon, its far bigger namesake. Nez Perce for a hundred generations had caught salmon and steelhead trout in the Little Salmon, as well as in the main Salmon and its higher tributaries. Nez Perce still live in Hells Canyon country: their reservation perches above the Salmon-Snake confluence, in north-central Idaho. Five miles above the confluence of the Little Salmon with the Salmon, invisible from Dry Diggins Lookout, the Rapid River—hardly more than a bracing brook, really—sluices through a salmon hatchery and into the Little Salmon. Built in 1964 by Idaho Power Company, Rapid River Hatchery now preserves remnant traces of the million-strong chinook runs that succored Lewis and Clark two centuries ago and occupied Nez Perce fishers for millennia.[43] After the Hells Canyon controversy ended, northwesterners tried to make topography the natural basis of a new strategy for preserving Snake Basin migratory fish. Rapid River Hatchery salmon follow the Little Salmon, which runs undammed into the lower Salmon at Chair Point. Flowing water then pushes the fish down the undammed lower Salmon into the undammed Snake below Hells Canyon. If this hopeful gamble succeeds in keeping life in the river—a question still open in our time—it will be because the Seven Devils pushed the Salmon north at Chair Point. Topography and geology, aided by law, may prevail in the long run over fish-killing power dams. Technology and money have bought only more time to let nature try to restore life to the water.[44]

Two distinctive northwestern societies occupy the region's two great watersheds. Their different relationships to water reflect the New Deal's disparate effects on natural systems and human societies in the Columbia and Snake basins. At the end of World War II, the Snake Basin still used water to irrigate the desert. The Columbia Basin, by contrast, distinctively depended on hydroelectricity to power its economy. The federal agencies that managed public power's domain believed they could replicate in the Snake Basin what they had accomplished in the Columbia Basin. Politicians devoted to public power's credo of maximum use at lowest cost endorsed their postwar upriver offensive. Together, the administrators and the politicians who governed the Columbia Basin reached out toward Hells Canyon. There, at the watershed boundary between two distinctive ways of valuing water, northwesterners had to decide whether the New Deal's transformation of the Columbia Basin should similarly rearrange the postwar Snake Basin. Ultimately, the whole nation became party to the Hells Canyon controversy. Its verdict against public power in what became a national referendum unplugged the New Deal public-power legacy in the postwar Northwest.[45]

3 NATIONALIZING NATURE

The New Deal Legacy of Snake Basin Hydropower

F
ederal plans to electrify Hells Canyon originated during the New Deal.
Public power's transformation of the Columbia Basin inspired
activists and ordinary citizens across America to dream of pushing
out hydroelectricity's frontiers. Building new federal dams became
more than matters of engineering judgment and cost-benefit analysis: they
made concrete statements about national progress toward the brighter future.
This New Deal legacy made the Hells Canyon High Dam controversy more
than a referendum about northwestern postwar natural-resources policy.
Public-power expansion engaged organizations and people far from the
region. Powerful ideological, economic, and legal currents invested this struggle about a big dam with remarkable durability and ferocity. These currents
traced their source far back into the American experience with capital and
nature, but the New Deal in the Northwest caused them to collide in the
Hells Canyon controversy.

In Hells Canyon, after World War II, the Snake River running west met
an expansive public-power domain pushing east. Abundant, inexpensive
hydroelectricity pouring from Bonneville and Grand Coulee dams had
spread new industry, farms, and people throughout the Columbia Basin after
1935. Almost overnight, Bonneville, built by the Army Corps of Engineers,
and Grand Coulee, property of the Interior Department's Bureau of Reclamation, unleashed an unprecedented jolt of energy. Public power transmitted through high-voltage lines built by the Department of Interior's
Bonneville Power Administration, re-created the Columbia Basin between
1935 and 1945. Power over Columbia Basin water, secured during the New
Deal, inspired federal agencies and their customers to look upriver, seeking control over Snake Basin hydroelectricity. Most downriver business
boosters and elected officials supported the quest by BPA, the Army Engi-

neers, and the Reclamation Bureau to secure more cheap hydroelectricity. Prosaic pursuit of price advantage dovetailed with planners' and publicists' hopes to reform virgin territory with public power. Federal turbines now did double duty as growth engines and dream machines.

Both wings of the postwar upriver offensive believed Hells Canyon's power potential, once annexed into the public-power domain, would make territorial expansion pay. Federalizing Hells Canyon hydropower would enable agency planners and their regional allies to attain five interlinked postwar ambitions: extend cheap public electricity into the Snake Basin, irrigate nearly a half-million acres of sagebrush desert on the Snake River Plain, diversify the Snake Basin's economy, satisfy the Columbia Basin's boundless energy appetite, and master the Snake's flow to prevent downstream floods and to carry barges upriver. Each goal enlisted a different segment of the public-power coalition that had redefined the objectives of natural-resources policy in the Columbia Basin.

The New Deal Northwest's grandest monument, Grand Coulee Dam, is central to understanding not only the New Deal in the Columbia Basin but also the postwar Hells Canyon controversy. The Bureau of Reclamation and Bonneville Power Administration used Coulee's power to drive a planned expansion of irrigated agriculture and industrial manufacturing throughout the Columbia Basin. That same vision inspired BPA and Reclamation planners, as soon as World War II ended, to plan a similar transformation of Snake Basin life. The New Deal's Columbia Basin strategy pivoted around cheap, abundant Grand Coulee hydropower. Postwar New Dealers' federal strategy for the Snake Basin likewise depended on cheap, abundant electricity generated by a new federal High Hells Canyon Dam.

The expanding public-power domain, formally known after 1946 as the Federal Columbia River Power System, innovated legal strategies and administrative techniques to try annexing Hells Canyon. The New Deal bequeathed not so much a new civic ethos about nature as a new administrative regime over nature. Executive agencies, ultimately responsible to the president and his cabinet, became the chief means for adapting nature to society. New Deal jurisprudence rationalized federal administrators' discretionary authority over nature. Law made during the New Deal magnified the postwar upriver offensive's striking power by neutralizing opponents' capacity to dissent. In targeting Hells Canyon, federal agency administrators deployed quasi-sovereign power over Northwest water and land.

New Deal statutes and administrative regulations committed the United

States to delivering cheap public power throughout the Columbia Basin. The trio of federal agencies that administered public power's domain—BPA, Army Engineers, and Reclamation Bureau—aggressively invoked the new laws to reach beyond the Columbia Basin. Lawmaking that created the public-power domain had often been urgent, ad hoc, driven by national emergencies. Somewhat belatedly, Congress tried to rationalize the New Deal fusion of federal dams and public power. The 1944 Flood Control Act recognized three distinctive innovations had transformed the Columbia Basin: mammoth multiple-purpose federal dams, subsidized power dedicated to maximizing consumption, and tripartite governance of this federal strategy.[1] The act directed the Army Corps of Engineers to design coordinated basinwide systems—dams, locks, levees, and docks—to develop all the water resources in the nation's great river valleys. To this charge the corps' North Pacific Division in Portland quickly turned when peace returned to the Northwest. The Snake River, which Congress and the corps had deemed navigable nearly to its source twenty years earlier, presented an unmatched opportunity to plan a basin's fate.[2]

The Flood Control Act also reaffirmed the role of public power in transforming the Columbia Basin. It directed the Corps of Engineers to provide all power generated at its new northwestern dams to the Department of Interior. Interior, which oversaw both BPA and the Reclamation Bureau, now commanded a nearly inexhaustible economic asset to fuel its campaign to push the New Deal into the postwar Snake Basin. All hydroelectricity generated at federal dams in the Northwest, whichever agency built them, would carry the same low price that had entrenched BPA as the primary power supplier in the Columbia Basin. An extensive array of public-power dependencies, organized into the Northwest Public Power Association, enjoyed a statutory "preference right" to claim as much new power as they could take from all new federal dams. Postwar expansion of public power into the Snake Basin thus mobilized a cavalcade of beneficiaries, each eager to obtain as much energy as possible from Hells Canyon at low, fixed "postage-stamp" rates enshrined as New Deal dogma. As *Public Power* magazine editorialized, "The reason for the preferences is obvious. Public funds are used to develop a public asset—the rivers of our nation. The most valuable product of the development is hydroelectric energy. . . . By permitting public bodies and cooperatives to buy the energy, the most widespread use is achieved."[3]

The 1944 Flood Control Act finally consolidated the multiagency regime that had managed Columbia Basin power. Bonneville Dam had been the

Army Engineers' chief contribution to New Deal hydroelectric strategy. Bonneville Power Administration sold its electricity as well as Coulee's and also promoted electrification of homes, industry, and farms. To mollify the Interior Department and its traditional constituents in irrigated agriculture, Congress had made BPA, like Reclamation, a subdivision of Interior in 1937. The 1944 act perpetuated this tripartite administrative alliance by directing the Corps of Engineers, Reclamation Bureau, and BPA to work in harness. Henceforward, the Bureau of Reclamation would own and BPA would sell all hydropower from new northwestern federal dams, including the Hells Canyon High Dam proposed in 1947.[4]

By consolidating federal hydroelectric administrators' discretionary authority over the Northwest's principal energy source, the Flood Control Act facilitated strategic planning for postwar expansion. It prompted the three agencies in 1946 to form the Columbia Basin Inter-Agency Committee (CBIAC). Pronounced "*sibeeack*" by those who knew the jargon of power, CBIAC drove the first phase of the Hells Canyon controversy through 1950. The committee met monthly in various cities around the Northwest, from Eugene, Oregon, to Great Falls, Montana. It acted as a clearinghouse for federal plans, a bazaar where local interests sought federal funds to advance a pet construction project, and a board of complaint for states and private groups protesting management of the hydroelectric empire. A federal body that has never been systematically studied or properly appreciated by historians or political scientists, CBIAC played a decisive part in extending the public-power domain during the Hells Canyon controversy. Until Dwight Eisenhower became president in 1953, CBIAC principally directed the campaign to federalize Hells Canyon hydroelectricity. Its decisions from 1946 through 1950—about construction plans, reclamation strategy, economic development, and the Northwest's anadromous fish—reflected shifting federal strategies for annexing the Snake Basin into the postwar New Deal.[5]

Wartime mobilization of federal water-development projects also influenced CBIAC's mission. Its national-security pedigree gave CBIAC additional influence whenever cold war defense strategy preoccupied the federal government. The Federal Power Commission, Interior and Agriculture Departments, and Army Engineers had created, in late 1943, the Federal Inter-Agency River Basin Committee. The committee was supposed to encourage agency cooperation "in the preparation of reports on the multiple-purpose development of national water resources."[6] Shortly after peace returned, CBIAC appeared, its birth announcement a dry, three-page resolution adopted on 5 February 1946 by the parent FIARBC.[7]

The member agencies of CBIAC agreed to "effectively interchange information and coordinate their activities among themselves and with those of the states . . . to assure coordination of activities and avoid duplication of effort."[8] Hydropower fueled the postwar upriver offensive, so Bonneville Power Administration became a charter member of CBIAC. Bonneville Power and CBIAC usually pursued complementary objectives in the first phase of the Hells Canyon controversy because the same men officered both enterprises: CBIAC's founding charter also required its agency members simultaneously to act as the Bonneville Advisory Board. Facing themselves, as it were, across the conference table, CBIAC and BPA were usually able "to assure coordination of activities and avoid duplication of effort."[9]

The Columbia Basin Inter-Agency Committee commanded a broad field of maneuver: "the Columbia River Basin, and the streams which enter the Pacific Ocean within the boundaries of the States of Washington and Oregon, and the closed basins in the State of Oregon." Its strategic objective was heroic: "planning and execution of works for the control and use of the waters of the Columbia River system and the streams of the coastal drainage areas." And its procedures subjected northwestern states to federal hydro-electric leadership: the seven states encompassed in CBIAC's theater of operations were "invited . . . to designate jointly five representatives . . . for the purpose of keeping the [federal agency] members advised of the interests of the states in the plans or proposals under discussion," but only the federal regional chieftains, or their Washington, D.C., superiors could act.[10]

Colonel Theron D. Weaver, commanding the Corps of Engineers' North Pacific Division from his Portland headquarters, first convened CBIAC in spring 1946. The committee's chairman enjoyed broad administrative powers during his one-year term. He selected its secretary, effectively making his agency the committee's secretariat. He thus enjoyed the bureaucrat's prerogatives: scheduling meetings, preparing agendas, publishing public notices, and writing up minutes and reports. During the Hells Canyon controversy's first phase, each agency that coveted the Snake Basin's hydropower potential had ample opportunity to influence federal policy. R. J. Newell, Region 1 director of the Bureau of Reclamation, succeeded Weaver as CBIAC chairman in July 1947, followed at yearly intervals through summer 1950 by Federal Power Commission regional engineer Lesher S. Wing and Agriculture Department field director Herbert M. Peet.[11]

Interior secretary Harold Ickes provided CBIAC its rationale for building a replica of the New Deal Columbia Basin in the postwar Snake Basin.
He issued in January 1946 a departmental power-policy memorandum that
linked low-cost New Deal hydroelectricity, federal multipurpose dams, and
expanded electricity use to diversify regional economies. Ickes ruled that a
decade of New Deal power policy now committed the Interior Department
to five broad objectives: new multipurpose federal dams, preference sales
of federal hydroelectricity to public agencies rather than to corporate utilities, transmission programs favoring reclamation and urban growth, electric prices low enough to stimulate demand by maximizing consumption,
and constant pressure against private utilities through low-cost public
power.[12]

Ickes's 1946 power-policy memorandum dedicated the Interior Department to stimulating electrical demand. Revenues from power sales would
not only retire federal dam-construction debt but also facilitate new irrigation works in areas using public power. In the Northwest, new federal
electricity would be sold wholesale at prices low enough to "bring power at
the lowest possible rates to distributors that are principally serving domestic and rural consumers." Wholesale contracts committed BPA to enforcing
its preference customers' retail power sales at rates "which shall reflect as
nearly as may be the cost of the service." In addition, to encourage power
consumption and spread the blessings of federal hydroelectricity, Ickes
directed Interior to promote "diversified development of the industries and
resources" of regions served by BPA and the Reclamation Bureau. Ickes's
successor as Interior secretary, Julius A. Krug, intensified the department's
drive to expand federal power primacy in the Northwest.[13]

In the first years of the Hells Canyon controversy, private power companies in the Columbia Basin shared Ickes's and Krug's expansionist fervor.
Their chief executives hitched their future to buying cheap wholesale public power from BPA and reselling it at steady profits, subject to regulation
by state public utility commissions in Oregon and Washington.[14] Their customers in the Puget Sound and Willamette Valley seemed likely to demand
ever more cheap electricity, so corporate utility leaders chorused BPA administrator Paul Raver's tune. Raver, testifying in favor of big boosts in his
agency's transmission-line budget, told Congress in spring 1946:

> The Bonneville Power Administration as I see it today is a public utility. . . . And
> when a public utility enters on the responsibility of serving the people of a given

area with an essential service it undertakes large responsibilities. . . . We are now in that position for the large part of the Northwest. The government, as I see it, is now in the position of having undertaken a responsibility of supplying the distributing agencies in the Northwest and therefore the people of the Northwest, through those distributing agencies, whether they are public or private, with an essential service, and we can't withdraw. We can't be too handicapped in the rendering of that service by appropriations.

In October, James H. Polhemus, president of Portland General Electric Company, conceded to BPA the field of generating and transmitting electricity from federal dams to load centers. The first and still the biggest customer for public power in the Columbia Basin, PGE pleaded with the federal government to fund Raver's construction budgets. Polhemus acknowledged that his utility had not expanded its own generating capacity during the Depression and World War II because of PGE's "sincere desire to cooperate in the program for Columbia river development in a way that would best serve the public interest." With Bonneville power available at cut-rate prices, Polhemus believed it "unpatriotic to our region [and] economically unsound, to build additional generating plants to compete with Federal projects." As PGE studied the future, Polhemus foresaw federal hydroelectric growth as the answer to his utility's supply needs, as well as to his customers' demands: "Our present rate structure is built upon the continuing availability of federally generated power in amounts adequate to meet not only the present but the future demands of our people. If these needs are not fulfilled, it is these people who will be hurt."[15]

During the winter of 1946–47, Columbia Basin power companies negotiated what became known as the "Tacoma Statement." Issued 22 January 1947, together with BPA's preference customers in the region, the Tacoma Statement urged consolidation of federal hydroelectric supremacy. By designating BPA as the Columbia Basin's sole utility for selling and transmitting power generated from new federal dams, the Tacoma Statement cleared the way for the federal upriver offensive: "The assumption of utility responsibility by the Federal government has caused investors and management of both publicly and privately owned industrial and power distribution enterprise in the states of Oregon and Washington to plan their investments and development programs in the belief that this Federal policy will continue."[16] Tacoma Statement signatories carried their plea to Congress, testifying in support of BPA's fiscal 1948 construction budget.[17] A disappointed northwestern utility executive admitted that "the Federal government has pre-empted the field so far as hydro generation is concerned."[18] A critic of the Tacoma Statement thought BPA planned "a steady drive to bring all electric power of Washington, Oregon, and Idaho into public ownership, the sources to be under the administration's control."[19]

New Deal policy—selling federal electricity at cost throughout the region—fed BPA administrator Paul Raver's postwar appetite for more power. He wanted to adorn the entire Northwest, from Montana to the Oregon-California border, with a concrete necklace of high multipurpose dams strung along 230-kilovolt steel cables. His "fundamental principles" for expanding the Federal Columbia River Power System stressed treating the entire Northwest as a single power-supply planning unit. Raver advised his CBIAC colleagues to act as if BPA were "the Pacific Northwest's public utility." He envisioned interconnecting the region's electrical system with federal power projects in the Missouri and Colorado river basins.[20]

Bonneville Power's partners in CBIAC shared Raver's enthusiastic expansionism. "Nature endowed the Pacific Northwest with an abundance of certain natural resources—land, water and minerals and the wealth which they produce," declared the interagency committee's strategic manual. "The basic long-term objective toward which this six-year program is directed is ultimately to meet the economic needs of this country—specifically, to provide through resource conservation and development, better living, greater opportunity for economic advancement, and more security for the individual, the family, the community, the Pacific Northwest, and the Nation."[21]

Both the Army Corps of Engineers and the Bureau of Reclamation pivoted their Snake Basin offensives around building the mightiest new dam in the region, and in the world for that matter. However, each agency pursued Hells Canyon High Dam so aggressively that their rivalry threatened to stall the upriver offensive before it really got untracked. The corps' North Pacific Division began formulating plans to build new dams almost as soon as Japan surrendered in September 1945. Region 1 of the Reclamation Bureau, based in Boise, also began circulating in the Northwest and Washington, D.C., its plans for new multipurpose federal dams athwart the Columbia and Snake.

Contemporary academic analysts, such as Harvard's Arthur Maas and Reed College's Charles McKinley, bemoaned the federal construction agencies' inability to cooperate. Maas and McKinley cited the Northwest as a prime example of wasteful bureaucratic pettiness and inertia.[22] Yet robust rivalry between Reclamation and Army Engineers was not the whole story, nor even the most important, during 1947. Steadily and patiently, CBIAC was massaging the agencies' water-management blueprints at its monthly public meetings, probing for common ends and complementary approaches. Away from the public eye, CBIAC's principals found that Reclamation, the corps, and BPA could easily agree on one big point: the United States had to federalize the Snake's hydroelectric potential to power any coordinated strategy for upriver expansion of the Federal Columbia River Power System.

Strategically vital as Hells Canyon was, maps of the region still denoted it simply as "Box Canyon" or "Snake River Canyon." An enterprising journalist and ambitious politician from Portland, Richard Neuberger, had begun calling the area "Hells Canyon" in 1940s travel magazine articles. But his efforts had not yet fixed the nation's eye, or its legendary place-name, on Hells Canyon. Anonymity quickly evaporated when political passion about Hells Canyon High Dam reached white heat. Flaring in the nation's capital early in 1947, and then erupting in the Northwest by midsummer, Hells Canyon became a national controversy. Fodder for national newspaper editorials and Sunday-afternoon radio public-affairs roundtables, it remained so for more than a decade.[23]

President Truman's January 1947 State of the Union address and Budget Message pledged to accelerate comprehensive river-basin planning and water-resources development. Truman's keen interest in public power coincided with Interior secretary Krug's philosophy. Krug had been Harold Ickes's wartime energy administrator. Since releasing the first sketch of Interior's Snake Basin plan in June 1946, Krug had been exhorting Reclamation commissioner Michael Straus and BPA's Raver to complete their agencies' strategic surveys of Hells Canyon. Assistant Interior secretary C. Girard Davidson managed Krug's daily relations with Reclamation and BPA. Formerly a legal counselor to both the Tennessee Valley Authority and Bonneville Power, "Jebby" Davidson believed in New Deal power policy with the zeal of a fanatic. Davidson and Raver, both Ickes protégés, shared the "Old Curmudgeon's" commitment to using federal power to transform the entire Northwest. Straus, himself a veteran New Dealer, dutifully kept pressing Reclamation's Region 1 chief, R. J. Newell, to get the Boise office's Snake Basin studies done.[24]

Straus formally published Reclamation's recommended plan for federalizing Snake River hydropower in mid-March 1947. The bureau sought public comment and got an earful. The Snake Plan's centerpiece amazed observers: Hells Canyon High Dam, nearly 750 feet tall, would be higher than Hoover Dam and store more water, 3.5 million acre-feet, than Grand Coulee. Reclamation thought big because High Hells Canyon was intended to accomplish much larger ends. The Snake Basin Plan proposed redirecting the paths of rivers over and under mountains, into canals gouged across miles of arid foothills, and then pouring them onto hundreds of thousands of rolling desert acres around Region 1 Boise headquarters. By marshalling High Hells Canyon's power revenues for this Mountain Home Project, Reclamation's Snake Basin Plan sought to extend its New Deal Columbia Basin strategy to jump-start urban growth and industrial diversification under federal direction (map 3).

"Continued strong westward migration and rapidly growing population in Western regions impose an expanding demand on the department of the interior to assist in an accelerated development of the region's resources of land, water, energy, and raw materials," Region 1's Snake Basin Plan declared. As nearly one million new mouths would have to be fed in the Northwest by 1960—25 percent more than its 1947 population—the Reclamation Bureau would have to bring irrigation to at least eight hundred thousand new acres of cropland in the region, half of that alone in the desert around Boise.

New agricultural production required more intensive fertilization. The Snake Plan identified phosphate rock—more than five billion tons deposited in southeast Idaho, 60 percent of the nation's known reserves—as "much the most valuable nonmetallic mineral resource, and probably the single most important of all the mineral resources in the Upper Snake River Basin." To transform rock into fertilizer took vast amounts of electricity. However, the Interior Department had solved a similar challenge in the New Deal. Cheap public power in the Columbia Basin had literally created a domestic aluminum industry, dependent on BPA electricity to fire its reduction furnaces. Experience gained with Columbia Basin aluminum assured Reclamation that High Hells Canyon could do the same for Snake Basin phosphate: "A further expansion of great magnitude in the phosphate industry of the Upper Snake River Basin . . . to meet requirements of the Region and Nation will be possible only when the large amounts of low cost electrical energy which are required for efficient, large-scale production by electrical methods can be made available."[25]

Hells Canyon High Dam had to generate revenue as well as power to drive this "far-flung program for raising the Pacific Northwest's industrial, power, agricultural, and mineral output to new heights by 1960." The Snake Plan was, BPA and Reclamation conceded, "one of the more difficult, higher cost projects which now remain after the less difficult, less costly projects have been constructed." Pooled with federal revenues generated in the Columbia Basin, High Dam earnings would be indispensable to the Mountain Home Project. High Hells Canyon thus served the same two purposes for the Interior Department in the postwar Snake Basin as Grand Coulee had in the New Deal Columbia Basin. By adding more than 1,000 megawatts of permanent capacity to the Federal Columbia River Power System, High Hells Canyon would enable BPA to meet growing electrical demands in Oregon and Washington for cheap public power. By earning money from selling this power to Columbia Basin customers, the High Dam would fund what Reclamation termed "the Columbia Basin Account." This fund, Reclamation's cashbox for the Snake Basin, would first pool all revenues earned by selling federal hydroelectricity. Then, after paying down debt incurred to build new dams, Interior would deploy this permanent subsidy to build and operate irrigation works like the Mountain Home Project. Reclamation commissioner Straus termed the hydroelectric pooling account "the major feature of the report."[26]

The Snake Basin Plan offered the Bureau of Reclamation's solution to southwest Idaho's perplexing problems of topography and hydrology. Nearly four hundred thousand acres of sagebrush plain rolled between the Snake River and the east-west mountain wall at the Snake Plain's northern margin. Reclamation planners projected twenty-five hundred new irrigated farms dappling this public land on the Mountain Home desert. Together, the Snake itself and two tributaries in the northern mountains, the Boise and Payette, carried more than enough water for the Mountain Home Project. Confoundingly, this water bypassed the land it was meant to irrigate. A deep canyon carried the Snake several hundred feet below the Mountain Home Desert, while a ragged skein of granite ridges pushed the Boise and Payette west, away from the desert. Early bureau projects had dammed both rivers, but delivered the storage to irrigated farms well west of the Mountain Home Desert. Getting these two wayward rivers running south instead of west, onto the Mountain Home Project instead of into the Snake 60–100 miles downstream, presented the natural problem Region 1's Snake Basin Plan intended to solve.

"Almost all of the water for irrigation," Newell told Straus, "would be supplied by transmountain diversions from the Payette River. . . . The remainder would be supplied from the portion of the water resources of the Boise River not now utilized." In short, the United States would create twenty-five hundred new farms on four hundred thousand acres of high desert southeast of Boise by rearranging nature in the Middle Snake Basin. Region 1's Mountain Home Project tapped central Idaho mountain water to irrigate southwest Idaho desert. Two new reservoirs, one on the Payette and the other on the Boise, linked by the Payette-Boise Aqueduct, would carry stored waters south from both drainages nearly one hundred miles to the rim of the Snake Basin. After punching beneath peaks topping eight thousand feet, the aqueduct would fill two new canals, each more than fifty miles long. They would transport mountain water south and west out onto the Hillcrest and Long Tom Divisions of the Mountain Home Desert, nurturing the project's twenty-five hundred new irrigated farms. Total estimated construction costs, Newell reported to Straus, would exceed $250 million; Reclamation would have to spend more than $1.5 million per year to service the works.[27]

Newell's staff estimated that irrigators who would settle the Mountain Home Project, many of them demobilized servicemen, could muster less than 10 percent of the construction costs, even by paying water charges for fifty years. To finance the project, therefore, Reclamation needed a lot of power revenues. E. N. Torbert, Region 1 planning director, carefully hedged his agency's bets. Some of the irrigation subsidy would come from Mountain Home itself. Reclamation planned three new hydroelectric generating stations along the water's fall line through the mountains. However, they would earn enough power-sale revenue to recoup merely 40 percent of the project's construction and operating expenses. Another cashbox had to be rapidly filled and repeatedly drained: the High Dam in Hells Canyon. Nearly half the financing of the Mountain Home Project depended on federalizing Hells Canyon. Without it, Reclamation's entire Snake Basin Plan foundered on costs so high even the bureau's notoriously rosy benefit projections could not obscure them.

Interior secretary Krug maintained that "revenues from power installations at the Hell's Canyon Dam would materially assist in the financing of irrigation developments. . . . Surplus revenues from that project will be required in the near future to permit the authorization and construction of needed irrigation developments."[28] Howard R. Stinson, Region 1 Reclamation legal counsel, testified that the High Dam was "one of the essential and key elements" in federal postwar power and reclamation strategy for the

Snake Basin and the entire Northwest. The High Dam enabled federal dam building, power marketing, and reclamation agencies to coordinate their plans "in order to achieve the fullest use of the water resources of the Snake River . . . [so as] to achieve a full development of the land and water resources of the Pacific Northwest."[29]

Straus sent Reclamation's draft Snake Basin Plan to Idaho governor C. A. Robins in mid-March 1947, rightly calling it "of great importance to the ultimate development of the Basin." Its prescription for "full, orderly basin-wide development" reflected not only BPA's demand for more hydropower to serve its Columbia Basin customers but also Harold Ickes's vision for using public power and federal expertise to remake society.[30] Interior and Reclamation Bureau staff then fanned out across the Northwest to sell Hells Canyon High Dam. Their pitch came with a warning: without the High Dam, the entire Northwest would soon confront disastrous shortages of its basic energy source. Bad as the power picture was in the Columbia Basin, Krug painted an equally grim portrait of a power-starved Snake Basin: "This area's power requirements for phosphate production, other mineral processing, and mining as well as commercial and domestic consumers will exceed the capacity of the existing and approved power installations in the area . . . by 1951. By 1956, . . . the initial power must be available from Hells's Canyon Project to meet both the loads in the eastern and western service areas of the Basin."[31]

Krug, Straus, and Newell dangled tempting bait before Snake Basin irrigators using water from existing Reclamation Bureau projects. The Snake Plan's Columbia Pooling Account would reduce charges to run these works as well as fund new projects like Mountain Home. "Power revenues in excess of those required for return of construction costs . . . may be utilized to return construction costs of worthy irrigation developments which water users cannot reasonably be expected to repay." Hells Canyon High Dam power sales would, in effect, operate as start-up capital for the Pooling Account: "Surplus revenues from that project will be required in the near future to permit the authorization and construction of needed irrigation developments. . . . The Hells's Canyon Dam is required to be undertaken as a Federal project in order to permit this Department to achieve the goal of the fullest economic development of the land and water resources of the Pacific Northwest."[32]

By early July 1947, Newell had mobilized the Idaho, Oregon, and Washington granges to plead for federalization of Hells Canyon "at the earliest possible date." For the grangers cheap public power from the Snake Basin promised more reclamation water as well as industrialization of southeast Idaho's phosphate rock deposits for fertilizer production.[33] The grange, however, carried little water in Snake Basin politics. The Idaho State Reclamation Association's (ISRA) annual late-spring meetings in Idaho Falls gathered the men whose views about the Snake Plan mattered most to Idaho politicians. Governor Robins therefore dispatched State Reclamation Engineer Mark Kulp to solicit ISRA's advice about how to respond to Reclamation's proposals.

Kulp's Idaho Falls mission planted him in the vortex of the Hells Canyon controversy for a decade. His agency decided who got Snake Basin irrigation water, how much, and when. He knew all the leading irrigators, their lenders, the politicians who represented them in Boise and Washington, D.C. Trained as a civil engineer in the Reclamation Bureau's Denver headquarters, he became Idaho's Reclamation engineer in the late 1930s after teaching for five years at the University of Idaho. Kulp's administrative discretion and professional training invested him with the kind of nonpartisan authority usually associated with British civil servants. He already was attending monthly CBIAC meetings as Governor Robins's eyes, ears, and, usually, voice. Robins, a Republican physician, knew little about irrigation. In his home region, the north Idaho panhandle, ample precipitation made irrigation unnecessary.[34]

Robins's dependence on Kulp became so total that, for the rest of his single term in the governor's office, his public comments on federal water and power policy simply repeated the state engineer's confidential advice. Through three successive administrations—from 1946 through 1958—Kulp represented Idaho on the Columbia Basin Inter-Agency Committee, advising state and federal politicians and administrators of both parties about reclamation and power strategy. Kulp negotiated regularly (and usually privately) with Idaho Power Company after it unveiled its plans in late 1947 to counter Hells Canyon High Dam with a smaller run-of-river dam. As much as any Idahoan, Kulp shaped and expressed irrigators' fierce opposition to Reclamation's Snake Plan. As influential as any Northwest elected official during the Hells Canyon controversy, Kulp used legal authority over Idaho water and credibility with irrigation leaders to help them stop the upriver federal offensive.

May in Idaho Falls affords crystal-blue views of the Snake's birthplace in the Tetons. After hearing Kulp's briefing, the Idaho State Reclamation

Association quickly began aligning against the Snake Basin Plan. Snake River Watermaster Lynn Crandall summarized ISRA's attitude as one part wait-and-see and one part fear of "the vast discretionary powers and authority contemplated by the proposed report." Snake Basin irrigators "are not dupes or agents of the power companies," he told Idaho senator Glen Taylor, but they "are inclined to be suspicious of the Bureau of Reclamation and Interior Department policies and look for some 'nigger in the Woodpile' in proposals that are made to them." Crandall voiced irritation with heavy-handed federal management. Irrigators felt water belonged to them, equitably if not exactly legally. He deplored Ickes's and Straus's overhaul of Reclamation's mission. From irrigating desert lands, the bureau now led "the determined Government drive to take over the northwest for public power." And he feared the Snake Basin Plan risked Idaho's well-entrenched system of reclamation water subsidies in the raging congressional debate over western water and power policy.[35]

The state's most powerful business and agricultural organization, the Idaho State Chamber of Commerce, advised Governor Robins that Crandall "seems to us to state the situation relative to the Columbia Basin report in a very clear-cut manner." Robins had to listen when the chamber spoke about water and power. Among its directors advising the governor to withhold endorsement of the Snake Plan were the state's leading banker, leading public-works contractor, ISRA's current and incoming presidents, the watermasters of the upper and lower Snake basins, and Idaho Power Company's board chairman and senior vice-president.[36]

For six months, Robins fended off Krug's demand that Idaho take a stand on the Snake Plan and High Hells Canyon. The Interior Department was busy trying to promote Reclamation's Snake Basin strategy ahead of the Army Engineers' study of the same terrain. When Krug finally set a drop-dead date for Idaho to comment formally, the governor told Interior in early August 1947 that the Snake Plan "has many interesting phases which would immensely benefit the development of the resources of the Columbia Basin in general and the State of Idaho specifically." Nevertheless, his definitive position depended on what the Army Corps recommended for the Snake Basin. Kulp wrote this letter, as well as the governor's last, and still non-committal, noncomment of 27 September. Since rivalry between Reclamation and the corps was cresting, Idaho saw no "unified program for watershed development" and thus had no reason to prefer one hydro/reclamation plan over another.

One "paramount consideration," however, motivated Robins to warn Krug, "The waters of the Snake River and its tributaries in the southern part of our state should be utilized and protected for utilization for the development of reclamation in the Snake River Basin." Hells Canyon hydroelectricity had to be permanently subordinated to future upstream diversions of the Snake for irrigation. Unless all stored water in Hells Canyon carried a permanent legal servitude in favor of Snake Basin irrigated farming, Idaho would refuse to grant any state-law right to appropriate water for power purposes.[37]

By autumn 1947, therefore, Snake Basin irrigation and business leaders had decided Idaho would oppose Hells Canyon's federalization. Together, they determined the legal, political, and economic rationale for Idaho's future policy. Any federal dam big enough to generate more than 1,000 megawatts of power, no matter which agency built it, would have to store so much water that Idaho irrigators believed it would menace their livelihood and political supremacy over the Snake. A reservoir that filled ninety miles of Hells Canyon would require so much water—3.5 million acre-feet—as to preclude nearly all future upstream diversions from the Snake and its tributaries. Whether that was so—and hydrologists would spend the next decade savaging one another to vindicate or demolish this argument—its mere possibility permanently unified Snake Basin irrigation leaders and their political allies against a federal dam in Hells Canyon.[38]

Secretary Krug might insist that High Hells Canyon and the Snake Basin Plan would never compromise irrigators' legal right to use water. "You may rest assured," the secretary protested to Governor Robins in October, "that this Department as illustrated by its long record of successful and harmonious cooperation with the States will be zealous in its compliance with Federal laws and regulations designed to protect the interest of the States."[39] However, Idaho and the ISRA never conceded their legal priority to the Snake. Prior appropriation and state ownership of water afforded Snake Basin irrigators an impregnable redoubt during the Hells Canyon controversy. Even Krug's clumsy threat to choke Idaho's existing federal water projects if state opposition delayed authorization of the Snake Basin Plan bounced off the irrigators' defensive crouch. The Idaho State Reclamation Association and Engineer Kulp were both deeply paranoid and remarkably savvy. Their bulldog defense of the sanctified right to divert water gave Idaho Power Company the crucial legal and political leverage to foreclose federal dam building in Hells Canyon.[40]

Privatizing Hells Canyon hydropower would meet Idaho Power's future growth needs for years, stabilizing its primacy in the Snake Basin by strengthening its ability to resist BPA encroachment. New company president Thomas E. Roach had just joined Idaho Power after managing a Portland-area utility company during the early 1940s. Roach had been an influential Portland businessman; wide contacts in the Willamette Valley made him prominent in the Portland Chamber of Commerce. Unlike Columbia Basin utilities that had signed the Tacoma Statement in early 1947, Idaho Power did not intend to capitulate to Paul Raver. Bonneville Power could serve its hydroelectric dependents. The Snake Basin secured Idaho Power's future generating base.[41]

The company's strategic growth plan called for doubling its system capacity over ten years by adding 100 megawatts of new hydropower. It would rebut BPA worries about Northwest power shortages by building just ahead of rising demand in its Snake Basin service area.[42] And Idaho Power certainly did not intend to mimic New Deal power pricing policy. Raver's philosophy of increasing power sales by keeping rates at cost had instead boosted demand well past BPA's capacity. Roach and his senior managers, led by general counsel and corporate secretary A. C. "Art" Inman, had "a profound and tenacious conviction that growing federal involvement in the power business was dangerous." Like Puget Sound Power's president Frank McLaughlin, Roach agreed that "there is no such thing as fair government competition [because] public and private power cannot competitively co-exist. . . . The end result of government competition in business is the destruction of private enterprise."[43]

Public hearings in July 1947 about Hells Canyon and the Snake Basin Plan had exposed squabbling between Reclamation and the Army Engineers over the upriver offensive's pace. One week later, Idaho Power exploited federal rivalry by filing its Federal Power Commission application for a preliminary permit to build a small run-of-river dam in Hells Canyon. Denoted FPC Project Number 1971, the "Oxbow Project" would be "a concrete dam across the Snake River . . . creating a reservoir about 11 miles long and with an area of about 1,000 acres . . . and a powerhouse with installed capacity of approximately 140,000 kilowatts [140 megawatts]."[44] Another private power company, hoping to spark a mining boom in Hells Canyon, had partly excavated a small tunnel some forty years earlier on the Oregon side of the river. To generate hydroelectricity, the Oxbow Project would push the Snake through turbines mounted in that widened tunnel. Idaho Power proposed using topography's trick at the Oxbow bend of the Snake to frustrate the federal upriver march to Hells Canyon. Barely one-seventh the size of Hells Canyon High Dam, and one-tenth as potent in making water into electricity, Oxbow almost seemed to mock BPA's Raver, Interior's Krug, and Reclamation's Straus.[45]

Shock them it did. Krug quickly protested Idaho Power's application, informing the FPC that "construction of a dam at the Ox Bow site is incompatible with the optimum, full development of the water resources of the Snake River Basin, and might preclude such development." Idaho Power's "proposed dam would be comparatively low (100–120 feet above river level); the reservoir to be created [would] have virtually no active storage capacity." By contrast, Hells Canyon High Dam, "approximately 750 feet high above foundation, would provide about 3,500,000 acre-feet of active storage capacity at that site, and develop a power head ranging from 360 to 600 feet." Neither Interior nor the Army Corps had yet formally unveiled their High Dam plans, but Krug insisted that "to provide the regulation required in the interests of the full use of the waters of the Snake, the Hell's Canyon Dam is a key, potential structure on the lower river."

Krug and his federal colleagues at once perceived Oxbow—a cheap, little, run-of-river, single-purpose, private power dam—might block the upriver offensive at Hells Canyon. Congress would be highly unlikely to authorize a federal dam in the very same river reach as a private project. Alarmed that Idaho Power had exploited patient federal fact-finding and embarrassing interagency rivalry, the Interior secretary warned the Federal Power Commission "the investment in the low dam would result in no permanent contribution to the power supply problem of the region . . . [and] could result in substantial delay in the building of the larger dam." Interior's protest unfurled the volatile mix of patriotic stump rhetoric that transformed the federal upriver campaign into a national referendum on the New Deal's postwar legacy. Oxbow would "delay and impair programs for development of land and water resources of the region to the detriment of the region and of the nation as a whole." High Hells Canyon "is required to be undertaken as a Federal project in order to permit this Department to achieve the goal of the fullest economic development of the land and water resources of the Pacific Northwest." But Idaho Power's Oxbow "would be inadequate within just a few years . . . [and] would deny to the people of the Pacific Northwest the maximum use of a great natural resource at a time when it is greatly needed."[46]

Hells Canyon High Dam and the Snake Basin Plan enflamed the New

Deal Northwest's partisan and social divisions. Idaho Democratic senator Glen Taylor, who had won election in 1944 as a dedicated New Deal proponent, blasted Oxbow and Idaho Power. "Our natural resources," Taylor told the FPC, "particularly those resources which belong to all of the people of the United States, . . . should be developed in conformity with the principle of the greatest good for the greatest number, and not for the benefit of any single private individual or corporation." The federal government had to capture Hells Canyon's "vast quantity of low-cost hydroelectric power . . . if the people themselves are to receive the benefits to which they are rightfully entitled." The High Dam was so vital to "the strategic water storage and power projects in the entire Columbia Basin development," Taylor argued, that "no action should be taken to prevent or delay its construction." Idaho Power's "low dam and power plant at the Ox Bow site would be a blow to sound public policy because of its effect upon Hell's Canyon development."[47]

Idaho Power's Oxbow filing stung the Corps of Engineers and Reclamation Bureau. Both agencies publicly released their preferred Snake Basin plans in December 1947 at CBIAC's monthly meeting in Baker, Oregon. By scheduling the committee's December meeting in Baker, Chairman Newell carefully chose a favorable forum for announcing Reclamation's Snake Basin Plan. High Dam boosters from Baker, forty-five miles southwest of Hells Canyon, had already been peppering the Federal Power Commission with protests against Idaho Power's Oxbow application. Union Pacific's main Northwest rail line linked Baker to Boise, but public power was quickly dividing them.[48]

Newell selected Roy F. Bessey to make Reclamation's best case for High Hells Canyon before an audience packed with its most enthusiastic supporters. Officially posted to Raver's Portland BPA headquarters, Bessey had spent a decade doing New Deal hydroelectric missionary work. A veteran of Harold Ickes's Natural Resources Planning Board during the 1930s, he had spent much of 1947 executing Secretary Krug's order to get Interior's multiple Northwest agencies into line behind President Truman's public-power expansion campaign. Thoroughly devoted to the cause of transforming the region with cheap electricity, he spoke with statistical passion about hydropower's capacity to diversify and industrialize the Northwest. Newell knew his CBIAC colleagues were trying to gauge local sentiment for the High Dam. Bessey, preaching the pure gospel of federalizing Hells Canyon, would have the job of earning "amens" from the Baker choir.

On 10 December, Bessey took the lectern in Baker City Hall. Reclamation's blueprint for transforming the postwar Snake Basin, he explained, required building the world's highest dam in Hells Canyon. Evoking the New Deal's legacy as regional social planner in a time of economic crisis, Bessey expressed Interior's belief "that only by a resources development program of the most intensive kind can a foundation be provided for the expansion in the region of opportunities for secure and gainful employment and for business enterprises of various kinds."[49]

Colonel O. E. Walsh, the Army Engineers' point man on the Columbia, may have lacked Bessey's sense of historical destiny. But when he strode before CBIAC the next day, Walsh also pitched his briefing as much to the wider community as to federal employees on the committee. The Corps of Engineers understood their "interim" survey of recommended dam projects seemed less concrete, less exciting, than Reclamation's bold Snake Basin Plan. However, Walsh, like his commander, Colonel Weaver, sensed that the metropolitan Columbia Basin, where public power's most numerous and voracious customers lived, could swing the debate toward the Army's High Hells Canyon alternative.

To this downriver audience, therefore, Walsh spoke when he characterized Hells Canyon as "one of the greatest hydroelectric possibilities on the continent." Bonneville Power administrator Raver had warned CBIAC just that morning that total northwestern electrical demand was rising so fast that "a critical power shortage" menaced the region. That was why the Army was designating Hells Canyon High Dam "the focal point" of its combined strategy to transform the Snake Basin into a fully managed, thoroughly developed river system. However, whereas Reclamation's Snake Plan pointed upstream, toward the Mountain Home Project and desert irrigation, the Corps of Engineers' version of High Hells Canyon spilled its principal benefits downriver, toward the millions who inhabited the Columbia Basin. The High Dam's ability to store and release huge quantities of water would reduce floods in Portland. By delivering precise downstream flows in the lower Snake, High Hells Canyon justified the new navigation locks that the corps planned to carry barges between Portland and the aluminum-manufacturing and wheat-growing areas in southeastern Washington. Timed releases of Snake water would boost power-generation capacity at the two other Army dams on the main Columbia: Bonneville, above Portland, and the new McNary, getting under way just below the mouth of the Snake.[50]

By the end of 1947, seemingly everyone in the Northwest agreed the Snake must be dammed in Hells Canyon. But by whom, and to what ends, still perplexed politicians and bedeviled boosters. Interior and the Army Engineers were soliciting regional and national support for their comprehensive, but contradictory, Snake Basin strategies. Federal hydroelectric agencies and Idaho Power were fanning the Hells Canyon controversy with mutually exclusive rhetoric and engineering data. Julius Krug contended that Idaho Power's low Oxbow would block full development of the Snake for the public benefit. Tom Roach countered that High Hells Canyon would socialize Idaho's lifeblood for the benefit of bureaucrats and city dwellers. There now seemed no way of compromising.

By Christmas, Idaho Power was distributing color movies throughout the Northwest: "The Story of the Snake River" hailed Idaho Power's service record in the Snake Basin. Steadily, week by week, BPA was selling more electricity than it could deliver. Paul Raver's dire warnings about inadequate generating capacity would become nearly hysterical in early 1948, giving the federal government the second-best argument it would ever have to justify nationalizing Hells Canyon. Nature itself was quietly providing the best case: Snow in the Snake Basin high country fell steadily all winter, piling up in the headwaters of the Clearwater, the Salmon, the Selway, the Weiser, and the Payette.

4 TAMING RIVERS AND PRESIDENTS

The Hells Canyon Controversy Goes National

B ig main-stem dams and levees had gentled the Snake and Columbia
rivers enough to encourage settlement along their banks. By the end
of World War II, nearly sixty thousand people inhabited Vanport,
Oregon, a low spot where the Willamette River swung westward into
the Columbia near Portland. Oregon's second-largest city—its name coined
to describe this new middle ground between Portland and Vancouver,
Washington—Vanport's wartime shipyards had given refuge to thousands
of Depression migrants. The ragged community straggled along the
Columbia's historic floodplain, but not since 1894 had spring runoff made
flooding a realistic concern. Dikes thrown up by the New Deal and extended
during wartime construction of Portland's airport appeared impregnable.[1]

Spring sunshine came early in 1948. In the Idaho high country, snow that
had gathered all winter came rushing downhill. Its power freed the Snake
to kick its traces. The Snake raced into the Columbia, and between mid-
May and early June, the larger river swept over its banks from Umatilla to
Astoria, Oregon. By mid-June, Columbia Basin flooding had swamped nearly
a half-million acres and a half-billion dollars' worth of property. Vanport's
dikes crumbled in a half-dozen places, drowning fifty. Fifteen perished
elsewhere in the basin.[2]

The great Columbia flood also broke the bureaucratic logjam that had
delayed federal plans to build Hells Canyon High Dam. From spring 1948
through spring 1950, caprices of snow and sun gave the public-power domain
its best opportunity ever to annex the Snake Basin. Once nature pushed the
Snake River full tilt into the Columbia and flooded Vanport, water policy
wore a human face. Politicians mournfully made campaign headlines. The
Hells Canyon controversy went national, surging out of the Northwest onto
the floor of Congress.

Lost lives and swamped property energized politicians. Statistical projections did not. During winter and spring, Bonneville Power Administration's strident warnings about scarce power seemed distant and abstract, annoying but not frightening. Twice, in December 1947 and again in April 1948, Paul Raver had hectored the Western Governors' Conference about looming power shortages. Perhaps because BPA's demand projections seemed obsolete as soon as announced, listeners heard the administrator's pleas skeptically. In February Raver again revised his recommendation for expanding the Federal Columbia River Power System, from 3,000 new megawatts of federal capacity to 4,000 megawatts by 1956. Even with all this new federal hydropower, he insisted the Northwest would still run short of electricity for six more years.[3]

Oregon congressmen chorused Bonneville's warnings. Representatives Homer Angell of Portland and Lowell Stockman of Pendleton, whose constituents depended most on BPA, pleaded for new dams to slake the region's power thirst.[4] Stockman specifically included Hells Canyon High Dam in his demands. Even though the Northwest possessed more than half the nation's hydropower potential, Angell declared on the House floor, "a great proportion of it is undeveloped and is wasting away to the sea without utilization." But Republicans, in a congressional majority for the first time in sixteen years, dismissed BPA's cries. Out of political power for so long, they had grown to loathe what they considered more New Deal pump-priming. A scathing report by the Republicans' leading public-power critic, House Interior appropriations subcommittee chairman Ben Jensen of Iowa, denounced federal hydroelectric expansion as "having all the earmarks of a Soviet power policy."[5]

Vanport's agony handed Raver a natural advantage in the Hells Canyon controversy. Its flooding supplied the argument he needed to force decisive action from the Columbia Basin Inter-Agency Committee. As dirty water sluggishly receded under Portland's pale June sun, BPA began patiently guiding CBIAC into refereeing Reclamation's dispute with the Army Corps of Engineers over federalizing Hells Canyon. Raver enjoyed crucial backing from President Harry Truman. The president decided to show his subordinates at the Interior Department and Pentagon that he outranked them. Truman, also eager to highlight his New Deal heritage, knew a political winner when he saw it. Desperate to evoke Rooseveltian imagery in his coming election campaign, he characterized High Hells Canyon as the logical extension of the New Deal's battle against massed forces of private privilege. Truman quickly and effectively used Vanport's flood to cut CBIAC's marching orders.[6]

The president hurried into the Northwest during the floods' aftermath. From Boise to the Pacific Coast, his "nonpolitical" speeches to rail-yard crowds and mealtime audiences emphasized that new dams would have stemmed the deluge. He toured stricken areas with Interior secretary Julius Krug and the corps' North Pacific commander, Colonel Theron Weaver. Before a crowd in Portland's Municipal Auditorium, Truman announced his commitment to unleash the federal upriver hydroelectric offensive. By linking New Deal public-power dams with both flood control and wartime victory, Truman implied his Republican adversaries bore responsibility for Vanport's tragedy. "I hope we can pass a program under which these disastrous floods will never happen again," the president promised. He neatly intertwined regional distress, his growing frustration with interagency bickering, and partisan sniping at congressional skeptics. "There is a plan for a Columbia river development program and I hope to see it outlined and completed," Truman pledged. Invoking sacrifices in his audience's memory, he claimed, "Had it not been for the immense power dams on the river, it would have been much more difficult for us to win the last war." As his train prepared to depart Portland on 10 June, Truman punctuated his personal interest in northwestern water control by dramatically signing a disaster-relief bill sent by air courier from Washington, D.C.[7]

Truman's "nonpolitical" stop in Portland rearranged Hells Canyon High Dam's bureaucratic landscape. As the presidential train steamed south toward California, federal public-works director Lewis Fleming assured reporters Truman was "interested in a long-term plan to prevent recurrence of floods as well as relief and rehabilitation." The president telegraphed Krug and Army Corps secretary Kenneth Royall as he left Portland, directing their agencies "to begin at once a review of the long-range plans . . . for the Columbia Basin development, with a view to proposing such modifications as might be appropriate in the light of the present disaster." Underscoring the partisanship of power, Truman accused Republicans of appeasing corporate utilities while northwesterners paid the costs with flooded homes and lost lives. "Had we had some of these projects which have been pending for several years," he told a Pocatello, Idaho, trackside audience, "we might to some extent have alleviated the Columbia flood which caused so much damage."[8]

Vanport became a code for aggressive presidential advocacy during the 1948 campaigns. Truman and liberal allies in the postwar Democratic coalition ratcheted power politics into one of the fall campaign's most divisive issues. At Truman's urging, forty-two prominent liberals petitioned the administration to speed up federal hydroelectric construction programs throughout the nation. Led by Eleanor Roosevelt, they called for extending multiple-purpose valley authorities, modeled on the Tennessee Valley Authority (TVA), into the Columbia-Snake Basin. Private electric utilities fought back, announcing an Edison Electric Institute study that condemned BPA's cut-price policy for provoking the nation's only acute shortage of electricity.[9]

By August, businesses in the Portland area were feeling enough political pressure to form their own lobbying group to stimulate regional opposition to High Hells Canyon. Directed by Daniel B. Noble, the Pacific Northwest Development Association wanted federal agencies to concentrate on meeting "very urgent" power and flood-control needs. Annexing new territory into the agencies' domain, PNDA asserted, would divert precious regional resources into a fruitless national battle. McNary Dam, said association spokesman Thomas M. Robins, "is our only real relief in the Northwest to take care of the power shortage which is gradually developing." Robins had retired from the Army Engineers as a general after World War II. The former commander of the corps' North Pacific Division during the New Deal, his views carried real weight in the Columbia Basin.[10]

In Port Angeles, Washington, the Northwest Public Power Association invited Raver and his senior BPA managers to its annual convention to present graphic proof of the region's "critical power shortage." The president of NWPPA warned of "brownouts," voluntary or mandatory power cutbacks being considered by the Columbia Basin's major public and private electric suppliers. The association affiliated dozens of BPA's "preference" customers, municipal and county-level public-power districts in Oregon, Washington, and north Idaho that enjoyed the right under federal law to buy nearly unlimited hydroelectricity for resale to end users at controlled wholesale prices. Its widespread local roots gave the association formidable economic and political influence in the Columbia Basin. Linked with public-power generators and distributors throughout the nation in the American Public Power Association, NWPPA counted Democrats from coast to coast, including the president himself, as allies and fellow enthusiasts for public power's expansion.[11]

Political pressure in late 1948—"No More Vanports!" "No Brownouts!"—complemented Raver's use of CBIAC to coordinate an Army Corps–

Reclamation Snake Basin Plan. In August, at a joint meeting of the Bonneville Advisory Board and CBIAC, Colonel Weaver pledged the corps' willingness to cooperate with the Reclamation Bureau. He promised to release the corps' "Main Control Plan" in the autumn. The Main Control Plan featured High Hells Canyon Dam as its linchpin. Its sheer bulk at a strategic location between the Snake and Columbia basins undergirded the North Pacific Division's stated aim to add 7,000 new megawatts of prime power to BPA's grid while "controlling all floods that have ever occurred on the Columbia."[12] Weaver's summer preview heralded November's formal release of the Engineers' Main Control Plan for the Snake and Columbia. Again, the Army Corps used a monthly CBIAC meeting as the forum to announce its preferred strategy.[13]

Now CBIAC went to work, seeking by year-end to fuse Reclamation's Mountain Home Project with the Army Engineers' Main Control Plan to harness the Snake for BPA's use and Vanport's protection. Neither agency could move upriver unless both approved the offensive's objectives and pace. The monthly meeting schedule of CBIAC supplied final impetus for meshing the corps' November 1948 Main Control Plan with Reclamation's December 1947 Snake Basin Plan. During late fall, planners from all three agencies met regularly to negotiate construction schedules and the necessary authorizing legislation from Congress. The interagency committee's rule of unanimity dictated that "coordinating" their hybrid battle plan meant agglomerating more than harmonizing.

The final 1948 meeting of CBIAC, scheduled for 8–9 December in Spokane, spurred Reclamation's Northwest director, R. J. Newell, to complete negotiations with Weaver and Raver. By striking a regional deal, which the press soon dubbed the "Weaver-Newell Accord," federal hydroelectric administrators could all report to their commander-in-chief: "Mission accomplished by the New Year." Reclamation spoke first in Spokane, with Newell telling the public session that "reconciliation is already practically complete" between "the great number of potential projects listed in the Reclamation Bureau's master plan announced in 1946 and the Army Engineers' revised report made last month." Weaver, leading off the committee's second day, politely ignored his regional rival's jab at the Army Engineers' more methodical planning, as well as the Reclamation chief's revisionist time line—the bureau had not even released its Snake Plan in draft form for public comment until spring 1947. He instead announced that the Army Engineers ambitiously intended to win Truman's approval of the Main Control Plan by July 1949.[14]

The federalizing of Hells Canyon featured prominently at Spokane's CBIAC meeting. The Army Corps projected asking Congress to appropriate more than $300 million to finish High Hells Canyon by 1955. If honored, that request would consume more than one-third of the Army Engineers' total five-year national construction budget.[15] The Columbia Basin Inter-Agency Committee's multiagency decision process, coupled with BPA's skillful manipulation of the "power crisis" that its pricing structure did so much to create, ensured High Hells Canyon power would drive a big load of federal initiatives. The corps' North Pacific Division promised the High Dam would not only help add 6,500 megawatts to BPA's capacity but would also fund thirteen Reclamation Bureau irrigation projects. Power revenues earned by fish-killing dams would pay a macabre form of tribute. High Hells Canyon would exterminate anadromous fish that spawned above it in the Snake Basin while funding the Interior Department's new experiment to focus conservation efforts on commercial salmon in the lower Columbia Basin.[16]

Vanport's soggy memory gave the upriver offensive its rallying cry after 1948. Colonel Weaver told navigation boosters from eastern Washington just before Christmas, "The multi-purpose dams proposed for construction along the Columbia and Snake rivers would provide a major bulwark against floods of the type which ravaged the area last spring." To achieve such comprehensive mastery over nature's varied forms, the Weaver-Newell Accord called for pouring more federal money into Northwest water projects between 1950 and 1955 than all the nation's private utility companies had spent building new generating capacity in the previous five years.[17]

The staff of CBIAC brokered the Weaver-Newell Accord behind closed doors. Their ungainly handiwork fully satisfied neither the Army Engineers nor Reclamation. The Bonneville Power Administration, however, welcomed the accord, although Paul Raver still believed his agency needed even more power faster than the dam builders proposed to provide it. Private logrolling by administrators now had to survive the intense public debate that Hells Canyon High Dam and the Snake Basin Plan were generating about federal power policy. The president still had to propose construction budgets, and a package of projects this expensive would face an uncertain reception by his budget office. Congress had to enact laws to execute the upriver offensive, and whether members from outside the Northwest would ratify such a massive commitment of federal resources depended on many fluid political factors. The Hells Canyon controversy, now defined by the Weaver-Newell

Accord, was going national in a very public way. Yet, by deciding what would be built, by which agency, and on which timetables, CBIAC's unelected administrators reigned as quasi sovereigns over northwestern waters.

In 1949 President Truman intended, as leader of the executive branch and head of the nation's new majority party, to make the key policy decisions about using water to develop the Northwest. Truman had risked his desperate political fortunes in 1948 by forcing Northwest power policy onto the national agenda. In return, he expected that his victory entitled him to some deference from federal agencies that managed hydroelectricity. He would reciprocate, of course. That was the style he had learned from Kansas City's rough-and-tumble Democratic world of threats and favors.[18]

The Columbia Basin Inter-Agency Committee resisted the president's challenge to its regional supremacy. Its objectives, enshrined in the Weaver-Newell Accord, grudgingly became White House objectives. Truman still wanted to federalize Hells Canyon. The High Dam symbolized his own passion for comprehensive planning, multiple-purpose dams, maximum economic growth, river-basin development, and public power. But his administrative subordinates actually decided how to capture the Snake Basin's hydroelectric and reclamation potential.

Truman would learn a hard lesson in 1949 about power in postwar politics. His 1948 whistle stop campaign mobilized partisan passions in the Northwest and across the country. By casting his election as a new birth of liberalism, Truman made New Deal public power a target for an array of interests that wanted little to do with federal planning and nothing to do with using hydroelectricity for social reform. This contest between postwar liberalism and resurgent conservatism bedeviled the president's bid to enfold High Hells Canyon into a new Columbia Valley Administration (CVA). Hells Canyon High Dam stimulated a national referendum about the New Deal's postwar legacy. Truman encouraged liberal Democrats to endorse the High Dam, CVA's centerpiece, as Franklin Roosevelt's fitting monument. Republicans and conservative Democrats aligned against both CVA and the dam because they had had enough of the New Deal. Embracing the Weaver-Newell Accord without the High Dam permitted CVA opponents to claim, with much justification, that they were not simply obstructionists, just practical developers. Truman's dream of a northwestern TVA fizzled in 1949. Its collapse engulfed Hells Canyon High Dam but left Weaver-Newell, the Army Engineers–Reclamation alternative, standing.[19]

Weaver-Newell not only undercut Truman's campaign for CVA but preempted the president's sweeping initiative to link basin planning with administrative reform. In his 1949 State of the Union message trumpeting the "Fair Deal," Truman proposed a fiscal 1950 budget with billions for starting new dams and reclamation projects. Included for the Northwest were both the High Dam and Snake Basin Plan. Truman wanted to remodel traditional bureaucracies as he built a new postwar society. His pledge to use CVA to accelerate water development promised radical restructuring of the New Deal agencies that administered public power's domain. Pursuant to Truman's orders, former president Herbert Hoover's government-reorganization commission recommended abolishing the Army Engineers' dam-building duties and reducing Reclamation Bureau independence over irrigation and public-power marketing.[20]

Truman instructed assistant Interior secretary C. Girard Davidson, a BPA and Tennessee Valley Authority veteran, to "draw on lessons of the past" by hammering out a new northwestern interagency power plan. The president had Weaver and Newell in mind when he advised Davidson's planners to "take into account the interests of all parts of the executive branch." Mindful of the Northwest's cool reception to Roosevelt's version of CVA in the 1930s, the president instructed Davidson to "take into account characteristics and needs of the region."[21]

Meanwhile CBIAC was patiently preparing to resist new threats to its authority, whether from the White House, the Hoover commission, or CVA. The committee's chieftains were already securing congressional support for their Weaver-Newell Accord by assembling a regional consensus to favor new works built by old friends. The Army Corps, BPA, and Reclamation Bureau calculated that they could stave off CVA and Hoover's restructuring better if they played active defense. These agencies were used to making policy as well as executing presidential orders. They shaped northwestern politics to suit their policy goals. Working in harness, Army Corps, Bonneville, and Reclamation staff conducted more than thirty public meetings, from Seattle to Idaho Falls, to demonstrate Weaver-Newell's superiority to anything the president and Jebby Davidson might offer. Representatives of CBIAC spent much of the first half of 1949 wheeling their charts and models around school auditoriums and booster clubs.[22]

For four weeks in February, CBIAC used Army Corps brass to line up northwestern commitments to the Weaver-Newell Accord. Seven field-grade officers, composing the board of directors for Rivers and Harbors, conducted public hearings that began in Portland and ended in Boise. The Columbia

Basin Inter-Agency Committee used the briefings to sell the accord. Unsubtly, its member agencies stoked regional sentiment against the president's rival bid to replace CBIAC with a presidentially appointed Columbia Valley Administration board. Since neither Idaho Power nor its Snake Basin irrigator allies supported CVA, they enjoyed the opportunity of linking opposition to Hells Canyon High Dam with support for Weaver-Newell.[23]

At their hearing in Boise on 4 February, the Army Corps generals heard welcome news. Snake Basin irrigators wanted more federal reclamation works, wanted downriver power customers to pay for them, but distrusted CVA. William Welsh, speaking for the Idaho State Reclamation Association, testified, "We feel that we cannot have a balanced economy in the Columbia River region without adequate [farm] production and that means we must develop reclamation resources concurrently and along with other water resources development." Other Snake Basin irrigation witnesses found the accord, executed by familiar federal agencies, far preferable to Truman's novel CVA. Idaho Power general counsel A. C. Inman seconded their judgment, telling the board, "We are of the opinion that the Corps of Engineers and Bureau of Reclamation are the agencies best qualified and equipped to undertake development of locally-endorsed multi-purpose projects in which reclamation and flood control are primary objectives."[24]

Inman's Boise testimony favoring Weaver-Newell also detailed Idaho Power's side of the Hells Canyon controversy. The company recognized that, by convincing the public that CVA and the High Dam hung together, defeating the unpopular CVA would probably drag down the dam as well. Inman warned the Army Rivers Board and CBIAC that Idaho Power would dissent vigorously if Hells Canyon High Dam remained the Weaver-Newell Accord's strategic pivot. The High Dam, he claimed, was "essentially a $3 billion subsidized public power development program and should be recognized as such." For the next eight years, the company and its allies relentlessly extended Inman's arguments against federalizing Hells Canyon.[25]

Inman advanced two basic arguments against the High Dam. Idaho Power's Snake Basin service territory suffered no electricity shortage like that which BPA had caused in the Columbia Basin. The company's postwar dam building, coupled with hydropower coming from federal projects already under way, would "amply supply the power needs of this area for years to come." Bonneville Power's profligate policy of selling public power at cost doubtless created acute shortages for its customers. Idaho Power, by contrast, "has never asked any customer to curtail service, or denied to any customer or potential customer all the power required for its existing or prospective operations."

Inman's second argument exploited Snake Basin irrigators' fear that federalizing Hells Canyon would imperil their hegemony over Snake Basin water. High Hells Canyon "would benefit Pacific coast areas at the expense of the Snake River Basin and the Intermountain territory." Citing Army Engineers' testimony at CBIAC hearings in 1947 and 1948, Inman charged that "Hells Canyon would require obtainment of a water right and require the use of all water comprising the entire remaining and unappropriated future flow of the Snake river at that location. It would not only pre-empt the site—as against future upstream power developments—but would also pre-empt all rights to unappropriated water for later upstream irrigation use." By waving the red flag of federal water seizure, Idaho Power challenged Reclamation's linkage between the High Dam and the Mountain Home Project. By assuming the role of irrigation fiduciary, the company enflamed upriver fears that CVA would subjugate the Snake Basin, relegating it to second-class status as the Columbia Basin's hydropower plantation.[26]

Truman's April special CVA message to Congress further polarized northwestern and national opinion. Oregon's Congress of Industrial Organizations executive secretary claimed that cheap CVA public power would bring "an enlarged and more prosperous Northwest, with an added increase in population and industry." In Seattle, a coalition of unions and liberal farm lobbies formed the CVA League to spread public power's gospel. The *Oregon Labor Press* saluted CVA's public-power potential as "the greatest asset we enjoy and the one that is essential to full development and utilization of every other resource. . . . [CVA] offers the best method of making a living a little more secure and a little finer for all Americans." The *Washington Post's* liberal cartoonist Herblock pictured a plucky Truman rescuing the nation's falling electrical reserves, his CVA "stepping it up a few jolts."[27]

All three northwestern governors were Republicans, so denouncing CVA took little political courage. Arthur Langlie of Washington, Douglas McKay of Oregon, and C. A. Robins of Idaho quickly attacked Truman's plan. McKay demanded, "What's the matter with the way we're doing it now? That's the American system. We don't need to delegate authority to a board or a commission to regulate the economy of the Northwestern states." Private-power backers in the Pacific Northwest Development Association called CVA "a socialistic scheme." In north Idaho, the *Wallace Miner* attacked CVA as "a federal power monopoly . . . that would hold the whip hand over industry and agriculture and regional development." Salem, Oregon's *Capital Journal* warned that, if CVA became law, "a three-man dictatorship would rule the Pacific Northwest." Back east, in Connecticut, the *New Haven Register* called CVA "another step toward creation of the superstate and the new society."[28]

Jebby Davidson zealously advocated Truman's spring directive to push CVA in the Northwest. By securing the public-power coalition's support, his work collided with emotional corporate and Republican rhetoric, steadily escalating regional partisan divisions. The New Deal's hydroelectric initiatives inspired the assistant Interior secretary. He believed in public power's transformative possibilities. Davidson contended economic security in the Northwest depended on increasing electricity consumption. Even more than BPA, CVA would further expand power use by lowering its price. As the TVA had done in the upper South, federal river-basin planning that promised economic abundance would accompany the march toward social justice. "States using little power are far from realizing the dream of life without drudgery," Davidson wrote in a newspaper column syndicated nationwide. "Even the areas with the highest average power consumption have a long way to go in making the fullest use of electricity."[29]

Davidson's mission first carried Truman's Columbia Valley plan into the public-power heartland in late April. Speaking in Seattle—home to CVA's Democratic sponsors, Representatives Hugh Mitchell and Henry Jackson and Senator Warren Magnuson—he stressed its authority to transfer private electric transmission systems to municipal power departments and public utility districts.[30] The next day, in Portland, Davidson reminded his audience of Vanport's tragedy. The president, he said, decided flood control and hydropower had to support northwestern economic growth when he watched Vanport's victims, most of whom were working people, trying to salvage their homes. In a region lacking both adequate industry and electricity, he contended, CVA promised new jobs by thoroughly subjugating the Snake's and Columbia's flow.[31]

Davidson encountered some of CVA's most hysterical opponents in Boise. The final stop on his mission to expand federal hydroelectric authority confronted the irrigator–Idaho Power coalition on its home ground. By carefully cultivating Snake Basin irrigation leaders, the company had convinced them that its opposition to Hells Canyon High Dam aided their campaign against the valley authority. Tying the High Dam to CVA was starting to pay off in the controversy over Hells Canyon. N. V. "Nick" Sharp of Filer, president of the Idaho State Reclamation Association, vowed to oppose CVA "stronger than ever." William Welsh, Boise River and lower Snake watermaster, thought CVA "proposed a strong centralized control over the water resources of the area [that would] take jurisdiction away from the state courts and grant unlimited powers of condemnation." The *Idaho Daily Statesman*, the state's leading paper, warned readers the day Davidson arrived, "We do hope the people who listen to Davidson's spiel will bear in mind the prime consideration underlying all this remarkably sudden hysteria to bring the Northwest more closely and tightly under government control. That consideration being: Is our Northwest, is our Idaho so economically and sociologically unfortunate and subnormal that we must, in desperation, pay the government extra millions of dollars to extend its regimentation to our hitherto comparatively free community?"[32]

More than twelve hundred packed Boise High School's auditorium on the cool evening of 21 April to hear Davidson's address. For those who could not squeeze into the little capital city's most spacious hall, a live radio hookup broadcast both the speech and the lively debate that followed. Unions, liberal farm groups, and state Democrats—gratified at the turnout they helped muster—announced before Davidson took the podium that they were forming an Idaho chapter of the CVA League. Introducing him as "one of the foremost authorities in the United States on the subject of reclamation and power" was legendary southwestern Idaho angler and hunter Clayton Davidson. No relation to the assistant Interior secretary, Clayton Davidson was one of Ernest Hemingway's favorite guides on shooting and drinking forays around Sun Valley. In a state where hunting and fishing were popular pastimes, his praise for the CVA's attention to fish and wildlife habitat carried weight.[33]

Secretary Davidson assured Boiseans that CVA "would have no effect on state rights or local political subdivisions." He characterized as "tommyrot" charges that CVA "would be a foot in the door for a northwest federal super state." In answering a hostile question shouted from the crowd, he claimed that "nothing in the bill interferes with state water rights, nor the Idaho constitutional provisions governing water rights."

Look at Idaho, Davidson urged his skeptical listeners. "Your industrial and population growth are lagging behind the rest of the Northwest." Despite holding 60 percent of the nation's phosphate rock, Idaho produced only 5 percent of its fertilizer because new factories could not be built without cheap public electricity. High Hells Canyon Dam would enable the federal government to direct nearly half of its generating capacity, 500 megawatts, to the phosphate industry alone. Power revenues from the dam would also assist the Reclamation Bureau to irrigate two million new acres of desert lands throughout the Northwest. Staffing those new factories and eating that new food would be two million new northwesterners. "We've got to get a power supply for full development," Davidson declared. Implicitly, he warned that a national job of this magnitude exceeded the traditional water and power agencies' competence. "What the [CVA] would do," he summarized, "is to provide a more effective structure to help the Northwest carry its own weight in development. . . . Potentials of the area are not being developed in proper proportion to the national need for them, and the executive and administrative branches of government must look to their responsibilities."[34]

As his emissary tried to convert northwestern supporters for the Weaver-Newell Accord into CVA believers, Truman tried in Washington, D.C., to prune CBIAC's authority. His Hoover Commission on the Organization of the Executive Branch of the Government proposed eliminating all Army Corps civilian construction responsibilities. A new service directly responsible to the Interior secretary would combine BPA's hydroelectric marketing and Reclamation's irrigation development. If Congress agreed with the last Republican president, CBIAC would never convene again. Executive-branch reorganization would eliminate the three principal northwestern hydroelectric agencies altogether. Critics savaged the Hoover commission, but Truman's warm thanks to its chairman reflected his conviction that the president should be commander in chief of the upriver hydroelectric offensive.[35]

Assessing the duel between the White House and the agencies that controlled northwestern hydropower, the *Idaho Daily Statesman*'s political correspondent observed, "The amazing thing is that neither the Bureau of Reclamation nor the Army Engineers approves [the CVA] bill. Officials of both branches are mum concerning the bill because it is an administration measure. . . . The CVA bill, of course, would virtually wipe the Reclamation Bureau out of existence [and] the Bonneville Power Administration would be taken over lock, stock and barrel by the proposed CVA." The *Statesman* editorialized that Truman's Columbia Valley bill "inspired the engineers and reclamation people to hang together lest they hang separately." However, "regardless of the motive for their cooperative spirit, the net result will be good for all of us if they carry out their proposed plan."[36]

In late April 1949, Army secretary Royall and Interior secretary Krug resolved the final dispute left from CBIAC's December Weaver-Newell Accord. The interagency committee had been unable to decide whether the corps or Reclamation should build Hells Canyon High Dam. Both agencies were pivoting their upriver offensive around the dam. However, much as pride of ownership meant to Army morale, it mattered little to actual execution of either Reclamation's Snake Basin Plan or the Army Engineers' Main Control Plan. Once the federal government federalized Hells Canyon hydroelectricity, dispensing its bounty became an Interior Department prerogative. That had been decided by the 1944 Flood Control Act and Interior's 1946 power-policy memorandum.

A joint announcement by the Defense and Interior Departments on 19 April confirmed the Reclamation Bureau would build Hells Canyon High Dam. The Army Engineers would finish McNary and begin constructing four new dams on the lower Snake. The corps would also build a new dam on the Boise River to store irrigation water and generate hydroelectricity for Reclamation's Mountain Home Project. Endorsed as well was the Columbia Basin Pooling Account. Power-sale revenues filling this Hells Canyon cash box confirmed the High Dam's intimate connection with Reclamation's grandiose plan to water the Mountain Home Desert. As the announcement noted, "The pooling of all power revenue producing projects in the Columbia Basin and coastal areas of the Pacific Northwest [will] extend financial assistance to irrigation in accordance with principles current in reclamation law."

The *Idaho Daily Statesman* bannered Weaver-Newell's ratification on page one. So vital to the Snake Basin was knowing who would lead the federal government's hydroelectric charge, and in what manner, that the paper's political correspondent had been in Washington, D.C., all week covering the struggle between Truman and his putative subordinates.[37]

Congressional hearings on CVA during summer revealed the Hells Canyon controversy had already arrayed northwesterners into two adversary coalitions. They pioneered tactics and rhetoric that drove the controversy for the next eight years. Backing CVA were labor unions, liberal farm groups such as National Farmers Union and the Grange, public-power preference customers allied in the Northwest and American Public Power Associations, and the Democratic Party. Against them fought the nation's corporate utilities led by the National Association of Electric Companies, probusiness lobbies such as the U.S. Chamber of Commerce and National Association of Manufacturers, and the Northwest's Republican governors.

The Washington secretary of state revealed utility companies were pouring thousands of dollars a month into organizing anti-CVA/anti–High Dam publicity blitzes. High Dam opponents deflected critics, who accused them of sabotaging full exploitation of regional hydropower, by embracing Weaver-Newell if it dropped the Hells Canyon dam. The president of NWPPA, Carl Moore, countered by branding the accord a bureaucratic bastard, "born in iniquity" without public oversight, that jeopardized full exploitation of Hells Canyon's power potential.[38]

By autumn, the White House conceded enactment of CVA was unlikely in the 1949 session of Congress. Still, Interior's Davidson soldiered on, rallying the Northwest's public-power alliance against corporate and state-government opposition. By uniting Democrats and liberal activists around CVA and tying the High Dam to its fate, Davidson and the president were encouraging politicians and ordinary citizens to understand the Hells Canyon controversy as a partisan litmus test. As Democrats and Republicans nationwide entered the struggle, they further polarized the controversy. In Spokane in October, Davidson clashed with Governor Langlie, who charged CVA "sets up a corporate state and places broad powers in the hands of a few without the usual checks and balances." At its Tacoma convention later that month, NWPPA gave Davidson a standing ovation. Representative Henry Jackson won NWPPA's strong resolution endorsing CVA as well as accelerated federal dam and transmission-line construction.

However, the real hero in Tacoma was Bonneville Power's Paul Raver. The Columbia River Boys barbershop quartet warbled a special version of "Old Man River" to mark his tenth year as BPA administrator. Raver basked serenely, eager to take the upriver offensive's battle plan to Congress in 1950. After all, "Old Man Raver" and CBIAC's other chieftains had done much good work during 1949. They had negotiated a truce between the Army Corps and Reclamation Bureau, used Weaver-Newell to blunt both CVA and the Hoover commission, and forced their president to accept their administrative vision for the Northwest.[39]

Meeting in early February 1950 in Salem, CBIAC learned Truman had capitulated to the power agencies' Weaver-Newell Accord. Newell's successor at Reclamation Region 1 headquarters, Harold T. Nelson, reported "presidential approval has been given to the main aspects of the Corps of Engineers–Bureau of Reclamation Columbia Basin plan, which includes region-wide power pooling plan." Raver confirmed that the Federal

Columbia River Power System's high-priority power-construction plans, BPA's "Schedule S," now contemplated the High Dam coming online in 1957. Raver outlined the lobbying tactics necessary to launch the upriver offensive: the Senate was taking up the Rivers and Harbors bill, passed by the House in late 1949, so "the procedure contemplated is to add the authorization of these projects [in Weaver-Newell] to the bill in the Senate and to endeavor to obtain concurrence of the House in final conference. Amending language to accomplish this has been approved by the Bureau of the Budget and transmitted by the Secretary of the Interior to Congress." New Interior secretary Oscar Chapman had already testified in favor of BPA's and Reclamation's portion of the accord. Raver and Nelson were flying to Washington, D.C., to make the case for the High Dam and Snake Plan to the Senate Interior Committee in late February. Colonel Weaver confirmed that the corps was methodically lining up its traditional allies on the Senate Public Works Committee, which customarily handled Rivers and Harbors authorizing legislation.[40]

National public-power advocates were mobilizing to ensure Congress ladled out billions for new northwestern dams. At their annual convention in Chicago in early March, rural electric cooperative delegates heard Interior secretary Chapman proclaim the Truman administration's commitment to robust expansion of public power. On behalf of 2.5 million members, concentrated in the South and Midwest, National Rural Electric Cooperative Association (NRECA) executive manager Clyde T. Ellis pledged to deploy their "militancy and effectiveness" on behalf of more cheap electricity. Senator Lister Hill (D-Ala.) urged NRECA to act "as if the fight is your fight whether a specific project is close to home or not. The fight is your fight— whether it is the fight for TVA, the St. Lawrence Seaway, the Columbia or Missouri valley developments, or regional power authorities of the Pacific Northwest." In a special message, President Truman challenged the co-ops to back his power policy.[41]

Two weeks later, the American Public Power Association (APPA) came to Washington. The association's five hundred delegates heard Senator Estes Kefauver (D-Tenn.) proclaim that "the orderly development of our water resources is highly necessary." C. Girard Davidson's speech promised that reclamation and hydropower would be mutually supportive in the West. Outgoing APPA president Samuel Morris, director of Los Angeles's giant utility department, cited the Northwest as an example of public hydropower's promise to attract industry and finance irrigation.[42] Capping this burst of national debate over the Northwest's power future, NRECA's Ellis and APPA's executive director Alex Radin vowed to coordinate their organizations' lobbying.[43]

Concentrated, effective national pressure secured CBIAC's most crucial objective yet when the Senate Interior Committee in March authorized Hells Canyon High Dam and dedicated its power revenues to Reclamation Bureau projects. Raver's and Nelson's testimony in late February had been persuasive: the committee pledged to use the High Dam's 1,000 megawatts to earn nearly $350 million for CBIAC. Raver reported to CBIAC's March meeting that BPA intended to use Hells Canyon power to "take care of all presently estimated potential industrial loads by 1957–58" and to extend a 230-kilovolt trunk line into the Snake Basin. "By this time the Administration will have power available to meet all utility requirements as well as a considerable amount of power for industrial development any place on the grid system."

From its share of the Columbia Basin Pooling Account, Nelson reported, Reclamation could spend $16 million to bring irrigation water to more than one hundred thousand acres in the Intermountain Northwest. The Senate Interior Committee had ordered Reclamation to delay the Mountain Home Project's costlier features, including the underground aqueduct planned to pour the Payette River onto the Mountain Home Desert. Still, Nelson told his CBIAC colleagues, winning congressional support for the pooling plan and Hells Canyon High Dam was "the most important single development from the standpoint of the Department of the Interior, . . . [for] if enacted into law, the account will very significantly affect resource development in the Northwest, particularly the power and irrigation aspects."[44]

Only final legislative merger between the Senate's two committees handling the Rivers and Harbors bill stood between CBIAC and Hells Canyon in spring 1950. While the Senate Interior Committee readied its High Dam/ Snake Plan amendment, the Public Works Committee had been marking up the House-passed 1949 version. With jurisdiction over the Army Corps of Engineers' share of the Weaver-Newell Accord, Public Works had incorporated all recommended corps projects into the Rivers and Harbors bill. Now, on the verge of victory, President Truman's doomed campaign for the Columbia Valley Administration blundered into CBIAC's delicate legislative dance. Unwilling to let the hydroelectric agencies secure the Snake Basin on their own terms, the president forced Congress to decide whether federalizing Hells Canyon in spring 1950 was worth surrendering its customary prerogative to negotiate water-development strategy with Army Corps generals and Reclamation Bureau planners.

Since January, Truman had been stoking another surge of public support for CVA by rallying Democrats against both jealous bureaucrats and disdainful congressmen. His public-relations vehicle was the new President's Water Resources Policy Commission. Although chaired by a respected former chairman of the Rural Electrification Commission, Morris Cooke, the WRPC's most energetic and outspoken member, Leland Olds, was also its least popular in the Senate. In late 1949, the Senate had twice voted down Olds's reconfirmation as a federal power commissioner. Powerful Democrats, led by Robert Kerr of Oklahoma and Lyndon Johnson of Texas, savaged Olds in committee hearings and during floor debate for his radical journalism in the 1920s and 1930s.

Truman's pique, never far beneath his skin, had been poked. The first jab came when the hydroelectric empire forced him to endorse the Weaver-Newell Accord in spring 1949. His own party's conservative wing had struck next, rejecting Olds despite the president's stubborn bid to make his confirmation a test of fidelity to the postwar New Deal. By creating his new Water Resources Policy Commission to rally support for the Hoover commission's sweeping recommendations to reorganize water and power agencies, Truman challenged both CBIAC and Congress to more debilitating combat over presidential powers and administrative discretion. Naming Olds to the WRPC almost before the bruises had healed from his humiliating defeat displayed little of the political wisdom, though some of the doggedness, that had seen the president through 1948's desperate campaign.[45]

Olds personified CVA and New Deal liberalism to senators who heartily detested both. Public Works chairman Dennis Chavez, one of CVA's and Olds's most contemptuous critics, carried the Rivers and Harbors bill to the full Senate. Like many conservative Democrats who customarily backed Army Corps of Engineers water projects to please home-state boosters, the New Mexican sympathized with the corps' construction agenda. Chavez feared entangling the Army Engineers in CVA. Reclamation's link between High Hells Canyon and the Snake Basin Plan drew unwanted attention to more controversial water projects. National controversy and regional divisions swirling around this high-profile package jeopardized powerful senators' less troublesome projects. During conference-committee negotiations to reconcile Senate and House versions of the 1950 Rivers and Harbor's bill, energy spent defending the High Dam would impair senators' bargaining influence. Chavez therefore declined Interior committee chairman Joseph O'Mahoney's (D-Wyo.) request to add the Hells Canyon/Snake Basin Plan amendment during Public Works' markup of the Rivers and Harbors bill.

Public-power liberals and CBIAC tried at the last minute to save the High Dam by appealing to the full Senate. O'Mahoney, a veteran New Dealer, offered Reclamation's share of the Weaver-Newell Accord as a floor amendment to the Rivers and Harbors bill cleared by Chavez's Public Works Committee. O'Mahoney and Warren Magnuson led the floor fight, but the CBIAC's careful congressional campaign for High Hells Canyon foundered on bitter sentiments left from Truman's heavy-handed lobbying for Olds and CVA. Both senators had alienated conservative Democrats by backing Olds's failed reconfirmation bid in 1949. Both demanded their Senate party colleagues endorse CVA. Like the president, they portrayed the High Dam and Snake Basin Plan as logical extensions of New Deal public-power social reform in the Northwest. Both underestimated party conservatives' alienation from CVA.

For a week in May, conservative and liberal Democratic senators struggled over the New Deal's hydroelectric legacy in the Northwest. Intraparty differences, heightened by Truman's bid to reignite passion for postwar liberalism, fatally wounded High Hells Canyon Dam. No Republicans felt any loyalty to either FDR's memory or Harry Truman's CVA. O'Mahoney claimed Hells Canyon High Dam's revenues, collected for the Snake Basin Plan by the Columbia Pooling Account, renewed the long national commitment to desert reclamation. For Magnuson, building the High Dam offered his constituents and their Columbia Basin neighbors in Oregon a lifeline of cable and concrete. Without the High Dam, BPA's cut-price public power would soon run out, forcing the cost of northwestern electricity up to national levels. Guy Cordon (R-Ore.), a long-time advocate of Army Engineers dams in the Northwest, countered with arguments pitched to fiscally conservative congressional Democrats. By saddling the High Dam with costly schemes like Reclamation's plan to water the Mountain Home Desert, Congress would subsidize wasteful irrigation and eliminate its right to make future decisions about northwestern water-development strategy. For, once authorized as the linchpin of federal postwar hydroelectric policy, Hells Canyon High Dam and the Pooling Account would "pave the way for CVA" and effectively liquidate the Army Engineers.[46]

Cordon exploited regional hostility to the Columbia Valley Authority, confounding CBIAC's thus far united front for its Weaver-Newell Accord.

The Oregon Republican also neatly sidestepped Magnuson's plea on behalf of Columbia Basin power customers. A fellow northwesterner, generally sympathetic to cheap public power's regional economic benefits, was essentially demanding that both the Senate and his constituents in public power's domain grasp the High Dam's real implications. "Defend your claim to low-cost electricity," ran Cordon's analysis. "Cut loose from the upriver offensive's ambitious, costly bid to annex the Snake Basin using a failed New Deal model. Build Columbia River dams, operated by the Army Corps to provide power to BPA. Reap the benefits of experience. Don't gratify Harry Truman's vendetta against corporate power and administrative authority by authorizing CVA in the guise of the Snake Plan, the Columbia Basin Pooling Account, and Hells Canyon High Dam." By 43–22, the Senate backed Cordon and Chavez, killing Reclamation's High Dam/Snake Basin amendment to the 1950 Rivers and Harbors Act. Only the most liberal Democrats supported O'Mahoney and Magnuson.[47]

The Senate had killed Hells Canyon High Dam and the Snake Basin Plan, but President Truman was present at their execution. His personal devotion to CVA, the spiritual heir to FDR's New Deal public-power legacy, created political divisions that doomed the High Dam. The president had stubbornly rejected a package of dams and reclamation projects he could have won in a vain pursuit of what he would never obtain. By spending political capital in 1949 and 1950 to found his own postwar TVA in the Northwest, he forfeited the Weaver-Newell Accord on CBIAC's terms. Perhaps his temper had blurred his considerable political acumen. Futile pursuit of his cherished CVA progressively strangled his best opportunity to federalize the Snake River's hydroelectric potential.

Federal agencies superintending the Columbia Basin's public-power domain could likely have overcome Snake Basin resistance to their upriver offensive. Their resources were plentiful. Their crafting of the Weaver-Newell Accord to capture northwestern public opinion reflected fifteen years' experience of balancing boosters' dreams against engineers' imperatives. Momentum generally favored the aggressor in most postwar struggles over exploiting natural systems to serve material demands. Yet the hydroelectric agencies' whole intricate structure—High Dam, Snake Basin Plan, Mountain Home Project— came crashing down when Truman chose to tie his unpopular Columbia Valley Administration to CBIAC's upriver offensive.

Emotional hostility to CVA poisoned many northwesterners against CBIAC's own designs on the Snake. Truman persistently identified Hells

Canyon High Dam as CVA's strongest lever to reorganize northwestern water administration. His chief sparkplug on public power, C. Girard Davidson, constantly reminded northwesterners how much the High Dam and CVA owed to FDR's New Deal. Yet, by 1949, a decisive majority in the region were losing interest in reviving the New Deal. The Columbia Valley Administration conveniently epitomized their fears of federal direction and their frustrations with Truman. The now-obsolete heritage of CVA undermined CBIAC's postwar lobbying for the Snake Basin Plan. The president's struggle to curb hydroelectric agencies' authority divided his administration during the crucial congressional negotiations. High Hells Canyon's most ardent opponents, led by Idaho Power, exploited administration dissension and shifting ideologies. Divisions over the purposes of public power helped undermine postwar liberalism. The Columbia Basin Inter-Agency Committee's Weaver-Newell Accord shattered amid the tensions generated when Harry Truman nationalized the Hells Canyon controversy.

5 PLANNING FOR PERMANENT CONTROL

The New Deal Legacy of Northwest Fishery Policy

T he New Deal in the Columbia Basin conditioned federal hydroelectric planners to manage fish as portable, temporary obstruc-
tions. Dams would eliminate the fish from watersheds dedicated
to power production. The survivors would then be transferred to
other waters where they could not impede public power's upriver march.
Experimental fish relocation at Grand Coulee Dam on the upper Columbia
River in the late 1930s would cast a long environmental shadow. Postwar
anadromous fish–conservation policy extended Coulee's engineering solution to the entire Northwest. The federal campaign to hydroelectrify the
Snake Basin after World War II sacrificed upriver anadromous fish runs
for economic growth by applying Depression-era experiments first tried at
Grand Coulee.

Federalizing the Columbia Basin's hydroelectric potential destroyed half
of the world's richest salmon and steelhead trout fishery. New Deal public
power policy sacrificed the entire population of these sea-run fish that
spawned above Grand Coulee Dam. The dam closed forever one thousand
miles of the upper Columbia Basin's watery web. Wild fish that had inhabited its waters for ten millennia simply disappeared during their five-year
life course, to be replaced by domesticated salmon bred in new hatcheries
on undammed rivers below Coulee. Interior secretary Harold Ickes decided
to employ destitute Americans and stimulate the regional economy by closing the upper Columbia watershed to migratory fish.

Late in October 1938, federal engineers directed their army of hourly laborers to pour the last tons of concrete into Grand Coulee. The new dam now
closed the upper Columbia River watershed in northeastern Washington,
eastern British Columbia, and northwestern Montana. John C. Veatch, Fish
Commission of Oregon (FCO) chairman, shared with Interior secretary

Ickes his state's concerns about the fate of the Columbia's anadromous fishery. Chinook salmon (*Oncorhynchus tshawytscha*) principally inhabited the upper Columbia Basin. Smaller numbers of other salmon races ascended into the watershed's higher-elevation reaches: bluebacks or sockeyes (*O. nerka*) swam the farthest; chums (*O. keta*) concentrated in lower reaches; silvers (*O. kisutch*) usually preferred middle-elevation waters. The steelhead trout's range encompassed nearly every reach of the Columbia and Snake basins (*Salmo gairdnerii*).[1]

Oregon worked cooperatively with the state of Washington to regulate fishing in the lower Columbia, which formed their common boundary. But, as Veatch wrote Ickes, "Since the fishery as a whole is composed of and depends for its continuance upon individual runs from the various tributaries of the Columbia river, we are equally as interested in the preservation of migratory fishes in tributaries of the Columbia river in British Columbia, Washington, or Idaho, as in those tributaries within the state of Oregon." Oregon respected Washington's sovereign power to negotiate with the United States over the biological crisis caused by a dam wholly within its territory. Nevertheless, FCO informed the Interior Department, "as a moral and legal responsibility it is our duty to preserve, protect and perpetuate such migratory fishes, not only for the present but for the future as well."[2]

Ickes wielded enormous power over the Pacific Northwest during the Depression. His department oversaw the Bureau of Reclamation, the agency building Grand Coulee. The secretary also directed the New Deal's Public Works Administration, which actually spent the emergency federal relief money Congress appropriated for the project. One of the New Deal's most aggressive proconsuls, as well as a self-described "Progressive conservationist," Ickes was driving men hard, in Washington State and in Washington, D.C., to complete Coulee Dam. Finished, the dam would operate like the giant mainspring of an ambitious federal scheme to harness cheap hydroelectricity to irrigate deserts. Ickes and Coulee's Reclamation planners envisioned using public power not only to irrigate new farms but also to employ dislocated workers and to diversify the inland Northwest's predominantly agricultural economy by attracting new industries. New Dealers believed abundant hydropower also promised social reform. By alleviating rural poverty and boosting living standards for people accustomed to manual toil, cheap electricity would give the poor a new sense of mastery over their environments. Public-power enthusiasts dreamed of a Northwest more economically secure and socially egalitarian. Since deciding how to use electricity as a public resource required community decision making, Ickes and his advisers hoped the Columbia Basin project would spark a new civic spirit.[3]

John Veatch of the Fish Commission of Oregon also wielded power, though he could not command water to run across arid lands or spin turbines. Instead, FCO decided when and how the four species of salmon and the sea-run steelhead trout that traversed the Columbia Basin lived and died. A detailed state statutory code empowered Veatch and his two other unpaid commission colleagues to "protect, preserve, and perpetuate" food fish inhabiting Oregon's coastal seas and freshwater rivers.[4] From its origin in 1878 as a one-man office dependent on cooperative county sheriffs to enforce catch laws, FCO had by the 1930s grown into a state bureau employing hundreds of enforcement officers, scientists, and engineers.[5] Master Fish Warden M. T. "Mike" Hoy, the agency's director since 1927, looked to the FCO commissioners, appointed by the governor and confirmed by the state senate, for broad policy guidance.[6] Hoy and his principal deputy, Hugh C. Mitchell, director of Hatcheries and Fish Culture, met the full commission at formal quarterly meetings. Hoy kept Chairman Veatch posted on a weekly or even daily basis, depending on the issue at hand. Veatch, a Portland attorney, had served on the commission for more than a decade. He would chair the FCO for nearly two more decades.[7]

Since June 1933, the FCO had pondered the Coulee project's effects on Columbia Basin anadromous fish.[8] More than fifty thousand summer chinook ascended the upper Columbia to spawn, along with at least as many steelhead trout and smaller runs of fall chinook. Ranging into more than one thousand miles of tributary waters braiding British Columbia, Washington, and Idaho, the great upriver fishery supplied a substantial share of the basin's total anadromous runs.[9] Oregon's legal power to safeguard its multibillion-dollar commercial and sport salmon fishing industry transcended state boundaries. As Veatch explained to Ickes on 26 October 1938, "We are directly responsible to the people of the state of Oregon for the preservation of salmon and other migratory fishes inhabiting the Columbia river."[10]

Inland Empire business and farming leaders for nearly thirty years had envisioned a big Columbia dam watering a vast, new irrigation project in the lava-rock scablands of eastern Washington. The New Deal, under President Franklin D. Roosevelt's prodding, transformed Grand Coulee from an irrigation reservoir into a high, multipurpose hydroelectric dam.[11] Though Ickes resented the Reclamation Bureau's touchy independence within his Interior Department, he persuaded the president its dam building prowess "would take hold of nature and shape it to human purposes as never before in history."[12]

Only one other dam spanned the Columbia River in 1938. Built by Puget Sound Power and Light Company five years earlier, Rock Island, some seventy-five miles below Coulee Dam, stored only enough water to spin a single turbine. Puget Sound Power had had to follow both federal and state fish-conservation laws. The 1934 Fish and Wildlife Coordination Act and 1920 Federal Water Power Act required Puget Sound Power to make "due and adequate provision . . . for the migration of fish life . . . by means of fish lifts, ladders, or other devices."[13] Puget Sound Power had agreed with the Washington Department of Fisheries and Federal Power Commission, which licensed nonfederal power dams on interstate rivers, to install fish passage facilities at Rock Island Dam.[14]

Grand Coulee, a federal dam authorized by Congress, fell outside the new 1935 Federal Power Act's mandate that private power dams use fishways to pass adult fish above and juvenile fingerlings below their structures. The Federal Power Act, enacted by the most pro–New Deal Congress of FDR's presidency, regulated only nonfederal dams licensed by the Federal Power Commission.[15] Congress thus enabled Interior to extinguish the Columbia's upriver anadromous fishery by authorizing Grand Coulee without fish passage facilities. The federal government imposed biological obligations on private dam builders that it did not have to observe. Ironically, the Interior Department had to rely on Rock Island Dam's fish ladders and counting stations—installed pursuant to federal license—when it imposed its Coulee fish-salvage plan between 1938 and 1940.[16]

Dam builders in the Bureau of Reclamation saw no reason to invent new duties when Congress had insulated the agency from old ones. Reclamation resisted taking responsibility for the fate of the upper Columbia fishery. Interior secretary Ickes considered fish protection entirely secondary to such cherished New Deal aims as social planning, rural resettlement of dispossessed midwestern farmers, widespread electrification at postage-stamp prices, and utility-company reform.[17] As Paul Pitzer's fine history of the Coulee project observes, "Although the Bureau [of Reclamation] took steps to preserve the salmon, had its measures failed, it was ready to see the salmon disappear, deeming the economic contribution of the dam as far more important than the fish."[18]

As early as 1934, Reclamation and the Commerce Department's Fisheries

Bureau realized Coulee's size and site created a fish-conservation crisis. The U.S. commissioner of fisheries told the Reclamation Bureau that passing fish over or around the dam "would probably fail." He recommended capturing fish blocked from the upper Columbia, transplanting them to undammed rivers, and artificially propagating their successors as "the only alternative." By summer 1938, federal administrators responsible for building Coulee Dam decided how to solve the fish crisis. Their plan assumed the dam would extinguish the upriver fishery. They would replace it with a re-created artificial downriver run dependent on hatcheries and transplantation into undammed tributaries.[19]

Since Reclamation was consumed with building the dam and the irrigation works it would support, the federal Fisheries Bureau prodded the Washington Department of Fisheries to request that the United States fund a $2.6 million fish-salvage plan. Its key elements called for catching adult fish at Rock Island Dam's fish ladders. Trucks would haul spawners to a new hatchery complex at Leavenworth, on the Wenatchee River. Fertilized eggs from the hatchery fish would then be replanted in the Entiat, Okanogan, Methow, and Wenatchee rivers, which all emptied into the Columbia downriver from Grand Coulee. Pitzer correctly terms fish culture on such a grand scope "speculative and experimental."[20]

Congress ratified administrators' transplantation experiment in spring 1938. The Mitchell Act authorized the U.S. Fisheries Bureau to build hatcheries in the Columbia Basin. Since no one had ever tried to eliminate an entire migratory fish population from one watershed and artificially re-create it in different waters, Congress directed the Fisheries Bureau to study the Coulee salvage plan's effects on fish conservation. If the experiment worked, federal dam building could avert the future string of biological crises it would trigger. Power-sale revenues would pay tribute to relocated fish.

An emergency measure enacted during the Depression's worst years, the Mitchell Act established two legal innovations with far-reaching consequences for anadromous fish inhabiting the upper Columbia and Snake basins. First, discretionary authority vested in federal hydroelectric agencies—Reclamation, the Army Corps of Engineers, and Bonneville Power Administration—supplanted northwestern state sovereignty in governing the region's migratory fishery. Second, New Deal fish-conservation policy essentially split the Northwest in half to accommodate new public-power dams. Federal hydroelectric managers consigned fish unlucky enough to spawn in higher elevations, above the dams, to extinction. They progressively sought to replace Snake Basin and upper Columbia populations with hatchery fish raised in the lower Columbia Basin.[21]

Oregon's Charles McNary, the Mitchell Act's floor sponsor in the Senate, believed federal relief could restore prosperity in the Northwest only by building both Coulee and Bonneville Dam, sixty miles above Portland. He acknowledged New Deal public-power policy meant closing the upper Columbia to fish. Coulee's 370-foot bulk "is so high that ladders or lifts to enable the salmon to negotiate the dam are not feasible." Above the dam, in the waters used by anadromous fish for more than ten thousand years, fish simply would not be permitted to go. "The territory, heretofore a breeding place of the salmon, . . . will be denied them." Adult fish that had spawned, and juvenile smolts that had been born, above Coulee Dam would now be replaced by transplants. The exact location of their new homes would be "left up to the experts in the Bureau of Fisheries," Oregon representative James Mott told the House Merchant Marine Committee in April 1938. If the federal experiment at Coulee failed to replenish upriver fisheries by transplanting hatchery fish, "then they will have to be established up on the tributaries of the Willamette River or some tributary of the Columbia below the Bonneville Dam."[22]

The Mitchell Act alarmed Oregon's Fish Commission. It implied Reclamation intended to solve the ecological crisis Coulee was causing by transplanting fish runs to open waters below Coulee Dam. "Frankly," Veatch wrote Ickes on 26 October 1938, "we are unable to share the optimism of the U.S. Bureau of Fisheries or of others regarding the success of the proposed plans for dealing with so vitally an important part of the fishery problem." He tried to appeal to Ickes' legendary frugality by advising him "continuing indefinitely to transfer all migratory fishes cut off by the barrier to tributaries of the Columbia river below that point" would be "prohibitively" expensive. Veatch instead urged federal plans for upper Columbia fish should "permit them to ascend beyond the barrier, thereby maintaining and preserving the runs in certain important tributaries of the Columbia river."[23]

By early 1939, Oregon's Fish Commission apparently conceded engineering Coulee to mimic an open river was politically impossible. The commission now sought simply to get the federal government to listen to state expertise. Veatch struggled to preserve a role for state management in the Coulee salvage plan. Writing the Interior secretary on 8 February 1939, he "offered the following suggestions and recommendations . . . [i]n order that those sharing the grave responsibilities of preserving the Columbia river salmon may have a voice in the acceptance and development" of the federal government's plans "for handling and safeguarding that portion of these runs as may be blocked by the Grand Coulee dam."[24]

He recommended Oregon and Washington join the U.S. Fisheries Bureau on a new "joint commission" charged with administering the federal hatchery/transplantation plan. This commission would "afford each of the several departments . . . an opportunity to voice their ideas and recommendations for perpetuating the fishery resource of the Columbia river." Downriver states could also work cooperatively with the federal government on research aimed at minimizing fish losses caused by "further development of water resources in the Columbia River Basin." Veatch noted as an example of such future developments the "projects now proposed on the Snake river." The Army Corps of Engineers' survey of the Snake Basin had already approvingly noted Hells Canyon's untapped hydropower potential.[25]

Oregon's Fish Commission had accepted elimination of upper Columbia runs by Coulee and their replacement by hatchery fish. The state was now willing to follow this fish conservation experiment when the federal government pushed dam building into the Snake Basin. Offered in the face of Coulee's imminent completion and the Depression's painful stimulus, Veatch's concession of upriver fish to federal management would haunt FCO and the other northwestern states in the postwar years.

Interior secretary Ickes never replied to Veatch's "suggestions and recommendations" about joint state-federal management of northwestern fish. New Deal public-power policy focused on building dams and stringing transmission lines, not conserving salmon. Reclamation had washed its hands of Coulee's ecological crisis, U.S. Fisheries Bureau acting commissioner Charles E. Jackson notified Veatch on 17 March 1939. "The Bureau of Reclamation is definitely withdrawing from this field anticipating, no doubt, the completion of its responsibility with the construction of the physical facilities required for salvage of the fish runs." The Mitchell Act, Jackson now informed Veatch, required FCO to deal with the Fisheries Bureau as the sole federal agency responsible for preserving what could be saved of the upriver fish.[26]

That chronically understaffed, underfunded federal agency faced its herculean task as a surly senior partner. States would be asked for their advice "and as much active cooperation as can be provided." Veatch's assertion of transboundary "moral and legal responsibility" for the fate of the Columbia anadromous fishery carried little weight with the Fisheries Bureau. Jackson instead consigned Oregon, Washington, and Idaho to a future as commercial regulators and industrial promoters:

> In our opinion the greatest unsolved problem which faces us today is to properly regulate the commercial fishery in order, first, to permit an adequate escapement of spawning fish to maintain the resource at the highest level the watershed will support, and second, to exploit this resource in the most economic manner. This is clearly the function of the state governments and until this problem is solved, the success of all the activities in the upper Columbia River may be completely nullified.[27]

Enclosed in Jackson's reply to Veatch was the Fisheries Bureau's 15 March blueprint for "a cooperative program of handling the runs of salmon and steelhead trout that will be prevented from reaching their natural spawning grounds in 1939 by Grand Coulee Dam." The final form of the federal salvage program was "guided chiefly by the recommendations of this Bureau's officers."[28]

The Fisheries Bureau's Coulee experiment eliminated the upriver chinook and steelhead fishery. It inaugurated a federally financed, federally managed fish conservation strategy dependent on hatcheries and transplantation:

> In view of the uncertain fate of downstream migrants from fish spawning above Grand Coulee Dam, it is recommended that the risk of losing the entire run by planting in this location be spread by distributing the fish taken from the traps at Rock Island equitably among the major tributaries of the Columbia River between Rock Island and Grand Coulee . . . as a major program of transplantation. . . .
>
> In carrying out such a program the Bureau of Fisheries proposes to invite the active cooperation of the fishery authorities in the States of Oregon and Washington.

Interior secretary Ickes spoke more profoundly than even he intended when, on 31 March 1939, he announced the federal government had adopted Jackson's blueprint as its "plan for permanent control of the migratory fish in the Columbia River." The secretary declared "no claim against the Grand Coulee Dam project for compensation or damage due to the loss of future potential runs in Upper Columbia waters, other than as provided in the plan, should be considered." The Coulee salvage strategy depended on federal money: $2.5 million would be spent immediately to build a four-hatchery complex servicing rivers that emptied into the Columbia below Coulee. Its executors would be federal agents: the Bureau of Fisheries (later renamed the Fish and Wildlife Service) would operate the "works" because of "the heavy Federal investment, . . . the fish are migratory, and . . . the commercial interests in the runs are interstate." State fish agencies in Oregon and Washington would merely serve as "advisers" to Reclamation and the Fisheries Bureau. Relocation's chances of success were speculative, Ickes conceded. "The program may be experimental in some respects," he admitted. "An important end to be held constantly in view should be the prosecution of important lines of research calculated to add to the useful knowledge in connection with fishery problems."[29]

Presented Ickes' federal salvage strategy as a fait accompli, the Fish Commission of Oregon tried to keep the high legal and moral ground it had first claimed in October 1938. Veatch told Ickes on 17 April 1939, "While we recognize the fact that your department may make any arrangements you may see fit with the State of Washington . . . and we need not be consulted in the matter, we desire to make our position clear as to the attitude we take on the Grand Coulee dam and on any future dams that may be constructed in the Columbia River Basin, regardless of the states within which such dams may lie." The commission's "opinion [is] that where dams are constructed by the federal government which interfere with the run of migratory fish, that the government should as far as possible remedy the damage done to fish life by the construction and operation of such facilities as may be necessary under the circumstances. . . . We are of the opinion that proper facilities for the propagation of fish below the Grand Coulee dam should be constructed with federal funds, and that these facilities be operated as a permanent program by the Bureau of Fisheries. . . . Also, we feel that with the operation of these facilities under the Bureau of Fisheries, we might have some voice as to the extent and the manner of their operation."[30]

Oregon's fish commissioners doubted from the outset Ickes' "plan for permanent control" would preserve viable fish runs that had inhabited the Columbia Basin above Grand Coulee. The federal government's assertion of legal primacy over anadromous fish irreparably weakened Veatch's negotiating position on future higher-elevation dams. By reluctantly accepting the central premise of New Deal hydroelectric fish conservation strategy, FCO foreclosed Oregon's future ability to safeguard anadromous runs that happened, because of biology and geography, to fall behind the concrete curtain of dams that the United States would erect after World War II. Eventual replacement of the upriver fishery with hatchery-reared and transplanted fish compelled downriver states to concentrate conservation efforts on the lower Columbia Basin. Ickes had cut the high constitutional and historic ground from beneath the Oregon Fish Commission. The commission in the postwar period retreated from its sweeping assertion of transboundary moral and legal responsibility. Like its northwestern state counterparts, the agency held only the low mound of construction debris shadowed by Grand Coulee's impassable bulk.

When the Federal Columbia River Power System tried expanding upriver to the foot of the Rockies after 1945, the Coulee Dam principle justified the extinction of wild Snake River chinook salmon and steelhead trout that swam through Hells Canyon. Federal public-power policy wrote off preserving upriver fisheries. Oregon and Washington had submitted to the New Deal experiment of using transplantation and hatchery technology to preserve remnant Columbia Basin fish runs. Conservation choices enforced by the Great Depression haunted Oregon's and Idaho's fish agencies when prosperity returned.

Pushing federal multipurpose dams beyond public power's domain in the Columbia Basin required more hard choices about the fate of Snake Basin fish in the immediate postwar years. The Columbia Basin Inter-Agency Committee made most of those choices. Congress in 1945 authorized building McNary Dam across the mid-Columbia, just below the Snake's mouth.[31] The interagency committee's administrators responded to this new ecological crisis by trying to save only fragments of the Northwest's anadromous fishery. Downriver fish, which spawned below McNary, became wards dependent on hatcheries built with power revenues generated by the federal upriver offensive. The Fish Commission of Oregon and Washington Department of Fisheries believed commercial fishing's economic survival depended on downriver fish. The Snake Basin's upriver fish, by contrast, had fewer and weaker advocates. Sport anglers and Indians proved no political match for commercial fishers, packers, and hydropower managers. The Idaho Fish and Game Department, custodian of the upriver fish, failed to grasp public-power expansion's ecological threat to Snake Basin fish. The Columbia Basin Inter-Agency Committee sacrificed Snake Basin fish by targeting Hells Canyon as the upriver offensive's chief strategic objective and by concentrating scarce conservation resources on preserving commercially valuable Columbia Basin fish.

Federal hydroelectric managers justified their postwar sacrifice of upriver fish by retooling Depression-fighting strategies devised at Grand Coulee. Their Lower Columbia River Fishery Development Program, written between 1947 and 1949 by CBIAC, supplanted state conservation of open water with federally funded hatcheries.

Experimental results from Coulee might have counseled caution by 1946. For seven years, Ickes' salvage strategy had necessitated complex, expensive human interventions into the upper Columbia's fishery. Adult salmon and steelhead destined for the upper Columbia Basin had to first climb Bonneville Dam's sixty-five-foot-high fish ladders. They then had to navigate the new obstacles created by construction of McNary Dam before reaching fish-counting stations at Puget Sound Power's Rock Island Dam, seventy-five miles below Grand Coulee. Each summer and fall, as seasonal runs tried to head upriver past Rock Island, men had to trap adult fish, force them to spawn in new federal hatcheries, and then transplant hatchery-reared juveniles into undammed tributaries that entered the Columbia below Coulee. Even after seven years, thousands of man-hours, and millions of individual battles for new life in Leavenworth Hatchery's concrete raceways and rearing pens, Ickes' New Deal conservation experiment was yielding ambiguous data, at best.[32]

Chinook runs in the upper Columbia had fallen below prewar, pre-Bonneville, pre-Coulee counts. If the Coulee salvage experiment were working as planned, fish numbers should have rebounded during World War II. Military restrictions on navigation in the North Pacific had diminished commercial fishing pressure. Older tribe members had migrated to urban defense jobs and many young men had served in the armed forces, which should have restrained Indian catches in the middle Columbia. Abundant winter snowfalls had begun swelling stream flows again after nearly a Depression decade of low water. Still, escapements past Bonneville and fish-trap counts at Rock Island had failed to reach pre-Depression levels. Ominously, both sockeye salmon and steelhead runs had plummeted by 50 percent since the United States had taken over the upper Columbia fishery.[33]

Congress' enactment of the Fish and Wildlife Coordination Act in 1946 offered some hope that state resistance could ameliorate fish losses caused by the federal upriver hydroelectric offensive.[34] Its Senate sponsor, Guy Cordon (R-Ore.), assured the Oregon Fish Commission the coordination act required the Army Engineers and Interior Department to include state-agency comments when briefing Congress about proposed new power dams and reservoirs. "Of course," the senator also pointed out, "under the constitution the federal government has control of navigable waters. . . . [W]ith reference to navigable waters, the states surrendered their rights to the federal government." When Oregon Master Fish Warden Arnie J. Suomela asked whether the federal government could "take over fisheries facilities" by flooding existing state hatcheries under reservoirs created by federal dams, Cordon replied, "It would not take over but it could. If your facilities are destroyed it could provide structures for the state's operation or could construct their own." At best, the new administrative tool presented by the act boosted northwestern states' bargaining power. They could leverage their fish-management expertise to maneuver hydroelectric agencies into building the best hatcheries federal money could buy.[35]

Coordinated postwar hydroelectric planning by CBIAC revealed a new purpose for building new dams. Dams made hydroelectricity, and electricity sales returned regular revenues to the federal power agencies. Dams that watered deserts could also save fish. With postwar prosperity spinning government turbines and filling BPA's cash register, northwesterners were starting to eye that income as a fund for fish conservation. Representative Henry Jackson (D-Wash.), an enthusiastic New Deal promoter of new federal multipurpose dams, believed power money could placate state conservation agencies and their commercial and sportfishing constituents. Just as public-power sales paid for building new dams to generate more public power, so power sales could pay for new fish-conservation measures. "I think enough money should be allocated out of power revenues to provide for extensive research into the fishery situation," Jackson declared. "I favor construction of dams for power production but before they are constructed ample revenue should be allocated from the power income to provide the assistance needed by the salmon industry along the river."[36]

6 SACRIFICING HELLS CANYON'S FISH

Death by Committee

Congress and President Truman feared rapid demobilization after World War II would throw thousands of northwesterners out of work. Worries about another economic slump impelled more of the federal pump priming that had built Bonneville and Grand Coulee dams. Just as the New Deal did, postwar public-power dams created ecological crises for northwestern anadromous fish. Congress authorized the Army Engineers to build McNary Dam on the main Columbia in late 1945.[1] Authorized as well was a multidam corps project to make the lower Snake in southeastern Washington navigable to Lewiston, Idaho, just downstream from Hells Canyon.[2] McNary, the first new federal dam to block the Columbia since the New Deal, once again forced fish managers to negotiate emergency conservation measures with the federal hydroelectric agencies. Designed to be one hundred feet taller than Bonneville, McNary menaced both Columbia and Snake basin fisheries because of its location just downstream from the Snake's mouth.

McNary triggered tough public and internal debates about federal hydroelectric dominance over northwestern fish. In midsummer 1946, the Oregon fish commissioners met Army Corps staff at the dam site near Umatilla to debate ways of passing adult fish above, and juvenile smolts below, the dam. Several days later, corps engineers in Portland briefed Oregon governor Earl Snell, Master Fish Warden Arnie Suomela, and state game director C. E. Lockwood about McNary fish passage. Corps engineers told the incredulous Oregonians current plans contemplated forcing downstream smolts against a screen over the turbine intakes. After first pinning the four-inch-long fish to screens, the Columbia's flow against the dam would "wash them off with pressures behind [a] screen into [a] trough." Upstream adult migrants would have to surmount fish ladders narrower and steeper than those at Bonneville.[3]

Congress' other postwar stimulus measure, the lower Snake navigation project, caused even more consternation in FCO. At a late-summer 1946 conference with Oregon fish managers and U.S. Fish and Wildlife Service salmon specialist J. T. Barnaby, corps planners revealed the army had not even settled on the number of new dams needed to carry ocean-going barges into Idaho. Congress had authorized at least six; the corps' North Pacific Division headquarters in Portland projected five; and a corps engineer closed the discussion "as to the number of dams desirable (5–4–6??)" by "point[ing] out nothing [was] known."[4]

Government biologists, commercial fishers, and sport anglers privately and publicly wondered whether such uncertainty warranted a pause before the upriver offensive rolled on. In autumn 1946, as Congress debated appropriations to start McNary Dam, Fish and Wildlife's Portland office leaked Barnaby's preliminary report on the ecological consequences of more dams. It presented grim data from the Coulee salvage experiment. Barnaby warned northwesterners accelerated dam building "would literally destroy the valuable Columbia River salmon fishery." His report infuriated higher-ups in Interior, who ordered the FWS to recall the study pending further discussions with the power agencies.[5]

The Oregon Fish Commission's official summary of its 1945–46 work reflected fish managers' new urgency. Suomela "viewed with alarm" gathering dam-building momentum. "The tremendous program of the army engineers, which calls for the construction of multi-purpose dams on most of the rivers of Oregon, threatens to deplete the salmon resource to a point where it will no longer exist in commercial abundance," Suomela warned. "I believe," he wrote, "that we are witnessing the most crucial period in the history of our fisheries, and that complete development of those plans may well spell the doom of the great salmon resource of the Northwest." Considering losses already caused by New Deal dams, "a continuation of the present trend of yield and abundance of our major fisheries, coupled with the unrestricted and improper planning of water uses, can only lead to virtual extinction of our great fishery resources, particularly the salmon."

Suomela outlined a postwar conservation strategy premised on the New Deal hatchery-transplantation model. Oregonians were "now entering a postwar era of expansion and industrialization," he wrote. The Oregon Fish Commission "is not opposed to the development of new industries for the betterment of the state." The new Fish and Wildlife Coordination Act required federal dam-building agencies to solicit state fish-agency views, so Suomela pledged Oregon's technical skill to reweave a new web of water to carry salmon to and from the Pacific. "The artificial propagation of fish as carried on by this Department becomes increasingly important," he vowed, "in view of the great number of proposed dams and hydroelectric plants in the Columbia River and its tributaries. The hope of maintaining the runs of salmon in the Columbia River and many of its tributaries will unquestionably be largely dependent upon artificial means of reproduction."[6]

Commercial salmon fishers in Oregon and Washington tried to temper state-agency confidence in more hatcheries. Industry leaders T. F. "Tom" Sandoz and James H. Cellars of Astoria began building regional support to delay new federal dams. Quietly encouraged by the Oregon Fish Commission, they announced in spring 1947 a new Columbia Basin Fisheries Development Association. To give fish time to adapt to Coulee and Bonneville, and to afford biologists more opportunity to assess federal fish-salvage experiments, Cellars urged Congress to enact a ten-year "moratorium" on new, high multipurpose dams. With McNary Dam already authorized but unbuilt, he argued the region had essentially stockpiled future hydroelectricity. Northwesterners could always complete McNary after scientists and engineers figured out how to light cities without extinguishing fish. Despite BPA's dire predictions of a "power crisis," Cellars believed new powerhouses already planned at Bonneville and Grand Coulee "would provide plenty of power for the next decade without building another dam."[7]

The Astorians swam upstream against a fast-moving regional hydroelectric consensus. Both political parties were proclaiming more federal power was good for the Columbia Basin, and not so bad for fish either. Business spokesmen clamored for more cheap public power. Ordinary consumers helped cement the hydroelectric consensus by quietly installing machines and constructing buildings that used more electricity. Federal administrators canvassed the Columbia Basin in late 1946 and early 1947, rounding up key congressional, business, and labor commitments to fund full-speed construction of McNary Dam. From McNary, the Federal Columbia River Power System could then press upriver into the Snake Basin.[8]

Still searching for coordination between Army Corps of Engineers and Reclamation Bureau upstream blueprints, the Columbia Basin Inter-Agency Committee had first to overcome agency rivalry and local political resistance. Colonel Theron D. Weaver, commander of the army corps' North Pacific Division, announced CBIAC would convene in late June 1947 in Walla Walla, Washington. Sitting as a quasi sovereign over northwestern water at this momentous meeting, the interagency committee would essentially judge the relative merits of "fish versus dams." At this two-day Walla Walla conference, the Portland *Oregon Journal* reported, "The future of the age-old salmon runs up the Columbia and Snake rivers may be decided."[9]

Colonel Weaver's public notice setting the Walla Walla hearings revealed a startling change in the Interior Department's position on fish and dams. Barely six months earlier, J. T. Barnaby of Fish and Wildlife had publicized federal biologists' plea for braking the upriver offensive. Now, in early summer 1947, the army's commander was announcing a meeting at which Interior would present its new conclusion "that the over-all benefits to the Pacific Northwest from a thorough-going development of the Snake and Columbia are such that the present salmon run must if necessary be sacrificed."[10]

Why had Interior reversed direction, from moratorium to upstream advance? Who or what was the "Pacific Northwest Field Committee," which now announced the department's new sacrificial policy? The "who" turned out to be Roy F. Bessey, one of the New Deal's most devoted Northwest servants. His decade in the memo-filled morass of interagency planning and intergovernmental relations equipped Bessey to define mission objectives and enforce them on bureaucratic dissidents. During the early New Deal, he had sought to coordinate all federal management of lands and waters in the region. When Congress eliminated this resources-planning effort in 1938, Bessey shifted to Bonneville Power Administration's Portland headquarters staff. He served as Paul Raver's speechwriter and executive special assistant. War militarized Bessey's mission. Even after 1945, he enjoyed being called "Colonel Bessey," testament to his commission as BPA's liaison to war-production industries and the Northwest Power Pool.

Bessey got new orders in peacetime. Administrator Raver delegated him to staff BPA's work with CBIAC. As clearly as any federal administrator, Bessey understood that expanding public power's domain dictated a truce between the federal government and worried state fish managers. But before CBIAC could craft that understanding, Interior had to speak with one voice. Fish and Wildlife thought existing dams threatened extinction of seagoing fish. Worse still, from Raver's perspective, FWS had publicized concerns about new dams in late 1946. To bring all of Interior's regional operations into line with BPA expansion policy, Raver requested Interior secretary Julius Krug to find consensus within the department, and to dictate it if necessary.

Krug oversaw both BPA and FWS, along with the Reclamation Bureau and Bureau of Indian Affairs. An Interior veteran himself, he knew just the man for the task. Early in 1947, the Interior secretary and his subordinates responsible for northwestern hydropower and natural resources, assistant Interior secretaries Girard Davidson and William Warne, instructed BPA administrator Raver to put Roy Bessey to work.[11]

Bessey leavened a bureaucrat's guile with a missionary's patience. To bend Interior's diverse, and often competing, constituencies to the cause of hydroelectric expansion, he had to overcome perennial friction among separate agencies. Interior's northwestern organizational chart looked nothing like BPA's clean, rational electric grid. Thinking the appearance of unity might incrementally generate unified action, Bessey marshaled delegates from the region's various Interior agencies—Fish and Wildlife, Reclamation, BPA, Indian Affairs, Bureau of Land Management—into a new ad hoc "Pacific Northwest Field Committee."

New Deal bureaucratic experience convinced Bessey the best decisions were made privately, then announced publicly with fanfare by confident administrators. None of the Pacific Northwest Field Committee's deliberations during the first half of 1947 were open to the public. Neither Astorians nor Indians could likely have swayed Bessey's conviction that public power promised the region a brighter, more secure future. His secretive methods never gave them the chance to try. Closed-door conferences prevented northwestern conservationists from enlisting national allies among the grassroots groups and state conservation agencies that had secured passage of the 1946 Fish and Wildlife Coordination Act. Neither the skeptical nor even the curious could influence federal administrators who concealed what they were doing. The New Deal epitome of the expert public servant, Roy Bessey enjoyed the deference still accorded government experts. He used secrecy, expertise, and deference to enforce public power's priorities against regional resistance in the Columbia-Snake Basin.[12]

Bessey's closed-door Pacific Northwest Field Committee enabled CBIAC to broker a plan to overcome conservationists' resistance. Krug squeezed Interior. Bessey applied the pressure. The field committee's disparate agencies now sang hydroelectric harmony. Distributed as background information for CBIAC's "fish versus dams" Walla Walla conference, Bessey's "preliminary recommendations" actually charted a hydroelectric expansion strategy targeting Hells Canyon. They recanted Fish and Wildlife's tentative dissent of autumn 1946. They excluded Indians and Astorians from decisions about dams. They allied Reclamation with the army on Bonneville Power's overriding objective: facilitating the Federal Columbia River Power System's march to the Rockies. The interagency committee's Walla Walla hearing could now split Oregon and Washington off from the salmon industry's alarming demand for a dam-building moratorium. By focusing federal resources on conserving commercially valuable downriver fish, the federal agencies would placate Columbia Basin state fish managers.

Bessey's fish-conservation strategy preempted any prospect of Oregon and Idaho, constitutional and historic keepers of the upriver fish runs, combining to oppose the giant new Hells Canyon High Dam. The Northwest Field Committee's decision to conserve downriver fish enmeshed the Oregon Fish Commission in meeting primarily the needs of commercial fishers working the lower Columbia and coastal waters. The commission surrendered what little political leverage it retained to fight upriver dams. Instead, beginning in summer 1947, John Veatch and his colleagues allowed the United States to sacrifice Snake Basin fish in favor of trying to re-create new runs in the lower Columbia Basin.

Interior's new June 1947 salmon policy reflected Bessey's New Deal heritage. It was now too late, his Northwest Field Committee concluded, to halt a decade-old drive to electrify the entire Northwest with public power from federal dams. Congress' 1945 approval of McNary and the lower Snake navigation dams had ratified the New Deal in the Northwest. The nation was committing still more resources to attain the power agencies' goals of pushing cheap hydropower and slack-water navigation to the foot of the Continental Divide. "It is difficult precisely to equate these potential benefits against the value of the present Columbia River salmon," Bessey mused. "But all concerned within the Department are agreed that they are the foundation of the ultimate development of the Pacific Northwest and that they considerably outweigh the resulting cost to the commercial fisheries, the Indians and the sportsmen." Agencies that Harold Ickes had used to plan the New Deal Northwest now stamped the "Old Curmudgeon's" utilitarian conservation philosophy on postwar fishery policy.[13]

Both Portland newspapers—the morning *Oregonian* and evening *Oregon Journal*—sent correspondents to cover the Walla Walla hearings. The Associated Press wired its stories immediately to papers around the Northwest. Journalists smelled news in this dramatic case of "fish versus dams." Tom Sandoz and James Cellars of the fishing industry had already guaranteed a clash with hydropower and navigation boosters. The Astorians' new pressure group was demanding work stop on McNary Dam. They wanted a moratorium on new dams. Restive Columbia Basin Indians planned to protest any plans to build a federal dam at the Dalles that would drown their ancestral Celilo Falls fishing grounds 120 miles up the Columbia from Portland. Controversy, especially one that pitted rubber boots and dip nets against slide rules and flip charts, meant good copy.

Colonel Weaver opened CBIAC's "fish versus dams" hearing on 25 June. Witnesses, spectators, and reporters packed Walla Walla's city hall. Tempers quickly flared, matching the early summer temperatures. Sensing trouble, Weaver took control. The colonel, resplendent in his summer-tan uniform bearing on its lapels the Army Corps' distinctive gold castle badges, ordered the interagency committee to decamp for a bigger venue. Aides rushed to gather their charts and models. Chamber of commerce organizers hustled their delegations down the street. Reporters sidled alongside the rival camps, trying to get comments from wary federal planners, noting the "colorful" Indian costumes, arranging lead paragraphs in their heads as they wiped sweat from beneath their fedoras.

Down the street streamed the hydroelectric cavalcade and its supplicants, heading for Walla Walla's biggest room available on such short notice, the Marcus Whitman Hotel's ballroom. After herding everyone inside, Colonel Weaver sized up the crowd. Accustomed to giving orders and receiving obedience, CBIAC's chair announced procedures designed to keep the United States firmly in control. He divided the hearing into three phases. Federal representatives would speak first, establishing their special competency, then dam opponents, and finally dam boosters. The colonel limited each witness to ten minutes' testimony.

Armed with charts, maps, and pointers, Reclamation's R. J. Newell helped BPA's Bessey outline Interior's new strategy to conserve downriver fish by building upriver dams. They maintained downriver salmon stood a better chance of survival if Hells Canyon High Dam were built immediately after McNary. That way, downriver conservation efforts could take hold before any other dams were built on the main Columbia. Representatives from the Fish and Wildlife Service and Bureau of Indian Affairs next dutifully testified how their work in the Northwest Field Committee during the spring had produced a plan to build dams that saved fish. They agreed with Bessey that damming the Snake in Hells Canyon adequately met their agencies' needs and responsibilities.

Bonneville Power administrator Paul Raver took the lectern immediately before lunch on the first day. Characteristically, he sounded ominous. His power-planning staff at Portland headquarters had already discarded its spring 1947 projections. Fast-rising demand made their power-use assumptions obsolete. In this era of hand fans and seersucker suits, summertime air-conditioning was not the culprit behind BPA's perennial shortages. Instead, Raver warned, nature might confound the Northwest by failing to deliver its accustomed winter snows and rains to swell the rivers and spin Coulee's and Bonneville's turbines. Raver reminded the committee, the crowd, and the entire region his agency still fought "a critical power situation that will become worse next winter." Much as Raver wanted more power now to serve his Columbia Basin customer base, Bonneville Power welcomed new upstream dams such as High Hells Canyon. Accelerating completion of Hungry Horse Dam in northwestern Montana and High Hells Canyon Dam met BPA's upriver objectives.[14]

Fish proponents pleaded their case to CBIAC the rest of the day. Thirty Indians, "most of them in their colorful costumes, braids, and beading," as the *Oregonian*'s Lawrence Barber wrote, gathered behind their designated spokesmen. They represented Columbia Basin tribes with century-old treaty fishing rights, the "Wy-Ums from Celilo, Nez Perces from Lewiston, Cayuses and Umatillas from Pendleton, Walla Wallas from this community, Warm Springs and Yakimas from their home areas." The "more vocal and militant" Astorians, who had chartered a special plane to fly in fishing industry leaders, followed the tribes. State fishery managers from Oregon and Washington went next. Finally, Weaver squeezed in a handful of citizens to speak for the Izaak Walton League, Oregon Wildlife Federation, and Washington Sportsmen's Council. "From their words and voluminous briefs," thought the *Oregonian*'s Barber, "much of the destiny of the area for years to come may be written."[15]

Tribal leaders declared they would not accept reparation payments if new U.S. dams inundated customary fishing sites. Postwar power-sale profits could not replace fishing rights guaranteed by treaties negotiated ten years before the Civil War. "Salmon straight from the river" was how his interpreter, Big John Whiz, translated Wy-Um chief Tommy Thompson's plea.

But, as the *Oregonian*'s reporter observed, "most of the day was taken up by white men," especially the Astorians flown in by Tom Sandoz to belittle Raver's dire warnings. Newell's rescheduling offer to build Hells Canyon High Dam before starting new Columbia dams seemed to ignore the fishers' main objection: all new dams interfered with migratory fish and posed

Franklin Roosevelt Inaugurates Bonneville Dam Construction, 1934. New Deal public-power policy transformed the Columbia Basin. Bonneville and Grand Coulee dams expressed a powerful vision that inspired engineers, politicians, and ordinary people for nearly two decades. Cheap public hydroelectricity had fascinated FDR since his Progressive Era entry into New York politics. *Courtesy BPA*

Bonneville against the Columbia River, 1936. Engineers convinced wary biologists that Bonneville's innovative fish ladders could pass adult salmon and steelhead trout upriver, over the dam. Young fish heading downriver toward the Pacific had to survive passage through the dam's turbines. Coulee Dam, 250 miles upriver, made no provision for fish passage in either direction. *Courtesy BPA*

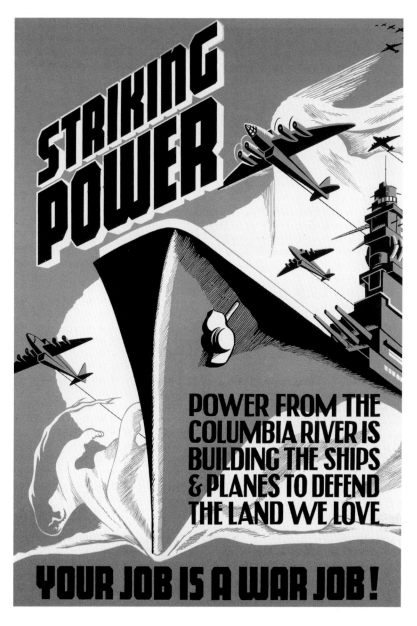

Bonneville Power Administration War Production Poster, 1944. BPA hydropower flowed into Portland shipyards, Seattle aircraft factories, and nuclear-bomb development in eastern Washington's desert near Coulee Dam. World War II speeded the industrialization and urbanization of the Columbia Basin, while the Snake Basin lost population. *Courtesy BPA*

BPA Administrator Paul J. Raver. Directing the Bonneville Power Administration throughout the Roosevelt-Truman era (1935–53), Raver's control of most northwestern electricity made BPA into a regional power. A formidable champion of federalizing Hells Canyon, Raver personified the New Deal Northwest. He was anathema to Eisenhower and regional Republicans after 1952. *Courtesy BPA*

Roy F. Bessey (left) with FDR's Uncle, F. A. Delano. Raver's indispensable assistant at Bonneville Power, Bessey epitomized bureaucratic esprit de corps in the public-power domain. After 1945, as staff director for the Columbia Basin Inter-Agency Committee, he used BPA influence to reconcile the Reclamation Bureau's and Army Corps of Engineers' competing plans to build High Hells Canyon. *Courtesy BPA*

(*Top*) Harry Truman Inspects Grand Coulee's New Powerhouse, 1950. FDR's successor argued Hells Canyon High Dam would strengthen cold war America. New Deal dams had enabled the Northwest, heretofore mostly rural, to become a key Allied production complex in World War II. Truman tried unsuccessfully for five years to convince Congress to authorize High Hells Canyon. *Courtesy Truman Presidential Library*

Hells Canyon of the Snake River. By many measures the deepest canyon in North America, this far-off place captured Americans' attention in the first postwar decade. This view looks downriver to the north into Hells Canyon High Dam's site, with Oregon to the west (left) and Idaho to the east (right). Peaks in both states top eight thousand feet barely three miles from the river's banks. *Courtesy Idaho State Historical Society*

(*Facing page*) High Dam Partisans, 1949. Surrounding Truman, as he ceremonially opens the line sending hydropower from Coulee's new turbines, are Interior Secretary Julius Krug (center) and Assistant Secretaries C. Girard Davidson (left) and William Warne (right). Davidson would devote the next decade, in and out of federal service, to the Hells Canyon controversy. He represented High Dam forces in the long dam licensing case against Idaho Power. *Courtesy Truman Presidential Library*

Truman Inspects Vanport Flood. The president went straight from this boat tour of the devastated community to a Portland motorcade that took him to a major speech about Northwest water and power. He compared the struggle to federalize the Columbia Basin hydropower to World War II by linking Hells Canyon High Dam to wartime triumphs in the region. *Courtesy Truman Presidential Library*

(*Facing page, top*) Planning the High Dam. Shortly after World War II, federal personnel began measuring Hells Canyon's water and rock. Until the 1949 "Weaver-Newell Accord" assigned the High Dam to Reclamation, its survey teams raced Army Engineers into the canyon as both agencies sought advantage in the intense bureaucratic politicking. *Courtesy Idaho State Historical Society*

(*Facing page, bottom*) Vanport's Agony, June 1948. Columbia River flooding killed dozens and damaged millions of dollars' worth of property. Hardest hit was this Portland industrial suburb at the confluence of the Columbia and Willamette rivers, inundated when dikes raised during World War II collapsed. Truman and other High Dam backers exploited the flood to pressure Congress to authorize Hells Canyon High Dam. *Courtesy BPA Library*

Federal Reclamation of the Snake Basin, 1936. Standing atop this huge new irrigation siphon, Reclamation Bureau Northwest director R. J. Newell (left) directed millions of dollars of federal subsidies into southern Idaho and eastern Oregon. The bureau's 1947 Snake Basin Plan proposed rerouting rivers beneath Idaho mountains to expand irrigated agriculture and cheap public power. *Courtesy Idaho State Historical Society*

(*Facing page, top*) Truman Dedicates FDR Plaque at Grand Coulee, 1950. Just two weeks after the Senate first defeated High Hells Canyon, Truman made a "nonpolitical" northwestern visit to link his Fair Deal power policy to Roosevelt's New Deal legacy. At Coulee, with Washington senator Warren Magnuson (left) and dam manager Frank Banks (center), the president insisted federalizing the Snake would realize FDR's vision for the Columbia Basin. *Courtesy Truman Presidential Library*

(*Facing page, bottom*) Reclamation Bureau Irrigation, Snake Basin, late 1940s. From its Boise office, the Northwest Region of the Reclamation Bureau oversaw some of the first federal irrigation efforts, such as these Minidoka Project fields along southern Idaho's middle Snake River. To bring big new swaths of Idaho high desert into production, the Bureau in 1947 envisioned Hells Canyon High Dam as a "cashbox" generating enormous power-sale revenues to subsidize new irrigated farms. *Courtesy Idaho State Historical Society*

Wayne Morse, Oregon Senator, Early 1950s. The "tiger of the Senate" championed the High Dam fiercely, first as a Republican, then an independent, and finally a liberal Democrat. He linked cheap public hydropower with social reform, industrial development, and political democracy. A savage critic of Idaho Power's bid to build small Hells Canyon dams, he accused private power of trying to "mutilate the Snake." *Courtesy Eisenhower Presidential Library*

Thomas E. Roach, Idaho Power president, 1955. Roach insisted the Hells Canyon controversy pitted liberty and property rights against socialism. Although leading Columbia Basin utility executives had accepted federal primacy after 1947 by profitably reselling cheap public hydroelectricity, Roach refused to surrender any of Idaho Power's Snake Basin service territory to BPA. *Courtesy Idaho Power Company*

Northwestern Governors Fight the High Dam, 1952. Idaho's Len B. Jordan spearheaded an intensely partisan, deeply conservative, phalanx of governors who opposed High Hells Canyon. Republicans Arthur Langlie of Washington (left), Paul Patterson of Oregon (second from left), and Hugo Aronson of Montana (right) join Jordan to welcome their party's presidential candidate, Dwight Eisenhower, to Boise. Jordan, who had ranched in Hells Canyon for several years, exploited this experience to appeal to irrigators. *Courtesy Idaho State Historical Society*

Bonneville Dam fish ladder (center), early 1940s. Federal administrators assured skeptical state-agency managers that technology and power-sale revenue would preserve anadromous fish. Postwar conservation efforts, however, failed to avert dams' ecological threats. *Courtesy Oregon Historical Society, OrHi50237.*

(*Facing page, bottom*) Ike on the Offensive, 1952. Eisenhower (seated, center) opened his presidential campaign in Boise in August. As the guest of the region's Republican governors (all pictured), he blistered High Hells Canyon in his public address. His managers chose the site and subject of Eisenhower's first campaign trip to symbolize Republican hostility to New Deal public-power policy. *Courtesy Idaho State Historical Society*

Idaho Power Chief Counsel R. P. Parry, Early 1950s. Parry directed Idaho Power's dam license case before the Federal Power Commission and federal courts for five years. This Kansas native, who migrated in the 1920s to the Snake Basin fresh from law school, became Idaho's most powerful lawyer during the postwar years. From his Twin Falls law firm, Parry simultaneously advised governors, corporate presidents, state administrators, irrigation companies, and their customer-owners. *Courtesy Ann Sensibaugh and Barker Rosholt and Simpson LLP*

Idahoans Greet Their Hero, August 1952. From the statehouse steps in Boise, Eisen-hower looked over the largest crowd ever gathered in the state, estimated at more than twenty thousand. Broadcast and telecast nationally, his address outlined conserva-tives' objections to public-power expansion. Just a month earlier, inside the statehouse, hundreds of Snake Basin people had testified before a Federal Power Commission for and against the High Dam. *Courtesy Idaho State Historical Society*

Eisenhower and Interior Secretary Douglas McKay. The new president announced the Oregon governor as his first cabinet appointment in December 1952 to signal his intent to kill High Hells Canyon. McKay thought the High Dam too big, too expensive, and too threatening to private enterprise. "Giveaway" McKay labored loyally during his two years as Interior Secretary to attain his president's objective. *Courtesy Eisenhower Presidential Library*

Idaho Power's Low Hells Canyon Dam. Built near the High Dam's planned site, but barely one-third its size, it was the last of Idaho Power's three Hells Canyon dams. Completed in the early 1960s, it was the last dam, private or public, built in the canyon. From 1947, when federal High Dam plans first emerged, until 1957, when the Supreme Court upheld Idaho Power's license and Congress rejected a final High Dam bill, the Hells Canyon controversy raged. It remodeled American attitudes about water, law, and power. *Courtesy Idaho Power Company*

unacceptable risks of their extinction. One after another, all afternoon, the Astorians challenged both BPA's threat of winter brownouts and Interior's hopeful program of research and downriver rehabilitation. Raver's past projections, Sandoz charged, had overestimated electricity usage by as much as 40 percent. The region's realistic hydropower needs "for the next ten years" could be fully met by installing all new turbines planned for Grand Coulee and Rock Island dams. Astoria mayor Orval Eaton and port president William McGregor testified that the cause of preserving wild salmon in the Columbia Basin had united even long-time economic adversaries. To dramatize this point, packing-plant owners James Cellars and Anton Sorensen symbolically shook hands with fishermen's union leaders Henry Niemela and William Puustinen before testifying together. A common thread linked the Astorians' Walla Walla testimony. All pleaded with federal hydroelectric administrators to declare a moratorium on "any more multiple purpose dams across the main thread of the Columbia below Foster Creek or on the Snake River below Swan Falls Dam."[16]

Master Fish Warden Suomela's nineteen-page brief summarized Oregon's conservation objectives. The fish commission now believed the federal upriver offensive could save the downriver spring-run chinook salmon both Astorians and Indians championed. Suomela's testimony blended prudence and optimism. The United States should preserve commercial and treaty fisheries in the lower Columbia. Delaying the lower Snake navigation dams and foregoing a new main-stem dam at the Dalles that drowned Celilo Falls would accomplish this objective. The public-power domain also owed the region "a comprehensive program of lower river development . . . to mitigate the losses to the salmon runs by main stem dams on the Columbia River or its tributaries."

Suomela emphasized that "the Fish Commission is not opposed to the orderly industrial and agricultural development of our northwest territory" because "it is their firm opinion that this expansion can be accomplished with little or no damage to the fisheries resource." The Oregon Fish Commission doubted even the best fish passage facilities at new dams could keep alive the Snake Basin's upriver spawning reaches. Rather than chasing this illusory, uneconomical mirage, Suomela recommended hydroelectric revenues and additional appropriations should build "hatchery, trapping, and holding facilities . . . when the normal migration is blocked." Results from the Grand Coulee salvage plan justified optimism rather than caution. The Fish Commission endorsed a strategy premised on using federal money and state expertise. "Present and future programs by the States of Washington and Oregon and the Fish and Wildlife Service," he concluded, "promise to arrest the observed decline in the blueback [sockeye] and spring chinook runs in spite of both Bonneville and Grand Coulee Dams, and given adequate funds and technical skill these runs can almost assuredly be rehabilitated, providing of course additional destructive factors are not encountered."[17]

What exactly Idaho—whose fish would be sacrificed above Hells Canyon— thought about moratoria, Indians, or hatcheries was not clear at Walla Walla. The *Oregon Journal* reported Idaho's Fish and Game Commission joined Oregon and Washington, as well as the Astorians' Columbia Basin Fisheries Development Association, in "spearheading opposition to any further dam construction in the lower Columbia and Snake." However, none of Idaho's citizen-commissioners even testified before CBIAC. Instead, according to the *Oregonian*, Idaho Fish and Game Department director "Mark" Murray did, "taking the stand in favor of dams."

The Idaho Fish and Game Department had a director named Murray, but his name was "Tom" Murray. He had been on the job barely six weeks following his predecessor's unexpected resignation. Uncertainty and confusion, about little matters like Murray's first name as well as far weightier problems, typified Idaho's entire approach to the Walla Walla conference in summer 1947. Murray might have been sharing his own view that downstream dams did not jeopardize Idaho fishing. Or he may have misunderstood his commissioners' position, assuming they had one. The Idaho Fish and Game Commission minutes for the year preceding June 1947 mentioned neither CBIAC nor its proposed upriver offensive into the Snake Basin. More than likely, Idaho failed to grasp the significance of the Walla Walla hearing for the state's anadromous fish. The public-power domain's eastern boundary was still well below the Snake Basin, so Idaho's fish managers probably missed the implications when Oregon acceded to Roy Bessey's plan linking downriver conservation to upriver offensive. Idaho's inattention and ignorance facilitated the sacrifice of steelhead and fall chinook that spawned above Hells Canyon. Rehabilitating downriver spring chinook using hatcheries was irrelevant to Idahoans.[18]

Life-and-death struggles over salmon, pitting Astorians against administrators and fish against dams, seemed someone else's problem to Idaho's conservation agency in the immediate postwar years. The state had no well-established industry to lobby for fish. Oregon Master Fish Warden Suomela and Washington Fisheries Department director Milo C. Moore criticized federal hydroelectric expansion because it menaced the commercial fishery they were sworn to preserve and perpetuate. Though the lion's—or chinook's share—of northwestern anadromous runs originated in Idaho's Snake Basin, the state had long forbidden the industrial fishing methods practiced by Astorians.[19] A cursory examination of Oregon's strategy, which was likely all Tom Murray's commission gave it before dispatching him to Walla Walla, may have even reassured the Idahoans. Oregon, after all, did specifically acknowledge the valuable Salmon Basin spawning grounds by opposing the Army Engineers' lower Snake dams. Suomela advised CBIAC to leave open to migratory fish "the Snake River below the confluence of the Salmon River."

What the master fish warden did *not* say should have alarmed Tom Murray, however. Suomela's proposed lower Snake moratorium remained silent about the rest of the Snake that ran through Hells Canyon *above* the confluence of the Salmon River. By implication, Oregon's Fish Commission was echoing Newell, Bessey, Weaver, and Raver. Their federal agencies were targeting precisely that river reach for High Hells Canyon Dam, to be built seventy-five miles *above* the Salmon's mouth. Suomela differed with Reclamation and the Army Engineers about the scope and pace of their postwar upriver offensive. He did second their judgment that a downriver dambuilding moratorium was acceptable only if "all other possible sources of water power are fully utilized." Arnie Suomela and Paul Raver were on the same page at last. Building High Hells Canyon held the strategic key to both of their objectives: concentrating conservation efforts on commercial fish and maximizing output of public power.

Colonel Weaver convened the second day of CBIAC's Walla Walla hearing to hear from dam boosters. Tom Humphrey wrote in that night's *Oregon Journal*, "Hard-hitting proponents of the program to build big dams on the Columbia and Snake rivers for power, navigation, irrigation, and recreation purposes fired double-barreled arguments back . . . against fishing and conservation interests which argued . . . for a ten-year moratorium on dambuilding in the interest of saving migratory fish runs." Humphrey's summary of Day Two's hearing must have pleased Weaver and Newell: "Shall there be a 10-year moratorium on dam building as suggested by fish-wildlife groups, or a 10-year moratorium on commercial fishing as suggested by power-reclamation groups, or a compromise between the two extreme views?"[20]

Roy Bessey's patient private committee work now offered federal hydroelectric agencies a chance to appear both aggressive and compassionate. By claiming what observers were now describing as the middle way "between the two extreme views," CBIAC could solidify Interior's and the Army Engineers' emerging coalition with Oregon and Washington. By allying federal dam builders with state fish managers around the principle of sacrificing Snake Basin fish for Columbia Basin conservation, Bessey and Newell had seemingly sliced the "fish versus dams" knot. This tactic of positioning the federal government as the only player seeking common ground between extreme views structured the United States' role in remodeling Northwest lands and waterways.

Walla Walla mayor Herbert G. West led the powerful Inland Waterways Association that had sought slack-water navigation up the Snake for twenty years. He denounced any talk of slowing dam construction to save fish. He charged any delay in building any dam was just "a well-devised scheme to kill Columbia and Snake river reclamation, power, navigation, irrigation and food development for our time." Twelve witnesses—metropolitan and hinterland chambers of commerce, Portland barge interests, and the Oregon and Washington granges—pleaded with the interagency committee to begin immediately building all new dams on the drawing board: McNary, the Dalles, and the Lower Snake projects.[21]

Gus Carlson of the Inland Navigation Company peppered his attack on the Astorians' moratorium with statistics produced by Frank Bell, U.S. fisheries commissioner during the New Deal. Bell's study maintained overfishing, encouraged by the Oregon Fish Commission, "is the real reason for declining fish catches."[22] Mayor West, citing enthusiastic backing given dam construction by business and agricultural leaders from Seattle to Boise, urged the federal power agencies to press on. He closed the second day's testimony by telling Colonel Weaver, "The people of Washington, Oregon, and Idaho are overwhelmingly opposed to any delay whatever in construction of authorized projects in [the] Columbia basin." Even the slightest deviation from a program of maximum expansion defied the consensus for hydroelectric expansion, West insisted. "If the fish and wildlife service was merely sending up a trial balloon when it suggested a moratorium," CBIAC's host declared, "we've shown them where we stand."[23]

Weaver and his CBIAC colleagues recessed their Walla Walla hearing with a promise to take thirty days to "pore over the record and come up with a recommendation that will have a direct bearing on the future development of the mid-Columbia and lower Snake rivers." On behalf of Interior's

Newell, BPA's Raver, Lesher S. Wing of the Federal Power Commission, G. T. Hudson of the Agriculture Department, and the Commerce Department's H. E. Waterbury, Weaver praised "one of the most comprehensive presentations ever made on the complicated dam-fish problem."[24] Any decision made by CBIAC would come under new leadership, though. Weaver ended the Walla Walla inquest into "fish versus dams" by announcing that, effective 1 July, CBIAC'S chairmanship for 1947–48 would pass to Newell.

Federal hydroelectric managers reconvened privately in Portland for two days in late July. The Columbia Basin Inter-Agency Committee's new chairman, R. J. Newell of the Reclamation Bureau, closed its meetings to facilitate tough negotiations. He had earlier appointed a temporary subcommittee, chaired by Roy Bessey, to work up the Walla Walla hearing record into an apologia for CBIAC's postwar fish policy. To permit Bessey's subcommittee to enforce consensus in favor of downriver conservation and upriver sacrifice, Newell did not convene CBIAC again until early October. This ten-week delay became the longest hiatus in CBIAC's eight-year history. The interagency committee held both its July and October meetings behind closed doors.[25]

Newell's secrecy worked. Dam builders and fish managers could speak frankly about the biological crises that upriver hydroelectric expansion was causing as each new dam blocked or delayed fish passage. Walla Walla had captured the region's attention for days. Passion made good copy, especially when the stakes were so high and the antagonists so adamant. Closed-door deliberations within Portland's federal building on 23–24 July and 8 October, by contrast, yielded scarcely any press coverage. Yet reporters aggressive enough to have cultivated sources in and out of government would have heard big news. The downriver states had now accepted CBIAC's plan, drafted by Bessey's Northwest Field Committee, for sacrificing upriver fish.[26]

Even before the Portland negotiations, Oregon's fish managers had essentially told CBIAC a deal could be struck between downriver states and the public-power domain. Dams and fish could coexist if the United States paid for both. Suomela's public statement at Walla Walla's "fish versus dams" hearing signaled FCO's private willingness to back the upriver hydroelectric offensive into the Snake Basin if expansion both protected and compensated the Columbia Basin. Oregon fish managers were willing to help Reclamation and the Army Engineers recast the Walla Walla issue from "fish versus dams" to "fish *and* dams."

This state-federal truce became the "Lower Columbia River Fishery Development Program." It focused postwar conservation efforts on adapting anadromous biology to public dam building. As its title indicated, the Lower River Program directed Oregon's efforts to downriver commercial fisheries. When Hells Canyon High Dam took the spotlight after December 1947, Oregon's Fish Commission had little time or energy to worry about the High Dam's impact on upriver fish. The Lower Columbia River Program expressed the postwar consequences of the "permanent program of control for migratory fish" first announced by Harold Ickes during the Grand Coulee crisis in 1939.

A joint federal-state pamphlet defended the Lower River Program's method of sustaining downriver anadromous fish runs with steady infusions of federal money. *A Program of Rehabilitation of the Columbia River Fisheries* confirmed Oregon's and Washington's downriver focus as the federal upriver offensive gathered momentum. Its analysis of dam building's biological consequences and rehabilitation's political feasibility synthesized Oregon's and Washington's Walla Walla testimony, as well as Bessey's June "preliminary recommendations." Publication of the pamphlet jointly by Oregon, Washington, and the U.S. Fish and Wildlife Service suggested its authors' shared purpose. *A Program of Rehabilitation* put the downriver states on record as backing an aggressive, costly plan to rebuild commercially valuable downriver fish runs with federal money and state expertise. It rationalized sacrificing upper-basin stocks imperiled by McNary, High Hells Canyon Dam, and the Army Engineers' lower Snake project.[27]

Central to the Lower Columbia River Program was the Oregon Fish Commission's conclusion that Snake River fish that migrated *above* the mouth of the Salmon River had no future. In other words, the runs to be extinguished by High Hells Canyon Dam were already doomed relics of northwestern history. A map of the Columbia River watershed, from the Fish Commission's files on the Lower Columbia River Program, documented the agency's belief that abandoning this family of Snake Basin fish cost little. Entitled "Remaining Salmon Spawning Grounds" and filed with other documents from summer 1947, the FCO map depicted the Snake River Basin bereft of fish habitat *above* the mouth of the Salmon. That being so, new dams on the Snake *below* the Salmon, such as the corps' navigation project on the lower Snake, threatened prime available habitat. Oregon's Fish Commission fought the corps until Congress overrode resistance in 1952 by appropriating construction funds to build four dams below Lewiston, Idaho.

However, damming the Snake *above* Lewiston and *above* the Salmon—in Hells Canyon, in other words—would block but a tiny remnant of the Snake Basin's fishery.[28]

Walla Walla's hearings and Portland's truce marked a new phase of managing fish to complement the postwar hydroelectric offensive. *A Program of Rehabilitation of the Columbia River Fisheries* announced, "The program of Federal dam construction for purposes of power, navigation, irrigation and flood control must progress consistently with the public need." To manage the biological crises this program would cause, Oregon and Washington "propose[d] that the Federal agencies involved should shoulder not only the responsibility for their share of the damage done to the fishery resource but their just share of the costs involved in the repair of these damages and the perpetuation of the northwest salmon industry."[29]

Downriver states and the federal hydroelectric agencies had already devised the outlines of "a unified over-all program of rehabilitation and perpetuation of the northwest salmon industry." Needed now was "immediate planned action and . . . adequate Federal appropriations to launch and maintain the rehabilitation program." *A Program of Rehabilitation* outlined a ten-year $6 million program to build thirteen new hatcheries in Washington below Grand Coulee and eleven new Oregon hatcheries on rivers emptying into the Columbia below McNary. After completing this first phase of capital investment, the United States would permanently appropriate $400,000 per year to the two states to operate the hatchery system.[30]

This "practical program of rehabilitation and full utilization of the *lower* Columbia watershed for the purpose of fish production" would mostly ignore the higher-elevation Snake Basin.[31] Although *A Program of Rehabilitation* indicated Idaho's Fish and Game Department shared its goals, fish caught by Idaho's sport anglers and Indians would be given only "limited consideration . . . in the proposed hatchery program." To justify sacrificing upriver chinook and steelhead, the Oregon and Washington fish agencies retold the inland Northwest's history of white conquest. Fifty years of dam building to irrigate Snake Basin farms, exacerbated by mining's and logging's high-country habitat destruction along spawning waters, had "destroyed completely" upriver fisheries "or reduced [them] to such an extent that they are of no commercial value." "In fact," the pamphlet concluded, "Idaho now has no commercial salmon fishery and it is doubtful if an adequate sport salmon fishery can be maintained in the face of planned Federal projects."[32]

Washington's Department of Fisheries helped Oregon conserve commercial fish stocks by sacrificing Snake Basin fish living in and above Hells Canyon. Department director Milo Moore agreed with Oregon's Arnie Suomela and John Veatch that merging federal money and state expertise in a hatchery strategy offered the Columbia Basin states' best chance to conserve salmon families that fed coastal commerce. *The Salmon Crisis*, published in 1949 by Moore's agency to explain the Lower Columbia River Program, assigned federal dams most responsibility for the fishery's crisis. "Hundreds of miles of spawning grounds have been cut off by the construction of power dams," *The Salmon Crisis* reported. "Power is the leading competitor of salmon for streams where water supply is still abundant." However, the Fisheries Department acknowledged that, after CBIAC's meetings in Walla Walla and Portland, more dams were the Northwest's destiny. "The policy of the Department of Fisheries is *not* in opposition to all hydroelectric development," *The Salmon Crisis* announced. "It is recognized that power is essential to regional and national prosperity."[33]

Washington endorsed a postwar conservation strategy premised on the federal model Harold Ickes had first forced on Columbia Basin states at Grand Coulee. "Most of the state's watersheds will be largely reliant upon mechanical fish passage devices and artificial propagation to perpetuate their migratory fish life," according to *The Salmon Crisis*. Hatcheries would produce fish for planting "back into their parent streams, or if that is not possible, into streams of like characteristics." Those streams were simply no longer available in the upper Columbia and Snake basins because "the Columbia and its tributaries, including the Snake River system, have a growing number of dams which are either total or partial blocks."[34]

The Columbia Basin Inter-Agency Committee formally adopted the Lower Columbia River Program in a closed-door executive session on 8 October. Its parent Federal Inter-Agency River Basin Committee ratified it on 21 November 1947. That autumn, the Reclamation Bureau and Army Corps began to formulate budget requests for coming fiscal years on the basis of the downriver strategy.[35] As their CBIAC counterparts did over northwestern water, federal fish managers began acting as quasi sovereigns over northwestern fish. The Lower Columbia River Program transferred discretionary authority to Fish and Wildlife Service director Albert M. Day and northwest regional director Leo L. Laythe, which far exceeded that retained by Suomela, Veatch, and Moore. Day and Laythe defined what had been agreed during the Portland negotiations. Their agency's budget experts translated states' needs into federal dollars. Fish and Wildlife Services's perceptions of the proper relationship between the states and the federal government defined state-agency tasks.[36]

Even before Idaho, Oregon, and Washington formally ratified the Lower Columbia River Program, Laythe explained to the American Fisheries Society annual conference how Fish and Wildlife intended to execute the downriver strategy. He conceded, "Of all factors causing decreases of salmon runs, dams have presented the greatest single obstacle that confronts the maintenance of the fishery resource." By the outset of the postwar years, public and private dams storing irrigation water and turning turbines had cut off two-thirds of historic anadromous fish habitat. Laythe's agency assumed "the present trend is toward greater development of the water resources of the basin." He expected the United States would "undoubtedly" build power and navigation dams blocking the Snake, as well as two more main-stem Columbia dams between McNary and Bonneville.[37]

Laythe believed Grand Coulee's Depression-driven hatchery/transplantation strategy began "a new era in the management of the anadromous fish of the Columbia River." The Coulee salvage experiment offered a workable postwar model for adapting fish to the upriver offensive. A decade of monitoring chinook, sockeye, and steelhead runs on the upper Columbia "provided sufficiently promising results to warrant similar operations . . . which would have as a goal the preservation of the fishery of the Columbia River." Coulee had blocked all fish runs into the upper Columbia Basin. The postwar dam-building drive would inevitably block the Snake Basin above the Salmon River. Political reality therefore dictated the biological expedient of making "the lower Columbia Basin . . . obviously the region in which to concentrate efforts toward maximum utilization of streams by fish."[38]

From the outset, the federal agency executing the Lower Columbia River Fishery Development Program assumed upper-elevation fish that inhabited Idaho waters had no commercial value. Fish and Wildlife and the Columbia Basin states would therefore sacrifice them to conserve downriver stocks that supported commercial fishing. A map illustrating Laythe's report to the Fisheries Society made clear FWS's rationale for the trade-off. It depicted the lower Columbia Basin in Oregon and Washington as the zone "where salmon rehabilitation will be concentrated." Laythe's speech indicated Idaho had conceded the downriver states' power to sacrifice its Snake Basin fishery. "Such a plan for the development of the lower Columbia Basin," he recounted, "was organized by the Fish and Wildlife Service and the States of Oregon and Washington as a program of restitution of losses incurred in the past." A moratorium on upriver dams endorsed by the Idaho Fish and Game Commission at CBIAC's Walla Walla hearing "was not deemed advisable . . . [i]n the face of existing demands for hydroelectric power and flood control." "As a result," concluded Laythe, "there came into being a concerted program for the development of the salmon and steelhead trout in the lower Columbia River watershed."[39]

Administrative inertia paralyzed Idaho's Department of Fish and Game during this crucial stage of Snake Basin fish policy. Still trying to find his footing as IDFG's new chief, Director Murray had not attended either of the crucial Portland CBIAC negotiating conferences in July and October 1947. State Reclamation engineer Mark Kulp had been Idaho's sole official CBIAC delegate. Murray had testified in Walla Walla only as an adviser to federal agencies running an informational hearing. In Portland, where CBIAC made the real conservation decisions, Idaho relied on Kulp. The state engineer had little interest in salmon because his duties blended only irrigation development with water appropriation. Kulp not surprisingly advised Idaho governor C. A. Robins to back the Lower Columbia River Program "specifically" to advance "the States' [sic] interest in the Snake River Navigation and Power dams between Lewiston and Pasco."[40] Dutifully, Murray signified Idaho's acceptance of the Lower Columbia River Program on 30 June 1948. As joint, but decidedly junior, architects of the downriver conservation strategy, Moore of Washington and Suomela of Oregon had already done so.[41]

From 1947 on, northwestern states would come as suppliants to the federal government. They depended on uncertain congressional appropriations for hatchery construction. The Lower Columbia River Program required states to request assistance from the director of the U.S. Fish and Wildlife Service. Fish and Wildlife would then decide which projects would "be suitable for inclusion in the general program contemplated to be carried out by the States of Washington, Oregon, and Idaho." Albert Day in the capital and Leo Laythe in the region would be "primarily . . . responsible for the coordination of activities contemplated in the general program . . . and for the supervision of the activities of the States covered by this agreement."[42]

The new federal guardians of Snake Basin fish expected that Hells Canyon High Dam, the means of their elimination, would not be long in coming. Even as CBIAC secretly devised the downriver conservation strategy in Portland, Fish and Wildlife cleared the way to federalize Hells Canyon's water and extinguish its fish. Acting regional director Alphonse Kemmerich submitted only two pages of vague "comments and recommendations" about High Hells Canyon to CBIAC. Fish and Wildlife's opinions were sketchy because it lacked funds for fish studies in the Snake Basin. Kemmerich informed CBIAC, "Definite information is lacking as to the exact magnitude of the salmon and steelhead runs which now spawn in the main Snake River and its tributaries above the site of the proposed dam." Nevertheless, FWS anticipated another Coulee would block the Snake in Hells Canyon. Kemmerich conceded, "In view of the height of the dam, no fishways are contemplated."[43]

Inadequate presidential budget requests and meager congressional appropriations soon dogged the downriver conservation effort. Early promises of federal-state cooperation frayed when the federal power agencies put higher priority on building dams than saving fish. State fish managers hoped to start building hatcheries as soon as they finished drafting the Lower Columbia River Program in fall 1947. However, federal dam-building budgets for fiscal 1948 spending had already been set. Downriver states had to wait until the next federal budget cycle. A pattern of parsimony soon appeared. Congress appropriated less than one-third of the money promised for 1948–49 construction work. It replenished none of the funds expected, but not received, during the program's first year of 1947–48. Barely two years into the Lower Columbia River Program, CBIAC's chairman conceded skimpy appropriations—$4 million less than budgeted—were placing it "already a year or more behind schedule." McNary was more than half closed. If new lower Columbia hatcheries were not soon operating, "serious dangers of resource depletion and economic dislocation" jeopardized the entire Lower Columbia River Program.[44]

Early in the federal budget cycle for fiscal 1949, Oregon's Fish Commission began lobbying for its share of fish-conservation money. The agency had to adapt its once-sovereign prerogatives to its federal supervisors' and paymasters' calendars. Fish Commission chairman John Veatch telegraphed Oregon's congressional delegation on 13 January 1948, "respectfully request-[ing] every assistance possible" in securing a specific $1.4 million allocation for the Lower Columbia River Program in the appropriation bill funding Army Corps dam building in the Northwest.[45] Commercial fishers fell into line behind the Fish Commission. Astorians' spokesmen James Cellars and Tom Sandoz echoed FCO's plea, wiring the Oregon and Washington delegation for "immediate action on your part to secure favorable considerations of this item." Sandoz's telegram warned, "If such steps [are] not taken existence of resource is threatened."[46] Master Fish Warden Arnie Suomela sent copies of *A Program of Rehabilitation* to key regional congressmen. He journeyed across the country to put his state's case to Fish and Wildlife director Albert M. Day. In Day's absence, Suomela had to meet with the assistant director Milton C. James.[47]

By the time the Lower Columbia River Program's first funding request had passed from the House to the Senate, Suomela was feeling frustration born of distance and dependence. He airmailed Day on 3 March, reporting that FWS's regional director Leo Laythe had advised him to plead the Fish Commission's case to the chairman of the Senate Appropriations Subcommittee overseeing Army Corps spending. Having done so, Suomela informed Day he and his Washington State counterpart, Milo Moore, were flying to Washington, D.C., later that month hoping to appear personally before the subcommittee. Suomela told Day, somewhat icily, "I trust that the Committee will see fit to have us appear before them sometime between the dates mentioned in my letter to Senator Gurney."[48]

Congress appropriated no fish-conservation money directly to the Fish and Wildlife Service. It never appropriated any funds to put lagging hatchery construction back on schedule. Instead, in early summer 1948, the Lower Columbia River Program appeared as a line item in the overall Army Corps appropriation. The initial $1 million was only two-thirds of that sought by Day. The FWS director nonetheless put an optimistic spin on the outcome. By emphasizing how the service had carved a slice of dam-building budgets to protect downriver runs, Day reminded northwestern states that the national sovereign now decided the fate of regional fish.

"Development of salmon spawning grounds on Columbia River tributaries located below the McNary Dam was assured when President Truman signed the Army Civil Functions Appropriation Bill for 1949," FWS's official release claimed. The money would be spent "for hatchery construction and river clearance by the Fish and Wildlife Service, cooperating with the states of Washington and Oregon." Since McNary and the lower Snake navigation dams "interfere with natural salmon and steelhead migratory movements," FWS would "transfer . . . fish-spawning areas from headwater Columbia River streams to a number of lower-river tributaries."

Fish and Wildlife was reaching back to the New Deal's Coulee salvage strategy. It characterized the Lower Columbia River Program as a federal campaign to mesh fish with hydroelectricity by deploying money and technology. Day's 1948 press release echoed Harold Ickes' confident New Deal promises about the Coulee salvage strategy. After juvenile fish—known as fingerlings—hatched in new federal facilities, Fish and Wildlife boasted, "they are then taken to the new spawning grounds to establish their habitat. Once acclimated, the fingerlings become so attached to these new areas that they return to them when they reach their spawning period."[49]

Suomela exploded when the federal blueprint for spending the Lower Columbia River Program's first million dollars reached Oregon in late July. His 4 August letter to Day belatedly sought to restore state management prerogatives over fish. Reminiscent of Veatch's fruitless pleading to Ickes during the New Deal, Suomela insisted postwar conservation planning for hydroelectric expansion had to consider the entire Columbia-Snake Basin as a unified biological network. A decade before, Veatch had unsuccessfully resisted the New Deal's Coulee salvage strategy by reminding Ickes that nature respected watersheds, not state boundaries.

"It is our intention," Suomela told Day, "to protest the method used here and point out that here again it appears that the States are being 'used' in setting up a gigantic program for the Fish and Wildlife Service and leaving a few crumbs on the outskirts of the program to appease the States." He complained, "Fundamentally, it would appear that Fish and Wildlife is still attempting to wrest the authority for fisheries management from State control." He told Day the federal government now was using the Lower Columbia River Program to overcome state resistance against the upriver hydroelectric offensive, "although it was not the intention of . . . the states in the original program."

In light of Oregon's plea for federally funded hatcheries at the Walla Walla "fish versus dams" hearing, and FCO's maneuvering behind closed doors at the follow-up Portland CBIAC conferences, Suomela's protest was disingenuous. The master fish warden ignored the FCO's role in writing the 1947 pamphlet, *A Program for Rehabilitation*. In it, the downriver states and Fish and Wildlife Service endorsed mitigating dams' impacts on fish with new hatcheries and transplantation. At Walla Walla FCO had backed new federal dams in the Snake Basin instead of stopping them with the ten-year moratorium proposed by the Astorians. Suomela's letter to Day now tried to portray FCO's pro-hatchery position in a new light. "We have not hitherto agreed and do not now agree with this," he insisted, "and will not participate in a program including such an outmoded and illogical approach to the problem of fish salvage until such time as the technical staffs of all three agencies agree."

Suomela and Veatch had conceded the postwar consensus driving the upriver offensive was too powerful to be stopped. Instead of losing what seemed a hopeless fight, they staked their expertise on the promise of federal funds to mitigate the ecological crises of dam building. Now their putative ally, the Fish and Wildlife Service, was flexing its sovereign authority to manage Northwest fish under the Lower Columbia River Program. The Oregonians realized their deal with the public-power domain rendered them nearly impotent to do more than beg funds and criticize federal decisions.

Suomela had hoped the Lower Columbia River Program would designate and protect downriver "fish refuges." In these undammed Columbia tributaries below McNary Dam, the state would try to reestablish fish runs by transplanting hatchery products. But the hope invested in refuge waters was chimerical, Suomela now charged in his August letter to Day, because a century of land and water use had deteriorated most lower Columbia tributaries' biological qualities. "Practically *none* of the important salmon-producing tributaries of the lower Columbia River remain untouched," he argued, "with the possible exception of the Cowlitz River. Most are in a deplorable state already." Oregon's master fish warden now demanded of Day, "Why not attack the problem at its crux and make the Columbia a 'refuge' stream [for the] the Snake, the Salmon, the Deschutes, and other really important streams? Why soft-soap the public into believing the saving of the Molalla will compensate for the loss of the Salmon River?"[50] His challenge must have astounded Fish and Wildlife. Oregon's Fish Commission, after all, had testified against a moratorium and in favor of accelerating upriver dam building at Walla Walla just the year before.

Day tried to pacify the Oregonian. He quickly dispatched Milton James, his deputy at Fish and Wildlife, to the Northwest. James tried to dispel Suomela's and Veatch's "misunderstandings" by proposing more frequent conferences be held between regional FWS staff and the Fish Commission. "There is really little point in our attempting to carry on a long-range debate of this nature," James informed FCO. "I think a half an hour's personal discussion will accomplish a great deal more than reams of correspondence. I want to take advantage of every opportunity for such discussion, both on the part of our Portland staff and ourselves in Washington." He understood how touchy Oregon was becoming about its diminished responsibility for Columbia Basin fish policy. He nonetheless restated his agency's prerogatives: "Inasmuch as the Service has a direct and unavoidable responsibility in the handling of a sizable Federal appropriation, we do have to be in a position to consider the biological aspects, particularly in the field of check-ing, reviewing, and bringing up to date studies which have been previously carried on by the Service itself, as well as the States, but this does not involve any intent to supplant the States."

James believed Suomela plainly understood how much the Lower Columbia River Program relied on transplanting hatchery fish to mitigate the ecological crises erupting in the postwar Northwest. "I am frankly sur-prised," he wrote Suomela on 8 August, "since there seemed to be an agree-ment among all concerned that the hatcheries projected for the States, as well as for the Federal Government, were vital key elements in the Lower River Program. . . . [There is] an apparently well established consensus of opinion that artificial propagation must carry an important part of the bur-den of developing and maintaining [chinook, silver, and sockeye] runs." Plans to relocate upriver fish populations displaced by new federal dams to lower-basin refuges "were specifically included in the original plan which I believe the States agreed upon."

James tried to soften this blunt bit of candor with his own disingenuous retelling of Northwest fish-conservation history. He told Suomela, "No one in the policy-making levels of this Service has any idea of using the Lower River Program or any other joint activity as a means of acquiring greater responsibility or authority in the regulation of coastal or anadromous fisheries. We simply do not have any such ideas, but hope to be able to work with you and the State of Washington in the upbuilding of the salmon resources and the other fishery resources where joint action is practicable."[51]

No federal funds for the Lower Columbia River Program reached Oregon and Washington until autumn 1948. More than a year had gone by since the Portland CBIAC meetings negotiated the state-federal understanding. Fish and Wildlife Service regional manager Leo Laythe informed Suomela on 6 October his agency was finally ready to start deciding which hatchery construction projects to support. He solicited "any suggestions which you may wish to make." Fish and Wildlife expected to direct hatchery building under the Lower Columbia River Program, Laythe made clear, by propos-ing the state managers come to his Portland office "where the files are read-ily available." Oregon and Washington could "submit suggested problems or general topics for discussion on the agenda," but FWS staff would "pre-pare answers to the questions."

Suomela and his Washington fisheries counterpart Milo Moore now had to work in the federal bureaucrat's natural habitat. Laythe proposed the lower river parties write "a procedural manual for reference purposes by all participants in the program." Invested with the discretionary authority of a federal fish proconsul, Laythe expected further disputes about the respective duties of the states and federal government. His proposal for a court reporter at the conference anticipated his state counterparts might want to renegotiate what they had bargained away the previous year in Portland.[52]

Personal grudges by now had soured professional courtesy among the state and federal fish managers. The first project agreements for federally funded hatcheries in Oregon stipulated the FWS director had to approve the plans. He retained full power to inspect the work and to withhold payment "as he may deem necessary to insure completion of the project in compliance with said plans."[53] Wariness replaced early optimism on all sides. Suomela's angry attack on FWS in August 1948 presaged rising state hostility as federal agencies assumed greater responsibility for fish management. Early hopes for comradeship and common enterprise dissolved in acrimony. Day addressed not "Dear Arnie" but "Mr. Suomela" when he reported bad news about the Budget Bureau's cut in fiscal 1950 funding requests. He signed his January 1949 letter not "Al," as before, but as "Albert M. Day." Truman's Budget Bureau, Day regretfully informed Suomela, had selected the precise hatcheries the states were to build. Choices made by staff accountants three thousand miles east of the Columbia Basin now bound Oregon to execute conservation policy made in Washington, D.C. "Under Federal budget policy," Day lectured his colleague from the hinterland, "deviation from the approved Bureau of the Budget figures is not permissible unless an appeal is made directly to the Bureau of the Budget and that agency approves modifications." "I am sure that you will be disappointed," Day surmised. "The rate of progress on the Lower Columbia development work will, of necessity, be curtailed as a result of these allowances, but the Fish and Wildlife Service is not in a position to bring about any change or increase."[54]

Federal dictation and state resentment symbolized how much had been done by CBIAC to resolve what journalists liked to call the "fish versus dams" issue. The committee took over northwestern public-power policy in 1946. It followed up by controlling fish policy by autumn 1947. Its two-day public hearing in Walla Walla in June 1947 let northwesterners speak about the economics of power and the culture of salmon. However, CBIAC's verdict for dams and against Hells Canyon fish came later, during two closed sessions in Portland. It rejected a moratorium on new federal dams by appearing to broker a compromise that mitigated hydroelectricity's ecological crises.

By negotiating the Lower Columbia River Fishery Development Program with Columbia Basin states, CBIAC sacrificed Snake Basin salmon and steelhead to power production. Preserving fish with commercial value seemed not only rational economics but also smart politics, given the downriver regional consensus that embraced more cheap hydropower.

The interagency committee's 1947 verdict looked backward to the New Deal, demonstrating how history still influenced fish and power policy in the Northwest. Harold Ickes' New Deal Coulee salmon-salvage program, his "plan for permanent control" of the Northwest's signature fish, gave CBIAC the historical precedent it needed to manage anadromous fish in the postwar years. By surrendering legal responsibility for migratory fish to the federal government during the Depression, northwestern states retained little power to object when the United States sacrificed upriver fisheries in favor of downstream runs in 1947. State capitulation to federal fish management, perhaps inevitable during the Depression's darkest hours, entrenched as postwar policy the belief that hatcheries could solve the "migratory fish problem." When Oregon ratified the Lower Columbia River Fishery Development Program in 1948 it endorsed a "program for salmon rehabilitation" premised on the Grand Coulee experiment.

The Columbia Basin Inter-Agency Committee's 1947 "fish versus dams" decisions also pointed forward, with two important consequences for the Hells Canyon controversy. By focusing conservation efforts on downriver fish, the Lower Columbia River Program helped condition northwesterners to see upriver expansion as both economically desirable and biologically inconsequential. Belief in public-power expansion's inevitability helped the Reclamation Bureau and Army Corps of Engineers reconcile their competing plans to electrify Hells Canyon. By focusing its conservation priorities on downriver fish, the Oregon Fish Commission eroded its future interest in protecting Snake River fish imperiled by both High Hells Canyon Dam and Idaho Power Company's low dams. Idaho, the other guardian of fish inhabiting the Snake, simply failed to grasp the implications of the Lower Columbia River Program. Oregon, Washington, and the Fish and Wildlife Service assumed higher-elevation anadromous fish mattered little, if they existed at all. Trading upriver fish for downriver federal hatcheries in 1947, northwestern state fish agencies missed their last clear chance to brake the public-power domain's race to the Rockies.

7 UNPLUGGING THE NEW DEAL

Hells Canyon High Dam and the Postwar Public-Power Debate

ells Canyon became a national controversy because the High Dam symbolized deep postwar political differences over electricity's ownership and water's social purposes. What might have been a regional scrap about the best dam to build across the Snake River fueled a wider national debate over the New Deal promise to transform watersheds and regulate capitalism with public hydropower. "High versus low dam" simplified the complex issue of whether government or business best served the public's need for electricity. This vibrant economic debate also raised two larger issues that still challenge American environmental policymakers: Where should the power to control nature reside, and how should that power be used?

Postwar liberals subscribed to the New Deal principle that public power constrained private profit making by invigorating popular government; some even wanted government electricity to supplant private power altogether. Conservatives believed New Deal public power threatened property rights and local self-determination; some even believed more government power dams portended socialism. The Hells Canyon controversy thus had immediate regional impacts and long-term national implications. Not only a referendum about public-power expansion in the Northwest, it also tested the New Deal's continuing relevance as Americans in the postwar years worked out new definitions of the public interest in nature.

Electric current generates heat as it encounters resistance. So did public-power expansion in the postwar Northwest. Hells Canyon High Dam mobilized the New Deal's most ardent backers and dedicated opponents. Idaho Power Company appeared locked in a head-to-head duel with the federal government. Idaho Power fought the federal dam as a proxy for conservatives in business and politics still fuming, after twenty years, about the

New Deal's intervention into American capitalism. President Truman made Hells Canyon High Dam a test of Democratic fidelity to the New Deal's faith in government planning and business regulation. Republicans matched Truman's partisan vigor. Each contestant agreed public power embodied the New Deal spirit. One side to the Hells Canyon controversy wanted to keep that spirit alive. The other wanted to snuff it out.[1]

The nation's natural-resources custodians agreed Hells Canyon had large implications. Julius Krug, Truman's Interior secretary from 1946 to 1949, backed the High Dam to extend public power's domain beyond the Columbia Basin. "In an area where Uncle Sam has become the dominant power supplier," Krug told the American Public Power Association's 1949 convention, "the Federal government has a responsibility to keep ahead of demand by providing facilities to assure an adequate power supply."[2] Douglas McKay, Dwight Eisenhower's first Interior secretary, abandoned federal efforts to build the High Dam shortly after taking office. Explaining his decision, McKay wrote in 1953, "The Department of Interior would be playing the reprehensible part of 'a dog in the manger' if it insisted on opposing a badly needed development that private capital is ready and willing to undertake if the plan proposed by the Idaho Power Company is reasonably comparable as to results, while the Department itself has no assurance that it can carry out its plan without extended delay."[3]

Senator Wayne Morse, Oregon's maverick liberal Republican, despised McKay for backing corporate capital. Morse thought nature and history enfolded the Snake Basin into the northwestern public-power domain. Private utilities, he charged, thwarted national goals by seizing public water resources to exact monopoly profits.[4] "We cannot and must not tolerate this mutilation of our rivers," Morse thundered to the Senate in May 1952. Public power in the postwar Snake Basin would solve "the problem of orderly resource development for the benefit of the people not only of Oregon but of those in neighboring states and for the nation at large." Hells Canyon High Dam had to be a federal project because "construction of large dams for multiple-purpose use of our rivers is the business of the United States."[5]

Morse extolled public power's promise in terms that inspired postwar liberals. He urged the Senate to push the New Deal upriver to guarantee "plenty of power for all" through "full public development of our hydroelectric resources so as to provide generating capacity well in advance of load growth." Cheap public hydropower from New Deal dams and transmission systems had transformed the Columbia Basin's economy and society. The High Dam would work similar magic in the Snake Basin, Morse believed. Thousands laboring to build it would purchase millions of dollars' worth of local goods and services. Like Grand Coulee and Bonneville, the High Dam would spin out billions of kilowatt-hours. Long-term low-cost electric supply contracts between Bonneville Power Administration and public distributors would market the current to rural and urban users.[6]

Two months before Morse spoke, a leading utility manager portrayed the New Deal's public-power legacy in sinister terms. Kinsey M. Robinson's Washington Water Power Company was building Cabinet Gorge Dam across the Clark Fork River on the Montana-Idaho border. At a North Idaho Chamber of Commerce meeting in Sandpoint, he claimed more federal dams menaced political liberty as well as power companies. He urged listeners to fight the Reclamation Bureau's Hells Canyon High Dam, "keeping in mind what can happen when we lose our freedom." He warned his audience, "Planned economy has stepped out from around the corner and is now waiting for us on the sidewalk unless we take a greater interest in the affairs of our communities, the state, and the nation."

At the groundbreaking ceremony for Cabinet Gorge in spring 1951, retired Army Corps of Engineers general Thomas M. Robins defined private power's case against the High Dam as a matter of conservative political philosophy. Under his command, the corps' North Pacific Division had built much of the New Deal's hydroelectric infrastructure in the Columbia Basin. Now, though, he worked for the Pacific Northwest Development Association, a new business lobby opposing the federal upriver offensive. Robins admired corporate utilities' willingness to challenge public power. "You have an opportunity here," he told the shivering crowd of four thousand gathered beneath the snow-clad Clark Fork canyon walls, "to make the last stand for state's rights . . . if you will stand firm and back up private initiative, private enterprise, and democratic ways of determining what your region will develop into." Spokane's largest daily paper thought Cabinet Gorge Dam, though far smaller than New Deal dams on the Columbia, "should also become an imposing monument to the persistence of men who still believe in the type of free enterprise that has made America a great nation."[7]

Business utilities anticipated a sharp fight over electricity's purposes after World War II. They helped provoke national debate about electricity's ownership by enlisting new allies against public-power expansion. The U.S. Chamber of Commerce, National Association of Manufacturers, and American Bankers Association all subscribed to the Edison Electric Institute's and

National Association of Electric Companies' goal of halting public-power expansion. In response to corporate organizing, Harry Truman's 1948 presidential campaign singled out utilities for biting criticism. Fierce partisan divisions over the proper relationship between the state and private capital arrayed most Republicans on private power's side while Democrats endorsed public power.[8]

Both economics and politics gave public power initial advantages in the clash over Hells Canyon. By 1950, Bonneville and Grand Coulee dams were generating 71 percent of all electricity in the Columbia Basin.[9] Distributed through BPA contracts, public power flowed to all of the region's private utilities as well as to preference customers such as municipal power departments and rural cooperatives.[10] Cheap power from public generating and transmitting facilities drove the region's rapid industrialization and urbanization.[11] Low-cost electricity also transformed regional agriculture. By 1930, Pacific Northwest farmers were five times more likely than were their counterparts nationwide to have electrified their homes and operations.[12] Customers of all types naturally preferred lower power prices. Even the private utilities' advertising adviser conceded its low cost sanctified public power as a northwestern icon.[13]

Corporate competitors not only sold electricity at a cost disadvantage. Public suspicion still tainted their reputations. Utility securities had been among the flimsiest during and after the 1929 stock market crash. Millions of investors lost billions of dollars when utility bond and share prices tumbled. Dubious utility mergers and outright corruption of securities markets and state utility regulatory commissions tarnished the companies' collective reputations. Samuel Insull, the most notorious utility tycoon, had fled the United States in 1931 to avoid prosecution on charges ranging from bribery to mail fraud. Although Insull was never convicted, his ghost haunted the power industry two decades after his disgrace. A stench of private greed, compounded by managerial incompetence, overhung the utility industry throughout the 1930s.[14]

Efficient service during World War II began restoring utilities' public standing. Industrial mobilization boosted power use nearly 50 percent between 1940 and 1945. Corporate utilities met new demands reliably, helping disperse suspicion that had clouded their business for more than a decade. Private power still supplied most American homes and businesses as the postwar years began. Even though TVA and BPA dominated their regional service areas, private utilities met 85 percent of the nation's total demand.[15]

Government electric providers "defin[ed] power as a public service." Corporate utilities treated it "as a profitable commodity." This distinction shaped the Hells Canyon controversy's environmental implications. Federal power agencies, acting through the Columbia Basin Inter-Agency Committee, envisioned the Columbia and Snake watersheds as a virtually limitless hydroelectric reservoir. They managed waterpower as a social dynamo capable of transforming regional life. Private power companies assessed the region's rivers more prosaically. Water was a fluctuating resource but a fixed asset. The electrical industry thrived on hydroelectric limits because utilities profited by selling a scarce commodity. "The two systems did not peacefully coexist," David Nye has found. "The generally lower rates of municipal systems were a constant embarrassment to private companies, who attacked public power as a dangerous form of socialism."[16]

Bonneville Power's status after the war preoccupied both sides in the Hells Canyon controversy. Its long-term electric supply contracts enabled regional corporate utilities to smooth out their demand peaks. Federal electricity supplies let utilities forego building their own costly dams. As long as BPA could be confined to serving the Columbia Basin's power demands, its utility customers could confidently project their future power costs and market low-cost electricity to new business and residential customers. Private power companies expected the agency to exist for the foreseeable future. Yet utilities considered BPA a historical accident—too large to be removed or avoided—not a model for regional waterpower development, social reform, or political governance. When liberals after the war tried to revive the New Deal dream of Bonneville Power as a northwestern version of the Tennessee Valley Authority, dedicated to social change and federal economic leadership, the utilities rebelled.

Northwestern utility executives began developing their strategy to unplug the New Deal by criticizing President Truman's efforts to remake BPA into a social-reform agency along TVA's lines. Frank McLaughlin, president of Puget Sound Power and Light Company, in June 1947 denounced public-power expansion as the vehicle to force TVA-style New Deal social planning on northwesterners. His arguments outlined regional utility executives' case against Hells Canyon High Dam a few years later.[17]

McLaughlin sensed that opposing more public power outright risked enflaming customers. Public discontent complicated the utilities' delicate relations with state politicians who appointed rate-setting regulators. "Regardless of their ideologies," he agreed, "the people will purchase their electricity wherever they can obtain it the cheapest. . . . Many people, while giving lip service to the cause of private power, use public power in their industries, businesses, and homes because of favors granted or reprisals feared. . . . Without customers there would be no public power."[18]

McLaughlin therefore framed private power's superiority as "an economic approach." He believed northwesterners needed "an unbiased and realistic picture" before they would consider limiting public-power growth. Government subsidies to public power—principally tax-free bonds, property-tax exemptions on operating assets, and low preferential power prices from BPA—distorted the region's economic priorities. Subsidies impeded private firms from efficiently serving customers' growing electric demands. Encouraged to expand by interest and tax subsidies, public-power agencies "cannot do otherwise than force electric rates too low, reduce earning capacity, impair credit" and encourage wasteful overproduction. McLaughlin contended public agencies exploited subsidies to build dams three times as cheaply as private utilities. "Any inefficiency of management on the part of the government agency could be easily absorbed."[19]

McLaughlin encased economic criticism within political rhetoric honed during the increasingly fierce postwar debate about the New Deal's regulation of business. Public-power advocates misled citizens, he charged. Their "appeals to the emotions . . . employ[ed] demagogic tactics and highly prejudiced propaganda." Federal hydroelectric agencies, abetted by liberal politicians, had unleashed "a private property–destroying cyclone." Public-power expansion threatened not only Puget Sound Power and Light's viability but also "the capitalistic system." Because "there is no such thing as fair government competition," he contended, "public and private power cannot competitively co-exist." In the Northwest, McLaughlin concluded, "a cancerous condition exists in the power industry. . . . [T]he present half-slave, half-free situation in the power field cannot long endure. . . . [T]he end result of government competition in business is the destruction of private enterprise."[20]

The utility industry's trade association, the Edison Electric Institute, formally echoed McLaughlin's critique at its 1947 annual convention. Outgoing EEI president Grover C. Neff told twenty-five hundred delegates: "We are up against heavily subsidized competition from governmental proprietary power systems. . . . As you know the power to tax is the power to destroy. There are in this country groups of people who are doing everything they can to put an end to the free enterprise system and particularly to have the government take over the electric power business."[21]

Truman's proposed Columbia Valley Administration further incited private utilities to fan northwestern resistance to public-power expansion after 1947. A centerpiece of the president's Fair Deal, CVA symbolized Truman's effort to link his presidency with New Deal power policy in the Northwest. Power companies pounced on CVA, arguing it would remodel BPA into another TVA, dedicated to federal direction of the region's economy and impervious to local political influences. Utility spokesmen and their conservative political allies then yoked CVA to the federal upriver offensive. They claimed Hells Canyon High Dam's promise of more public power concealed CVA's threat of more federal control over the region's economy and society.

Truman unsuccessfully urged the Eightieth Congress in 1947 and 1948 to create new "basin authorities" modeled on TVA. They would stimulate hydropower production, economic growth, and social reform in watersheds as geographically diverse as the Missouri, Red River, and Colorado basins. Throughout these two crucial years of the postwar power debate, national utility leaders joined their northwestern counterparts in a coordinated attack on TVA's legacy. They used TVA to symbolize their critique of New Deal public power as economically inefficient, politically insensitive, and philosophically utopian. Truman proposed a specific basin authority for the Northwest in 1949. Utilities by then had used costly public-relations campaigns to caricature CVA as bumbling and costly, an overbearing menace to northwestern ratepayers and citizens. Widespread regional resistance to Truman's CVA originated from many sources. However, the utility industry capitalized on the discontent to link a popular New Deal program—cheap public power—with an unpopular New Deal legacy: social reform planned by federal administrators.[22]

Northwestern corporate utilities charged CVA would suffer from the same interlocking economic and political flaws that had made TVA their nemesis for fifteen years. Idaho Power and its allies insisted BPA's upriver offensive targeting Hells Canyon would extend these flaws into the Snake Basin. Deep ideological differences over public power colored the Hells Canyon controversy from 1949 forward, its peculiar intensity and durability reflecting vigorous national debate about the New Deal's relevance in the postwar years. By muddling together CVA, TVA, and BPA, the private-power critique of New Deal public-power policy stiffened popular resistance to Hells Canyon High Dam.

Regional federal power authorities specialized in generating cut-rate electricity, so private rivals claimed they had to waste expensive borrowed capital to match subsidized federal prices. The Bonneville Power Act maintained long-standing federal "preferences" for public-power retailers.[23] Rural cooperatives and municipal utility districts enjoyed guaranteed access to electricity costing less than that available from investor-owned utilities. At the Edison Electric Institute's 1953 annual convention, outgoing president Bayard L. England listed statutes, agency rules, and judicial decisions that "heavily discriminated against investor-owned power companies." Their combined effect encouraged "selling power below cost to preference customers." Cut-rate power multiplied the customers for publicly generated electricity, distorting power demand and supply dynamics. Price subsidies encouraged rising consumption, which in turn, encouraged more and bigger federal dams. By saddling utility investors and customers with "hidden" costs, in the form of higher taxes and lower sales, public-power preferential prices discouraged smaller, private dams.[24]

Tax exemptions further penalized private companies that tried carefully to expand generating and transmitting capacity. Settled constitutional doctrine exempted public entities, such as federal generating facilities and municipal distribution systems, from paying federal, state, and local taxes on income, sales, and property. England estimated the combined effect of tax exemptions forced private utilities to charge up to 23 percent more for their power than that marketed from federal dams and municipal sources. His successor as EEI president for 1953–54, Walter H. Sammis, pledged in his inaugural address to "exert every effort to have the Federal government tax government enterprises competing with the private power industry on a basis equivalent to the electric utility companies." England noted inflation was boosting the cost of private borrowing for utility construction programs. Unsaid, but plainly implied in his warning about high capital costs, was the fear that federal power agencies, freed from the market costs of borrowed capital, would surpass private construction schedules and preempt future corporate dams in areas where demand was booming.[25]

W. C. Mullendore, president of Southern California Edison Company, hammered on three New Deal subsidies that promoted public power. Federal power agencies gained a "grossly unfair advantage" from borrowing construction money at low interest rates, property-tax exemptions for public-power facilities, and deficit spending to disguise losses incurred in selling cut-rate electricity. "Agents of government boast of the cheaper housing, the lower lending rates, or the lower rates for utility service which government thus provides," according to Mullendore, "and use these citizen subsidized rates as an argument for further encroachment upon the field of private enterprise." Fifteen years after "the American people were swept along upon a flood of promises and even bribes (with their own money) . . . Government, as a competitor with its own citizens in various lines of endeavor, has now become so commonplace as scarcely to excite notice."[26]

Private utilities seethed about public-power agencies' apparent disdain for ordinary accounting practices. Both state public-utility codes and federal statutes required corporate power companies to observe accounting conventions that facilitated scrutiny of their rates. The enormous costs of building dams and transmission lines necessitated private utilities' borrowing and raising substantial capital. Private-power executives believed oversight by money-center lenders and institutional stock investors ensured new private construction projects "penciled out" by matching generating capacity to customer needs and tailoring kilowatt-hour prices to supply and demand. By contrast, utilities complained, federal agencies such as TVA and Reclamation had only to convince a handful of key congressmen and presidential appointees before winning massive appropriations to build dams. According to industry publicists, federal power agencies in the Northwest and upper South had learned to employ their political power to set wholesale electricity prices well below market levels to attract customers, expand service areas, and reward preference customers. Public-power users then petitioned their elected officials to demand new federal projects.

John P. Callahan, utilities editor for the *New York Times*, sought to counter "the widespread erroneous impression that hydroelectric generation is cheaper than steam" for producing electricity. Backers of TVA peddled "that false impression" by insisting that "the government was harnessing 'natural' or 'free' power." However, according to Callahan's research, hydroelectricity incurred huge fixed charges because of "the tremendous cost of constructing and maintaining these sites." The ambitious federal postwar dam-building campaign "does not seem to consider the rise in construction costs an economic barrier." Generating costs were only half the equation. Given the Northwest's dispersed population, extensive transmission lines had to take the power from dams to end users. Their high cost, and the diminishing value of electricity transmitted over 250 miles, actually made public power up to twice as expensive, in real economic terms, as power produced nearer the customers. Callahan summarized the economic case against public hydroelectric expansion by quoting a utility engineer's exasperated lament: "The government is ahead of the industry in hydro developments because it is running a subsidized plant."[27]

A June 1951 study by the Council of State Chambers of Commerce attacked cheap federal power as a "myth" premised on "large hidden costs." The council drew on the 1946–48 Hoover commission's work on executive-branch reorganization to claim, "When the large hidden costs of Federal power operations are taken into account, the differential in favor of government rates is soon wiped away." By disguising interest subsidies for federal dams, avoiding taxes on federal property, and juggling project accounts to charge power-generation costs against flood-control and navigation benefits from dams, the Federal government and public-power advocates were "attempting to socialize America's electric power industry."[28]

Northwesterners bragged their region had nothing in common with the upper South except language, and even that was open to debate. By praising the region's "independence" and "prosperity," utility publicists tried to convince northwesterners that TVA-type power policy ignored Columbia-Snake Basin political culture. Tom Humphrey, who covered power issues for the Portland Oregon Journal, painted a lyrical portrait of a Northwest that disdained both TVA and CVA:

> The Pacific Northwest is one of the most progressive and prosperous regions in the United States, in marked contrast with the Tennessee valley states. It has the highest per-capita income; TVA states have only 60 per cent of the national average, despite fifteen years of TVA. Oregon, Washington, and Idaho are among the top eight states in rural electrification, without TVA, while Tennessee is forty-fourth. . . . The fastest-growing region, [the Pacific Northwest] needs at least 6,000,000 more kilowatts of power in the next ten years. But TVA is short of power, too. . . . Imagine that, in a so-called hydroelectric haven![29]

Writing in April 1949, Daniel B. Noble, the Oregon spokesman for a coalition contesting Hells Canyon High Dam, argued CVA was the wrong model for his region. "By all economic, social, and health standards," he claimed, "the Pacific Northwest without a valley authority has a better record than the TVA states before and during the 15-year jurisdiction of a valley authority. . . . [O]ur states' rights American system is superior to an authority method of conservation and development."[30]

Northwestern utility critiques of CVA and TVA acknowledged that Depression-era job-creation strategies may have been appropriate for the upper South in the 1930s. Noble noted TVA employed more than forty thousand day laborers when construction was at its peak.[31] Utility analysts thought alliances between southern congressmen and TVA ensured politics would "inevitably" cause federal dam construction projects to employ the maximum number of employees rather than a workforce measured by the project's size and schedule: "Politics inevitably play a large part, inevitably because most of the executives and 'higher ups' are appointed by politicians who in turn are elected. The politicians are humanly interested in votes and when they appoint people to well-paying positions it is not surprising if they hope to get political support in return. . . . It is a commentary on human behavior."[32]

Montana Power Company president J. E. Corette compared his firm's Kerr Dam with the Reclamation Bureau's Hungry Horse project on the Flathead River to contrast private power's alleged discipline with public agencies' profligacy. To build just over twice as much generating capacity, the federal project had spent ten times as much money and was still trying to complete Hungry Horse after six years of work. "Which is 'cheap' power? . . . The socialized power program of the Federal government lacks a firm foundation of integrity and economics. All the facts are on the side of the electric companies."[33] *Public Utilities Fortnightly*, the industry trade journal, regularly reported labor unions' endorsement of new public-power programs as proof that jobs mattered more to federal agencies than providing electricity as and where needed.[34]

Ambitious federal hydroelectric proposals for the Northwest spilling from the Truman administration alarmed corporate power interests. Their enormous cost seemed indicative of federal agencies' capacity to mobilize nearly unlimited resources to expand the public-power domain. In late 1948, the Army Corps of Engineers announced it would ask Congress to appropriate more than $3 billion to build seven new Northwest generating dams and associated transmission lines. If fully funded and built, the Army Corps' Main Control Plan would more than double the region's generating capacity.[35]

In Truman's final year in office, Interior secretary Oscar Chapman revealed his department was studying its most ambitious engineering plan ever, "United Western," which envisioned diverting Columbia-Snake Basin water across the Oregon-Nevada-Idaho high desert to central California. *Public Utilities Fortnightly*, assessing this $4 billion proposal, reprinted a speech by Los Angeles Republican congressman Norris Poulson damning Interior's report as "fantastic . . . reckless and desperate." Poulson predicted the "taxpayers of America will hit the ceiling" when they learned of this "wild proposal of the Reclamation Bureau," advocated "without regard to what it would cost the nation's taxpayers."[36] Charles Tatham Jr., writing in late 1951 about federal power projects generally, voiced a characteristic corporate utility view about schemes such as "United Western": "Once embarked on a program of expanding its control over the citizens' economic lives, it is extremely difficult for the government to retreat, or even to call a halt."[37]

The American West throughout its modern history has simultaneously hungered for and resented federal spending to stimulate its economy. Its elected representatives, by the middle of the twentieth century, had perfected rhetorical strategies and political techniques to secure public money for regional projects while denouncing "dictation" by the same federal agencies that delivered the appropriations. In the postwar conflict between government and private hydroelectricity, private-power advocates deployed this traditional western political trope. Federal power authorities, they claimed, spawned a distant and resistant new bureaucracy that either distorted or defied local interests.[38]

Conservative politicians claimed CVA would mimic TVA's novel governance methods. They equated their presidentially appointed administrators and governing boards with regional emperors and courtiers, indifferent to local views and resistant to customary means of influence. United States senator "Chan" Gurney (R-S.D.) in October 1947 reported all ten state governors in the Missouri Basin had resolved earlier that summer to oppose any new federal power authority in their region. "The 7,000,000 persons in the 10 Missouri valley states wanted a voice in their authorized development," he proclaimed. "[E]lected officials, big and little business, and the general populace of the Missouri basin had gone on record through their state legislatures in opposition to an MVA."

They told him, Gurney declared, that "a grandiose new authority with vague powers and unknown plans could disrupt the whole economy of the region." The South Dakotan found especially ominous the TVA-type governing board, "a 3-man autocracy":

> The people of this country, I believe, have had more than enough of government by the bureaucrats. They want the light of day to shine on the spending of their taxes. They do not want any super-executives telling them what to buy and what to build without any scrutiny as to appropriations, audits of funds, and

supervision through chosen representatives of operations in connection with public expenditures. . . .

I feel sure that the American public today does not want any more valley authorities presided over by super-executives who are unresponsive to the will of valley residents and to their duly elected local, state, and Federal officials.[39]

Conservatives escalated their criticism of federal power administration in 1949, when President Truman presented draft legislation to create CVA. Tom Humphrey, whose *Oregon Journal* also opposed High Hells Canyon, predicted "plenty of argument in the Pacific Northwest . . . when the President says that 'we should apply the lessons of our Tennessee valley experience to our other great river basins.'" He found the region's governors unanimously opposed to a new TVA in the Columbia and Snake basins. Republican Arthur B. Langlie of Washington accused his state's pro-CVA congressional delegation of truckling to distant bureaucrats. He warned against "the overpaternalistic interest of Federal government. . . . [I]f the people of the state don't mind their own power business today, the Federal government is going to come in and do it for them and we are not going to have local control; control of our resources and economy will come from Washington, D.C."

Humphrey's report noted businesses large and small chorused regional governors and private power companies. The Portland, Seattle, and Spokane chambers of commerce had formally resolved to fight CVA in the Northwest, "recalling that TVA engages in 30 different business enterprises in competition with private industry." Humphrey observed, "Every power company president is actively antagonistic, remembering, no doubt, that TVA has elbowed 32 privately owned utilities out of the picture, either in whole or in part, in the Tennessee valley." He summarized memorials and statements from an array of regional irrigation, livestock, mining, and conservation organizations: "They declare in forthright resolutions and statements that they want no super-state to threaten their state, water, and mineral rights or to supersede existing Federal agencies such as the Army Engineers, Bureau of Reclamation, and the soil conservation and forest services with which they have dealt satisfactorily for years and which are susceptible to local demands."

Even Oregon's liberal Republican senator Wayne Morse, who advocated public-power expansion, refused to endorse CVA. He opposed "government agencies in control of our rivers based upon the Tennessee valley pattern." Morse's rationale, thought Humphrey, captured the essence of the governance critique: "Our economy is very much different and our people are strong believers in a maximum of local self-government."[40]

Corporate utilities admitted that few northwesterners wanted to dismantle BPA or to transfer ownership of Grand Coulee and Bonneville dams to private owners. Yet the utility press complained that federal agencies, their preference customers, and liberal politicians spread half-truths, propaganda, and downright lies to politicize their customer base.[41] During congressional debate in summer 1947 over Federal Power Commission policies, Francis X. Welch, *Public Utilities Fortnightly*'s pugnacious editor, surmised commerce secretary Henry Wallace and FPC chairman Nelson Lee Smith had convened a Washington social gathering simply to lobby sympathetic journalists. These public-power enthusiasts "'briefed' if not indoctrinated the group on the inequities of the electric power industry." Representative William J. Miller (R-Conn.) denounced the meeting from the House floor as "a clever piece of propaganda work." He demanded the special committee on "Publicity and Propaganda in the Executive Agencies" investigate "these propaganda activities," which "cheapened the Federal service, and free press, and the principles of self-government."[42] In that same issue of the *Fortnightly,* Welch's review called John Gunther's best-selling *Inside the U.S.A.* "misleading propaganda . . . in the sophisticated manner of some pinko cocktail party in New York City." Gunther's offense: "a lyrical admiration for public power with its 'cheap and abundant electricity,' a la TVA, supplemented by a bitter animus against privately owned electric utility companies."[43]

Corporate utility rhetoric during the CVA debate sometimes anticipated the most lurid McCarthyite fantasies of the early 1950s. Criticism of Democratic power policy equated TVA-style public power with foreign socialism and domestic subversion. These early postwar critiques of TVA and CVA would fuel later, shriller assaults on the entire New Deal legacy of regulated capitalism and social reform. Corporate critics of cut-price federal hydroelectricity stooped to questioning public-power advocates' patriotism. Southern California Edison's president W. C. Mullendore sharpened this harsher edge to the private-utility critique of public power. In early summer 1947, he saw "American industry today . . . threatened by a foreign invasion . . . of foreign ideas . . . which would have us surrender our birthright for the chains of slavery." Public power meant "the program of collectivism" which, unless checked, "will lead to the loss of America's contribution to our civilization, to the degradation, and it may well be to the enslavement of our children."[44]

Grover C. Neff, president of the Edison Electric Institute, told its 1947 annual convention that utilities were besieged by "groups of people who are doing everything they can to put an end to the free enterprise system and particularly to have the government take over the electric power business." To emphasize the global dimension of the public-power threat, EEI invited a British utility executive, Brigadier-General Wade H. Hayes, to report on the Labour Government's power nationalization plans. "The mounting growth of socialized power in this country in recent years," *Public Utilities Fortnightly*'s Welch opined, made Hayes's warnings "of special interest to the electric industry here."[45]

Truman's 1948 campaign criticism of private power convinced utility executives the struggle against public power posed fundamental ideological issues. During that summer's intense politicking, EEI president Charles E. Oakes told the group's convention that "government in business" delineated the difference between "individual rights and statism." He claimed utilities "find ourselves in common with other businesses, but in the forefront, standing against a drive for the socialization of our society."[46] A key political ally of the utility industry, Representative George A. Dondero (R-Mich.), told *Public Utilities Fortnightly* readers just before Election Day that a Republican victory "will help restore confidence in the American system of free enterprise and will halt the march of socialization of a vital segment of American industry." Truman's Interior Department and Federal Power Commission, Dondero charged, were led by "socialists at heart, at least on the issue of public power." These regulators "want to make over America into a state not too dissimilar to the Soviet Russia [*sic*] which tyrannizes so many millions of the world's citizens today."[47]

The postwar power-policy debate may illustrate the political and economic consequences of radical restructuring presently underway in the electric-energy system. The struggle to electrify Hells Canyon fifty years ago also generated hard thinking about electricity's economic and social implications. Private power presented an alternative to the New Deal's policy of using cheap public power to stimulate basinwide transformations. Instead of treating waterpower as a social resource capable of limitless exploitation, power companies stressed prudent expansion constrained by market forces. Corporate utilities had to raise investment capital to build new dams and transmission systems. Electricity had to be priced high enough to enable utilities to repay lenders and distribute dividends to shareholders. State public-utility regulators controlled prices to ensure both public convenience and continued profitability. Utility executives supporting Idaho Power Company challenged federal planners and liberal officeholders to a serious debate over the merits of this energy system. The Hells Canyon controversy framed their debate, and its resolution deserves careful assessment.

Idaho Power and its allies bested public-power advocates at a crucial point in postwar northwestern hydroelectrification. Idaho Power's popular triumph—at law, in politics, and through the mass media—suggests the need to reevaluate histories that portray postwar corporate motives as inimical to popular aspirations.[48] Private utilities' campaign to preserve their financial independence and political power also suggests reconsidering the sources and motives of postwar environmentalism. Corporate resistance to federal hydroelectricity unintentionally aroused in unexpected ways citizens' interest in the cost, control, and consequences of natural-resource development.[49]

Environmental histories of common resources—such as the Columbia and Snake rivers—often blame their degradation on private profit-making unfettered by conservation customs or laws. Paul Hirt has traced overlogging of the Intermountain West's public forests to corporations seeking maximum profits by bullying Congress and the federal agency that supervised forest health.[50] Arthur F. McEvoy has chronicled how innovative profit-maximizing investors eroded communal regulation of Pacific fisheries to cause overfishing.[51] Earlier, J. Willard Hurst had portrayed profit-hungry capitalists commanding the nineteenth-century legal system to mine Wisconsin's forests in little more than five decades.[52] Donald Worster's environmental history of the Dust Bowl indicted the agricultural branch of American capitalism for plundering the Plains.[53]

Hydroelectricity in the postwar Northwest presents another prospect. The Reclamation Bureau designed Hells Canyon High Dam to be big enough to remodel the Snake Basin's topography and society. Idaho Power's alternate plan for electrifying Hells Canyon aimed lower. Public-power advocates accused the company of timidly proposing "little dams for a big river." Private utilities projected fewer and smaller dams for the Northwest. Unlike federal hydroelectric agencies, which wanted to build new dams to stimulate demand, utilities wanted to build dams only fast enough to meet demand. Even though Idaho Power and its corporate allies projected adding more generating capacity to keep up with the region's bustling economy, they expected to move incrementally. By contrast, the Columbia Basin Inter-

Agency Committee's 1949 Weaver-Newell Accord sought to plant new dams as fast as Congress could appropriate construction funds.

New Deal public-power strategies minimized or ignored natural obstacles to hydroelectric expansion. Agency planners and their political allies overpromised how easily engineering expertise and public money could transform free-running rivers into domesticated draft animals. Federal dam builders too often squandered natural values as well as public capital. By ignoring river basins' cyclical propensities to flood in heavy snowmelt years and to run low following drier winters, the public-power domain pursued the dream of unlimited electricity at ever-lower prices.

Utilities in the postwar years anticipated environmental criticism of big dams. During their campaign to restrain public power, they outlined two important arguments that shaped future resistance to new, large federal dams in the Columbia-Snake Basin. According to their trade journal, federal dams' massive bulk, needed to demonstrate "multiple-use" benefits for flood control and navigation as well as hydroelectricity, "would have the effect of ruining the nation's valuable salmon industry."[54] New Deal monuments the size of Grand Coulee, as well as more modest postwar federal dams, raised barriers to anadromous fish movements that even the best technology could only partly mitigate. Corporate utilities sought smaller dams, built less frequently, and selling more expensive electricity. More modest dams would better mesh human demands, company profits, and fishery imperatives with the Northwest's rhythmic winter snows and spring runoffs. In addition, the potent combination of engineering hubris, bureaucratic "propaganda," and unlimited federal appropriations ignored what South Dakota senator Chan Gurney called "natural phenomena that can never be eradicated."[55] Public-power critics deplored federal agencies' penchant for blaming natural events on political causes. Gurney thought New Dealers—"advocates of more and more 'authority' for, and over, the people of this or that section"—weighed "neither the lessons of history nor the simple logic of economics."

> So subtle has been the propaganda of many "valley authority" enthusiasts that even the average American frequently is misled into believing that floods are not natural phenomena that never can be wholly eradicated, but really are the result of some nefarious activities by stock market manipulators or private exploiters. Many Americans who were led to believe early in the New Deal that a government agency could perform any type of miracle are surprised to learn that losses from excessive rainfall long since have not been declared unconstitutional.[56]

Corporate publications opened their pages to northwestern conservationists who shared their concerns about large federal dams' threat to oceangoing fish. *Public Utilities Fortnightly* reported famed wildlife biologist Dr. Olaus Murie's criticism of "over-ambitious" federal dam-building plans. In 1951, as the upriver hydroelectric offensive accelerated, *Fortnightly* readers learned of the National Wildlife Federation's growing concern about "dam foolishness," characterized by "the great race to bury the Northwest in concrete."[57]

In March 1948, *Public Utilities Fortnightly* published James H. Cellars's article about the ecological impacts of power dams in the Columbia-Snake Basin. Cellars, an Astoria, Oregon, salmon packer, had organized ocean fishers operating near the mouth of the Columbia into a political lobby. He had vainly pleaded with CBIAC in 1947 to adopt a dam-building moratorium. Cellars saw private-power companies as crucial allies in conservationists' campaign to slow the pace of federal dam building. He introduced readers across the nation to the salmon's prized place in both native and European-American traditions in the region. He noted Oregon and Washington state fish agencies estimated the annual dollar values of fish harvested by commercial, Indian, and recreational anglers exceeded $10 million.

> These millions of dollars of income . . . are the harvest from a great natural resource which has replenished itself year after year, and will continue to do so if not destroyed in an unrealistic effort to replace *existing* values with *expected* benefits. . . . [B]y adjusting the upriver development program, the great existing values as represented by the salmon fishery resource could be retained, and an opportunity given for realization of the expected benefits from power and reclamation projects.

"Salmon runs cannot pass high dams without losses," Cellars argued, revealing a 1947 U.S. Fish and Wildlife Service study that estimated minimum annual migrating salmon losses of 10 percent at Bonneville Dam and 15 percent at McNary Dam, just below the Snake-Columbia confluence. State biologists predicted even more grievous losses at both dams "and declare[d] that losses from additional dams would mount in geometric proportions."[58] If the federal government funded McNary Dam's accelerated completion, as President Truman was urging, dollar losses from fish-run destruction would total 75 percent of its estimated electric-power benefits.

Steady growth in private hydroelectric generating capacity, boosted by completing powerhouses already at Bonneville and Grand Coulee, offered a wiser solution to the region's "fish versus dams" dilemma, Cellars maintained. Frustrating postwar conservation efforts, though, was BPA. Its mission of expanding low-cost hydropower guaranteed decimation of the region's fishery. The New Deal had bequeathed this "experiment in socialization" to the Northwest. According to Cellars, Bonneville Power deflected scrutiny of its ecological impacts by disseminating spurious multiple-use benefits and phony estimates of future electricity demand. "Standard BPA procedure is to get Congress to build the power-generating sources, and then to go out and find a sale for the power." Cellars told his utility audience why fishers, sport anglers, and Indians entitled to catch fish under longstanding treaties were backing a private-power alternative to further expansion of the public-power empire into the Snake Basin: "No further dam construction should be undertaken until private enterprise has been given definite assurance that it can go ahead, and, that if it meets actual needs, no more government competition will be forced upon it."[59]

Ernest Clifford Potts, writing in late 1947, had already warned industry executives, "The Pacific Northwest's blessing of cheap Federal power needs certain reservations in the appraisal." A well-known Washington State outdoor writer, Potts saw corporate utilities as powerful, though unexpected, allies against the public-power domain's upriver strategy. Potts estimated the average annual value of the Columbia Basin anadromous fishery at $30 million, triple the figure cited by Cellars. Potts argued cost-benefit calculations should encourage private power companies to reach out to sport and commercial fishing interests. In a utility/fishing alliance, each partner could mobilize its own constituencies against CBIAC's ambitious strategy to push public power into every corner of the postwar Northwest.

Potts focused on BPA's policy of pricing public hydropower well below rates set by state regulators on utility companies. Cut-price public power, intended by the New Deal to spark economic recovery in the hard-hit region, had now crowded out hydroelectricity generated at more realistic costs by private utilities. Potts urged closer study of federal dams' "severe curtailment of the region's multimillion-dollar salmon industry." He recounted how BPA administrator Paul Raver had testified during CBIAC's dramatic June 1947 "fish versus dams" hearings in Walla Walla, Washington, that "if there must be a choice between dams and fish, the fish must go."

Potts believed ecological damage already caused by New Deal public power in the Columbia Basin warranted slowing the postwar federal upriver offensive. Grand Coulee Dam, "that great monolithic fish barricade, already has eliminated probably 30 per cent of the river system's vast spawning grounds." Despite Fish and Wildlife Service and state biologists discovering that "salmon thrive in rough, moving water," Bonneville Dam "and its 70 miles of repugnant slack water lake reduce the river salmon run no less than 10 per cent." McNary Dam, now rising on the Columbia 150 river miles upstream, promised to further slash runs another 15 percent. Now, Potts marveled, CBIAC was trying to convince the White House to recommend, and Congress to appropriate, enough funds to build four new main-stem Columbia dams. If this concrete gauntlet became a northwestern reality, "salmon, delayed and baffled, would die before negotiating the scores of miles of reservoirs."

He urged utility executives to appreciate how building smaller dams in tributaries and upgrading turbines at Bonneville and Grand Coulee met both regional power needs and environmental imperatives. Federal power agencies were fixated on damming big rivers, the Columbia and Snake, which migratory fish needed as highways between mountain spawning areas and the life-giving ocean. If private utilities prevailed in their struggle against public power, however, salmon and steelhead trout stood a far better chance of coexisting with a robust human society, for "smaller dams on branch streams would make possible their preservation."[60]

Senator Gurney of South Dakota challenged federal basin planning and water-resources development on more prosaic grounds than did Potts and Cellars. He supported Missouri River power and irrigation plans, memorialized in the 1947 Pick-Sloan concordat between the Bureau of Reclamation and Corps of Engineers. His environmental history lesson about riverine realities lacked the northwesterners' critical bite. Yet *Public Utilities Fortnightly*'s publication of Gurney's 1947 article dramatized private utilities' willingness to mobilize novel arguments against federal plans to transform river basins into electric grids.[61]

"No lesson of geologic or recorded history is plainer than that of the regular recurrence of floods," Gurney observed. Although his reading of Missouri Basin natural history inclined him to favor "large flood-control projects" built under Pick-Sloan's mandate, he urged corporate utilities and their political allies to advance arguments against public-power expansion based on "the lessons of history" and "the simple logic of economics."[62]

Gurney's attack on federal hydroelectric strategy expanded arguments usually offered by corporate enemies of CVA and cut-rate public power. By using language redolent with concepts of social cost and ecological consequences, the South Dakotan anticipated later postwar conservationist resistance to pell-mell federal construction of power dams. In tandem with conservative anti–New Deal politicians, private utility critiques of public power during the Hells Canyon controversy encouraged deeper reevaluations of dams' natural impacts.

Motivated mostly by self-interest, corporations generating and transmitting hydroelectricity in the Columbia-Snake Basin effectively illuminated public power's destructive environmental impacts. Utility executives, inveighing against phantom socialists staffing spectral Columbia Valley authorities, actually engaged northwesterners in real debates about the consequences of cheap, almost infinitely abundant, electricity. At stake in the Hells Canyon controversy, and in the larger national conflict between private and public power, were the future dimensions of northwestern society, economics, and ecology. Utility corporations' public-relations rhetoric unexpectedly posed hard questions about economic and environmental trade-offs in river basins rich with salmon and steelhead trout. Corporate criticism of public subsidies to hydroelectricity dignified dissent to pell-mell power expansion. Utility campaigns against engineering hubris and federal dictation laid down a postwar substructure of imagery and interests that encouraged new political alliances for environmental restraint after 1960.[63]

At a more basic level of historical morality, the private critique of public power in the postwar Northwest offers tantalizing possibilities of courses not taken and choices unexplored. The region today still wrestles with difficult problems summarized as "salmon versus dams." Those with a stake in the outcome—which must include nearly every human inhabitant in the Columbia-Snake Basin and most of the nonhuman species as well—might profit from reconsidering choices made in the postwar years.[64]

Had Idaho Power's Hells Canyon Complex, its three dams together only a fraction of the size of the federal High Hells Canyon Dam proposed for the same site, been replicated elsewhere, the market's capacity to discipline hydroelectric expansion would have undergone more rigorous testing. Corporate opposition to the Columbia Valley Administration—premised on concerns about cost, control, and consequences—derailed a hydroelectric strategy riddled with unexamined assumptions about natural forces. By critiquing the New Deal legacy so fiercely in the postwar, private-power advocates unintentionally laid the groundwork for later critics of pell-mell electrification. Challenging federal hydroelectric planners as distant and profligate, Idaho Power's allies in the utility industry unexpectedly posed hard questions about the consequences of abundant electricity on Northwest society, economics, and ecology.[65]

8 CLAIMING THE PUBLIC INTEREST

Idaho Power Moves on Hells Canyon

lanning + power = hydroelectric expansion. Since 1946, federal power agencies had been trying to apply this formula in the Snake Basin. The Columbia Basin Inter-Agency Committee's 1951 *Comprehensive Plan for the Development of the Natural Resources of the Northwest* proclaimed, "Development must provide for maximum returns from regional resource potentials. . . . Nothing less than full and well-coordinated development and management of these resources can be accepted." The agencies of CBIAC—the Interior Department, Army Corps of Engineers, and Federal Power Commission—expected the Northwest "to continue to grow in population and business activity." But without "comprehensive advance planning for development of its natural resources to meet present and oncoming demands, irreplaceable opportunities will be lost." To seize those irreplaceable opportunities, the *Comprehensive Plan* specified "immediate objectives to meet the needs of the region, including defense requirements." Hells Canyon High Dam and the Mountain Home Project came first on the list. "Immediate authorization should be sought for the facilities."[1]

President Truman titled his domestic agenda "the Fair Deal," but its dedication to planning nature's comprehensive development mirrored Franklin Roosevelt's New Deal. Comprehensive federal river-basin plans, with cheap public power maximizing exploitation of nature, would secure national prosperity. By turning a symbolic key to ignite the first blast of construction dynamite, Truman intended the High Dam to define the Fair Deal in the Northwest, as Grand Coulee had the New Deal. During the first phase of the controversy, he had designated Hells Canyon as the linchpin to expanding public power's domain. By fueling the Reclamation Bureau's ambitious Mountain Home Project, its hydropower would put federal planners "on the right road to a full, unified and coordinated development of the rich natural resources of the Northwest." Truman believed the High Dam's electric bounty would transform the postwar Snake Basin to resemble the Columbia Basin: "richer farmlands, more prosperous cities and industries, cheaper power, and healthier opportunities for a better standard of living in this whole area." Senate defeat of Hells Canyon High Dam, in April 1950, stung the president.[2]

Truman's refusal to accept this setback opened a new phase of the Hells Canyon controversy that extended from spring 1950 through the 1952 presidential election. Idaho Power Company replied by pursuing its private dam on the same reach of the Snake River. The company had two goals. The first was reactive and defensive. Idaho Power president Thomas E. "Tom" Roach and general counsel A. C. "Art" Inman sought to block Congress from reviving the Reclamation Bureau's High Dam, Columbia Basin Account irrigation subsidy, and Mountain Home Project. However, playing defense against the president would not secure the necessary federal license to build Idaho Power's dam. Roach and his supporters therefore pursued a second, more offensive goal, by making the legal and political case for privatizing Hells Canyon.

Like their adversaries in the Truman administration, Roach and Inman mixed power politics, public relations, and legal advocacy. Like the Snake itself, the Hells Canyon controversy's second phase flowed through diverse landscapes: noisy public meetings, quiet administrative conference rooms, often bursting into the mass-media glare. To decide the fate of natural systems at the center of the controversy—rivers, deserts, canyons, fish—northwestern people had to navigate political currents that poured life into dry legal questions. As people assessed their choices, running water—and the life it carried and promised— continuously impelled political action. Across this braided riverscape of politics and law, the Snake River reshaped culture as northwestern people sought to reshape Hells Canyon.

Faced with determined political opposition to Idaho Power's dam, Roach, his managers, and their lawyers introduced new methods. The Hells Canyon controversy simultaneously energized legal venues and political campaigns. It foreshadowed modern public-interest litigation over environmental issues. A significant chapter in the emergence of modern environmental law, the Hells Canyon controversy taught partisans how to use the legal system to develop political choices. They discovered that politics made environmental law. Control over water in an arid region, its economy dependent on hydroelectricity and irrigation, conferred unrivaled power to define the public interest. The Bureau of Reclamation and Idaho Power Company each tried to control the Snake Basin's hydroelectric and irrigation destiny. Americans weighed which contestant best expressed their changing values. Defining the public interest in the Snake River reflected the constant inter-penetration of politics and law. The Hells Canyon controversy revealed culture's inescapable conversation with nature.

Law not only reflected political choices Americans made about Hells Canyon's fate. Law also structured the way they made their choices. Truman and his allies portrayed Hells Canyon as public property, a vast national store-house of public power. They contended federal administrative agencies, devising plans to execute federal statutes, should capture and superintend the Snake's power. To Roach, however, the Snake Basin promised to secure his company future profits to enable it to maintain its legal status as a util-ity corporation. If the public-power domain federalized Hells Canyon hydro-power, Idaho Power, its irrigator allies, and the local officeholders they supported would lose command over vital decisions about land and water. Instead, federal executive-branch agencies, staffed by employees who believed private power impeded planned maximization of national wealth, would define the basin's public interest.

As Americans celebrated V-E day's fifth anniversary, President Truman tried to convince them that federalizing Hells Canyon expressed the pub-lic interest. Congressional elections, fast approaching, sharpened his hope of electing more liberal Democrats who shared his commitment to public-power expansion and federal river-basin planning. In May 1950, two weeks after Congress defeated the High Dam, he made a quick "non-political" tour of the Northwest: Boise, Idaho; Baker, Oregon; Pasco, Washington; and then on to Seattle. From there, his special armored train, the Magellan, rumbled back over the Cascades toward the Rockies, through Spokane, Washington; Sandpoint, Idaho; and Columbia Falls, Montana. Once across the Continental Divide, Truman's route to the capital followed the Missouri Basin. There, since 1946, federal water agencies—the Reclamation Bureau and Army Engineers—had been raising dams and dikes to realize his dream of comprehensive, planned resource maximization to secure national wealth.

At each stop, the president invoked New Deal public power's blessings. Hells Canyon High Dam became a great, unredeemed, national pledge to deliver abundant electricity, at rock-bottom prices, throughout the Northwest. Truman told audiences that building the High Dam was a fitting memorial to Franklin Roosevelt. Gone now five years, the late president's legacy loomed over the Columbia Basin. His successor urged listeners to do all they could—lobby their representatives in Washington, D.C., persuade the press, organize their community leaders—to weave the Snake Basin, up to the Continental Divide, into FDR's vision of a prosperous, secure, economically modern Northwest.

"I am not running for anything now," the president told a Twin Falls, Idaho, trackside audience. His wry jest drew appreciative laughter in this GOP bastion. He was there to explain the need for more power and irrigation water. "I am out here to report to you on exactly what I am trying to do and I want your help to help me put it over."[3]

In Boise, on a sunny morning, a crowd engulfed the handsome Spanish Revival Union Pacific station on the bluff above the little city. From the Magellan's rear car, Truman told them how disappointed he had been when the Senate voted against High Hells Canyon and the Mountain Home Project. "The pennypinchers who want to cut all funds for reclamation simply don't understand good business principles," the president observed. "We have done a great deal of good pioneering work in resource development, but we need more power dams to develop mineral resources, and to bring cheap power to all the communities of this area." His reference to minerals reflected the Reclamation Bureau's plan to use cheap hydroelectricity to create a Snake Basin phosphate fertilizer industry. Public power had already founded an aluminum industry in the New Deal Columbia Basin.

Roosevelt's dams and dreams inspired Truman. "I want to say to you that if we hadn't had the power projects in the Tennessee Valley, if we hadn't had the Bonneville and Grand Coulee Dams and other power projects, it would have taken us much longer to win the war. . . . Now I want to see a Northwest power development. . . . I want to say to you that if we get that done, nothing in the world can prevent this country from accomplishing its purpose. It will mean an economic development that will keep us the most powerful nation in the world." The president told Boiseans, "What I want you to understand [is] that I am working for world peace on a basis that will make our economic setup the greatest in the history of the world, as it is right now. I want to keep it that way. I want to keep on developing it."[4]

Three hours later, in Baker, the president returned to his recent defeat at Hells Canyon. "Your city, like all of the great state of Oregon, has been growing fast in recent years," Truman reminded trackside listeners. "That is splendid, and I hope that you keep right on growing. To do that, however, there must be continued development of the natural resources of the Northwest." Senate rejection of Hells Canyon High Dam was "an obstacle in the way of sensible development of the country's and your resources." Hells Canyon's ambitious combination of hydropower, flood control, and reclamation irrigation promised "full, unified and coordinated development of the rich natural resources of the Northwest." To those who suspected he might abandon the High Dam, the president pledged, "I am sure we will get Hells Canyon Dam before we quit. We have got to have it. It will add close to a million kilowatts of power to this section of the country. It will help control flood waters, it will help bring a higher standard of living to this entire region." The next afternoon, Truman identified his foes as "those who do not understand the greatness of our goals, and who fear some impairment of their selfish interests."[5]

Truman's itinerary included a pilgrimage to a New Deal shrine, Grand Coulee Dam. Installation of new turbines to boost Grand Coulee's hydroelectric capacity encouraged him to identify his Fair Deal public-power program with this New Deal northwestern icon. Truman told assembled federal managers and local boosters the Northwest would "always need more power from our great rivers." For fifteen years, he charged, private power companies had tried to stop people in the region from getting cheap hydropower they desperately needed. Selfishness, Truman observed, motivated his adversaries. Private utilities profited by selling a public resource, so they naturally fought the New Deal. Despite regional prosperity fueled by public power, corporations still insisted on fighting his Fair Deal plan "to put the energy of our rivers to use as power and sell it to the people at cost."[6]

Just a year and a half earlier, Truman had won Idaho and Washington. He had nearly broken the historic Republican presidential hammerlock over Oregon. Swept into office along with the president in 1948 was the Eighty-first Congress, more Democratic than any since FDR's second term. Although northwestern Democratic senators had unanimously backed Hells Canyon High Dam in April 1950, conservative southern Democrats had deserted the president. Truman thus redoubled his partisan efforts to remind Democrats the High Dam would stamp their imprint on postwar power policy. The president still described High Hells Canyon as the keystone to public power's expanded northwestern domain.[7]

Despite balking at the High Dam, the Eighty-first Congress had mostly endorsed Truman's Fair Deal water program. The 1950 Rivers and Harbors

Act authorized nearly all big new federal dams and irrigation projects he had been seeking since his first State of the Union address in 1946. In all, Congress approved more than 150 new federal construction projects. *Congressional Quarterly* calculated that, if future appropriations bills matched authorization totals, the nation had just committed a record $1.5 billion to making America's rivers work harder to serve the goals of power production, reclamation of arid lands, and flood control. The Army Corps of Engineers and Bureau of Reclamation could anticipate years of busy labor in the basins of the nation. In the Northwest alone, federal construction would exceed $75 million.[8]

Truman exhorted liberal allies in the Fair Deal coalition to make basin planning and public power partisan litmus tests. He anticipated the midterm elections in 1950 would reenergize the coalition that had elected him in 1948. Liberal Democrats, Progressive Party refugees, trade unions in the North, southern and midwestern farm lobbies of the Populist persuasion, and urban wage earners had all answered his whistle-stop crusade against corporate power, expensive electricity, and selfish Republicans.[9]

Truman intended to rally them again to win Hells Canyon High Dam. By nationalizing the Hells Canyon controversy in 1950, the president tried to unite public power's many supporters outside the Northwest. The White House's full array of political incentives and public-relations techniques focused national attention on the Snake. Using his own speeches, steady pressure on reliable Democratic constituencies, and a high-profile presidential commission on river-basin development, Truman took his plea for federalizing Snake River power to the nation.

The 1950 Rivers and Harbors Act came to the White House in due course. The president quietly signed the bill on 17 May, just after returning from his northwestern swing. But press aides hinted the boss might be inclined to make a little news himself in just a few days.[10] Five days later, in the Rose Garden, Truman squared his shoulders and fixed his wire-rimmed gaze on the newsreel cameras and print reporters. When he tightened his mouth like that, not even a jaunty spring bow tie and matching pocket square could mask his dedication. He had signed the Rivers and Harbors Act, Truman told the press, even though many of his advisers and congressional leaders thought a veto would pry loose enough votes to revive Hells Canyon High Dam. However, he signed reluctantly. "In a number of particulars, this act is seriously deficient," Truman said. Without the High Dam and the Reclamation Bureau's Mountain Home Project, it failed to meet the nation's obligation to comprehensively develop the Snake Basin's water resources "in a sensible and practical operating system." Of course, the president admitted, the High Dam and Mountain Home Project had been bold. But they represented "the kind of comprehensive planning and action that is required if we are to conserve, develop and use our natural resources so that they will be increasingly useful to us as the years go by." He vowed to send the High Dam to Congress again in his fiscal 1952 budget.[11]

The Korean War's unexpected outbreak, in late June, sharpened Truman's interest in northwestern public power. He ordered Interior secretary Oscar Chapman to mobilize public support for new dams to drive the region's defense factories and federal atomic weapons sites. Chapman quickly assembled an advisory board, drawn from both public-power customers and corporate utilities. Among the Defense Electric Power Agency's (DEPA's) tasks, the Interior secretary told its first meeting in September, was figuring out how to build congressional coalitions to authorize more new northwestern dams. "All segments of the industry are in this defense program together and the industry must work together—both public and private power—to perform this job. This is a national defense emergency problem and it has nothing to do with ideologies with respect to public and private power."[12]

Chapman assigned BPA's assistant administrator, D. L. Marlett, to the advisory board as interim staff director. Bonneville Power's administrator Paul Raver became a full DEPA member. He was also chairing the Columbia Basin Inter-Agency Committee. From these two key posts, Raver helped Truman and Chapman portray Hells Canyon High Dam as a vital national defense asset, patriotism cast in concrete.

Raver told CBIAC at its regular October session, in Wallace, Idaho, that northwestern public-power expansion now commanded national, even global, significance. "The problem of expansion of power supply at a pace that will parallel the power needs that will be increasing with the enlarging defense program . . . is one thing that makes this Committee's speedup program of great importance to this region." Fortunately, Raver believed, expansion planning had been a CBIAC priority for the past three years. "Because of this work . . . we are in a position to move as quickly as anyone."

Raver asked his aide, Roy F. Bessey, to update CBIAC on the work of his Accelerated Program Subcommittee. Created in July, shortly after the Korean fighting began, and meeting in closed executive sessions, the subcommittee was superseding the full committee on issues of power planning and construction scheduling. Bessey, a long-time New Deal planner, knew how to forge interagency consensus. He had been Raver's staff liaison to CBIAC since its formation in 1946. He had devised the fish-conservation plan in 1947 that overrode state and federal biologists' concerns about the postwar hydroelectric offensive. Since midsummer 1950, Bessey's subcommittee had been pressing federal and state conservation agencies to mute their concerns about hydroelectric expansion. First a casualty of postwar optimism, the region's migratory fish were now captives of the Korean War.

The Accelerated Program Subcommittee seized responsibility for identifying new federal power dams that could come on line as quickly as possible. Into category 1, Bessey's subcommittee placed those projects "which are not in conflict with other resources programs," a euphemism for salmon and steelhead trout. If fully funded by Congress, Bessey told CBIAC, category 1 dams would generate another 9,800 megawatts, more than doubling the federal hydroelectric capacity in the Northwest. Raver thanked his aide for the subcommittee's "splendid job pulling this information together and classifying it into the different categories so that if the Pacific Northwest is called upon, we will have the best chance of going ahead on those projects which do not have any controversy."

Raver then asked about Hells Canyon High Dam. "It is in the first group," Bessey replied, "which includes those which are not in conflict with other resources programs." That was the answer Raver wanted CBIAC and the two-dozen business executives, public officials, academics, and reporters to hear. He had opened the committee's afternoon deliberations to broadcast its thinking across the region. "With the requirements coming on this region for defense purposes," Raver announced, "I consider Hells Canyon a key dam in the major river system development program. It is a key dam not only for power, but it is also a major dam in the flood control picture and to delay that dam any further would be a very serious matter for the entire Pacific Northwest and will affect its economy for many years to come."

He endorsed accelerated construction of Hells Canyon High Dam as an urgent national priority. "Business is being hurt today and expansion in the Pacific Northwest is being hurt today because of lack of adequate power supply and it will continue to be hurt until some of these major projects are completed. Hells Canyon is a major project. . . . It should be authorized immediately and construction started *in this year* in order that storage water can be available by 1955."[13] By December, Raver felt confident enough in the Accelerated Program Subcommittee's work to project High Dam hydropower entering BPA's grid in fall 1956.[14]

Like the president, federal power agencies—DEPA and CBIAC—tried to make Hells Canyon a test of patriotism. Measured by the November elections, their effort foundered. Republican congressional candidates won 52 percent of the national vote. Democrats barely retained control of both houses of the Eighty-second Congress, their majority in the House of Representatives cut from seventeen to twelve, and in the Senate from twelve to two.[15] The 1950 elections brightened Idaho Power's prospects for defeating the High Dam. Incumbent Republican governors in Oregon and Washington, Douglas McKay and Arthur Langlie, were already among the West's most outspoken and reliable critics of New and Fair Deal power policy. Each had opposed High Hells Canyon and the Columbia Valley Administration. Both used their state party organizations to slow the federal upriver hydroelectric offensive.[16]

Idaho voters in 1950 consolidated Idaho Power's home-state base. They ousted Democratic senator Glen Taylor, one of the company's most persistent congressional critics. In concert with most other Idaho businesses, the company deployed considerable financial and media resources to help defeat the one-term senator. Taylor had earned national notoriety by campaigning as Henry Wallace's Progressive Party running mate in 1948. Elected in 1944 as a passionate New Deal liberal, Taylor courted grave political risks in Idaho by backing a party that earned less than 5 percent of his state's presidential vote.[17]

Idaho Power timed its attack on Taylor for maximum disruptive effect. On the Thursday before Idaho's 1950 August Democratic primary, the company coordinated with Snake Basin irrigators a southern Idaho media attack on the senator. In Twin Falls, the irrigators' two leading public spokesmen, Charles Welteroth of Jerome and Nick Sharp of Filer, accused Taylor of "vicious misrepresentations in every sense of the word, designed to mislead the people of this area." Taylor had been claiming since 1947 that Idaho Power opposed Hells Canyon High Dam solely to keep its power rates and profits too high. Welteroth and Sharp defended the company's service record, demanded the senator name any company that had complained about high electric costs, and charged him with "deliberate misrepresentations" intended to transfer legal authority over Idaho water from the state to federal government. The next day, on the statehouse steps in Boise, Taylor replied. He agreed he favored public power and the Reclamation Bureau's High Dam. "It would bring cheap public power and great industries to the Northwest," he declared.[18]

Taylor was swept away in the primary by D. Worth Clark, a conservative from the upper Snake valley, home to the High Dam's most vocal irrigator enemies. An even more conservative Republican, Herman E. Welker, handily defeated Clark in November. Another conservative Republican endorsed by Idaho Power, Henry C. Dworshak, also won a Senate seat in November to replace a Democrat who had died in office. Idaho's Senate delegation would now chorus Roach's bid to block Hells Canyon High Dam for at least the next four years.[19]

Idaho Power also picked up a crucial state political ally by supporting in Idaho's Republican gubernatorial primary rancher and car dealer Len B. Jordan. Deeply hostile to Truman, Jordan had lived for a time in and along Hells Canyon. He spoke passionately about the Snake River's power potential for Idaho. He epitomized the Northwest farmer's and rancher's reflex suspicion of federal natural-resources management. Nominated and elected with Idaho Power's financial backing, Jordan fully shared its managers' belief that Hells Canyon High Dam menaced state prior-appropriation law and water administration. During his one four-year term in the statehouse, Governor Jordan labored loyally to block High Hells Canyon.[20]

Election reverses intensified Interior secretary Chapman's efforts to drape a wartime flag atop Hells Canyon. In late autumn 1950, he dispatched assistant Interior secretary C. Girard Davidson, an intensely partisan public-power veteran, to mobilize northwestern political support for the High Dam. Jebby Davidson had canvassed the region in 1949 on behalf of the Columbia Valley Administration. A former BPA general counsel, he knew the Northwest's electricity and water politics well. Davidson agreed that a politically savvy federal emissary skilled in the arts of interagency lobbying could help Paul Raver make High Hells Canyon a national-defense priority. He welcomed his new opportunity to carry on the liberal crusade for Hells Canyon.

By December, Truman, Chapman, and Davidson had agreed on the mission's objectives. "We are faced with an urgent problem," Chapman told Davidson. "Defense industry desperately needs the large blocks of cheap hydroelectric power that can be developed from the Columbia River system. While everyone in the region would like to see that latent power developed, there is as yet no large body of opinion united behind a single program for accomplishing this." Davidson's charge, wrote the president and Chapman, was "to consult with the public and private agencies and other individuals in the region." Davidson would then deliver to Interior "as soon as possible a unified plan which will result in the quickest and most effective development of the great power resources of the area for defense purposes."[21]

As 1950 ended, Davidson wrote to the Northwest's governors. He enclosed the president's and Interior secretary's directives. "I have been asked," Davidson wrote, "to consult with individuals in the Pacific Northwest with a view towards recommending a unified plan for the most effective development of the electric power resources of the region for defense purposes." To Idaho's governor, Davidson added, "I am anxious to meet with you at an early date to obtain your views on this subject which is of such importance to the Northwest and to the nation."[22]

For the next two years, Davidson would use his special commission from the president as a base to rally public-power supporters around Hells Canyon. Dwight Eisenhower's 1952 victory abruptly terminated his mission. Davidson left Interior to associate with a Portland labor-law firm. However, he soon became even more deeply engaged in the Hells Canyon controversy. Beginning in 1953, he would battle Idaho Power general counsel Art Inman for five years during the Federal Power Commission and federal court legal case about Idaho Power's bid for a Hells Canyon dam license.

While Davidson tried to rally the partisan faithful in the Northwest, Truman's aides quietly worked through DEPA and CBIAC to exhort electric-industry leaders to stop opposing High Hells Canyon. The president also worked the national stage to build political support for public-power expansion. With the chief executive's unmatched power to set the nation's agenda, he intended to keep the High Dam high on that list of unmet tasks. Whenever possible, Truman reminded Fair Deal supporters that Hells Canyon was a litmus test of loyalty to his program of social reform and material security.

Some of his most reliable allies needed little prodding, although they welcomed the administration's new resolve. In the nation's two public-power lobbies, Truman found his most enthusiastic and effective backers. In less than a decade, rural public-power customers, especially in the South and Midwest, had built one of the country's most tenacious lobbies, the National Rural Electric Cooperative Association. The association allied 2.5 million customers of the nation's 850 electricity cooperatives. By working in tandem with the Rural Electrification Administration, one of the New Deal's most popular initiatives, NRECA—or "En-Reeka," as Capitol Hill habitués pronounced it—often acted as a shadow government in public-power policymaking. Rural Electrification Administration administrator

Claude Wickard regularly appointed association leaders to key advisory boards that shaped and executed presidential power strategy. The association's executive manager Clyde Ellis first came to Washington, D. C., early in the New Deal as a young Arkansas Democratic congressman. Defeated in his bid for a Senate seat after two terms, he remained in the capital to lobby for more federal dams and public power.[23]

Rural co-ops identified private utility companies as both business rivals and ideological enemies. Members of NRECA generated little of their own power. The Rural Electrification Act entitled co-ops to first call on hydroelectricity generated at federal dams. The act obligated the dams' operators, either the Reclamation Bureau or Army Corps, to set a price for this preference power at the lowest feasible level. Corporate generating facilities supplied that portion of the co-ops' demand that they could not meet with federal power. Preferential power prices undercut wholesale power generated by private electric utilities by up to 33 percent.[24]

In the Northwest, the 1934 Bonneville Project Act as well as the 1944 Flood Control Act gave co-ops, along with other public-power distributors, first right to take as much hydropower as they could afford. By contrast, state regulators required private utilities to repay borrowed capital with interest and distribute dividends to shareholders, thus forcing higher charges for power they generated at their own dams. Private firms dependent on BPA for large blocks of firm power also had to pay up to 25 percent more per kilowatt-year for hydroelectricity left over after preference customers had satisfied their needs.[25]

Co-ops exploited their Progressive and New Deal heritage to compete for new business in the postwar electricity market. They claimed their statutory preferences required the federal government to meet their demands by electrifying Hells Canyon. A sympathetic contemporary scholar, Arthur Cushman Coyle, found NRECA's members displayed "the unbounded faith and enthusiasm of men who believed in the cause" of public power. The two Roosevelts had inspired co-ops to define conservation in economic terms. In Coyle's estimation, co-ops thought "using publicly owned resources to benefit the people makes possible an achievement that was held to be impossible from the narrowly commercial point of view." By promoting "area coverage," the provision of electricity to all residents regardless of ability to pay, rural co-ops had amassed capital assets exceeding $2 billion by the early 1950s. To ensure their continued growth, the federal government had to plan comprehensive river-basin developments "for the benefit of all the people."[26]

These economic and political facts, to which Clyde Ellis devoted his professional life, made "more electricity for less money" an apt theme for the NRECA 1950 annual convention. Ellis described Hells Canyon as "the finest remaining undeveloped dam site in America." Its 1,000 megawatts promised a huge infusion of competitive capital into co-ops throughout the Northwest. "By almost any standard," he boasted, it would be the most impressive dam in America." Hells Canyon was pivotal if Bonneville Power were to expand upriver to satisfy public-power demands. All of its output would "be fed directly into the BPA system of the Columbia River Basin." Under federal preference law, its "very low-cost power" would go immediately to rural co-ops and public utility districts that usually lacked their own generating facilities. The High Dam would enable rural northwestern co-ops to win new customers in growing suburban areas, perhaps even pry loose customers from established utility-company service areas.[27]

Urban public-power distributors enjoyed their own powerful interest group, the American Public Power Association (APPA). Its membership ranged from the nation's second-largest city, Los Angeles, to tiny villages in New England and the upper Midwest. Its elected leaders, though, came from big cities—especially in the West and upper South—where public power had been long established.

The association anticipated political conflict over public-power expansion during the Truman presidency. Its leadership reflected the charged atmosphere. From 1949 to 1950, Samuel Morris, general manager of Los Angeles's Department of Water and Power, presided. In January 1950, he also served as urban public power's representative on Truman's new Water Resources Policy Commission. At APPA's April 1950 convention, States R. Finley, who managed Chattanooga, Tennessee's power division, took over as president. Chattanooga was the biggest urban area completely served by Tennessee Valley Authority power. The association's national convention, meeting in Washington, D.C., tapped two more urban power managers to succeed Finley as the 1952 elections approached. Kansas City, Kansas's public-utility director, Ralph Duvall, would head APPA for the 1951–52 term, followed by Tacoma, Washington's municipal power manager, J. Frank Ward, during the critical 1952–53 period. Duvall was one of Truman's most outspoken defenders in the president's home area. Ward's agency purchased more BPA wholesale electricity than did any other municipal customer.

Clyde Ellis of NRECA understood the capital's folkways. He knew the public-power lobby had lost an important first round when Congress refused to authorize Hells Canyon High Dam in April 1950. To revive the dam before the 1952 elections, or to make its fate a major campaign issue, demanded extensive, aggressive public-relations work. Already, Ellis thought, the Hells Canyon controversy looked like it was becoming "the longest and most emotional controversy" over natural-resources policy in the postwar years. High Dam proponents had "a fundamental difference in philosophy" with Idaho Power and its allies. Americans who supported "comprehensive development of river basins by the federal government" were represented by NRECA and APPA. Truman's Fair Deal understood "the navigable rivers of this nation are a great natural resource that should be developed for the benefit of the people." Rural cooperatives as well as urban electricity customers were desperate for power at cost, and rivers such as the Snake promised what they craved. "But before they can benefit anyone," Ellis contended, "they must somehow be harnessed, usually by the construction of large multi-purpose dams."

NRECA mobilized co-op members throughout the nation to embrace the High Dam as their own cause. Ellis wrote and spoke extensively about Hells Canyon. During the early 1950s, "I had to make our members see Hells Canyon as more than a local issue." As he appraised the political and economic setting between 1950 and 1952, Hells Canyon High Dam promised to fulfill the New Deal dream of abundant, inexpensive electricity for greater national wealth. Once Congress appropriated construction funds, High Dam power sales to preference customers at cut-rate prices—"the lowest possible cost to the public"—would ignite intensive agricultural and industrial development throughout the Northwest. Idaho Power's private-dam alternative, which would block the High Dam, posed a question about national principles. The Hells Canyon controversy was becoming "clearly a battle for the public interest and for principle." Even Tom Roach and his allies, Ellis conceded, "were also fighting for principle, as they saw it."[28]

During the second phase of the Hells Canyon controversy between 1950 and 1952, NRECA and APPA closely coordinated public relations and political lobbying. By late 1951, they had launched what Ellis called "their national campaign" for the High Dam. "Hells Canyon had to become a rallying point and a slogan—a symbol of our determination to fight for our convictions."[29] *Public Power*, their combined monthly journal, read like a High Dam campaign flyer. Both Reclamation commissioner Michael Straus and Interior secretary Oscar Chapman authored articles identifying High Hells Canyon with the Truman administration's goals to boost hydropower capacity, control Columbia Basin floods, and ignite a new Snake Basin phosphate fertilizer industry. As the Korean War intensified, NRECA and APPA contended that Idaho Power's opposition to the High Dam weakened the nation's military. With Columbia Basin defense industries demanding ever-greater supplies of cheap hydropower, Ellis charged, "We could not afford the waste of resources which the failure to build Hells Canyon High Dam would represent." Idaho Power's "small" dams on the Snake would plunder more than $1 billion in public electric resources alone, he claimed.[30]

Clyde Ellis grasped the fundamental political and environmental differences dividing Idaho Power and Fair Deal public power. In Hells Canyon, nature presented Americans a grand opportunity to turn flowing water into national power. "Where a site on a river lends itself to a multi-purpose development," he wrote, "and engineers have determined that a large federal dam would be feasible, and its construction is opposed by the power companies, the question of the public interest becomes paramount." If Idaho Power prevailed, it would simply "build small, run-of-the-river dams of [its] own to generate power for [its] own use. These small structures," Ellis warned, "are useless so far as multiple public benefits are concerned." Hells Canyon encouraged Americans to decide what was the public interest in water. The High Dam controversy was "simply a matter of whether the river should be developed in the public interest or exploited for private gain."[31]

President Truman enlisted two other key elements of the Fair Deal coalition, intellectuals and urban liberals in the Northeast and Middle West, in his push for Hells Canyon High Dam. He named a new Water Resources Policy Commission in early 1950, and Interior secretary Chapman, Reclamation commissioner Straus, and Eleanor Roosevelt promptly urged him to select commissioners devoted to public-power expansion.

Prominent educators dominated the WRPC. Four college presidents—from Arizona, Arkansas, Montana, and Pennsylvania—joined Morris Cooke, Leland Olds, and Los Angeles Water and Power's Samuel Morris. Cooke, a protégé of Gifford Pinchot, had managed Pennsylvania's public-power system before the New Deal lured him to Washington. He directed FDR's National Resources Planning Board, and then administered the Rural Electrification Administration until the end of World War II. Cooke had written widely on the theory of utility regulation and the economics of electricity. Olds, before joining the Federal Power Commission in Roosevelt's second term, had been a progressive journalist and popular lecturer about energy and social reform. Eleanor Roosevelt was his most powerful patron. Olds had consulted with New York City's electricity department after failing to win Senate confirmation for a third six-year term on the Federal Power Commission in late 1949.[32]

Gilbert White, a geographer and president of Haverford College in suburban Philadelphia, quickly became WRPC's most outspoken academic defender. An expert on water's use, administration, and control, he advocated the commission's central finding in speeches and writings for the rest of the 1950s: "We all want the integrated development of multi-purpose projects for entire river basins for the public good." Two years later, White contended that WRPC expressed a popular and scholarly "consensus" for managing multistate watersheds as administrative and political units. Federal basin plans had to emphasize multipurpose projects. The Reclamation Bureau's High Dam and Mountain Home Project properly conceived of the Snake Basin as an integrated system of human and natural resources. "The chief problems of wisely developing water resources," White wrote in 1953, "are thus ones of using an expanded knowledge of the basic resources so as to meet human needs wisely at the suitable time and by methods that will promote healthy economic and political processes." White promoted using interlocking water supplies for "urban growth, river navigation, swamp drainage, flood control, pollution control, recreation, hydropower, and wildlife protection."[33] Apportioning competing water uses and defining the public interest in river basins was a job too big for states and communities. Instead, White endorsed New Deal agencies as best suited to make postwar water policy: Roosevelt's Natural Resources Council, National Resources Planning Board, and Tennessee Valley Authority best integrated federal authority with local needs.[34]

Chairman Cooke promised WRPC members would travel throughout the country during 1950. He invited all groups interested in federal water-resources development to attend WRPC hearings and to submit written testimony. Cooke summarized the commission's charge by echoing many of Truman's themes: "The Commission considers that the objective of a sound national water policy is to promote the full use of the water resources of the country for all useful purposes so combined as to yield for the people maximum benefits at minimum costs."[35]

The Cooke commission fanned out across the country in summer 1950, sparking debate about how to electrify the nation's rivers. The National Association of Electric Companies kicked off an expensive public-relations blitz to eliminate public-power distributors' preference right to federal hydropower at the lowest possible rates. Alex Radin, who edited *Public Power,* observed in June, "The controversy between public and private power is rising to a fever pitch . . . with this fight more intense today than ever before, and moving to a climax."[36]

Truman public-power officials focused their efforts on High Hells Canyon. On a far West tour in late summer, Reclamation commissioner Straus sought to reassure key public-power and reclamation constituencies that April's Senate setback had only whetted the president's combative spirit. The Truman administration was just beginning to fight for the High Dam, he insisted. In Portland, Straus predicted, "Hells Canyon Dam will probably be the next great Western power dam to be undertaken." Every executive-branch player—the White House Budget Office, Army Corps, Reclamation, Interior's other regional agencies—still played on the High Dam team.[37] Straus promised the Columbia Basin the High Dam would anchor the Northwest's public-power grid. "Hells Canyon," Straus said, "will be a very large dam, larger than Boulder Dam. Its generators are to be larger than those at Grand Coulee for cheaper power." His Portland audiences knew how BPA hydroelectricity had powered area defense industries in the Second World War. Now that American boys were fighting in Korea, Straus reminded them, "kilowatts are materials of war, just as much as machine gun bullets and airplanes."[38]

Three days later, his party boarded boats in Weiser, Idaho, and motored downstream to inspect Hells Canyon's dam site. Seeing the Snake River roll through its canyon made Straus even more optimistic. American soldiers were clinging to the Pusan perimeter. No one in Washington knew how the fighting would turn out. But Straus believed the "critical national situation in Korea" actually improved the administration's chance of changing enough votes in Congress to secure High Hells Canyon's authorization in 1951. He reminded a joint meeting of the Boise and Mountain Home chambers of commerce how Reclamation had accelerated completion of Grand Coulee by ten years to help win World War II.

As he had in Portland, Pendleton, and Baker, Oregon, Straus appealed to Boiseans' patriotism. An old newspaperman, he had learned from his mentor, Harold Ickes, how to portray public power in golden tones. "It's the last great natural dam site of that scope on the continent," Straus proclaimed of Hells Canyon. "I believe it will be the next great dam in the Northwest to be built by the government. The geology of the site is almost perfect for dam building. There are 93 miles of river behind it that are nothing but a reservoir site—no roads or railroads to move, no towns or farms to be flooded." In "the present emergency," a big new federal dam operated by his agency would again serve the nation's needs for power and food. "The 50-year-old Reclamation service has been through several hot and cold wars. Our program can be bent to any requirements."[39]

Straus and his aides made a special effort to remind Snake Basin businessmen and farmers how future federal reclamation projects depended on the High Dam. It was, Straus told the Boise chamber of commerce's special reclamation committee, "the cash box" for the Mountain Home Project. Reclamation boosters from Mountain Home, led by Mayor John Glasby and car dealer R. M. "Bob" Wetherell, smiled with Straus for a news photograph. But none of the big irrigation farmers in the basin attended his conference with the chambers of commerce. Neither did Idaho state reclamation engineer Mark R. Kulp, who allocated water rights.

Traveling with Straus in mid-August were the two federal administrators most responsible for packaging the High Dam and Mountain Home Project as a Reclamation Bureau job: Harold T. Nelson, Reclamation's Northwest director, and R. J. Newell, his predecessor. Newell had won for his agency control over the High Dam during tense negotiations with the Army Engineers in 1948 and 1949. At Region 1's Boise headquarters, Nelson would drain the Hells Canyon "cash box" to build the Mountain Home Project's tunnels, aqueducts, canals, and headgates.

Hopeful reclamation boosters and public-power consumers welcomed Straus's pugnacious pleas for the High Dam. Nelson and Newell had a different mission, though, on Reclamation's promotional tour. They had to reach Snake Basin interests who had not attended Straus's Boise event: prosperous irrigators who ran the Idaho State Reclamation Association and controlled water districts along the Snake. If Reclamation could persuade elite irrigators that Hells Canyon High Dam helped them, then the Truman administration might harvest more votes when the High Dam came up on Capitol Hill again in early 1951.

On the evening after the Hells Canyon boat tour, Nelson reminded a Weiser audience how the High Dam keyed Reclamation's Mountain Home Project. Weiser lay at the edge of the Snake River Plain. Most ISRA members farmed upstream, around and above Twin Falls. But the Reclamation Bureau had built small projects in the area, so Nelson's listeners included irrigators, their bankers, and various businesses dependent on reclamation farming. He therefore emphasized the High Dam's compatibility with irrigation and its fealty to state laws allocating water from the Snake.

That summer evening, in Weiser's Washington Hotel, Nelson met what he judged to be the federal government's main adversary: fear. Irrigators holding established Idaho and Oregon water-appropriation rights feared the High Dam would condemn their water to fill its reservoir. Hopeful reclamationists feared hydroelectric demands at Hells Canyon would require so much stored water as to block future upstream diversions to expand agriculture. State water managers feared federalizing Hells Canyon would unhinge their structure of law and policy favoring Snake Basin farmers.

Nelson tried to allay all of these fears, many nurtured and exaggerated by Idaho Power Company, some of which were valid. By federalizing Hells Canyon hydroelectricity, he explained, the Bureau of Reclamation did not intend to overthrow irrigation farming. "Consumptive use of water will come first," Nelson vowed. Irrigators would still be first in line at the edge of the Snake. They would still enjoy legal hegemony over water, still wield social and political prerogatives that flowed from this command. He pledged his agency would respect state prior-appropriation law's preference for irrigation. Making Hells Canyon High Dam the region's premier power site would not impede future irrigation expansion. "There will be no 'power filings' to pre-empt water for the High Dam," Nelson pledged.[40]

Reclamation Bureau leaders spent so much time soothing irrigators' paranoia because Idaho Power Company was winning the battle to label the Hells Canyon controversy. Not only had it defined the national contest as one pitting "free enterprise versus government planning," but Snake Basin people increasingly understood the controversy as one between "Columbia Basin public power versus Idaho irrigation." Idaho Power had discovered its most potent argument: the High Dam menaced Snake Basin irrigators' state-law water rights and future expansion opportunities. General counsel Art Inman's testimony at the Army Corps' Lewiston and Boise hearings in early 1949 paralleled criticisms from the Idaho State Reclamation Association, the Snake Basin's principal irrigator lobby. After the Senate vote in April 1950 against Hells Canyon High Dam, the company enjoyed crucial breathing space to perfect its own designs for damming the Snake. By splitting Hells Canyon from the biggest federal dam-building push since the Depression, Idaho Power had more time to develop its theme that economics, politics, and geography distinguished the Snake and Columbia basins.

Idaho Power now took the offensive, counterattacking the fundamental premises of New Deal hydroelectric policy in the Northwest. The utility fought public power as the champion of Snake Basin irrigators and the enemy of federal agency planners. It hammered relentlessly on its theme that planners who projected the High Dam wanted to take water from agriculture to make cheap public power for downriver urbanites. Though at least as simplistic as most political slogans, Idaho Power's "local irrigators versus distant dependents" caricature posed two important questions: What kind of world did Snake Basin residents want to build in the postwar years? And, who should be their architects: prosperous farmers and the local public officials they supported or federal executive-branch planners allied with national politicians?[41]

President Truman intended Hells Canyon to be the Fair Deal's fighting symbol, as well as a patriotic priority. Idaho Power's own emotional symbolism matched the president's. While Truman rallied postwar liberals around public power, and BPA's Paul Raver demanded more electricity for national defense, Idaho Power made Hells Canyon High Dam symbolize popular resentment against federal planning and regulation.

Like many environmental issues in our time, the Hells Canyon controversy's second phase, between 1950 and 1952, mixed popular aspirations and positive law. High Dam advocates celebrated cheap electricity, national economic strength, and federal natural-resources planning. Idaho Power invoked private enterprise, financial prudence, and local decision making. The contestants tried to win enough political power to write their preferences into law as statutes, regulations, and judicial opinions. Idaho Power waged a two-front campaign. Its lawyers, led by Art Inman, sought a federal license to build private dams in Hells Canyon. Meanwhile, Tom Roach enlisted national political allies to make High Hells Canyon a test case for changing New Deal hydroelectric policy. Since the president was portraying Hells Canyon as a national asset, Idaho Power managers understood their audience now included the entire political nation.

The company's two-front campaign hinged on getting Idaho state reclamation engineer Mark R. Kulp to endorse privatizing Hells Canyon hydropower. Responsible for both adjudicating rival water claims and popularizing irrigated agriculture, his post fused law and politics. Since 1946, Kulp had attended nearly every CBIAC meeting as Idaho's near plenipotentiary. Governor C. A. Robins, who had not sought renomination, was a lame duck in 1950. Loosely supervised by a weak governor, Kulp now made many of the state's decisions about Hells Canyon.[42]

Idaho Power enjoyed warm relations with the state engineer. Both worshipped the powerful Snake Basin trinity: prior-appropriation doctrine, irrigators' state constitutional preference over water, and state river management. Kulp's close relations with Snake Basin irrigation leaders made him indispensable to Idaho Power. Befitting his status, Kulp took the lead in assembling a united front of northwestern governors and state water managers to testify to Truman's Water Resources Policy Commission in summer 1950. He willingly served as the pivot around which state governments, irrigators, and private utilities coordinated strategy against the High Dam. More than any elected official, Kulp brokered Idaho Power's alliance with Snake Basin irrigators.

Kulp reported to Governor Robins in late May that northwestern state officials had agreed on the substance of testimony for the Cooke commission's late June field hearings in Spokane. First among their agreed points was water ownership: "We believe in maintaining State control of waters within State boundaries and control of inter-state streams through agreements among the States involved." Next, Kulp reported the states "consider it a fundamental principle that river development be done cooperatively with local interests and in agreement with existing conditions." Finally, the states affirmed their position that prior-appropriation law subordinated all water stored in federal power reservoirs to future irrigation.[43]

The day before the WRPC convened, Kulp assembled a strategy conference in Spokane's palatial Davenport Hotel. No Idaho Power personnel were there, but regional private-power interests were well represented. Daniel Noble and Thomas Robins attended for the Pacific Northwest Development Association. Columbia Basin utilities and industries, as well as Idaho Power, had created the association in 1948 specifically to fight High Hells Canyon. Present as well were emissaries from southern Idaho's business and irrigation elite: Earl W. Murphy, manager of the Idaho State Chamber of Commerce; Nick Sharp, Harry Yost, and Charles Welteroth for the Idaho State Reclamation Association; and George Crookham, a leading lower Snake irrigator. Counterparts from Washington, Oregon, and Montana shared the Idahoans' concerns. Murphy reported that night to Governor Robins the conferees had written a joint statement for the governors of Idaho, Montana, Nevada, Oregon, Washington, and Wyoming.[44]

The six northwestern governors' joint statement told the Cooke commission that "fundamental principles common to all the States of the Columbia Basin" motivated their concerns about the High Dam and federal river-basin planning. Each principle reflected Kulp's May negotiations: state management of interstate rivers through interstate compacts, federal jurisdiction only over navigation and international rivers, state veto of new federal water projects, and state-law priorities that favored irrigation over hydropower. Idaho governor Robins then testified separately against the High Dam and Mountain Home Project. His statement measured how well Idaho Power and its allies had demonized postwar public-power expansion as New Deal resources planning in a postwar guise. Robins denied the Snake Basin needed, or wanted, the urban growth and industrial development envisioned in the Reclamation Bureau's Snake Basin Plan. Columbia Basin states needed more hydropower, he agreed, but "power development in Idaho has kept pace with the demand. . . . There is no present power shortage in Idaho." While industrial development in the Columbia Basin reflected public power's hegemony, in the Snake Basin "there are millions of acres of fertile highly productive desert lands and water enough when fully developed and regulated to . . . irrigate up to two million additional acres." To ensure the Snake Basin's future as an irrigation society, "no water should be dedicated for power and industrial use that will restrict full ultimate feasible irrigation development."[45]

After the WRPC completed its western hearings, Cooke probed Robins to determine what the governors meant by preferring interstate compacts to federal planning. Kulp replied for the governor. Idaho's water manager told Cooke that delegates from the northwestern states had discussed a draft Snake-Columbia River compact in early July. The version he sent Cooke reflected the deepening alliance between Snake Basin irrigators and Idaho Power. Kulp had asked R. P. "Pat" Parry, a leading irrigation-district lawyer from Twin Falls, to review the draft compact. Parry was also beginning to advise Idaho Power about winning a federal dam license to thwart the High Dam.[46]

"Fundamental principles" that were announced in the northwestern governors' WRPC testimony became the draft compact's legal authority. State water law should allocate the Snake among competing users. New federal dams on "waters of the Columbia River and its tributaries . . . shall be subservient to the use of such waters for domestic stock and irrigation purposes and shall not interfere with or prevent the use of water for such preferred purposes." To ensure federal planners did not use power reservoirs to manage upstream water, "the duty . . . to administer the distribution of water in their respective states under the terms of this compact" shall reside in "the official in each state who is now or may hereafter be charged with the administration of the public water."[47]

Idaho's new governor, Len Jordan, jumped into the Hells Canyon controversy feet first as soon as he succeeded Robins in early 1951. "The time has come to stop federal government expansion in the region until all avenues of development by private enterprise have been fully explored," one of his characteristic blasts against federal water policy declared. Federal basin plans were "conceived on a national level and only remotely related to the local economy." Public power from federal dams was less expensive only because "it is merely subsidized by general taxation." Bonneville Power's primacy had caused power shortages in the Columbia Basin. In the Snake Basin, by contrast, "government power is not needed for development of the state's resources."[48]

Shortly after Jordan's election, Tom Roach and Art Inman opened Idaho Power's second front to privatize the Snake's hydropower in Hells Canyon. To counter public-power's appeal to boosters who eagerly sought more economic growth, Idaho Power demonstrated it also wanted more electricity. To meet public power's undeniable popular appeal, the company had tapped its own vein of public enthusiasm. To keep expanding its strategic options to block the High Dam, Idaho Power now had to couple public relations with legal advocacy.

The Hells Canyon controversy spilled out of the public arena into the arcane field of administrative law when Roach directed his lawyers and engineers to apply formally for a federal license to build one or more dams in Hells Canyon. Idaho Power's licensing case—denominated "Project No. 1971" by the Federal Power Commission—would last seven years. The Truman administration contested the license application. The president, Interior secretary, and Reclamation commissioner sought to slow the FPC while administration allies tried again to win congressional authorization for High Hells Canyon.

On 15 December 1950, general counsel Inman filed Idaho Power's formal FPC application to build a low dam in Hells Canyon. The Oxbow project would be about ten miles upstream from the site proposed for the High Dam. Oxbow would not interfere with Idaho Power's future plans to build more small dams on the Snake, but Inman conceded it would preempt the federal dam. Nevertheless, he argued, Oxbow met the Federal Power Act's "public interest" test for damming an interstate river. The company's customers needed its electricity within two years. Its small size meant it could be completed quickly and cheaply to aid war production. Being so small, it "does not interfere with the economic development of related sites on the Snake River." Up to four other run-of-river dams could be added later, "as future power demands dictate, without the necessity of expenditure of Government funds."[49]

Oxbow Dam, as initially proposed, would rise about 115 feet above the Snake. Less than one-sixth the height of Hells Canyon High Dam, Oxbow would generate about 140 megawatts, about one-seventh the capacity of the High Dam. Its thirteen-mile-long pond, even when filled to the brim to meet peaking power demands, would hold only about one-seventh as much impounded water as the federal reservoir. Idaho Power had never built a dam as big as Oxbow: it would generate 25 percent more hydropower than the company's next largest facility, Bliss Dam. Still, its projected cost of $25 million was about one-tenth of the total costs projected for building the High Dam and Mountain Home Project. A shot glass beside Reclamation's five-gallon bucket, Oxbow would still boost Idaho Power's total system generating capacity by nearly half. Even then, the company's capacity would still be less than one-twentieth that of the Federal Columbia River Power System overseen by BPA.[50]

Inman's letter to the FPC emphasized Oxbow's modesty. To reassure utility regulators in Oregon and Idaho, he noted its cheap construction cost promised "the lowest cost major power site anywhere in the West." To distinguish between the High Dam's 3.8 million acre-feet reservoir and Oxbow's minimal impoundment, he noted that "plant water rights and operation of the project will not preempt the stream against future upstream irrigation development, as might be the result were the project to require water rights for high spring runoffs into the reservoir to make up a large volume of annual storage necessary for plant operation and to justify plant investment." Oxbow's very modesty recommended it to nervous defense planners because, within twenty-four months from beginning construction, Idaho Power would be able to deliver "immediate emergency power requirements for national defense and other purposes in the Northwest."[51]

Just two days after Idaho Power's license filing, the Truman administration shot back. Cooke's WRPC released an advance version of its report. It specifically recommended early construction of Hells Canyon High Dam and dedication of its revenues to the Mountain Home Project. Cooke reaffirmed Truman's Fair Deal commitment to use public power to transform the Snake Basin. The High Dam's cheap public hydroelectricity "holds out the promise of new and expanded industrial use in the region." Full development of the Snake, according to comprehensive federal plans, "will eventually transform the area into one with a healthy balance between agriculture, forestry and industry."[52]

An Idaho delegation replied, "No, thanks!" In Washington to confer with Interior secretary Chapman, Reclamation commissioner Straus, and Reclamation's Northwest director Nelson, the Idahoans charged the High Dam would cause "severe and perpetual financial injury" by "commandeering" Idaho's water to benefit power customers in the Columbia Basin. This delegation packed considerable punch. Along with outgoing governor Robins, it included irrigation leaders Harry Yost, Ival Goslin, and Dan Cavanagh; construction magnate Harry W. Morrison; and wartime potato and fertilizer millionaire Jack Simplot. Tom Roach had to be pleased. The company's outside attorney, R. P. Parry, and Washington lobbyist E. W. Rising joined the delegation. Even after hearing the federal administrators' plea for High Hells Canyon, the Idahoans still declared Idaho Power's dam filing would best meet the state's power needs for the foreseeable future.[53]

In 1951, the furious, seesawing war in Korea dominated national policy. Chinese intervention just before the year began made military defeat a terrible, very real, possibility. President Truman struggled to hold the United Nations campaign together. His dismissal of General Douglas MacArthur in April ignited a domestic crisis that began eroding the president's hold on office. Until the military situation on the Korean peninsula stabilized, the administration focused on the battlefield. Regional power policy seemed less crucial when the nation confronted military defeat. Amid domestic and international fears that the Soviet Union—or the United States—would use atomic weapons in Asia, the Hells Canyon controversy slipped for a time to the national periphery.[54] The High Dam receded from the headlines. Interior Department lawyers drafted a new High Dam bill and Truman's State of the Union message recommended its enactment, but the administration sent no authorizing legislation to Congress in 1951.[55]

This Hells Canyon interlude encouraged federal and state administrators in the Northwest to grapple with hydroelectricity's recurring, unresolved ecological crises. Since its inception in 1947, the upriver public-power offensive had posed a grave question that seemed to defy solution: How could power dams be designed, built, and operated to do the least damage to Northwest anadromous fish? In the Snake Basin alone, more than two hundred thousand salmon and steelhead trout spawned each spring and fall.

They laid as many as one billion eggs. Each new dam blocked at least 15 percent of the down-running juveniles from reaching the Pacific, even with fish-passage facilities. High Hells Canyon would be built without passage facilities because, at more than seven hundred feet tall, no adult migrants could ever surmount it. Hatcheries, the preferred solution since the New Deal, simply could not replace the Snake Basin fishery. Even all the new hatcheries built since 1948, under the Lower Columbia River Fishery Development Program, could handle less than 10 percent of the eggs laid by wild fish in the great Snake nursery.[56]

In 1951, Oregon's Fish Commission and Washington's Department of Fisheries tried to force federal power agencies to honor their promise to balance cheap public power with a vibrant fishery. Hells Canyon's uncertain fate sharpened the issue. All agreed the High Dam would obliterate Snake Basin fish upstream, as Grand Coulee had done in the upper Columbia after 1940. Idaho Power's low Oxbow project seemed more hopeful. State fish managers still had grave doubts about any new Snake Basin dams. As Fish Commission of Oregon chairman John Veatch pointed out, "Important salmon and steelhead runs now proceed past and spawn above the proposed Hells Canyon damsite." However, compared to the High Dam, the private-power alternative offered some hope for maintaining Snake Basin fish. When the FPC solicited public comment on Idaho Power's application, FCO and the Idaho Fish and Game Department quickly replied that, bad as it might be, Oxbow certainly gave them reason to hope power and fish could coexist.[57]

"The Oxbow development will be superior from a fisheries standpoint to the other proposed developments on the Snake River that are being considered in that the Oxbow Dam would be much lower than certain others contemplated for the same general area," Veatch told the FPC. Of course, any dam posed fish-passage problems, and Oregon was not yet prepared to bless Idaho Power's dam. Yet, "we wish to reiterate that there is a better chance to maintain the upper Snake River salmon runs at a low dam such as Oxbow than at some of the high dams planned for this portion of the Snake River."[58]

Idaho Fish and Game director T. B. Murray praised Oxbow's run-of-river design that impounded fairly little water to spin turbines. Its low height not only simplified fish passage but kept the Snake's flow reasonably constant, a significant plus for both upstream migrants and down-running juveniles. Idaho foresaw another advantage. Fish transplanted from Hells Canyon could provide the nucleus to reestablish salmon in a downstream tributary, the Clearwater River. Since the late 1940s, Fish and Game had been focusing its anadromous fish program on the Clearwater.[59] Budget constraints kept the program rudimentary, but Murray saw gold in Idaho Power's project. He recommended the FPC require the company to fund an ambitious fish salvage operation aimed at relocating Snake River populations into Clearwater country. Like his counterparts in the Columbia Basin, Murray seemed resigned to more dams. Like them, he tried to make dams in one area pay for fish in another.[60]

Idaho Power's Oxbow application encouraged public-power opponents to escalate their criticism of federal resource planning. Late in 1951, Oregon governor Douglas McKay attacked CBIAC's comprehensive plan for terming the High Dam a matter of immediate, patriotic urgency. McKay instead contended Idaho Power's private alternative deserved fair consideration. Until "the differences of opinion prevailing within the region . . . involving as they do a conflict of resources" could be harmonized, CBIAC should delete the High Dam from its Comprehensive Plan. He estimated that harmonization "may necessarily take a little time."[61]

McKay was being disingenuous. He cared nothing for harmony. He would fight the High Dam until Hell froze. His gubernatorial counterpart across the Snake spoke for them both when he wrote an old ranching friend about the Hells Canyon controversy. "I feel sure," Idaho governor Jordan declared, "that Dr. Raver and other socialist planners are insisting on the construction of Hell's Canyon Dam only because it will throttle further river development by private enterprise." Since Raver's comprehensive plan "has all the earmarks of a Columbia River Authority, I am sure that these socialistic planners have never lost their interest in the final objective to set up a regional authority that would transcend state boundaries and state governments. There is no place in their program for private enterprise and they point with suspicion to anyone who espouses free enterprise."[62]

The year 1952 being a presidential election year, partisan politics on all levels shaped the legal aspects of Hells Canyon hydropower. Idaho Power Company was using, and fomenting, widespread local resistance against federal planning to redefine "the public interest" in the Snake River. President Truman insisted on the nation's paramount interest in Hells Canyon, raising the political stakes. The Hells Canyon controversy had by now finally swept regional differences about rival dams into a national referendum on the New Deal legacy.

The FPC would discover, in summer 1952, just how polarized power policies had become in the Snake Basin. The Federal Power Act directed the agency to decide whether Idaho Power's Oxbow project was "in the public interest." The commission therefore announced that a hearing examiner would visit Hells Canyon country "for the purpose of permitting the introduction of views and evidence of a non-technical nature." William J. Costello, a veteran FPC legal officer, got the job in May 1952. He would spend the next three years sorting out rival claims, searching methodically, often pedantically, for the public interest.[63]

For a week in mid-July, northwesterners traveled to Baker, Oregon, and Boise, Idaho, to voice their opinions about Hells Canyon High Dam and Oxbow. Costello heard scores of citizens testify, some eloquently, about the rivalry between the Bureau of Reclamation and Idaho Power Company. Hundreds of spectators packed Baker's Central School auditorium and the Idaho House of Representatives chamber, often cheering when they liked what they heard, sometimes booing opponents.

Shortly before Costello opened his hearings, Interior secretary Chapman formally joined the FPC licensing case by intervening as a party entitled to question witnesses and present evidence. In 1951, Chapman had formally protested Idaho Power's license application. "Strongly urging that the application of the Idaho Power Company for a license to construct the proposed Oxbow water power project on the Snake River be denied," the Interior secretary had called it "a major economic loss to the nation and to the region." Too modest to "fully and properly develop" the Snake Basin's hydroelectric potential, Oxbow "would violate the concept of multiple-purpose comprehensive river basin development of the nation's water resources." Worse still, when American troops were bleeding in Korea, Idaho Power's small private dam "would reduce the Northwest potential of power for defense."[64]

Interior explained it was becoming a party to Idaho Power's licensing case to show the FPC how Oxbow "would most definitely interfere with and be inconsistent with" Reclamation's Mountain Home Project. Oxbow "would conflict with and obstruct the construction of the Hells Canyon project . . . thereby conflicting with and obstructing the most comprehensive development for multiple purposes of the Snake River Basin." The High Dam's 1,400 megawatts underlay federal resource plans throughout the Northwest. They were needed "to meet the electric power requirements of the Pacific Northwest, to alleviate the long-run power shortage, to support expansion of industries essential to the national defense, to contribute to the general agricultural and industrial development and employment in that region, and to stimulate the large-scale development of the mineral resources of the Pacific Northwest."[65]

Chapman enjoyed the backing of a powerful, national coalition. Two years of Fair Deal partisanship had mobilized the Grange and National Farmers Union, organized labor, public-power users, and reclamation boosters behind Chapman's plea for the High Dam. Beginning in mid-1951, dozens of individual Granges had filed FPC protests against Oxbow. Often using identical language drafted by the national office, northwestern Granges spoke for "the people of the Snake River Valley [who] will be deprived of a million kilowatts of power in order that the private power company may produce a measly little 140,000 kilowatts." Without Hells Canyon High Dam, the Plaza, Washington, Grange claimed, "the development of the valley as a whole will be dealt a blow from which it will not recover in 50 years."[66]

"We do not believe that the selfish interests of a few individuals should be allowed to interfere with the development that could benefit all of the people instead of a private power company," Volney Martin of the Oregon Building and Construction Trades Council argued. "The Northwest is desperately in need of more power and to use a site such as Hells Canyon for a series of small dams would be a tragic waste of natural resources."[67]

Gus Norwood intervened in the FPC's Oxbow case for the Northwest Public Power Association. His public-power members—cities, public utility districts, rural co-ops—depended on wholesale BPA power. The High Dam would keep wholesale rates at "actual cost," whereas Oxbow would not only raise the price of power but also "interfere with the program of comprehensive development of the Hells Canyon of the Snake River for all purposes."[68]

Small farmers who needed Mountain Home Project water to start desert farms and Snake Basin businesses that hoped to supply them feared Oxbow would dash their dreams of agricultural plenty. Mountain Home mayor John Glasby, for the Mountain Home Reclamation Chapter, intervened in the FPC case because "the only feasible manner in which to achieve the realization of the Mountain Home Project . . . is through the development of the Snake River water resources through a comprehensive plan including the construction of the Hells Canyon Dam." Oxbow would snap shut the High Dam's cash box. Without its subsidies, the Mountain Home Project could not spill mountain rivers onto "1,000,000 acres of irrigable land in the Central and Upper Snake River Basin."[69]

Across the Snake, in eastern Oregon, an ambitious real-estate agent, newspaper publisher, and hotel keeper had formed the Hells Canyon Development Association "to secure the . . . construction of Hells Canyon Dam." Albert C. Ullman, Byron C. Brinton, and Clint Haight Jr., catalogued for the FPC the High Dam's benefits to their area: "cheap and plentiful electricity delivered to distributors and industries under established federal postage-stamp rates, major construction benefits, tourist and recreation stimulus, indirect flood control, navigation, and irrigation assistance." Their association was "very much concerned that this application of the Idaho Power Company be denied because of its adverse effects on [Reclamation's] comprehensive river development plan."[70]

As Costello convened the first day's hearings in Baker on 14 July, Idaho Power formally replied to the intervenors. General counsel Inman reminded the FPC that Congress had never authorized the CBIAC, let alone its comprehensive plan for the High Dam and Mountain Home Project. Even Interior Department planning was administrative daydreaming: until Congress approved the High Dam, none of Chapman's ambitious blueprints "confer upon him, or pre-empt for him, any rights with respect to the development of the Snake River . . . or with respect to the construction of the Secretary's proposed high dam at Hells Canyon, or lands required for such purposes." Inman asserted the High Dam's reservoir was actually intended to become a powerhouse for the Columbia Basin public-power domain, "inconsistent and in conflict with and inimical to the interests of future and further reclamation and irrigation development in the Snake River Valley." So much of the Snake's flow would be needed to justify the High Dam's power potential "that irrigation development now going on in Idaho, and reasonably to be expected in the future, will be jeopardized, rather than assisted, if the proposed High Dam at Hells Canyon is constructed."[71]

Costello's first comments in Baker reflected the Hells Canyon controversy's divisions. His file review "revealed a very definite cleavage in the matter here as to those who are supporting the applicant Idaho Power and those who are opposing the applicant." Less than an hour into the hearing, Costello had to admonish spectators to stop cheering and hooting witnesses. Baker businessman David C. Silven had just testified that he and his associates, who had organized the Snake River Free Enterprise Association of 1950, saw the "main issue is how socialistic we want to get." Costello announced, "Mr. Silven's statement has brought up something that we had better straighten out here and now. This Examiner, being a member of the public himself, is very well aware of the great controversy that has raged over the years with respect to the relative merits of private development as against public development. Unfortunately, this hearing cannot be a sounding-board for the philosophies on either side of that issue. . . . This is not going to a public debate on private vs. public power. We just can't get into it."[72]

In spite of trying to keep popular politics out of legal administration, Costello spent the next three days refereeing partisans who wanted to debate the Hells Canyon controversy. Two decades of New Deal public-power expansion had inspired many northwesterners to believe cheap electricity promised both economic abundance and more democratic politics. Five years' worth of anti-Communist paranoia had persuaded at least as many that public power threatened both capitalism and political liberty. More than just an artist's rendering and mimeographed charts, Hells Canyon High Dam inspired debate about the New Deal legacy in an anxious postwar nation. In summer 1952, "comprehensive, planned development" warred with "free enterprise," each a convenient slogan for clashing popular values about America's contested future.

F. R. Schank, a Portland engineer, testified that 98 percent of his profession in the region opposed the High Dam. Federal planners, led by Jebby Davidson, were simply "cooking up" power-potential statistics. High Dam proponents "apparently just have an intention to deceive the FPC as to the facts." Reclamation Bureau counsel Howard R. Stinson had testified that High Hells Canyon could generate at least 1,400 megawatts. Outraged, Schank cried, "I do object to having one of the public servants of the Interior Department get up here and say, don't you know that the power to be developed at Hells Canyon is twice that of the five [proposed Idaho Power] dams, when he knows that that isn't the fact."[73]

Power figures also concerned Ken Billington, state director for Washington's public utility districts. "This is not public vs. private power. The question here is whether the water resources of the region shall be developed to a maximum degree on a comprehensive multi-purpose basis, or whether the comprehensive development will be disrupted." Idaho Power's small Oxbow dam "will destroy or remove in excess of half a million kilowatts from the maximum potential power development." License Idaho Power and the FPC will become party to "destroying the full potential of the Snake River."[74]

Some farmers and ranchers hoped the High Dam meant a new era for the Snake Basin. Clarence Carter, a LaGrande, Oregon, farmer, told Costello how his region had languished since the Depression. Cheap public power brightened the future for "a farmer who is interested in the development of my community, State and Nation, one who is interested in having available sufficient cheap power to attract new industries. These industries attract people here, and thus increase the markets for the produce from our farms." But Wayne Phillips, a Baker-area rancher, thought "free enterprise is the main issue anyway," and Harney County rancher Lee Williams dismissed cheap power as a snare: "My main interest in this controversy is free enterprise, first, last, and all the time. . . . So far as I am concerned, if it was only a fourth of the power under free enterprise, I would still vote for it as against public power."[75]

Five hundred pages of testimony later, Costello climbed off Union Pacific's Portland Rose in Boise. He reconvened his public hearing in the Idaho House of Representatives chamber on 16 July. Again, he pleaded with the hundreds of spectators to stick to the facts. "If you are going to speak today and tell us what you feel about Socialism, or private power, or private enterprise being the American way of life, . . . we simply cannot entertain that kind of matter here." He knew the lawyers were prepared to make an administrative law case, but he suspected many in the crowd "wanted to express their views as to the creeping paralysis of Socialism, and other such things."

As he spoke, Democrats and Republicans were gearing up for the fall elections. Each nominating convention had cast the Hells Canyon controversy as a referendum on the New Deal's postwar viability. That was fine with Costello: "The FPC cannot decide that great issue which is now before the people of the United States, and also before the Congress of the United States, and it will avail you nothing to make such representations here."[76]

As in Baker, the Boise hearings soon pitted public power and federal water planning versus private capital and prior appropriation. Reclamation's regional counsel, Howard R. Stinson, declared at the outset the High Dam would undergird, not undermine, Snake Basin irrigation. "Water rights are not an issue in this hearing, and I agree they are irrelevant to this hearing." The High Dam's authorizing statute would stipulate that water to produce power was subordinate "to all validly established water rights for consumptive upstream use." Congress would reserve enough Snake River water to irrigate another 1.1 million acres of desert lands and to supplement irrigation on 1.2 million acres.[77]

Idaho Power's cultivation of Snake Basin irrigators bore fruit at the FPC Boise hearing. One after another, irrigation leaders lectured Costello and

Stinson about the High Dam's menace to their water, their way of life, and their satisfactory commercial and political relationship with the utility that powered their operations. Idaho State Reclamation Association president Charles Welteroth led off. Its forty-seven water districts in the middle Snake opposed the High Dam. "This grass-roots organization represents Idaho farmers on some 2 million acres of land" who share "a firm determination to protect their all-important use of water and water rights." Upstream from Welteroth, the Committee of Nine water districts covered the upper Snake Basin. Alex O. Coleman of St. Anthony testified his Committee of Nine associates "are somewhat resentful of the disposition of nonagriculturists within the state and foreigners from our neighboring states, who for selfish gain are trying to encourage legislation which will deprive us of our heritage and our dowry to future generations. We feel that they are infringing on our personal property rights which were guaranteed by the State Constitution."[78]

Idaho State Reclamation Association and the Committee of Nine did not command the loyalties of all irrigators, however. Those belonging to liberal national agricultural organizations welcomed the prospect of cheaper power and federal water. These groups were generally less prosperous and influential in Snake Basin politics. Truman Styner from Paul, Idaho, introduced himself as "a dirt farmer who from farming earns a living for myself and my family." He had been a Granger and National Farmers Union booster for years. Hells Canyon's fabulous public-power potential tantalized him. Compared to the High Dam, Oxbow "would be a little lump of concrete below several hundred feet of water."

Local business boosters confessed that, without the High Dam's irrigation subsidy from power sales into the Columbia Basin, the Mountain Home Project was doomed. Mountain Home's leading car dealer and mayor, John Glasby, frankly told Costello, "If we were to realize that project, we would have to have some sort of subsidy. Now the most natural and the most logical seemed to be through the development of hydroelectric power on the Snake River. . . . A thorough and comprehensive survey was made, and it was the unanimous choice of both the Army Engineers and the Bureau of Reclamation, and of practically everybody interested in the reclaiming of the new land, that this site was Hells Canyon."[79]

Hardly anyone in either Baker or Boise spoke of salmon. The bureau's High Dam plan earmarked $5 million toward fish conservation, Stinson mentioned in passing. Oregon conservation agency witnesses casually told

Costello in Baker, "We are here to put in an appearance, and to express our interest in the project, . . . and we want very much to hear the expressions and arguments both for and against." An elderly Snake River boatman, John Flynn of Weiser, spoke briefly but passionately about Hells Canyon's scenic beauty: "We have one of the greatest canyons in the US, I believe I would be safe to say in the world, and if we put a dam in we destroy it, we are destroying nature's gift to us." However, his chief concern was how the High Dam would flood mining claims he serviced with his motor launches.[80]

More typical of the stray comments about the Canyon's life-forms were Joseph, Oregon, hotel keeper Max Wilson's. He hoped a gigantic federal dam would draw tourists away from Grand Coulee. "In addition to the dam itself, which will be spectacular and inspiring, they will see the deepest gorge in the United States. Before they get there they can see the wondrous beauties of the Salmon River in Idaho, . . . and unless development is brought about, by means of access, and seasonal roads, these beautiful spots will never be visited by a great number of people as they deserve to be."[81]

Even two legendary Snake Basin anglers and hunters, Ted Trueblood and Clayton Davidson, portrayed the Hells Canyon controversy as a fight about recreational access rather than ecological consequences. Trueblood, a Nampa, Idaho, native, was the outdoors editor of *Field and Stream,* read monthly by millions of eager sports enthusiasts. Davidson, from his base near Sun Valley, was the guide to the stars: Ernest Hemingway and Gary Cooper preferred his company on trout streams, on hunting jaunts, and over a bottle and cards.

Speaking for Trueblood and the Ada County Fish and Game League, Davidson "believed the proposed Bureau of Reclamation High Dam in Hells Canyon would be far superior for future recreational development to Idaho Power's suggested low dam at Oxbow." Anadromous fish sacrificed in Hells Canyon were negligible. Fifty years of dam building above Hells Canyon had decimated their spawning grounds. "Therefore I believe," Davidson concluded, "that granting a permit for construction of a lowhead dam at Oxbow would merely add one more destructive dam to an already badly despoiled river. Such a permit would surely tend to delay the construction of the High Dam, which should produce the most outstanding recreation area in the world." The last witness to speak, Davidson was the only witness in two days of Boise hearings to mention how either of the warring Hells Canyon dams would affect Snake Basin migratory fish.[82]

One month after the FPC witnesses sweltered on hard chairs in the stuffy, windowless House of Representatives chamber, General Dwight Eisenhower, the Republican presidential nominee, marched onto the Idaho statehouse's front steps. Like the FPC witnesses, he also sensed the nation's uncertainty and nervous excitement. Unlike them, he addressed the largest crowd in Idaho history. Eisenhower spoke about Korea and the cold war, of course. Yet his first formal speech of his first campaign trip chiefly addressed a different national problem, although one at least as divisive and perplexing. More than twenty thousand listeners assembled in front of the statehouse and a national radio audience heard Eisenhower make Hells Canyon High Dam the theme of his first campaign speech. The Hells Canyon controversy had gone national.[83]

In the two years preceding Eisenhower's address, between spring 1950 and summer 1952, Idaho Power Company won the political initiative to redefine the Snake Basin's "public interest." By making its case for an FPC license for Oxbow dam outside agency hearing rooms, Idaho Power nationalized the Hells Canyon controversy. Company resistance to Hells Canyon High Dam elevated an administrative licensing case into a national referendum about the New Deal.

High Hells Canyon and the Mountain Home Project distilled Roosevelt's and Truman's essential New Deal vision. Federal power-agency planners, dedicated to realizing that vision in the postwar era, treated northwestern water and the life it sustained as national economic resources to secure perpetual material prosperity. So vital were those resources to national wealth that experts enjoyed legal discretion to command their transformation. Local interests would interfere with planned disposition of natural means to national power.

Idaho Power mobilized a broad, popular coalition to contest that vision. Passionate, popular dissent against what many citizens believed the New Deal had done, and Truman's Fair Deal intended, sustained opposition to the High Dam. Intense debates during the Hells Canyon controversy between 1950 and 1952 marked an environmental policy crisis, though no one explicitly used this term in the early postwar years. Americans would resolve the crisis using democratic methods to redefine the public interest. They pioneered new ways of adapting enduring cultural values—private liberty and public welfare—to natural systems.

Harry Truman proposed one definition of the public interest in the Snake River: Federalize Hells Canyon with the High Dam, dedicate its power sales to remodeling the Mountain Home Desert under Reclamation Bureau planning, and spread Bonneville Power's cheap public hydroelectricity to the Continental Divide. Tom Roach built a political movement that offered a different kind of public interest: Keep Snake Basin hydropower local, require new Hells Canyon dams to subordinate their stored water to state-sanctioned irrigation rights, and let Idaho Power serve its customers using a mix of market capital and state price-regulation.

Roach not only proposed Idaho Power's version of the public interest privately, by lobbying politicians and briefing administrators behind closed doors. The company's case for the Oxbow project and against the High Dam courted wider popular support for letting capitalists handle people's relations with natural systems. The company's private-power alternative tapped deep resistance to national control of the Snake Basin's fate. Roach captured the political initiative to redefine the public interest in water because people wanted a national referendum on New Deal environmental policy.

9 PRIVATIZING HELLS CANYON

Dwight Eisenhower's Partnership with Idaho Power

The postwar West still seemed a New Deal stronghold as the parties plotted their 1952 campaigns. Controlling the White House and Congress for two decades had entrenched the Democrats. In 1948 Harry Truman, like Franklin Roosevelt in 1944, had carried all but one state between the High Plains and Pacific. Even popular California governor Earl Warren, Thomas Dewey's vice-presidential candidate, had not lured enough westerners to vote Republican. However, the veneer of Democratic presidential voting overlay a core of conservative popular dissent. Despite presidential reverses, Republicans had elected nine of ten western governors after 1946. Dwight Eisenhower, who had probably never voted in an American election, finally discovered how his new party could transform dissenters into majorities. He and the Republicans won the West in 1952 by enflaming popular frustrations with the New Deal, especially federal land and water management. Eisenhower and his campaign advisers recognized accumulated resentment against federal regulation was combustible after 1950.[1]

Republican strategists carefully selected Boise, Idaho, for their candidate's first campaign speech after the July nominating convention. Idaho's ambitious young attorney general, Robert Smylie, persuaded them that politics and geography made Boise an ideal kickoff spot. There, at the center of resistance to Hells Canyon High Dam, Eisenhower would confer with western governors and address natural-resources policy. Idaho's four electoral votes mattered hardly at all. Boise, though, was the biggest city, and only state capital, near Hells Canyon. By spending nearly half his time with the governors, Eisenhower would contrast his respect for local governments with what he claimed was Democrats' "absentee landlord" attitude. By attacking New Deal public-power policy at the outset of the campaign, the can-

didate would show westerners how the Hells Canyon controversy symbolized his fundamental philosophical differences with Roosevelt and Truman.[2]
Eisenhower and his aides launched their campaign by attacking public-power
policy because Republicans sensed an opportunity to recruit disaffected western voters. Hells Canyon High Dam had already enmeshed both political
parties in a referendum about the New Deal's postwar legacy. The 1952 elections, coming amid Idaho Power Company's Federal Power Commission
licensing case, invited Americans to ratify or reject two decades of federal
planning and regulation of the national economy.

The Republican candidate wanted to stop public-power expansion as a
way of reducing the government's role in the economy. Beginning in the
New Deal and then accelerating under the Fair Deal, hydroelectricity had
become a "political football," Eisenhower believed. "Federal power zealots,"
as he termed them, distrusted local people and pursued national economic
centralization under White House direction. Selfish congressional barons,
eager to reward their regional supporters, approved costly, unnecessary
water projects to gain "a federal monopoly over power." Hells Canyon High
Dam would be "a massive Snake River monument to political maneuver
and federal pre-emption," an expensive tribute to "a theory which had
failed." If elected, Eisenhower vowed to "liberate the Pacific Northwest."
If Idaho Power won an FPC license to dam the Snake in Hells Canyon,
that would truly be "public power," as Eisenhower redefined it: "regulated
power, freely chosen in each instance by the citizens of each area, with the
federal government coming in as a cooperating partner where this seems
necessary or desirable."[3]

His Boise campaign speech in late August outlined Republicans' new
definition of the public interest in rivers. Eisenhower wanted to replace
federal control with a "partnership policy" for hydroelectricity. "We have
had for a long time in power a government that implies the philosophy of
the left." Of course, the Northwest needed more electricity, but "for every
problem the party in power has only one solution: further extension of the
power of the federal government. To reach every social goal it knows only
one means: a new, bigger, and more highly concentrated bureau in Washington." For twenty years, the Democrats' "answer to the problems of this
western area is to make of the West a federal province and make its people
economic dependents governed by remote control." If elected, he would
work with Republican congressional majorities so "we can have a government that does not grow complacent, that does not grow away from people

and become indifferent to them, and does not become arrogant in the exercise of its powers, but strives to be the partner and servant of the people and not their master."[4]

As a campaign slogan, "partnership" packed a punch. Eisenhower and his allies stressed Republicans would consult frequently and sincerely with a range of local interests before deciding how, or whether, to build federal dams and irrigation projects. Since 1932, federal-agency planners had made the crucial decisions about northwestern water. In Eisenhower's homely imagery, that pattern made the public-power domain an intrusive, domineering know-it-all: "The Government will build power dams. The Government will tell you how to distribute your power. Why, the Government does everything but come in and wash the dishes for the housewife." When he was president, he told the delighted throng in Boise, "We are not going to gear the West to Washington. We will simply gear Washington in its proper sphere to the West—as a partner."[5]

As a principle for changing New Deal public-power policy, partnership proved elastic. Eisenhower and the Republicans agreed westerners still needed federal money and advice to make water serve the region's people. "Let Washington participate in this great transformation," he assured his Boise audience. The level of federal participation would vary during Eisenhower's presidency, depending on the goals and methods proposed for particular hydropower and irrigation projects. In partnership's elasticity lay the rationale that explains Eisenhower's support for Idaho Power's plans to electrify Hells Canyon, as well as his endorsement, midway through his presidency, of the massive Upper Colorado Project's network of public dams and reclamation subsidies. He found Hells Canyon High Dam would have made Bonneville Power Administration too big a power seller over too much of the country. By contrast, he believed corporate utilities serving the Colorado Plateau could distribute hydroelectricity generated by the Upper Colorado Project. No Bonneville Power Administration threatened to become the Southwest's imperial electric overlord.[6]

Democrats welcomed Eisenhower's Boise attack on public power. If the Republicans wanted Hells Canyon to symbolize the New Deal in the Northwest, then Democrats appreciated the gift. They claimed the politically naive general, captive of the corporate bosses, was desecrating the New Deal Northwest's sacred icon. Democrats campaigned again as the "people's power party," as Truman had done brilliantly in 1948. From the president on down, they tore into Republican hydroelectric policies. One of the most polarizing postwar social and economic problems, power policy renewed Democrats' covenant with their New Deal heritage. *Public Utilities Fortnightly* correctly predicted, as the traditional Labor Day campaign season neared, Democrats "intend to play the power issue for all it is worth."

The Democratic Party platform pledged "sound, progressive development of the Nation's land and water resources" and praised "the wise policy of the Democratic Party in encouraging multipurpose projects throughout the country." Fair Deal public-power policy aimed to realize Roosevelt's commitment "that the Nation and its people receive maximum benefits from these resources to which they have an inherent right." Those opposing "acceleration of all such projects" sought "to prevent or retard utilization of the Nation's power and water resources for the benefit of the people." "Wider and more equitable distribution of electric energy at the lowest cost to the consumer with continuing preference to public agencies and REA [rural electric] co-operatives . . . is responsible for America's productive security over any nation in the world."[7]

President Truman used an October speech dedicating a new power dam at Bull Shoals, Arkansas, to pledge, "No matter what the private power companies say, if I have my way about it, we are going right ahead and develop our resources all over this country." On a campaign swing through the West, he charged that Republicans intended to privatize federal dams and public waters so "the resources of this country will no longer be developed for the people." If Eisenhower carried Republican majorities into Congress, the president warned a Bonners Ferry, Idaho, trackside audience, "Hells Canyon Dam will be out the window." His listeners knew he had battled for the High Dam, and "I'm going to keep right on fighting for it."[8]

Crucial elements of the postwar Democratic Party coalition—especially urban labor unions and liberal farm groups—portrayed public power at a crossroads in the 1952 elections. They insisted Eisenhower the president would replace maximum, planned, federal hydropower expansion with corporate-enforced scarcity. James G. Patton, president of the National Farmers Union, charged public-power opponents favored "dictatorship control of the power companies over electricity." United Automobile Workers president Walter Reuther accused power companies of "trying to commit America to the economics of scarcity by trying to erect major road blocks in the achievement of economic abundance."

Reuther's speech to the July 1952 Electric Consumers Conference—called by labor, farm, and public-power groups to back Truman's public-power campaign—illustrated how Democrats hoped cheap power spelled partisan victory. By identifying the postwar Fair Deal with the New Deal, labor leaders sought to persuade union members their future economic security depended on perpetually exploiting nature. According to Reuther, "The basic concept of public power says that we ought to take our resources and utilize them to the fullest, applying our most advanced technology, so that the people can have the benefits of the highest volume of power at the lowest possible cost. That is the concept of abundance translated into practical achievement." Corporate utilities, by contrast, hoped to profit from scarcity: "Keep the production down as low as possible and the rates up as high as possible," Reuther characterized private utilities' strategy. If "private monopolies" prevailed, Interior secretary Oscar Chapman warned the Electric Consumers Conference, their high power prices would "further accentuate inequality."[9] Just in time for the fall campaign, the conference published *The People's Fight for Low Cost Power*. Described by *Public Power*'s Alex Radin as "a vital document which deserves the widest possible audience—in and out of the power field," *The People's Fight* hailed "the important role of Federal power in meeting the nation's power requirements." It blasted "the private power companies' assault on public and cooperative power programs."[10]

New Deal stalwart Warren Magnuson (D-Wash.), campaigning in southwest Idaho, emphasized Democrats' postwar commitment to public-power expansion and federal resources planning. Hells Canyon High Dam, the senator told a campaign rally in Nampa, "would provide new payrolls, open up vast new phosphate deposits to provide low-cost fertilizer, cut power rates, and aid flood control and navigation." Its power revenues, flowing into the Reclamation Bureau's Mountain Home Project, "would leave upstream water sufficient to irrigate more than a million new acres of land and supply supplemental irrigation to a million and a quarter acres." He told his audience of High Dam boosters he "wanted to steer away from politics as much as possible," but then urged listeners to elect Idaho Democratic congressional candidates Gracie J. Pfost and W. H. Jensen to help him authorize High Hells Canyon in 1953. Magnuson ridiculed Idaho Power Company's Oxbow project. Electrifying Hells Canyon Tom Roach's way meant "little dams with little power . . . built by little minds for little private profits." The company had duped Eisenhower and Republicans throughout the West "into their selfish war against government multi-purpose projects such as Hells Canyon."[11]

Duped or not, Eisenhower detested what he believed was the New Deal legacy of costly dams, comprehensive plans, and federal supervision. In Seattle, in October, he delivered what aides billed as the Republican's second major address about water and power. Eight thousand packed the Civic Ice Arena. Another five thousand, unable to secure seats, flocked to Memorial Stadium across the street to listen on loudspeakers. For twenty years, Eisenhower contended, Democrats have subscribed to the "idea of whole-hog federal government." By planning mammoth new federal dams, Truman's Interior Department "is seeking a monopoly not just in the West but throughout the nation." Of course, "water and power are the lifeblood of the great northwest." But "the sly apostles of Fair Dealism" are "far more interested in empire-building than in the conclusions and convictions of responsible officials of the regions where all these facilities should be owned and operated."

Eisenhower's Seattle address did not mention the Columbia Basin Inter-Agency Committee or Bonneville Power Administration by name. But he plainly signaled Republicans' intent to leaven CBIAC's and BPA's federal plans with a larger measure of local opinion. "The hard-core difference between those power-seeking politicians and the rest of us who still believe in basic American institutions" lies in "the whole-hog theory that the federal government must do everything for us and to us." If elected, he vowed to replace CBIAC with "a new interstate body, its members chosen in accordance with state law, [who] should have full equality with the federal members who sit in to advise and assist."[12]

Across the Snake, the *Idaho Daily Statesman* welcomed the Republicans' initiative. Eisenhower understood "natural resource development is an important part of the Republican program." His plan "for development by the states, with federal assistance, rather than federal domination, is encouraging." "President Truman has led the pack of socialist wolves who have deliberately misrepresented the natural resource problem at every opportunity." A Republican victory in November "will lead to a housecleaning in the Interior Department which will put an end to socialism in natural resources, and return development to the states."[13]

One week before the election, northwestern New Deal loyalists reaffirmed that hydroelectric expansion and federal planning symbolized Democrats' partisan goals. Meeting in Nampa, the Idaho-Oregon Hells Canyon Association endorsed only Democrats in key races across the region. The association had coordinated testimony on behalf of the High Dam at the

July FPC hearings. Its leaders—Baker realtor Albert C. Ullman, Mountain Home mayor John Glasby, and Vale judge Sewell Stanton—had all testified against Idaho Power. The association closed its election rally by endorsing "immediate authorization and construction" of the High Dam and opposing Idaho Power's Oxbow project.[14]

High Dam opponents also pinned their own hopes on the voters' will. Idaho governor Len B. Jordan told Idaho Power's outside counsel R. P. Parry, one week before Election Day, he "expected to win." But if "the Democrats should win on November 4, however, I think they will not waste any time in getting underway with their program" to federalize Hells Canyon hydropower. Jordan asked Parry to recommend "delaying tactics" he could use at an early November CBIAC meeting, called by the Reclamation Bureau to obtain governors' endorsement of a comprehensive Northwest water plan.[15]

Voters went to the polls in record numbers in 1952. Eighty percent of Idaho adults cast ballots for president. Eisenhower matched Roosevelt's 1936 record victory margin in Idaho, taking 67 percent of the vote. Oregonians also backed the general. Eastern Oregon's Republican congressman, Sam Coon, won handily after campaigning vigorously against the High Dam. However, energetic union get-out-the-vote efforts in Idaho's congressional district embracing Hells Canyon pushed Democrat Gracie Pfost past one-term Republican John Wood by fewer than one thousand votes. Upstream, in the heart of the Snake Basin's irrigation society, incumbent Hamer Budge defeated his Democratic opponent by better than 2:1.

Pfost interpreted her narrow win as a High Dam mandate. "I will do whatever I can to get approval of Hells Canyon Dam," she promised the day after the election. So fiercely did Pfost pursue her chief campaign theme that she soon earned the sobriquet "Hell's Belle," a backhanded compliment she cheerfully accepted. If she could secure the giant federal dam, "Idaho and her citizens may benefit to the utmost in the development of hydroelectric power, water transportation, and prevention of soil erosion and floods."[16]

Hell's Belle would find good intentions in short supply on her road to Washington. Sweeping Republican victories in 1952 changed everything about the Hells Canyon controversy. Dwight Eisenhower knew it, as did Governors Jordan of Idaho and McKay of Oregon. So did Idaho Power president Tom Roach and general counsel Arthur Inman. Gone—or going— would be Truman, Interior secretary Oscar Chapman, Reclamation commissioner Michael Straus, public-power sparkplug C. Girard Davidson, and

BPA administrator Paul Raver. Gone—or going—would be FPC chairman Thomas Buchanan. An unconfirmed Truman appointee, Buchanan had resisted processing Idaho Power's Oxbow license application. He and his presidential patron agreed to act only after concluding that election-year FPC field hearings would be public-power pep rallies in the Northwest. Gone—or going—would be CBIAC's primacy in deciding the Snake Basin's fate.[17]

Even before Eisenhower was inaugurated in January 1953, he had initiated detailed secret planning to remodel the federal administrative agencies responsible for power policy, the Interior Department and FPC. Republican corporate executives had funded a study of the entire executive branch by McKinsey Company, a leading business strategy consultant, during the campaign. McKinsey's report, *Restaffing the Executive Branch of the Federal Government at the Policy Level*, warned Eisenhower, "In order to effectuate the will of the people, . . . [you] must—within a brief period of time—substitute a new and different philosophy in the executive management of domestic and international affairs." Simply by replacing key administrators, "the new president can make the will of the people effective. Full control of policy and programs can be obtained through proper restaffing of no more than [610] positions—and probably fewer." The president-elect "fully appreciated" McKinsey's advice.[18]

A new Interior secretary would wield "high influence over the formation and approval of policies of national importance." McKinsey's report identified the FPC chairman, undersecretary of Interior, and assistant Interior secretary for water and power as second in importance only to the Interior secretary "in achieving the objective of implanting a new philosophy in the management of the executive branch of the federal government." For FPC chairman, McKinsey urged Eisenhower to identify someone with "an executive background in business, government, or law with experience in the fields of electric or gas utilities and familiar with the process of regulation." A new FPC chairman could at once "exert a strong or decisive influence on the administration's policies," so this post "should be restaffed *immediately*." McKinsey also advised Eisenhower to replace promptly the Interior Department's chief legal officer as well as the BPA administrator and Reclamation commissioner with "individuals sharing the philosophy of the new administration."[19]

Public Utilities Fortnightly, the industry trade journal, speculated about the president's new public-power personnel. "It is to be expected politically that General Eisenhower will not permit Chairman Buchanan's appointment to stand after President Truman leaves office. . . . While the policies of the FPC, let alone the entire new administration—with respect to utilities—would hardly seem to turn on that of an individual member, observers are beginning to regard it as a weather vane."[20] Eisenhower's first cabinet appointment electrified the weather vane, especially in the Northwest. Oregon governor Douglas McKay's nomination for Interior secretary dominated the headlines. A third-generation Oregonian whose grandfather had been a Hudson's Bay Company fur-trade factor, his term signaled "the end of an era of active government involvement in the development of the country's natural resources," according to the *New York Times*. Talking with Portland's *Oregonian*, McKay said, "I am against monopolies of any kind, in the department of Interior or in private enterprise. It seems to me there ought to be room for both public and private power."[21]

Gary S. Reichard, who closely studied Eisenhower's first term, has judged McKay "the most conservative" of Eisenhower's cabinet secretaries. Sherman Adams, the president's first staff chief, deemed the successful auto dealer "probably more conservative than anyone else in the conservative Eisenhower Cabinet." Adams, and the president-elect himself, originally favored Washington governor Arthur Langlie for Interior, but he had just been reelected and considered himself duty bound to remain in Olympia for four years. The leading historian of Eisenhower-era natural resources policy, Elmo Richardson, has concluded that McKay, hair carefully parted down the middle, "suffered foot-in-the-mouth affliction." But McKay was loyal, even deferential, to the triumphant general, reliable on public power, and eager to serve his chief.[22]

Public-power advocates tried to sound conciliatory. McKay, *Public Power* opined, "has played an important role in charting the development of the Columbia and its tributaries." Bonneville Power administrator Paul Raver quickly issued a press release praising the Oregonian's "faithful and generous work" on CBIAC. "It is my sincere conviction that the Pacific Northwest can feel secure in the furtherance of this development program under the guidance and leadership" of the new Interior secretary. Salem sources told United Press that McKay's interest in hydroelectrifying the Willamette Valley hinted at his flexibility on public-power policy.[23]

Governor Jordan's reaction to McKay's nomination offered a more accurate clue to the new Interior secretary's priorities: "He's a good businessman and outstanding governor. I'm as pleased as I can be." Oregon's rebellious Republican senator, Wayne Morse, warned public-power supporters they faced desperate fights ahead on Hells Canyon with McKay at Interior. "This is a great day for the reactionaries that are out to plunder the people," Morse fumed. "McKay is a well-recognized stooge of the tidelands thieves, the private utility gang and the selfish interests which place materialistic values above human values." Oregon's state Democratic chairman, Howard Morgan, warned that the governor sympathized "with the knifing of projects such as Hells Canyon."[24]

Hopeful his nomination promised a major power-policy shift at Interior after Eisenhower's inauguration, *Public Utilities Fortnightly* hailed McKay as "a man who believes in local responsibilities, . . . a free enterprise man . . . who has equal respect for [the people's] right to choose to have service by tax-paying private ownership." *Fortnightly*'s editor, Francis X. Welch, advised, "The main thing the utility industry has to do to get along with him is to keep the public interest as the top objective." Edison Electric Institute president Bayard L. England spoke for the utility industry when he confessed he was "looking ahead to the next five years."[25]

Idaho Power quickly heeded Welch's and Bayard's advice to "look ahead." During the 1952 campaign, public-power forces had ridiculed the company's modest, run-of-river Oxbow dam. "With a power capability only a fraction of that of Hells Canyon," it could never "provide maximum public benefits from this valuable public resource," *Public Power* charged. One week after Election Day, Tom Roach and Arthur Inman abruptly unveiled a major expansion of Idaho Power's Oxbow plan: it had become a three-dam complex combining flood-control storage with more power production.[26]

"Plan A," a totally new design for hydroelectrifying Hells Canyon, replaced the low-head Oxbow dam with three dams, to be built at about the same time, both above and below Oxbow. The uppermost, Brownlee Dam, would create a 55-mile-long reservoir storing up to 1.5 million acre-feet of spring runoff behind a 227-foot-high earth structure. The middle dam, still called Oxbow, would generate slightly more power than the original proposal. Eight miles below Oxbow, another low dam, Hells Canyon, would generate 270 megawatts, about 50 percent more than the original Oxbow proposal. Together, though, the three-dam Hells Canyon Complex would still generate less power and store less runoff than would the Reclamation Bureau's High Dam. Even if stacked one atop the other, Idaho Power's proposed three dams would still be lower than the federal behemoth.

Dated 28 October, the new three-dam supplemental application demonstrated Idaho Power had closely watched the elections. If Eisenhower won,

Plan A could be filed immediately after Election Day; if not, it could be with-held or filed later, depending on how the FPC assessed the original Oxbow proposal during licensing. Intimately involved with northwestern public life, Roach and his managers had spent five years mobilizing national opinions about power. They drafted Plan A for political as much as economic rea-sons. Adding a storage reservoir behind Brownlee Dam neutralized the Army Engineers' flood-control and navigation concerns about the Snake. Boosting low Oxbow's generating capacity with two more dams acknowledged BPA had raised real fears in the Northwest about electricity shortages if the Korean War intensified.[27]

Plan A also capitalized on Eisenhower's campaign promise that public-private power partnerships served the public interest. Inman emphasized Plan A enabled "private enterprise . . . to develop the river fully for power without injury to irrigation and reclamation, and provide accompanying flood control benefits. It will also provide maximum feasible power benefits downstream in critical power years."[28] The bigger Hells Canyon plan sug-gests how relentless campaign criticism of "little" Oxbow had stung Idaho Power. The timing of the company's announcement suggests cooperation, or at least consultation, with victorious Republicans now assembling their new presidential administration and congressional majorities. Outgoing Reclamation Bureau officials grudgingly praised Idaho Power's "shrewdness" in meshing its new plan to Eisenhower's partnership strategy.[29]

High Dam advocates, in and out of the federal government, exploded. Idaho-Oregon Hells Canyon Association termed Plan A "an attempt to silence the Bureau of Reclamation's fight against the company's Oxbow license." Outgoing Interior secretary Chapman, together with the Idaho-Oregon Hells Canyon Association, asked the FPC to dismiss Idaho Power's license case because Plan A materially changed its Oxbow proposal. Interior wanted the company to start over by filing a new license application so the department could brief and argue against it.[30]

Federal Power Commission staff approved Plan A as an amendment to Idaho Power's original Oxbow project application. The full commission agreed on 3 December, ruling "an applicant for license has the right to sup-plement its application." The commissioners also approved Idaho Power's request to delay the technical evidence phase of the license hearing until 13 April 1953.[31]

As 1952 ended, Eisenhower's win meant Idaho Power's strategic victory. The company could now shift the Hells Canyon controversy's third phase from electoral politics to administrative law. For the next three years, Idaho Power's three-dam plan dominated the FPC license hearing's focus and pace. Plan A won the crucial fight to define the hearing's legal and technical issues. Having lost the strategic initiative, the Reclamation Bureau and its public-power allies lost the political initiative as well. Idaho Power's legal gambit enabled the Eisenhower administration to shape the Hells Canyon controversy to emphasize private power's merits. The new Hells Canyon Complex proposal offered about two-thirds of the High Dam's power potential, instead of Oxbow's paltry one-seventh. Brownlee Dam's storage capacity placated the Army Corps and regional navigation boosters.

High Dam advocates tried to preserve their eroding legal position in the month before Eisenhower took office. In late December 1952 and early January 1953, the National Farmers Union (NFU), National Rural Electric Cooperative Association, and Department of Agriculture petitioned the FPC to intervene as full parties when the evidentiary phase of Idaho Power's license hearing resumed. National Farmers Union's petition outlined their common argument: Idaho Power's private dams "would interfere with the program of comprehensive development of the Hells Canyon of the Snake River for all purposes, and with full utilization of the hydroelectric power potential thereof." At risk were cheap public power, which would "stimulate the growth of population and industry [and] . . . permit fuller electrification of farms," as well as the nation's fertilizer industry, which required ample supplies of inexpensive electricity to exploit Idaho's and Utah's phosphate deposits. Outgoing agriculture secretary Charles Brannan contended Northwest preference customers could not meet future demands without cheap public power.[32]

Alex Radin's new-year preview column in *Public Power* began, "1953 will be a decisive year for public power." Utility companies were spoiling for a fight against federal power preference laws. A Republican Congress looked set to slow dam construction and delay new starts. The Supreme Court had heard oral arguments in the controversial "Roanoke Rapids" case, testing whether the FPC could license private dams on interstate rivers targeted for public power by federal comprehensive plans. Interior secretary-designate Douglas McKay "has indicated that he will place greater emphasis on State and local participation in regional development programs."

The Truman administration's final budget message still urged Congress to authorize Hells Canyon High Dam. But no one really noticed. In the Northwest, even Bonneville Power sensed 1953's political changes counseled both caution and adaptation. Bonneville Power administrator Paul Raver surprised his own advisory committee by requesting they study a plan to abolish the agency, replacing it with a new interstate compact that would use power-revenue bonds to "construct dams and operate the present Federal power system."[33]

"There has been a tendency in the past to give the breaks to all the public deals," McKay told the Senate Interior Committee at his January confirmation hearing, when questioned about New and Fair Deal policies. He believed federal power policy had "throttled" private dams in the Northwest. Even before Inauguration Day, the committee unanimously recommended McKay's confirmation by the full Senate.[34] Len Jordan whooped to his old friend J. C. "Jep" Jeppson of Lewiston, "I have so much confidence in the new administration and in Secretary of Interior-Designate McKay that I feel sure that we can work out a resource program that will make sense and stand the test of practicality as well." Things were moving so well in Washington, D.C., that Jordan even hoped McKay would heed his recommendation to appoint Idaho Power outside counsel R. P. Parry to "a top-level position in the Department of Interior, in which case Idaho's interests will be in good hands."[35]

Parry was not headed to Washington, D.C., quite yet. He was helping, though, to remake postwar natural-resources policy in the crowded intersection where law and politics collide. By early 1953, he wielded legal and political power few attorneys in Idaho history have ever rivaled. His Twin Falls firm was at once negotiating Idaho Power's water-rights applications for its Hells Canyon dams with state engineer Mark Kulp, readying the company's FPC licensing case, and representing Governor Jordan on the Columbia River Interstate Compact Commission. Parry's legal authority defied conventional rules that separated private rights from public service. He simultaneously represented two clients with different, likely inimical, interests to the Snake's flow: the state of Idaho during Interstate Compact Commission negotiations and Idaho Power in water-rights and dam-license matters. As Idaho Power's chief trial counsel in the FPC case, he was dedicating more of his practice to the crucial task of winning a Hells Canyon dam license. Although corporate general counsel Arthur Inman still exercised substantial responsibility, Parry was, by early spring 1953, managing the legal offensive designed to attain both the company's, and Governor Jordan's, most important political project.[36]

Eisenhower and McKay's new power-policy team complemented Parry's legal work. In March, the president nominated four westerners to key posts: Jerome K. Kuykendall to chair the Federal Power Commission, Ralph Tudor as undersecretary of Interior, Fred Aandahl as assistant Interior secretary for lands and water, and Clarence A. Davis as department solicitor. Tudor's and Davis's engineering and legal experience supported McKay's effort to end the New Deal public-power era. Aandahl now held Jebby Davidson's old job. A former North Dakota governor and congressman, he supplied McKay vital congressional credibility.[37]

Kuykendall would head an independent regulatory agency, theoretically responsible to neither the president nor any cabinet officer. However, the Eisenhower team carefully chose him to redeem the campaign's partnership pledge on northwestern power. Kuykendall had chaired Washington's state utility regulatory agency, ideally suiting him to achieve the McKinsey Company's goal of helping the president find experienced state regulators who shared the Republicans' distaste for federal hydropower.[38] When the young Tacoma attorney faced a long list of questions during his one-day confirmation hearing before the Senate Commerce Committee, he offered specific answers to few of them, simply promising to "use my best and independent judgment to decide what is in the public interest." Washington's Democrats, Magnuson and Jackson, questioned Kuykendall vigorously about the Hells Canyon license case. He cheerfully admitted he had anticipated their questions, but declined detailed answers because he could not prejudge a case he would have to decide. Of course, he assured the committee, he would make sure FPC gathered all relevant facts before deciding to license or deny Idaho Power's application. On close calls, Kuykendall admitted he would probably side with the administration, but as a principle of regulatory independence "my own judgment will guide me." The Senate confirmed him the next day.[39]

Ralph Tudor became Interior undersecretary free from Kuykendall's need to appear independent and dispassionate. For eighteen months, until he returned to private life in autumn 1954, he zealously executed Eisenhower's pledge to reduce federal influence over Hells Canyon's fate. Principal owner of a San Francisco engineering firm, Tudor had served the Army Corps of Engineers with distinction after graduating from West Point. He had had firsthand experience with massive New Deal public-works projects, supervising construction of the Oakland–San Francisco Bay Bridge during the late 1930s and Portland's new municipal-military airport and Vanport dikes along the Columbia in the early 1940s. As commander of the corps' North

Pacific Division during the war, Tudor had initiated the Columbia and Snake basin studies underlying the corps' abortive push in the late 1940s to construct Hells Canyon High Dam. Familiarity with Northwest hydropower suited him for his first postwar civilian job as chief engineer for the construction firm that had built most of Idaho Power's Snake River dams, Morrison-Knudsen Company. Harry Morrison's recommendation confirmed McKay's instincts about Tudor, whom he had known for at least a decade.[40]

Tudor and McKay relied heavily on Clarence Davis, the new Interior solicitor, for legal and policy advice as they considered dramatic changes in the department's New Deal hydropower philosophy. Davis, a Lincoln, Nebraska, attorney, was a protégé of Senator Hugh Butler, the conservative Nebraska Republican who now chaired the Senate Interior Committee. Davis had advised both local governments and the Nebraska state public-power agency. After Tudor retired in autumn 1954, Davis replaced him as undersecretary of Interior.[41]

Like any good lawyer who encounters a complicated problem for the first time, Davis quickly decided McKay, Tudor, and Aandahl needed more time to study Interior's options in the Hells Canyon FPC case. On 3 March, Davis asked FPC hearing examiner William Costello, who would preside during the evidentiary phase of the license case, to extend for at least one month the hearing's 13 April resumption. Idaho Power's Inman "regretted the delay" and hoped Interior would "cooperate fully to expedite hearing and final disposition [of] our application."[42]

Idaho Power did not have long to wait. A three-month fusillade of Eisenhower administration decisions soon vindicated Idaho Power's hopes for "full cooperation." New agriculture secretary Ezra Taft Benson signaled the coming Hells Canyon upheaval. On 11 February, he withdrew his department from the FPC case, reversing his predecessor's last-minute intervention in December 1952. Agriculture solicitor Karl Loos advised Costello that any information the department had to offer could be presented by other parties.[43]

In early March, McKay ordered Fish and Wildlife Service's Northwest office to restudy Hells Canyon by comparing Idaho Power's three-dam plan with Hells Canyon High Dam. By 10 March, Fish and Wildlife and Idaho's Fish and Game Department agreed the company's dams would best protect migratory fish if they complied with "reasonable" FPC license conditions recommended by state conservation agencies. Fish and Wildlife asked

Idaho and Oregon to suggest "means and measures for the prevention or mitigation of fishery losses" in Hells Canyon. Idaho Fish and Game director T. B. Murray welcomed the invitation. Since the end of the war, federal biologists had had to clear regional fish policy with Roy Bessey's omnipotent Northwest Field Committee. The Columbia Basin Inter-Agency Committee had operated as if adapting salmon and steelhead to Snake Basin dams was solely a federal responsibility. Now, if the FPC licensed Idaho Power's Hells Canyon Complex, then legally enforceable conditions, negotiated between state and federal agencies, "should give ample protection to the anadromous fishes."[44]

In early April, Tudor recommended that McKay make the Hells Canyon controversy's single most dramatic decision. He concluded Interior should no longer support the Reclamation Bureau's High Hells Canyon plan or oppose Idaho Power's Hells Canyon Complex. By formally withdrawing from the FPC case, the department would dramatize its commitment to Eisenhower's new "partnership" policy. The Supreme Court's recent "Roanoke Rapids" decision against Interior in *Chapman v. Federal Power Commission* convinced the undersecretary that both law and public opinion now opposed public-power expansion. The *Oregonian* editorialized, *Chapman* "virtually wiped out the new deal theory that the federal government has primary responsibility to provide power to any area or group of people." In the diary he sent weekly to colleagues in his former San Francisco firm, Tudor explained, "I am sure that a fight on Hells Canyon would result in exactly the same result. . . . In light of this legal record, Congress' failure to authorize [it] as a Federal project, and our own philosophies, we are simply going to withdraw our opposition and accept whatever ruling the Federal Power Commission may render." Such a step, thought the *Oregonian*, "will stir up a hornet's nest of vociferous protestations" because it is "a major change in the policy of the past administration on one of the most explosive private vs. public power questions in the Pacific Northwest and the nation."[45]

McKay and Tudor expected many angry hornets to buzz them and their president when Interior withdrew from the Hells Canyon controversy. Solicitor Davis borrowed time for the department and White House to coordinate damage control, asking FPC for two more weeks "to complete its review" of Hells Canyon's status. Even a commission still controlled 4–1 by Democratic appointees could sense something big was up. It granted Davis's request the next business day. A commissioner called on Tudor, trying to find out what he and McKay intended. The previous week, public-power supporters had introduced a new High Dam authorization bill in both houses of Congress. The unnamed commissioner "suggested that we drag our feet on the Hell's Canyon matter and thus, perhaps some of the controversy and excitement would die out." Highly improper, this ex parte contact convinced Tudor that the FPC was desperately trying to dodge the political heat erupting from Hells Canyon. "I was not very sympathetic to that idea for I would like to get it cleaned up."

Shortly after this startling conversation, the commission, on its own motion, again delayed resumption of the case until 7 July. To Tudor, the explanation for suddenly changing a hearing date the commission had just set three days before rang hollow. "Their excuse, believe it or not, is that they have run out of funds to transport their witnesses back here to Washington. . . . I suspect they are doing just what they suggested we do and this is 'dragging their feet.' That is a regular type of operation here in Washington."[46]

Eisenhower and his cabinet authorized McKay to announce Interior's withdrawal from the Idaho Power case as long as the western governors agreed. At noon on 5 May, McKay and Tudor outlined their decision at a private lunch with the governors. All eleven—all Republicans—concurred, although California's Earl Warren and Colorado's Dan Thornton sought, and got, assurances that Eisenhower and McKay were not completely abandoning federal hydropower generation. The northwesterners—Jordan, Langlie, and new Oregon governor Paul Patterson—told Interior's leaders "they were well pleased."

Nearly 175 reporters clustered at 1:00 P.M. in Interior's auditorium to hear McKay and Tudor explain why Eisenhower's drive to cut the federal budget deficit made it impossible to justify spending upwards of $1 billion to build and operate the High Dam and Mountain Home Project. "The Department of the Interior would be playing the reprehensible part of a 'dog in the manger,'" McKay announced, "if it insisted on opposing a badly needed development that private capital is ready and willing to undertake, if the plan proposed by the Idaho Power Company is reasonably comparable as to results, while the Department itself has no assurance that it can carry out its own plan without extended delay."

Tudor handled most questions, but McKay could not resist telling the press conference, "If Congress asks me, I would say 'no' to the Hells Canyon project." Asked if Interior was now considering abandoning the High Dam altogether, even if the FPC denied Idaho Power's license, McKay shot back, "Could be." Even though he deemed many of the questions either confused or hostile, Tudor "thought it was a very excellent press conference and although it was a very rough and tumble affair, I felt that we were treated fairly."[47]

That afternoon, Solicitor Davis informed FPC chairman Kuykendall that Interior "respectfully requested that the petition of intervention heretofore filed on behalf of this Department be withdrawn." Interior would open its Hells Canyon files to assist the commission in "a full and complete examination of the merits" of Idaho Power's three-dam plan. But "the granting of licenses for the construction of dams and hydroelectric plants on the rivers of the United States is the primary function and responsibility of the Federal Power Commission and not of this Department."[48]

"We are, of course, being criticized by a number of the columnists who, strangely enough, all seem to be New Dealers," Tudor mused during the week after Interior's bombshell. *Public Power* accused Interior of suppressing studies supportive of High Hells Canyon and "throwing in the sponge on a plan which would provide more power and flood storage than the Idaho Power Co. plan." Representative Pfost of Idaho bemoaned the possible loss of a federal project that would subsidize irrigation of one million acres, attract new industry to the Snake Basin, and "firm up power all the way to Portland, Oregon." Democratic National Committee chairman Stephen Mitchell flew to Idaho to proclaim, "Hells Canyon looks like a natural place for a high dam." Senator Morse, on the brink of officially joining the Democratic Party, called McKay's decision "a shocking betrayal of the public interest. It is further proof of what I warned during the campaign—that the Eisenhower administration would be a tool of American monopolies." Senator Magnuson called Hells Canyon "one of the greatest power sites in the world. It belongs to all the people and it is the duty of the Department of Interior to represent the people's interests in these natural resources."[49]

To the American Public Power Association convention, one week after his Hells Canyon announcement, McKay pleaded for "sweeping aside the emotions of public power and entering into the discussion of the problems ahead with one goal in sight—get the facts and then act accordingly." He believed the federal upriver hydroelectric offensive would have required Congress ultimately to spend $1.7 billion and federalize all available Snake water to secure High Hells Canyon. To justify the High Dam's size, the Reclamation Bureau had coupled it to the Mountain Home Project. To earn enough power-sale revenues to subsidize Mountain Home, Reclamation insisted on selling cut-rate hydropower to a growing class of preference customers in the Columbia Basin. To reach those customers, Reclamation needed new transmission lines tying Hells Canyon into BPA's grid. To attain the High Dam's claimed 1,500 megawatts capacity, the Army Corps would have to build five more new Columbia River dams. To command the water necessary to fill the High Dam's immense reservoir, the Reclamation Bureau had to get rights to store all unappropriated flows of the Snake.

To execute a project so vast, McKay claimed, New Deal planners built up the Interior Department "with one idea in mind, that of a completely federalized electric generating system, a Government monopoly in large areas of the United States." Even though the Eisenhower administration had to accept what had already been done by Democrats for twenty years, "it is incumbent on us to establish new trends that will lead us in what we believe is the right direction." Unmoved, APPA resolved to fight Idaho Power's FPC license application, still favoring "the full and early development by public agencies of [the Snake River's] feasible hydro-electric potentialities." As for preferences enjoyed by public-power distributors, Congress and the hydro-electric agencies should meet their needs first and "bring benefits of Federal power to all preference customers in the area on an equitable basis."[50]

Idaho Power lawyers smoothly exploited Interior's withdrawal from the FPC case. The company's timing suggests its executives either had advance notice about McKay's 5 May announcement or were given remarkably prescient legal advice. One day after McKay and Tudor's press conference, the company formally filed with FPC two more license applications covering Brownlee and low Hells Canyon dams. As with Plan A, abruptly unveiled the week after the 1952 election, the new legal steps meshed with political events. Idaho Power committed to build all three dams as soon as the commission licensed them. Company consultant M. O. Leighton indicated engineering studies, only just finished, prompted filing the new three-dam application. But he, attorney Pat Parry, and their clients were politically sophisticated enough to see McKay's reversal had essentially invited Idaho Power to control how the FPC case would unfold.[51]

One week later, the FPC approved Interior's withdrawal from the Idaho Power case. On 26 May, the commission ruled the company's new three-dam license application presented no new issues justifying more public hearings in the Northwest. The FPC ordered the technical evidence phase of Idaho Power's case to begin in Washington, D.C., on 7 July. Roach and Parry, with McKay's and Eisenhower's help, had used their new political leverage to structure the administrative-law case they sought. Company lawyers could now argue private power was willing and able to electrify Hells Canyon. Interior's withdrawal from the case limited the federal role to disinterested adviser—Interior's mission—and impartial judge—FPC's task under the Federal Power Act.[52]

Governor Jordan and Idaho's chief water engineer Mark Kulp officially endorsed Idaho Power's three-dam plan. The company was satisfying all Idaho water laws. Kulp had already negotiated with Inman and Roach a subordination clause in water-appropriation permits needed by the Hells Canyon Complex. Idaho Power permanently guaranteed Snake Basin irrigators could claim all presently undiverted upstream flows. "The restrictions written into the permits under authority of the Idaho Constitution and statutes," Jordan and Kulp informed the FPC, "adequately safeguard future upstream irrigation development."[53]

Jordan, Kulp, McKay, and Tudor defined the public interest in the Snake as a blend of local control, business enterprise, and state regulation of water and power. McKay and Tudor, like Eisenhower, believed New Deal power policy consolidated too much authority in the hands of unelected federal planners and administrators. Far from being a "Hells Canyon give-away," as Democrats were charging, "what we are doing is taking these things away from the bureaucrats and giving them back to the people," Tudor confided to his diary. "If there ever was a 'give-away' program in existence in this country, it has been during the last twenty years when the regime here in Washington has been 'giving away' the assets of the country for the benefit of a few."[54]

From his office facing Jordan's across the statehouse rotunda, secretary of state Ira H. Masters, a Democrat, reminded FPC that the governor was not the only statewide-elected official representing Idahoans. "On behalf of the masses of the common people," Masters argued, "The remaining undeveloped land in the Snake River Basin, like the Mountain Home area, will lose its last best chance for irrigation if Idaho loses the chance of having the big Hells Canyon Dam built as a Federal project so that the surplus revenues can help finance the irrigation programs." The "power trust and the predatory interests of our State" had so corrupted Jordan and Kulp that Masters urged further public hearings "to support the fact that the company's small Oxbow dam would forever ruin the great God-given damsite at Hells Canyon."[55]

Handwritten letters to the FPC echoed Masters's evocation of "the people's interest" in Hells Canyon. J. B. Redford, born in Jerome, Idaho, twenty years before the 1902 Newlands Reclamation Act, believed "it would be a crime to let Idaho Power Company establish power plants on the Snake River, thereby nocking [sic] out the Hells Canyon Dam." Pocatello Plumbers Union business representative W. C. Mansell termed the High Dam "a vital asset to any state, if it is to grow and expand. Small dams will not do this and it [sic] only helps a few people." L. W. Dianey, a Clarkston, Washington, Republican, told the commission, "Not only *this* but *all* dams where the water can be used for reclamation later on should be built by the Government." Tudor might mock agency planners' aspirations as the antithesis of democracy, but Masters and his allies celebrated administrative might. Strong agencies could dam big rivers, build monumental irrigation projects. Douglas McKay worried about government stifling private enterprise, but to J. B. Redford and W. C. Mansell, and many more like them, strong government was necessary to exploit nature's material potential. Like so much of the New Deal, its public-power legacy endured because federal actions promised more people wider access to material security.[56]

Interior's withdrawal from the Idaho Power case caused public-power advocates to found the National Hells Canyon Association (NHCA) one month later. Incorporated in Boise by Democratic activists George Greenfield and George H. R. Taylor, NHCA affiliated nearly every interest that had fought against Eisenhower's election and for Hells Canyon High Dam: the Oregon and Washington Granges; state labor associations, both AFL and CIO, from Washington, Oregon, and Idaho; rural electric co-op associations from Montana and Idaho; the Northwest Public Power Association and Washington's associated public utility districts; and High Dam boosters in the Idaho-Oregon Hells Canyon Association and Hells Canyon Development Association.[57]

Reclamation Bureau engineers and Interior Department attorneys could no longer plead the High Dam's case, so public-power supporters scrambled to find legal counsel and hire expert witnesses. Using advances from Oregon State Federation of Labor secretary J. T. Marr, Washington State Federation of Labor president E. M. Weston, and Washington Public Utilities District president Owen Hurd, NHCA retained two attorneys who shared its members' politics and belief in hydropower's social values: C. Girard Davidson, Truman's former public-power cheerleader who now practiced labor law in Portland, and New Deal Interior Department veteran Evelyn N. Cooper, one of the few female attorneys in Washington, D.C.[58]

Public-power forces raced to keep abreast of Idaho Power. Cooper and Davidson quickly filed NHCA's request for full intervenor status in the FPC license case. More time is a lawyer's lifeboat. Cooper and Davidson had to interview witnesses, draft pleadings, develop a theory of their case against Idaho Power, raise money for fees, and craft a public-relations strategy to counter their adversary's head start. Their first frantic plea to delay the hearing for at least ninety more days failed. On 17 June, having postponed its hearing three times already at the Eisenhower administration's request, the FPC ruled "to delay unnecessarily is not in the public interest." McKay's offer to supply all Interior Department evidence to any interested party undercut NHCA's contention it needed time to prepare witnesses. The FPC was eager, six years after Idaho Power and the Reclamation Bureau began their duel, to start resolving the Hells Canyon controversy.[59]

For trial attorneys and judges, the last weeks before a big trial whirl past. An adrenalized blur of stale coffee, yellow legal-pad pages, pink phone messages, and endless conferences in windowless rooms tests physical stamina and mental acuity. For Idaho Power's and NHCA's counsel as well as FPC hearing officer William Costello, the Hells Canyon controversy's intense publicity added another dimension. "Opponents have ripped into each other with undiminished vigor for many years," the *Oregonian* observed. Syndicated columnist Drew Pearson accused Secretary McKay of surrendering all BPA hydropower to "avaricious" private utilities, "with the co-ops and municipalities pretty much left out in the cold." In Portland to dedicate a new Army Corps dam, McKay rushed a Tudor-drafted column to the papers, defending BPA's policy and protesting his deep devotion to the region's welfare. "My grandparents were pioneers in this country. All I have I owe to this region. I would never do anything to hurt it." At a rally in Portland, McKay advised supporters to "keep cool." "I hope no one falls for the smears of some New Dealers and columnists. . . . When some people run out of arguments, they start calling you a crook."[60]

In late June, Idaho's Public Utilities Commission formally endorsed Idaho Power's three-dam complex. "A bipartisan, non-political body, not interested in or concerned with the ideologies and politics of the Hells Canyon-Oxbow controversy," the commission urged "full and speedy development of the power resources of this area, as a requirement of immediate necessity." Three days later, irrigation boosters committed to the Mountain Home Project resolved to keep fighting for High Hells Canyon. To bring more than one million acres of Snake Basin public lands into production required the

High Dam's cheap public power, "as opposed to the low dams and their nebulous plans for construction."[61]

National Hells Canyon Association attorneys Davidson and Cooper, assisted by the rural co-ops' general counsel Laurence Potamkin, faced every trial advocate's living nightmare: absorbing mountains of data under intense time pressure. They worked feverishly, throughout late June and early July, under another burden. Since their main technical witnesses were Interior Department employees, they had to coax hostile senior Eisenhower appointees into grudging cooperation to secure access to career employees who supported High Hells Canyon. In Portland, NHCA president J. T. Marr accused McKay of discouraging Interior employees from assisting his attorneys. Unless they received assurances of immunity, he claimed, "a fair decision will be impossible by the commission without full government testimony."[62]

Solicitor Davis assured FPC chairman Kuykendall that Interior would release all relevant material to any party and encourage all department employees to cooperate fully during the hearing. Of special interest to NHCA's attorneys was the so-called Cotton Report, prepared in late 1952 by a California engineer for outgoing Interior secretary Chapman and Reclamation commissioner Straus. Public-power supporters accused McKay and Tudor of trying to suppress the Cotton Report as well as others by the bureau's Denver and Boise regional offices that touted the High Dam's power and irrigation features. When released, the reports largely confirmed Davis's wry observation, "I would not be surprised if they all favor federal development. I assume that they are at least not unfavorable."[63]

Out West, and in the sultry national capital, partisans predictably were polarized about whether the reports offered enough dramatic new information to warrant canceling the 7 July hearing. Oregon State Grange master Elmer McClure, an NHCA founder, told reporters, "The Cotton report bears out our assertion that a federal high dam at Hells Canyon is the only logical method of developing Snake River hydroelectric resources. . . . Such a dam is vital to the comprehensive development of the Columbia River and its tributaries." Roach, however, was "glad" the reports were on the table. He accused NHCA and its constituents of wasting their attorneys' time on politics when they should have been preparing their case. "It has not used due or any diligence whatsoever . . . if said Association, at any time, had any real intention, as a bona fide and independent intervenor, to make any showing or present any facts in this proceeding."[64]

In Idaho Power's temporary legal bunker, room 602 of the Washington

Statler Hotel, trial counsel Pat Parry readied his opening statement on Sunday afternoon, 5 July. Eight blocks away, in the Cafritz Building, Jebby Davidson and Evelyn Cooper outlined their first-day strategy.

Costello applied the Federal Power Act and FPC procedural rules to structure a three-sided Hells Canyon license hearing. Idaho Power would argue for dam licenses. The public-power intervenors, allied as National Hells Canyon Association, would oppose licensure. Federal Power Commission staff counsel would independently assess the two contestants' evidence and arguments, helping Costello frame the key issues he had to decide in his recommended licensure decision. The Federal Power Act authorized the FPC to license private utilities to dam interstate rivers. The act also empowered the FPC to deny Idaho Power a license and to instead advise Congress and the president that the federal government should electrify Hells Canyon. If any party, or two of the commissioners, disagreed with the examiner's recommended decision, the full commission would reconsider it at another hearing. If any party still disagreed with the commission's decision, it could appeal to the intermediate level of the federal court system. Finally, an appellant armed with money and zeal could ask the U.S. Supreme Court to review an adverse court of appeals decision. Few FPC licensure decisions went through all four levels. Idaho Power's Hells Canyon case would.[65]

William Costello convened the technical evidence phase of *In re Idaho Power Company*, on Tuesday, 7 July, at 10:00 A.M., in the FPC's spartan hearing room on Constitution Avenue, midway between Capitol Hill and the White House. A career civil-service attorney from Great Falls, Montana, the thirty-eight-year-old Costello understood how touchy northwesterners could be about rivers, dams, power, and fish. He had already presided over two controversial license cases in Oregon and Washington State during the previous three years. Each had raised ecological and political storms, though none as threatening as the Hells Canyon controversy.[66]

In re Idaho Power Company anticipated by nearly two decades the legal proceedings that became public-interest theater. More than a case at law, it tested the combatants' political will and public-relations expertise. As they dueled before the agency examiner, the Hells Canyon advocates were engaging the nation beyond the hearing-room doors in a referendum about the New Deal's postwar legacy. As in the Baker and Boise public hearings that he had managed a year earlier, Costello struggled to keep the parties focused on facts. However, facts never really decided the Hells Canyon controversy. From July 1953 until he adjourned the hearing in July 1954, Costello listened to evidence under oath that restated and amplified the Hells Canyon controversy's long, fierce political debate. Try as he might to elicit engineering and economic data from the contestants, the hearing examiner found even those provoked intense dispute, in and out of the conference room.

Over Idaho Power's objection, Costello granted National Hells Canyon Association full intervenor status. That meant association attorneys Davidson and Cooper could interrogate witnesses, argue legal points to the examiner, and enter documentary and oral evidence into the administrative record. The association pioneered environmental public-interest legal tactics that became commonplace in the 1970s. A purpose-built public-private coalition, its members united by a political cause, NHCA brought legal theories to life. It acted as the Reclamation Bureau's litigious ghost if Oscar Chapman had still been Interior secretary. Davidson immediately rattled New Deal chains by challenging the hearing's impartiality. He argued that McKay surprised High Dam backers by repudiating settled Interior public-power policy. They needed three more months to overcome the strategic legal advantage the secretary's apostasy had given Idaho Power. Costello denied NHCA's plea, offered Davidson an opportunity to refine his case during a lengthy late-summer recess, then briskly prompted Parry and his adversary to get on with their opening statements.[67]

As much political activists as officers of the court, the Hells Canyon attorneys began a yearlong practice of relaying their hearing-room arguments to a waiting press. When he failed to secure his ninety-day delay, Davidson told reporters, "We feel this is a substantial miscarriage of justice and we can reach but one conclusion: The Commission does not want an adversary proceeding; the Commission does not want a full hearing on the relative merits of a high Hells Canyon dam and three small dams on the Snake River. The Commission does not want the public interest represented." Idaho congressional representative Gracie Pfost reinforced Davidson's position, telling Costello at the outset of opening statements that Tom Roach was playing with the FPC, "sending up so-called plans like so many toy balloons and, as each one explodes, patching it up and sending it aloft again for another trial." Even Idaho Power's three-dam plan, Davidson claimed, was just "a little plan for a big river."[68]

Parry's opening statement contended Idaho Power's three-dam plan was cheaper, faster, and simpler than the "grandiose and terrifically expensive" High Dam. He quickly struck at what made Hells Canyon High Dam anathema to Snake Basin irrigators. Above Hells Canyon, in the Snake Plain of southern Idaho, "irrigation, present and future, is paramount. . . . Any attempt to use this section of the Snake River for a vast storage reservoir, intended primarily to assist in downstream power production, would be an economic and engineering mistake." Truman's Reclamation Bureau contemplated industrializing the Snake Basin by selling Hells Canyon's power to Columbia Basin customers. By contrast, "[Idaho Power] has always conceded that the water rights for future irrigation development shall have precedence over their hydro-electric rights. . . . The applicant has long lived with irrigation people on the Snake River. . . . In its planning for the development of this stretch of the river, this paramount and primary irrigation situation has been kept always in mind."[69]

The hearing's first week set the pattern for the next year. Parry methodically laid out Idaho Power's plans. He demonstrated the Northwest's need for quick boosts in electricity. He explained how the company could afford to build three dams in less than four years. Cooper and Davidson countered by making speeches, in concert with NHCA's backers, trying the Hells Canyon controversy in the wider court of national opinion.

Parry's first witness, retired Army Corps North Pacific commander Thomas Robins, challenged the need for the High Dam. He denied that comprehensive development of power, flood control, and navigation in the Northwest required it. The next witnesses—Roach, his construction and planning manager, and the general contractor—all stuck to the company's plans. If permitted to go ahead in Hells Canyon, Roach assured Costello, Idaho Power could meet its service area's entire future needs and sell some surplus power into the Columbia Basin. He intended to keep Idaho Power independent of BPA's dominion, but would pitch in, as a good neighbor, to help alleviate the hydroelectric empire's chronic, worsening supply shortages.[70]

Davidson preceded his cross-examination of Roach by renewing his pretrial attack on Interior Department duplicity. Despite assuring FPC that federal witnesses and studies would be disclosed, he charged, Secretary McKay was quietly bullying agency lawyers and backpedaling on his pledge to release pro–High Dam reports prepared for Straus and Chapman. The claims of NHCA prompted Tudor to send FPC another letter formally restating the department's promise to supply legal analyses and factual evidence, even if they favored the High Dam. "No witness," he assured the FPC, "is being controlled in any way in this matter and no employee who may be called as a witness need be concerned that his testimony in this case will have any effect on his future with the Department." When Interior deputy solicitor Edward Weinberg, "who has always been a strong advocate of the Federal project," asked Tudor point-blank about intimidation, the undersecretary instructed him to advise agency employees to testify fully and freely. If Costello suspected improper pressure, he should ask "under oath if you so desire, if any witness from this Department has been influenced as to his testimony in the matter." To his confidantes in San Francisco, Tudor crowed, "This I think was a satisfactory challenge in the matter and we have heard no more of it."[71]

Costello opened the second week of testimony by declaring Interior's assurances satisfied him. Brusquely, he rejected Cooper's effort to introduce evidence about McKay's preference for private power. He wanted to get to what he deemed the heart of the case. The examiner instructed FPC's attorneys to call John S. Cotton to testify about the relative economic merits of public and corporate power in Hells Canyon. Now in private engineering practice in northern California, Cotton had been hired in October 1952 to advise Reclamation about criticizing Idaho Power's original low-dam Oxbow proposal. For the rest of the week, Cotton's report dominated the hearing. For the next year, his case for Hells Canyon High Dam polarized the parties around the political issue of public versus private hydroelectricity in the Northwest.

Of course, Cotton testified, a definite plan to build three low private dams in Hells Canyon was superior to the company's original one-dam license application. But Hells Canyon High Dam "is from all points of view superior to the scheme proposed by the Idaho Power Company." The High Dam "would completely develop the power resources" of the Snake, as well as fully integrate the Snake Basin into the federal hydroelectric system managed by BPA. That he had only surveyed Hells Canyon from the air, once, on a commercial flight from Boise to Portland, in 1942, did not shake his conviction. He thought that reams of federal-agency studies more than documented the High Dam's fitness.

Parry cross-examined Cotton for three full days, mostly to establish his bias for public power and his reliance on debatable cost-benefit estimates favoring the High Dam. On Tuesday, Cotton admitted he had never spoken to or corresponded with any Idaho Power employee or consultant. On Wednesday, he agreed BPA and Reclamation Bureau employees had supplied nearly all of the studies he used to write his report. On Thursday, he conceded that he estimated construction costs using hypothetical private dams built as he assumed they would be, rather than examining Idaho

Power's license applications. "You really haven't compared the projects Idaho Power proposes to construct with the government proposals, have you?" Parry asked. "Not exactly," Cotton replied.

On Friday, at the end of his cross-examination, he agreed federal dams elsewhere in the Northwest, coupled with Idaho Power's Hells Canyon Complex, would add as much new capacity as the High Dam. "In other words," Parry concluded, "there is no magic in which particular place we put the storage?" "No," Cotton admitted.[72]

Cooper, still miffed that Costello would not recess the hearing to give NHCA time to prepare its case, asked only a few perfunctory questions on redirect. As direct testimony resumed late Friday, focusing on Hells Canyon's geological suitability for dam building, the regional press thrashed out the much-awaited, hotly debated Cotton Report's significance. In Portland, the *Oregonian*'s two-week-long series of Hells Canyon analyses wearily observed, "Both Snake River Projects Would Utilize Full Power." High Dam proponents were leveraging their hydroelectric estimates by assuming construction of more new federal dams downstream. "Claims made in the Hells Canyon high dam v. low dams fight are confusing even to engineers," correspondent Paul F. Ewing admitted. The *Idaho Daily Statesman*, however, breezily dismissed Cotton's report and testimony as "just another of the endless number of deceptions used by public power proponents in behalf of Hells Canyon dam." Both Cotton and his report "should be investigated by Congress" for fraud. Writing specially for Portland's *Oregon Journal*, Democratic state legislator and author Richard Neuberger believed Cotton's report established the High Dam's superiority to Idaho Power's "pygmy" dam. "The future of the Northwest is geared directly to an abundant supply of low-cost hydroelectricity. If the government abandons the magnificent damsite in Hells Canyon, are other similar power sites safe?"[73]

Washington, D.C., in late July, encases inhabitants in a semitropical terrarium. Before air-conditioning, attorneys tried to beat the heat and humidity by wearing cotton seersucker suits and perforated white shoes. They sported straw boaters—or, for Cooper, broad-brimmed hats—when they ventured outside. Costello nevertheless pressed on, lengthening the trial day at the third week's outset by one-half hour, to six hours.

Parry now turned his case to focus on Snake Basin irrigation. Idaho state engineer Kulp and former deputy engineer Harry M. Dewey defended the Idaho Power complex's water-rights subordination to expanded upstream irrigation. Kulp projected at least thirty thousand new acres of desert land coming into irrigated production per year through 1977. To water those additional nine hundred thousand acres, Idaho Power had willingly subordinated its hydroelectric operations.[74] Evelyn Cooper finally waded in the next day, cross-examining Kulp and Dewey thoroughly. With Davidson absent all week, one of the handful of women practicing law in the nation's capital decided NHCA needed to stop sulking and start making its own record. She got Kulp to admit his estimates of future irrigation growth were somewhat speculative. Reluctantly, Kulp agreed Idaho Power and his agency were cooperating quite closely, and somewhat quietly, to structure water rights. Though Dewey defended his elaborate charts projecting future upstream diversion rates, Cooper successfully persuaded Costello to exclude them from the record because debatable assumptions permeated their conclusions against the High Dam.[75]

As the third week of testimony closed, Costello focused the combatants on what he deemed the decisive licensing issue: Were the company dams as effective as Hells Canyon High Dam in comprehensively developing all of the Snake Basin's water resources? Retired corps general Robins returned to the stand for two days. Parry walked him through the High Dam's stated objectives—navigation, flood control, reclamation, power—and to each, the former deputy chief of engineers objected. Reclamation and Army Corps planners had never deemed the High Dam essential to the corps' lower Snake navigation dams. Better flood-control dam sites speckled the Clearwater and Salmon watersheds: "The money [Reclamation] proposes to put into Hells Canyon to get that storage just doesn't produce the results." By spending more than three times as much to build the High Dam as it did on standard flood-control dams, the federal government would have to sell its hydroelectricity at more than twice BPA's Columbia Basin wholesale price. Robins doubted that equation would fund much new Snake Basin irrigation. Downstream customers simply would not buy enough power to fill the High Dam cash box so Reclamation could drain it to pay for the Mountain Home Project.[76]

Parry called Idaho Power construction and power-sale managers to outline the recreational consequences of the three-dam project. Ralph E. Gale waxed poetic in describing how the three reservoirs "will be more in proportion to the surrounding mountains" than the High Dam's ninety-three-mile-long pool. Shallower and shorter than the single federal reservoir, they would entice vacationers into Hells Canyon to fish, boat, and picnic. He explained how the company had developed all of its Snake River dam sites into "outstanding" recreation areas. To this, in her cross-examination, Cooper snorted, "Criminal." Idaho Power built dams and filled reservoirs simply to make more kilowatts. Now assisted at counsel table by Baker, Oregon, publisher Byron Brinton, Cooper interrogated Gale to contrast the High Dam's tourism potential with the company's bleak power-production reservoirs upstream in the Snake Basin.[77]

Long trials stretch the participants' nerves, testing the advocates' professional courtesy and the judge's personal patience. Bathed in the capital's unremitting summer heat, scrutinized by a bank of reporters, playing to larger audiences beyond the hearing room, the combatants in the FPC case finally snapped during the hearing's fourth week.

Both Parry and Cooper seemed to have half hoped for such an eruption. The Idahoan bristled when former FPC commissioner Leland Olds began sitting at counsel table to help Cooper cross-examine General Robins. Seated in a row, at three tables pushed end to end, the attorneys and their aides could hardly escape hearing whispered asides; for Olds, Parry had little more than contempt. On Cooper's part, she was struggling with some of the densest technical testimony of the entire proceeding while her partner, Davidson, combed the country trying to prepare NHCA's case for the High Dam.

Her repeated requests for more time on Tuesday, 29 July, to prepare adequate cross-examination provoked Parry to question his adversary's competence and motives. Had she not a law partner, Davidson, who could have effectively interrogated Robins and other Idaho Power witnesses? The former assistant Interior secretary, after all, had been the Northwest's leading public-power attorney during the New Deal. When Cooper protested Davidson knew too little about the High Dam to participate at this point, Parry incredulously reviewed his long service with federal power agencies and barked, "To me it is such a fiction that it offends intelligence." Cooper, Davidson, and Olds were national utility-law experts, while "this small, independent power company out there in the West, represented by us lawyers from this faraway small state, has come in here and in good faith brought our [sic] facts in."

Costello tried to defuse the confrontation, explaining he simply needed Cooper and Parry to agree on a schedule for questioning the company's remaining witnesses and moving on to the public-power case-in-chief. But NHCA's repeated theatrics seem to have frayed his judicial temperament. Inadvertently or not, Costello belittled Cooper, complaining her leisurely cross-examination style forced the hearing's pace to be dictated by "the slowest or the smallest element of it." Cooper had doubtless read press accounts openly scorning the "woman attorney" and describing her as "Davidson's red-headed assistant." Cross-examining engineers was hard enough for any trial lawyer. Now she had to justify her mere presence before dozens of male attorneys, clerks, and reporters. After lunch, Cooper read into the record a lengthy defense of her handling of the case. She demanded Parry retract his "contemptuous, abusive," and unethical criticisms. She mocked his modesty: "While he and his associates may be just country lawyers, let the record show that he and his company have the support and resources of the whole private power trust behind them."

By day's end, Costello had denied Cooper's motion to eject Parry from the hearing and encouraged the advocates to meet that evening to sort out a procedure for questioning the remaining Idaho Power and pro–High Dam witnesses. When the hearing reconvened on Wednesday, 30 July, Costello apologized to Cooper for implying her gender rendered her incapable of conducting NHCA's case. He reminded counsel to stay with the facts. He also indicated he expected Idaho Power to complete its case within ten days or less.[78]

Parry met the deadline with two days to spare. Idaho Power's final witnesses in the hearing's first phase—Wall Street bankers and bond brokers, New York and Portland engineers—explained how a "small, independent power company way out West" could finance a construction project costing more than all of its existing dams combined. To be sure, private capital would pay for the concrete and steel, bulldozers and laborers, but much of that investment would flow into Hells Canyon only because federal defense policy encouraged utility construction. In late 1950, Congress had enacted a generous subsidy for private-power expansion. The Defense and Interior Departments could certify to the Internal Revenue Service that utilities building qualifying projects were entitled to depreciate their capital investment rapidly, thus reducing their taxable income. With their income-tax liability so drastically cut, utilities became attractive investments to more than the proverbial widows and orphans. The industry quickly absorbed nearly $2 billion worth of construction subsidies. Idaho Power, despite its virtuous claims of thrift, sought and received so-called fast tax depreciation certificates for its Hells Canyon Complex.

Throughout 1953, High Dam proponents effectively scourged Roach's pious sermons about "market discipline" for their hypocrisy. Senators Magnuson, Jackson, and Morse termed Idaho Power's tax-favored financing of the Hells Canyon Complex "a subsidy of shocking magnitude." In October, Magnuson estimated the dams would save Idaho Power, over their fifty-year license period, more income-tax liability than their construction cost. The most effective argument leveled against Idaho Power during the Hells Canyon controversy, the "tax subsidy" charge ultimately prompted Roach in 1957—after the Supreme Court had upheld FPC's dam license—grudgingly to renounce all federal financial assistance.[79]

Costello's license hearing ground on through the autumn, punctuated with lengthy recesses, granted over Parry's ill-tempered objections, to enable NHCA's attorneys to prepare cross-examinations of Idaho Power's witnesses. Parry calculated, in the midst of NHCA's own presentation of High Dam testimony in spring 1954, the hearing had been in session 110 days, and in recess 70. Cooper and Davidson still complained regularly about the hearing's structure. Parry matched their protests with his own periodic remonstrances against Costello for plodding through testimony while the Northwest demanded more power.[80]

By late October, NHCA was soliciting additional funds from public-power advocates nationwide and readying its own case for the High Dam. Davidson and Cooper would begin calling FPC attorneys in early January 1954 to give testimony based on Truman administration studies. New Deal public-power crusaders pitched in to help where they could. Former BPA and Interior Department northwestern majordomo Roy Bessey joined Leland Olds at counsel table during examinations of power engineers. For two decades one of the New Deal's most committed servants, Bessey undoubtedly recognized his cue to leave public service. Interior's new power policy, announced by Undersecretary Tudor in August, steadily reduced BPA's mission of fostering public-power expansion in the Northwest. Tudor delightedly told a longtime San Francisco business associate the department's new policy was eliciting "screams of pain from the new-dealing left-wingers."[81]

In November 1953, NHCA agreed to a time-saving procedural innovation suggested by Costello. Davidson had fanned out across the country to verify the continued loyalty of BPA and Reclamation Bureau public-power advocates. He thus consented to have FPC staff counsel present federal-agency employees' testimony shortly after the New Year. By then cross-examining the employees, Cooper and Davidson would lay the foundation for their own case-in-chief, scheduled to begin sometime in spring 1954.

On 6 January 1954, Costello gaveled the next phase of his Hells Canyon hearing back into session. For three months, in four separate sessions, FPC counsel paraded twenty current and former federal employees onto the witness chair. The first, FPC staff engineer Ralph Coomes, earnestly outlined the Northwest's electricity situation and admitted that adding some more capacity was urgent, whether it came from Idaho Power or the High Dam. The rest used this opportunity to tell Costello just what Harry Truman, Michael Straus, and R. J. Newell had envisioned when they termed Hells Canyon the linchpin to planned federal maximization of Snake Basin waterpower. On and on, for thousands of transcript pages, Reclamation Bureau and BPA employees and consultants matched Idaho Power's witnesses, demand graph for demand graph.

On 13 January came this phase of the hearing's most dramatic confrontation on the Hells Canyon controversy's most volatile issue: hydropower's impact on future Snake Basin irrigation expansion. John R. Ritter, Reclamation's chief hydrological engineer, explained the High Dam would actually accelerate irrigated farming's growth. That had been one of Straus's and Newell's original objectives when they issued the 1947 Mountain Home Plan. Filling the High Dam's reservoir to generate hydropower for sale into the Columbia Basin would not menace water needed to irrigate the desert, Ritter testified. Lynn Crandall followed Ritter to the witness chair. Employed by both the state of Idaho as deputy state reclamation engineer and the U.S. Geological Survey as district engineer, he apportioned irrigation water from federal Snake River reservoirs between Wyoming's Jackson Lake and southern Idaho's Minidoka Dam. Crandall scoffed at Ritter's reassuring words. He insisted filling Hells Canyon would siphon vital irrigation water from existing Idaho farmers and breach the federal government's duty to respect state water laws.

Bonneville Power got its chance to educate Costello in February. Five senior staff from Portland BPA headquarters renewed Paul Raver's jeremiad on the critical Northwest electricity shortage. System planner, hydroelectric water engineer, chief—power supply, chief load economist, regional economist: their titles bespoke twenty years of federal hydroelectric dominion over the region's rivers. All agreed Idaho Power and BPA shared a common, overriding objective: pumping more electricity into the Northwest Power Pool. All also agreed that, if it was hydroelectricity the FPC wanted, the High Dam would generate a lot of it.

Five years earlier, Interior and the Army Corps of Engineers had jousted for control of the world's largest dam project. Now, serving a president who vowed the High Dam would never be built on his watch, veterans from these old interagency power wars returned to Washington to renew their debates about comprehensive basin planning. Roscoe E. Bell had directed federal land planning in the Northwest during the last years of the Truman administration. Exiled to Alaska when the Republicans swept into Washington, he recalled for Costello Reclamation's grand plans to irrigate one million more acres of Snake Basin public lands using funds piled up in the High Dam cash box. But Gordon Fernald, the Army Corps' chief Northwest water planner, nursed no grudges from old political fights. His Washington superiors had smoothly retreated from the Hells Canyon controversy. They preferred not to confront their former commander, who now sat in the White House. Fernald testified that the Army Corps now saw Idaho Power's dams complementing its Main Control Plan ("no more Vanports!"). The Hells Canyon Complex could release water to enhance navigation on the lower Snake if only Congress would outflank Eisenhower's "no new starts" policy by appropriating money to build the necessary corps dams.[82]

Finally, on 10 May, Jebby Davidson got his chance to show Costello, as well as Congress and the nation, why the National Hells Canyon Association had rallied a broad movement of labor, farmers, and liberal reformers. He got the hearing examiner to let Andrew Biemiller introduce the American Federation of Labor's 1952 convention resolution favoring immediate construction of the High Dam. Then Davidson delivered a sixty-page opening statement, dedicated to showing that Hells Canyon was big enough to hold so many dreamers' fondest hopes for northwestern growth.

Eleven witnesses spoke passionately, often eloquently, for NHCA's constituencies as Davidson and Cooper laid out their case to federalize Hells Canyon. Owen Hurd, John George, and Vincent Cleaveland, representing northwestern public-utility districts and rural co-ops, outlined why public-power wholesalers' preference claims for public power required a big new Snake River dam. Elmer McClure and Charles Baker, on behalf of the Grange, linked cheap High Dam power to industrializing Snake Basin phosphate fertilizer resources. Clyde Ellis, the feisty New Deal lobbyist for the nation's rural electric cooperatives, unleashed his finest Ozark rhetoric on behalf of Hells Canyon. E. M. Weston, Washington's senior labor leader, reviewed the reasons why organized labor felt deeply committed to public-power expansion. Reed College political scientist Charles McKinley wove his recent book, extolling robust federal planning for maximum resource use, into his 12 May testimony.[83]

The National Hells Canyon Association's final three witnesses brought the ghost of New Deal public power to life. Michael Straus, Truman's Reclamation commissioner, detailed the planning and politicking that produced the 1949 Weaver-Newell Accord that had assigned his agency to build Hells Canyon. Leland Olds had been harried off the FPC in 1949 by red-baiters and oil companies eager to forestall federal regulation of natural gas. He began by telling Costello what the Federal Power Act obligated FPC to do when weighing competing private and public dam plans. Before Davidson could get Olds fully untracked on the witness stand, Pat Parry objected. Mere legal opinions, even those of a former power commissioner, were irrelevant to Costello's task, he argued. Davidson and Parry jabbed, each trying to get his adversary's best, the former assistant Interior secretary and BPA general counsel icily informing the Twin Falls water lawyer not to lecture him about the FPC's rules of practice.

Costello resolved the debate by striking from the record Olds's testimony about federal power history and policy. Although interesting, it simply offered irrelevant opinions about legal issues properly the commission's and the courts' province. Davidson appealed Costello's decision to the full FPC. Three weeks later, the commission agreed with Parry, who huffed that Olds's testimony "might provide an appropriate argument in the case, or perhaps an illuminating article to submit for magazine publication, [but] it contains few, if any, facts relating to the license applications now before the Commission."[84]

Samuel Moment's testimony offered less history, but more political and personal drama. Four months earlier, the Eisenhower administration had forced his boss, BPA administrator Paul Raver, to resign. Again, Interior undersecretary Ralph Tudor eagerly played the heavy, pestering McKay to take Raver's measure. The former Oregon governor, who personally liked the imperious Northwest power titan, finally consented. He replaced Raver with little-known Washington State College engineering dean William A. Pearl. Raver's departure infuriated Moment, who knew his boss's demise heralded his own departure from BPA.[85]

Some time later, Moment unburdened himself in *Public Power*, sharpening his FPC testimony and laying bare the raw political passions that had fueled the Hells Canyon controversy throughout the postwar years. Privatizing the Snake's power potential was "a crime, the destruction of the principle of full development of the river." Tudor and Roach, partners in crime, "are destroying the principle of full conservation." New and Fair

Dealers in BPA, Reclamation, and the Army Corps of Engineers, just after peace returned, had prepared "a Federal program of full development" for public power's domain. By 1949, Moment, Raver, and their fellow hydroelectric administrators had brought Columbia-Snake Basin people to the brink of "the brightest period in Northwest history." Hells Canyon High Dam would have joined the honor roll of great Northwest federal power dams: Bonneville, Grand Coulee, McNary, Chief Joseph, the Dalles. Now, under penny-pinchers like Eisenhower and free-enterprise car dealers like his Interior secretary, federal power agencies scrapped for bits and pieces of "partial development." Unlike Moment and his administrative-agency colleagues throughout the public-power domain, Tom Roach and Ralph Tudor "have no responsibility for replacing the jobs, the flood control, and the greater prosperity they would take away from the Northwest." So much did Moment try to tell William Costello in his brief appearance under Davidson's respectful examination, and Pat Parry's contemptuously brief cross-examination.[86]

Nearly lost, in what had become the longest-running federal administrative case to date, were the migratory fish still swimming up and drifting down the Snake River through Hells Canyon. A three-cornered licensing procedure had presented only a two-sided argument about electricity. None of the interested parties—Idaho Power, NHCA, and FPC staff—had the legal objective of presenting biological evidence about power dams' effects on Snake Basin fish. Oregon, Idaho, and Washington fish agencies had never formally intervened in the FPC case. Only Oregon's had even sent representatives to the July 1952 public hearings, and they did not testify. Northwestern state fish agencies did send letters to the commission recommending license conditions to bind Idaho Power to protect the Snake River's fisheries. Idaho and Washington cautiously endorsed the company's dams over Hells Canyon High Dam. The Oregon Fish Commission endorsed neither private nor public power.

In one of his last official actions before being dismissed as Idaho Fish and Game director, T. B. Murray informed the FPC that his state sought eight specific Idaho Power dam-license conditions. Among them were provisions looking toward "the possibility and practicability of fish salvage operations" to reestablish the Hells Canyon salmon and steelhead runs below the dam site, in the Salmon and Clearwater basins. Murray doubted whether fish ladders could maintain spawning populations "in view of the three dams of medium height, and the probable future installation of various other large dams on the Lower Snake and Columbia." Fish and Game wanted Idaho Power to pay for at least four years of fish-conservation measures.[87]

Washington Fisheries Department seconded Idaho's comments about license conditions. Director Robert J. Schoettler, however, urged FPC to require Idaho Power to pay all costs necessary, "until such time as the agencies concerned are agreed that the maximum level of migratory fish protection is achieved." Achieving that level of assurance might require the state agencies to oversee the company's dams for at least eight years, maybe longer.[88]

Oregon's Fish Commission tried a different approach. Its chairman, John Veatch, told the FPC his state still knew too little to approve Idaho Power's three-dam plans. Despite requests to conduct studies and to consult with FCO personnel, the utility had simply gone ahead with its license applications. Veatch urged the FPC to withhold approval of dam licenses until the company "disclose[s] the projected elements of their plans." Oregon was not taking sides between private and public dams, for "the stipulations for the preservation of the fisheries resources are required equally of all prospective applicants." What those "stipulations" might be, FCO could not presently say, as "we are currently unable to provide any advice concerning how the problems of fish protection may be met."[89]

Undersecretary Tudor prepared Interior's formal FPC comments about Hells Canyon fish. He drafted Secretary McKay's letter, which was entered into evidence on the hearing's opening day. Tudor felt the FPC should not require Idaho Power simply to write "a blank check" for funding conservation efforts. After all, Reclamation and Fish and Wildlife had dedicated only $4 million to protect anadromous fish in the High Dam's construction budget, less than 1 percent of its total cost. "It seems [now] that the Snake River suddenly became a very important fish stream when we abandoned the Federal dam and somebody else asked to build a dam." Given FWS's "cursory" studies of Snake Basin fish, Interior advised FPC it "is not in a position to recommend definitely what means and measures should be specified in the project licenses for the protection of the fishery." Interior requested any license issued to Idaho Power compel the company to spend "about $250,000" investigating the matter. Its contribution to "salmon trapping devices, trout and salmon hatcheries, holding ponds, and other facilities" should be capped at "approximately $5,000,000." Fish, therefore, were now negotiable, their fate largely left to the Federal Power Commission, state conservation agencies, and Idaho Power.[90]

Only three actual witnesses testified in any detail about fish conservation during the technical evidence phase of the license case. Their views left Costello and the full FPC wide latitude to decide how to accommodate Snake Basin fish to power production. The Fish and Wildlife Service still wanted to use New Deal methods to handle Hells Canyon fish. James T. McBroom, FWS liaison with northwestern state fish agencies, testified that Grand Coulee demonstrated his agency's preferred model for adapting migratory fish to power dams. "Would your experience at the Grand Coulee Dam offer any guide for the Service in this problem?" asked NHCA counsel. "Indeed it would," McBroom replied. Passing fish over Idaho Power's dams—ranging from two hundred to four hundred feet high—with ladders was "not feasible in the sense that no strip of river has ever been successfully laddered at those heights." Fish and Wildlife therefore suggested replacing natural processes with technology and capital: an "egg-taking station somewhere below the lower downstream dam," the "possibility of transplantation of adult fish, and "the possibility of construction of a hatchery with appurtenant facilities in the stream near the downstream dam." Although FWS had given only a little study to either Idaho Power's or Reclamation's dam plans, "the same type of measures would be examined and evaluated and, perhaps, undertaken."[91]

According to Idaho Power's Ralph Gale, Idaho and Oregon fish agencies offered little more than FWS's "purely reconnaissance" study to guide the company's conservation duties. "There is a great deal of argument between the fish people. . . . I have had conferences with those fellows to see what their opinion is, and they are frank to say they do not have an opinion." Answering Cooper's question about his own views, Gale confessed, "I am entirely confused after conferring with [Idaho Fish and Game, the Oregon Fish Commission, and the Oregon State Game Commission]." He could learn only that state regulators were "particularly concerned about those fish" and "feel that what there are should be relocated, as their term is, 'by some method.'"[92]

Faced with federal and state biologists' uncertainty, Idaho Power president Tom Roach consigned what could be saved of the Snake River's fishery to the FPC. He agreed either his company's dams or the High Dam would "interfere with the fish migration." Company cost estimates were left purposely blank on the line item marked "Fishery Future." So, asked his attorney Pat Parry, "what is the position of your company with reference to its willingness to comply with whatever may be the requirements in the license with respect to handling fish?" On 4 August 1953, in a federal building in

Washington, D.C., Roach put Hells Canyon's anadromous fish up to bid. The FPC and northwestern state conservation agencies would have to decide what they were worth. "We are pressing our applications for these licenses," he testified, "with a full awareness that we are under obligations, whatever the remedy may be, to do that which the Commission would direct us to as a part of providing that remedy, and we so propose, if and when the license is granted, to conform to whatever requirements may be laid down in the license for meeting that particular problem."[93]

To make his initial decision about licensing Idaho Power's three-dam plan, Costello had to wade through thirteen thousand pages of trial transcript, some 450 documentary exhibits, and nearly five hundred pages of written briefs, filed in summer and fall 1954. For nearly a year, he pondered his options, testing his discretion against his statutory duties. Finally, on 6 May 1955, the presiding examiner issued his decision. He recommended FPC license Idaho Power to dam the Snake in Hells Canyon. He declined to recommend Congress authorize the High Dam as a federal project. Costello recommended Idaho Power be licensed only to build Brownlee Dam, the largest of the three-dam complex. Idaho Power could find a ready market, through the Northwest Power Pool, for Brownlee's 400 megawatts. The dam's storage capacity fitted it for service in the Army Corps' navigation and flood-control strategies farther downstream. Much as the Northwest needed power, southern Idaho did not need as much as the three-dam complex would generate. Besides, neither Oxbow nor low Hells Canyon "would provide flood control or navigation benefits and therefore . . . would not be adapted to a comprehensive plan for beneficial public uses" as required by the Federal Power Act's "public interest test." Tom Roach and Pat Parry seemed to have won their great prize. National Hells Canyon Association appeared to have suffered what would become its decisive defeat.[94]

However, Costello's initial decision left enough uncertainty that both NHCA and Idaho Power appealed to the full commission. In August 1955, the commission affirmed the license. Sympathetic commissioners ensured Idaho Power's complete triumph, ruling all three dams were "in the public interest" because the Northwest needed all of the power that the Hells Canyon Complex could generate. Down to its last appeal, NHCA asked the District of Columbia Circuit Court of Appeals to reverse FPC's licensing decision. In 1956, a three-judge circuit court panel unanimously affirmed. Public power's final, desperate toss of the judicial dice failed as well. Early in April 1957, the U.S. Supreme Court declined discretionary review of the appeals court's decision. By cooperating as partners and colliding as adversaries, in politics and at law, Tom Roach and Pat Parry, Dwight Eisenhower and Douglas McKay, William Costello and Earl Warren, even Evelyn Cooper and Jebby Davidson, had redefined the public's interest in the Snake River as it pounded through Hells Canyon.[95]

Costello's 1955 decision indicated a new postwar public interest in Snake Basin water was taking shape. Congress, by enacting the Federal Power Act, intended the Federal Power Commission to determine "within rather wide limits . . . that a proposed project fits within the 'comprehensive plan' of waterway development." To serve "the public interest" required administrative judgment and expertise. "The licensing provisions of the Federal Power Act may not be administered with a slide rule no matter how desirable this method might be." Costello understood the Hells Canyon controversy had engaged the nation, as well as the contestants before him, in a political debate that required choices. "'Facts' . . . of course, are very important, [but] it is quite obvious that the Congress . . . intended that the Commission administer the rather broad provisions of the licensing law with a view to achieving the greatest good for the greatest number."

Costello's analysis of the American public's greatest good demonstrated how far the "public interest" in the Snake Basin had shifted since 1947. Franklin Roosevelt, Harold Ickes, Harry Truman, and Michael Straus had made the federal government the Northwest's greatest electricity supplier. The High Dam and Reclamation's Mountain Home Project contemplated transforming the Snake Basin with more huge jolts of cheap public power. By 1955, however, Costello ruled Congress had never intended "that the United States itself would ever be a major developer of electric power or that the United States would assume the role that it has in some of the regions of the nation. There was no intent in the minds of the Congress at that time that electric power would some day be made an instrument of social reform."[96]

Bonneville Power administrator Paul Raver and Northwest Public Power Association manager Gus Norwood had tried, since 1937, to stimulate industrial growth and economic development with cheap public power. Leading with supply that exceeded demand, they transformed the Columbia Basin into a new kind of water-dependent society, a public-power domain, where per capita use of electricity doubled the national average. "Most of the industrial growth of the Northwest," Costello acknowledged, "has been based upon the cheapness of water power." Ten years after World War II, though, Costello found Idaho Power's three dams would generate too much power for its customers. "It would clearly not be in the public interest to license the three proposed dams when there is only a market reasonably predicted for the production of one of them."[97]

R. J. Newell and H. T. Nelson hoped the High Dam's cash box would fund the Reclamation Bureau's ambitious plans to remodel southern Idaho topography to spill water onto the Mountain Home Desert. To earn enough power-sale revenue to irrigate these arid lands, their agency projected the world's biggest dam, creating a ninety-three-mile-long reservoir. To fill that reservoir to generate enough hydroelectricity to raise enough revenue to subsidize the Mountain Home Project, Reclamation anticipated storing more than four million acre-feet of the Snake's flow. Costello, sensitive to engineering testimony and irrigators' fears, concluded the High Dam recruited too much water into federal service. The Federal Power Commission's license to Idaho Power would leave to Idaho and Oregon the task of "prohibit[ing] Applicant Idaho Power from interfering with future depletions of the Snake River or with future upstream diversion."[98]

10 FROM ENERGY TO ENVIRONMENT

The Aftermath of the Hells Canyon Controversy

Just months after the U.S. Supreme Court and Congress ratified Idaho Power's triumph in the Hells Canyon controversy, the Eisenhower administration redefined northwestern hydropower's central issue. Speaking to managers of western state conservation agencies at their 1957 annual conference, U.S. Fish and Wildlife Service director Ross Leffler announced the Interior Department's startling new direction. He urged the states and federal government to "stake out appropriate areas of both land and water all over the west as being primarily suited for fish and wildlife—as being of more value for fish and wildlife than for any other purpose." Ten years earlier, Leffler's agency had meekly withdrawn its northwestern salmon biologists' protest against new federal dams on the Columbia. Interior secretary Julius Krug had overruled his scientists and suppressed their alarming study because it conflicted with President Truman's drive for more public power and flood control. Now the Hells Canyon controversy had helped tip the politics and law that favored hydroelectricity toward fish conservation. Fish and Wildlife's new policy indicated the Interior Department, for the rest of Eisenhower's presidency, was steadily shifting its principal northwestern mission from producing energy to protecting environmental quality.

Interior secretary Fred A. Seaton, who replaced Douglas McKay in spring 1956, sharpened Leffler's point in October 1958. Hells Canyon was again making news. A three-way struggle had erupted over another proposed chain of Snake River power dams below Idaho Power's Hells Canyon Complex. Private and public rivals were once more jousting over the proper method of electrifying the canyon's remaining undammed reach.[1] Seaton shocked the rivals, and the Northwest, by urging the Federal Power Commission to defer licensing any new dams on the Snake "pending a solution to the problem of fish passage and the preservation of the fishery value in connection with this type of river development."

The next year, Leffler amplified Seaton's warning by proposing an outright federal-state ban on new dams in Snake Basin rivers vital to preserving chinook salmon and steelhead trout. "I believe it is especially critical here on the Columbia River," he wrote in 1959 in Oregon's wildlife magazine, "that we stake out a claim for an anadromous fish sanctuary in the Snake Basin. . . . Certainly it should include the Salmon River in Idaho and parts, if not all, of such rivers as the Clearwater, the Grande Ronde, and the Imnaha. These rivers, particularly the Salmon, are the mainstay of the spring chinook and summer steelhead runs." A decade's worth of hydroelectric expansion raised troubling ecological consequences that undercut the postwar push to make more energy. "If, in the end," Leffler warned, "we conclude that there cannot be any satisfactory solution to fish passage over high dams in important fish production streams, we can and should forthrightly declare that certain river basins of the Pacific Northwest should be dedicated to the conservation and development of fish and wildlife resources as their highest and best use."[2]

Leffler, Seaton, and President Eisenhower were all on the way out of power by November 1960. The prospect of powerlessness probably emboldened the Interior secretary to share his conviction that federal hydroelectric expansion had exacted too high a price in the Snake Basin. To the Federal Power Commission, still wrestling with three competing applications to dam the Snake in Hells Canyon, the Interior secretary urged a long-term ban on any new dams. The Northwest now had enough hydroelectricity: a new treaty with Canada promised transborder power wheeling. Energy sufficiency now gave the region, and the nation, a breathing space. "In light of this Department's responsibility for the protection and conservation of the vital Northwest anadromous fishery resource . . . ," Seaton informed the FPC, "we believe that it is unnecessary at this time and for some years to come to undertake any project in this area."[3]

Seaton's and Leffler's pleas for restraint mobilized a volley of legal and political objections to new dams in the Snake Basin. During Idaho Power's decade-long battle with the federal hydroelectric agencies, economics and ideology dominated the national debate. After 1958, conservationists streamed off the sidelines into the fray. Not a single private or state party dedicated to biological values had formally intervened in the FPC case between Hells Canyon High Dam and Idaho Power's low dams. In just six months, between November 1959 and May 1960, sixteen parties asserted legal interests in the fate of Snake Basin fish menaced by proposed new dams. Idaho's, Oregon's, and Washington's state fish agencies all intervened in the FPC's *Pacific Northwest Power* case. So did downriver commercial fishers—led by the Columbia River Salmon and Tuna Packers Association and Fishermen's Cooperative Association, Tom Sandoz's and James Cellars's old outfits. Intervenors came from the Pacific Coast—led by the Pacific Fish Conservation League, Inc.—and arid Intermountain West—represented by the Idaho Wildlife Federation. White sport anglers in the Washington Sportsmen's Council made common cause with the Makah Indian Tribe from Washington's Olympic Peninsula.[4]

These new voices, making legal arguments rooted in both ecology and culture, revealed how the Hells Canyon controversy destabilized the regional consensus that propelled public power upriver in the postwar years. Idaho Power's confrontation with the postwar New Deal sparked unexpectedly fierce resistance, from unexpected sources, to the Federal Columbia River Power System's designs on the Snake. Born of New Deal laws and administrative policies, the upriver federal offensive stumbled to a halt when the legal system began reconsidering the methods, and ultimately, the assumptions of the administrative state.

Resistance to New Deal economic planning and federal regulation unleashed new pressures, from within the legal system itself, that began eroding federal primacy over water in the Northwest. Even before Republicans won their first congressional majorities in sixteen years at the 1946 elections, they had united with conservative Democrats to enact the Administrative Procedure Act.[5] New Deal critics forced the executive agencies to observe new procedures that restrained their discretion to alter natural systems. New procedures stimulated the growth of novel forms of political action. New participants in lawmaking both reflected and encouraged emergence of new values. These new voices—state conservation agencies, commercial fishers, Indians, sport anglers—began to shift the legal balance that favored public hydroelectric expansion. This new relationship became more adversarial, transparent, and democratic. New legal disputes between public power and its foes provoked northwesterners to reassess their views about the long-term health of natural systems in the region.

Legal battles, such as the Hells Canyon controversy, encouraged northwesterners to question whether more dams were always necessarily better. That skepticism of the later 1950s would have been heretical during the New

Deal and early postwar years. As federal judges grew increasingly familiar with the Administrative Procedure Act's judicial-review provisions during the fifties, their concerns about unfettered agency discretion helped transform natural-resources regulation. The act exposed administrative discretion to heightened scrutiny, encouraging courts to widen the range of interests entitled to participate in agency actions and to seek judicial review.

Northwestern state fish and wildlife agencies contested the hydroelectric empire's upriver offensive most doggedly. State agencies revived their long-standing constitutional and historic duty to "preserve, protect, and perpetuate" riverine fisheries by using federal administrative procedures to defend the habitat on which salmon and steelhead trout depended.[6] Ecological testimony about public-power dams' impact on Snake Basin fish runs had convinced the FPC to require in its 1955 license that state fish agencies scrutinize Idaho Power's Hells Canyon dams. From this unaccustomed vantage point, Oregon's and Idaho's conservation agencies directed almost perpetual criticism against hydroelectricity's toll on northwestern anadromous fish. Exploiting this crucial breach in the legal consensus that undergirded public power, fish advocates—Indians, sport anglers, commercial fishers, and state regulators—forced their way into future decisions about federal dams on the Snake River.

Had the states been less interested during the 1960s in clashing with Columbia and Snake basin Indians over the boundaries of their coequal sovereignties, they might have formed a powerful legal coalition. Both state agencies and Indian people wanted federal hydro policy to balance more justly the needs of migratory fish. By trying to work alone, the treaty tribes encountered deep-rooted judicial and administrative racism that inhibited their postwar legal options. For example, in 1948, the Nez Perce Tribe had had to retain private counsel to try to halt construction of McNary Dam on the Columbia River. Even though the Nez Perce asserted their federal treaty rights were imperiled by the dam's impacts on anadromous fish, the Bureau of Indian Affairs and Department of Justice represented the general contractor, not the tribe. The U.S. District Court in Spokane dismissed the Nez Perce case before trial without writing a formal opinion.[7]

The legal revolution triggered by the 1946 Administrative Procedure Act, and confirmed by Idaho Power's 1955 FPC license, thwarted public hydroelectricity's final upstream push in the 1960s. The Hells Canyon controversy's decade of administrative fact-finding and judicial review destabilized the hydroelectric legal consensus. In 1967, the Supreme Court disapproved an

FPC license for High Mountain Sheep, a new federal hydroelectric dam planned just below Idaho Power's Hells Canyon Complex.[8] *Udall v. Federal Power Commission* shocked many northwesterners, who had become accustomed to BPA, the Army Engineers, the Reclamation Bureau, and Columbia Basin public-power districts forging a chain of federal dams that had reached the very gates of Hells Canyon.[9]

The Supreme Court, for the first time since the Federal Water Power Act in 1920 conferred broad authority on the FPC to electrify America's rivers, had disapproved licensure of a new hydroelectric dam. Its wide-ranging opinion demonstrated how disparate legal and political movements had expanded judicial review. Federal courts, which had deferred to administrative expertise since the New Deal, now felt confident enough in their roles under the Administrative Procedure Act to restrain agencies' power to transform nature. *Udall* consolidated postwar administrative jurisprudence and political strategies. Until 1967, the legal system merely acknowledged citizens' aspirations for balance between production and restraint. Now those aspirations were part of the law, binding on a federal agency that had long claimed unreviewable authority to superintend Americans' relationship to their rivers.[10]

Two decades of administrative-law evolution enabled *Udall* to establish a new definition of "public interest" in running water. Two forces, legally unrelated but practically intertwined, drove that evolution: expanding legal interests, which all administrative agencies were supposed to weigh when discharging their statutory mandates, and state governments' advocacy of their constitutional interests in fish conservation. Sponsors of the Administrative Procedure Act of 1946 did not specifically intend to change how the FPC assessed proposals to build nonfederal dams on navigable and interstate rivers. Yet the act's dual command—that agencies involve more interests in regulatory practice and that federal courts supervise the executive branch more closely—encouraged critics of pell-mell hydroelectric expansion to articulate a new "public interest." Cursory dismissals of state-agency and private-group pleas on behalf of the Northwest's anadromous fish gave way to detailed assessments of dams' effects on riverine ecology. Brusque rejections of state-law claims for fish conservation and recreational opportunity became respectful consideration of biological, economic, and engineering opinions offered by state-agency experts.[11]

Law—statutes, regulations and judicial decisions—guided this unexpected outcome of the Hells Canyon controversy. The legal dispute pitting the High Dam against Idaho Power's low dams went all the way to the U.S. Supreme Court. Every sort of lawmaking institution contributed to resolving the controversy: Congress and president, Idaho and Oregon legislatures, governors and administrators in those two states, as well as their trial and appellate courts. Ultimately, legal institutions, expressing the preferences and prejudices of Americans, endorsed the three small dams over one very big one. Hells Canyon's legal history is important. After all, the canyon became historically significant to me as I handled a legal case. More important, the law made before, during, and in consequence of the Hells Canyon controversy still shapes our choices and informs our beliefs about water and power, fish and dams, nature and technology.

The postwar period saw ordinary Americans more comfortable than they are now with leaving big, complicated decisions to organizations: business corporations, government agencies, labor unions, and political lobbies. The story of Hells Canyon requires entering deeply into the minds and hearts of groups. To understand why the Truman administration fought so hard to federalize Hells Canyon, we must appreciate the American Public Power Association's role in the postwar New Deal coalition. Without peeling back layers of memos documenting the Columbia Basin Inter-Agency Committee's work in the postwar Northwest, we cannot grasp the significance of federal control over hydroelectricity, and over the rivers that generated that power.

A powerful political consensus, rooted in the New Deal's celebration of public power, propelled federal hydroelectric ambitions upriver toward Hells Canyon and the Snake Basin after 1945. Growing resistance to both federal ambition and public dam building derailed the upriver offensive. Snake Basin irrigators, Columbia River fishers, state governors and conservation managers tentatively challenged the consensus that sanctified public power. A rival for Snake River hydropower—Idaho Power—bested the Bureau of Reclamation's High Dam. However, Idaho Power won only the right to dam Hells Canyon because a decisive segment of the American people lost faith in the New Deal dream of building the world's biggest dam to generate more of the world's cheapest electricity.

The Hells Canyon controversy thus encouraged more widespread resistance after the 1950s to the postwar consensus for dam building on other rivers. High Dam opponents, by challenging the public-power consensus, opened new space within American politics for dissenters to challenge an array of public and private actions that sacrificed natural systems to meet humans' material needs. However, deep and lasting changes in environmental politics awaited future developments. Although Idaho Power's allies challenged the deference due experts and celebrated a limited type of democratic dissent, a power company, a conservative war hero, and a coalition of irrigation farmers circumscribed strict limits to resistance and deplored more ambitious possibilities for reforming the politics of power.

In the Northwest today, migratory fish that once thrived in rivers dedicated to producing power are dying out. Americans have to make hard decisions about the region's rivers. Human communities touched by the waters are implicated in their fate. Those decisions will be at least as controversial as any made in the fifties about whether public power or private capital should electrify Hells Canyon. After half a century, the minority dissenters have seized the initiative to force new decisions about dam building. Dissent has become decisive, and the language of ecology shapes the discussion, because expert opinion has penetrated the public discourse. The most acute, substantive critics of pell-mell postwar public dam building were the flannel-shirted scientists who worked in state agencies during the Hells Canyon controversy. Primarily, between 1945 and 1957, the northwestern state conservation agencies dueled with both the federal government and Idaho Power over the size, location, and operation of Hells Canyon power dams. Although their colleagues in federal service often seconded their criticism, scientists in the Oregon Fish Commission, Idaho Fish and Game Department, Washington Department of Fisheries, and Idaho State Engineer's Office outlined the arguments that today shape the Northwest's debate about rivers' fate.

Idaho Power Company's victory in the Hells Canyon controversy changed the Snake River and its watershed forever. Its three-dam complex ultimately eliminated salmon and steelhead trout races that had inhabited the Snake Basin above Hells Canyon for ten millennia. Its hydroelectricity encouraged both more intensive urban settlement and extensive irrigated agriculture. However, corporate victory and federal defeat preserved natural features of the basin and left Snake Basin politics mostly unchanged. Things forever changed, coupled with those that endured, make the Hells Canyon controversy worth understanding. Antagonists on one of the first "modern" environmental battlegrounds contested old issues rooted in the New Deal's transformation of the Pacific Northwest. But the outcome of their fierce decade-long struggle shaped future controversies over power, water, fish, and land.

Private power's victory at Hells Canyon unplugged the postwar New Deal in the Northwest before it annexed the Snake Basin. Unable to turn the Snake's hydropower to the cause of industrialization and widespread desert reclamation, federal planners in the Bureau of Reclamation and BPA left the Snake Basin almost as they had found it at the dawn of the postwar. High Hells Canyon's defeat preserved Snake Basin irrigators' distinctive relationship to the water they controlled.

What did *not* happen at Hells Canyon is at least as important to the contemporary environmental history of the Northern Rockies as what did. Mountain rivers—the Boise and Payette—stayed in their canyons instead of being forced through turbines into tunnels under granite peaks and onto rolling deserts. More than one million acres of sagebrush plain remained arid but biologically diverse. The United States' largest wild-river system, the Salmon, remained free flowing. Its waters, instead of pooling behind a concrete necklace of federal dams, continued to nurse the world's richest anadromous fishery. Phosphate beds, piled against the Continental Divide at the head of the Snake Basin, did not vanish abruptly into the maw of an industrial complex tied umbilically into a federal hydropower grid. They steadily, but slowly, disappeared into two small fertilizer plants.

Had the Federal Columbia River Power System won the Hells Canyon controversy, the Bonneville Power Administration would have mastered Snake Basin hydropower, as it had the Columbia Basin's energy grid during the Depression and Second World War. Under BPA dominion, the Snake Basin—southern Idaho, eastern Oregon, and northern Utah and Nevada—would likely have urbanized more thoroughly and quickly during the postwar. More Snake Basin people would have worked in more factories and offices. Downriver political influences from the Columbia Basin would probably have nudged Snake Basin life after 1957 in directions being pioneered by Oregonians and Washingtonians. The irrigators who dominated Snake Basin life would have had to share power sooner with industrialists, labor unions, and urban salaried workers. Indeed, victory in Hells Canyon for Idaho Power ensured two more generations of political and cultural primacy for Snake Basin agricultural leaders.

The Hells Canyon controversy deserves understanding because the long postwar debate over its fate reflected both northwesterners and the larger American nation struggling to craft a new balance between private capital, public authority, and natural features. The chief combatants—engineers and planners, industrialists and irrigators, biologists and fishers, politicians and publicists—tried to make and use law to serve their competing claims to reshape a natural system in the public interest. They advanced their competing visions in a multitude of places where American law is made. People seeking legal advantages in each of those places exerted some influence over the course of the Snake through Hells Canyon. However, taken together, acting and reacting constantly on one another, northwestern people and the region's natural features and forces made history in Hells Canyon. The Snake River Basin's natural system of rivers and canyons, basalt plains, and silvery fish persistently bent human interests into new forms that reflected nature's own imperatives.

The Hells Canyon controversy divides the history of the modern Northwest. Roughly at the midpoint of the twentieth century, northwesterners appraised dams more critically. They grasped more clearly cheap hydroelectricity's ecological consequences. They helped lead all Americans to begin exploring different ways of living along all of the waters that bind places on earth together. They displayed a new willingness to ask less from rivers, to let them do more of the work they had been doing before people dammed them to make electricity and diverted them to irrigate fields. Idaho Power Company's campaign for a federal license illustrated how customary legal tools—administrative agencies and courts—could yield unexpected legal consequences when social values were rapidly changing. The Hells Canyon controversy led directly, a decade later, to the Supreme Court's *Udall* decision that declared a new legal definition of "the public interest."

Changing popular hopes and beliefs, fears and frustrations, during the decade or so following World War II revised the meaning of legal rules that resolved the Hells Canyon controversy. Social and environmental changes stimulated legal change. They still do. In Idaho and Oregon, and in the nation as a whole, Americans have still not rendered a final decision about the respective legal preferences due environment and capital. With luck and skill, we never will.

NOTES

1 / INTRODUCTION

1. Mark W. T. Harvey, *A Symbol of Wilderness: Echo Park and the American Conservation Movement* (Albuquerque: University of New Mexico Press, 1994). Stephen Fox, *The American Conservation Movement: John Muir and His Legacy* (Madison: University of Wisconsin Press, 1981), explores an earlier dam controversy, that over Hetch Hetchy in the Yosemite Valley. Echo Park's protagonists fought in the long shadow cast by Hetch Hetchy's giant antagonists, John Muir and Gifford Pinchot.

2. Federal dam advocates claimed its minimum output of 686 megawatts would almost triple Idaho Power Company's 1951 capacity. Congressional Quarterly, "The Hells Canyon Controversy," in *Congress and the Nation: A Review of Government and Politics in the Postwar Years, 1945–1964* (Washington, D.C.: Congressional Quarterly Service, 1966), 948; Susan M. Stacy, *Legacy of Light: A History of Idaho Power Company* (Boise: Idaho Power Co., 1991), 232.

3. Julius A. Krug to Nelson Lee Smith (FPC chairman), 29 August 1947, and Glen Taylor to Nelson Lee Smith, 16 August 1947, Formal File 100–2: Part 1, box 253, FPC Project No. 1971, FERC Accession No. 138–88–006.

4. Quoted in Roscoe Ames, "Private Enterprise Builds a Hydro Dam in the Northwest," *Public Utilities Fortnightly* 49 (3 January 1952): 21–29 (hereafter cited as *PUFN*); *Idaho Daily Statesman* (Boise), 5 February 1949, 1–2; Tom Humphrey, "The Northwest Power Puzzle," *PUFN* 43 (14 April 1949): 465–69.

5. American Public Power Association, "Federal Power Policy," *Public Power* 7 (November 1949): 7–8, 24–25.

6. "More Public Power for Private Utility Distribution?" *PUFN* 39 (10 April 1947): 511–12.

7. Reproduced in Gus Norwood, *Columbia River Power for the People: A History*

of the Policies of the Bonneville Power Administration (Portland, Ore.: Bonneville Power Administration, 1980), 165 (emphasis in original).

8. Three-quarters of all northwestern wageworkers labored in the wood products industry and agriculture at the Depression's onset, a proportion unchanged in nearly a half century. Robert E. Ficken, "Grand Coulee and Hanford: The Atomic Bomb and the Development of the Columbia River," in *The Atomic West,* ed. Bruce Hevly and John M. Findlay, 21–38, 25 (Seattle: University of Washington Press, 1998).

9. Richard White, *The Organic Machine: The Remaking of the Columbia River* (New York: Hill and Wang, 1995); John Gunther, *Inside U.S.A.* (New York: Harper Bros., 1947), chaps. 6–9.

10. T. H. Watkins, *Righteous Pilgrim: The Life and Times of Harold L. Ickes, 1874–1952* (New York: Henry Holt and Co., 1990).

11. Paul J. Raver to Columbia Basin Inter-Agency Committee, 6 May 1946, folder 14–2, box 14, CBIAC Papers, Accession No. 1659–2, University of Washington Archives.

12. Lesher S. Wing (FPC) to William E. Warne (assistant Interior secretary), 1 November 1948, folder 14–4, ibid.

13. Richard Lowitt, *The New Deal in the West* (Bloomington: Indiana University Press, 1984); Jeanne Nienaber Clarke, *Roosevelt's Warrior: Harold L. Ickes and the New Deal* (Baltimore: Johns Hopkins University Press, 1996); John G. Clark, *Energy and the Federal Government: Fossil Fuel Policies, 1900–1946* (Urbana: University of Illinois Press, 1987).

14. *Oregon Journal* (Portland), 10 August 1950, 11; *Idaho Daily Statesman,* 16 August 1950, 6.

15. Paul C. Pitzer, *Grand Coulee: Harnessing a Dream* (Pullman: Washington State University Press, 1994); *Oregon Journal,* 10 December 1947, 1, 20.

16. Region 1 Director (Newell) to Reclamation Commissioner, Supplemental Report on the Payette Unit/Mountain Home Project, 18 May 1949, Formal File 100–2: Part 1, box 253, FPC Project No. 1971.

17. Krug to Smith, 29 August 1947, Formal File 100–2: Part 1, FPC Project No. 1971.

18. U.S. House of Representatives, Document No. 473 (81st Cong., 2d sess., 1950), sets forth Reclamation's Snake Basin Plan.

19. Region 1 Director to Reclamation Commissioner, "Supplemental Report on the Payette Unit/Mountain Home Project," 18 May 1949, Formal File 100–2: Part 1, box 253, FPC Project No. 1971.

20. *Hearing Transcript,* 1:40–46 (14 July 1952), 885–87 (17 July 1952), FPC Project No. 1971, box 210, FERC Accession No. 58–A-161.

21. Anthony Netboy, *The Columbia River Salmon and Steelhead Trout: Their Fight for Survival* (Seattle: University of Washington Press, 1980), together with White, *Organic Machine*, and Joseph E. Taylor III, *Making Salmon: An Environmental History of the Northwest Fisheries Crisis* (Seattle: University of Washington Press, 2000), ably chronicle the region's fishery history. Joseph Cone and Sandy Ridlington, eds., *The Northwest Salmon Crisis: A Documentary History* (Corvallis: Oregon State University Press, 1996), supplies indispensable primary sources.

22. J. H. Gutride (FPC acting secretary) to Army Engineers Chief, 14 July 1947, Formal File 100–2: Part 1, FPC Project No. 1971; Leon Fuqua (FPC secretary) to Idaho Department of Fish and Game, 14 July 1947 (hereafter cited as IDFG), and Murray (IDFG director) to Newell (Reclamation Bureau), 9 June 1948, folders IIA/B (Hells Canyon Dams), Natural Resources Policy Bureau Archives, IDFG.

23. Veatch to J. H. Gutride (FPC secretary), 4 May 1951, *Nez Perce Tribe v. Idaho Power Co.*, CV 91–0517, court files, U.S. District Court for District of Idaho; Murray to Gutride, 4 June 1951, folders IIA/B (Hells Canyon Dams), Natural Resources Policy Bureau Archives, IDFG.

24. *Idaho Daily Statesman*, 26 October 1952, 6 (Magnuson); Pitzer, *Grand Coulee*, 223–26.

25. Public Notice, Office of the CBIAC Chairman, 13 June 1947, *Nez Perce Tribe v. Idaho Power Co.*, CV 91–0517, court files, U.S. District Court for District of Idaho.

26. Idaho Power Supplement to Application, 28 October 1952, Formal File 100–2: Part 3, FPC Project No. 1971; *Idaho Daily Statesman*, 19 November 1952, 2.

27. James B. Haas, *Fishery Problems Associated with Brownlee, Oxbow, and Hells Canyon Dams on the Middle Snake River*, Investigational Report No. 4 (Portland: Fish Commission of Oregon, 1965), is the standard administrative report. "The Oxbow Incident," in William Ashworth, *Hells Canyon: The Deepest Gorge on Earth* (New York: Hawthorn Books, 1977), 107–20, bitterly arraigns Idaho Power and the governmental fish managers.

28. U.S. House of Representatives Document No. 531 (81st Cong. 2d sess., 1950), contains the Corps of Engineers' Main Control Plan.

29. Brig. Gen. C. H. Chorpening to FPC, 5 August 1953, Formal File 100–2: Part 5, FPC Project No. 1971. *Idaho Daily Statesman*, 3 July 1953, 4; 7 August 1953, 12.

30. Idaho Power constructed no new Snake Basin dams after completing the Hells Canyon Complex in 1965. Stacy, *Legacy of Light*, vi, 207 (map). Ashworth, *Hells Canyon*, discusses later struggles over Hells Canyon dams, culminating in *Udall v. FPC*, 387 U.S. 428 (1967).

31. *Idaho Power Company*, 14 F.P.C. 55 (1955).

32. Idaho Power's dams were designed to generate a total of 565 megawatts; both

Grand Coulee's and Bonneville's installed capacity in 1955 exceeded the Hells Canyon Complex's designed capacity. Vera Springer, *Power and the Pacific Northwest: A History of the Bonneville Power Administration* (Portland, Ore.: Bonneville Power Administration, 1976), 52; Congressional Quarterly, "Hells Canyon Controversy," 948.

33. *National Hells Canyon Assn. v. FPC*, 237 F.2d 777 (D.C. Cir. 1956), cert. denied, 353 U.S. 924 (1957); *Oregonian* (Portland), 23 July 1957, 1; 25 July 1957, 1.

34. Federal Power Act, secs. 4(e) and 10, 16 U.S.C.S. secs. 797(e) and 803(a).

35. Changing historiographical approaches to postwar consensus can be traced in Thomas J. Sugrue, "Reassessing the History of Postwar America," *Prospects* 20 (1995): 493–510; Robert M. Collins, "David Potter's *People of Plenty* and the Recycling of Consensus History," *Reviews in American History* 16 (June 1988): 321–35; William A. Leuchtenburg, *A Troubled Feast: American Society since 1945*, updated ed. (Boston: Little, Brown, 1983); and Eric F. Goldman, *The Crucial Decade, 1945–1955* (New York: Knopf, 1956). Useful studies of Western attitudes toward federal authority are William G. Robbins, *Landscapes of Promise: The Oregon Story, 1800–1940* (Seattle: University of Washington Press, 1997); Patricia Nelson Limerick, Clyde A. Milner II, and Charles E. Rankin, eds., *Trails: Toward a New Western History* (Lawrence: University Press of Kansas, 1991); Patricia Nelson Limerick, *The Legacy of Conquest: The Unbroken Past of the American West* (New York: W. W. Norton, 1987).

36. Elizabeth A. Fones-Wolf, *Selling Free Enterprise: The Business Assault on Labor and Liberalism, 1945–1960* (Urbana: University of Illinois Press, 1994), and Lary May, ed., *Recasting America: Culture and Politics in the Age of Cold War* (Chicago: University of Chicago Press, 1989), explore the postwar debate about the New Deal. Carlos A. Schwantes, *The Pacific Northwest: An Interpretive History* (Lincoln: University of Nebraska Press, 1989), assesses the regional impacts of postwar ideological debate.

37. Examples include Alonzo L. Hamby, *Beyond the New Deal: Harry S. Truman and American Liberalism* (New York: Columbia University Press, 1973); Robert Griffith, "Dwight D. Eisenhower and the Corporate Commonwealth," *American Historical Review* 87 (February 1982): 87–122; Robert Griffith, "Forging America's Postwar Order: Domestic Politics and Political Economy in the Age of Truman," in *The Truman Presidency*, ed. Michael J. Lacey, 57–88 (Cambridge: Cambridge University Press, 1989); and David Halberstam, *The Fifties* (New York: Villard Books, 1993). Neither of the best recent biographies of the cold war presidents even mentions the Hells Canyon controversy: David McCullough, *Truman* (New York: Simon and Schuster, 1992); and Stephen E. Ambrose, *Eisenhower*, vol. 2, *The President* (New York: Simon and Schuster, 1984). The standard interpretive history of American

natural-resource politics after World War II, Samuel P. Hays, *Beauty, Health and Permanence: Environmental Politics in the United States, 1955–1985* (New York: Cambridge University Press, 1987), does not discuss the controversy. Nor does a more compact recent introduction to postwar environmental history: Hal K. Rothman, *The Greening of a Nation? Environmentalism in the United States since 1945* (Fort Worth, Tex.: Harcourt Brace, 1998).

38. Kevin J. Fernlund, ed., *The Cold War American West, 1945–1989* (Albuquerque: University of New Mexico Press, 1998); Hevly and Findlay, *The Atomic West.*

39. Michael C. Blumm, "The Northwest's Hydroelectric Heritage," in *Northwest Lands, Northwest Peoples: Readings in Environmental History,* ed. Dale D. Goble and Paul W. Hirt, 264–94 (Seattle: University of Washington Press, 1999). Even Blumm's excellent survey largely restates his fifteen-year-old findings originally published in "The Northwest's Hydroelectric Heritage: Prologue to the Pacific Northwest Power Planning and Conservation Act," *Washington Law Review* 58 (1983): 175–244.

40. Elmo Richardson, *Dams, Parks and Politics: Resource Development and Preservation in the Truman-Eisenhower Era* (Lexington: University Press of Kentucky, 1973).

41. Hells Canyon's absence from White's massive *"It's Your Misfortune and None of My Own": A New History of the American West* (Norman: University of Oklahoma Press, 1991), is scarcely remedied in his bold interpretation of northwestern hydroelectric history, *Organic Machine.* High Hells Canyon would have fit neatly into Worster's *Rivers of Empire: Water, Aridity and the Growth of the American West* (New York: Pantheon Press, 1985), as an example of state enterprise run amok.

42. James T. Patterson, *Grand Expectations: The United States, 1945–1974* (New York: Oxford University Press, 1996); Daniel Horowitz, *Vance Packard and American Social Criticism* (Chapel Hill: University of North Carolina Press, 1994); William H. Chafe, "Postwar American Society: Dissent and Social Reform," in Lacey, *The Truman Presidency,* 156–73; Joanne J. Meyerowitz, ed., *Not June Cleaver: Women and Gender in Postwar America, 1945–1960* (Philadelphia: Temple University Press, 1994).

43. Hays, *Beauty, Health and Permanence.*

2 / AT HELL'S GATES

1. Tim Palmer, *The Snake River: Window to the West* (Washington, D.C.: Island Press, 1991); Ashworth, *Hells Canyon*; Boyd Norton, *Snake Wilderness* (San Francisco: Sierra Club, 1972).

2. John C. Veatch (chairman, Fish Commission of Oregon) to J. H. Gutride (FPC secretary), 4 May 1951, Formal File No. 100–2: Part 2, FPC Project No. 1971, box 253, FERC Accession No. 138–88–006; T. B. Murray (director, IDFG) to FPC, 4 June 1951, ibid.

3. Charles F. Wilkinson and Daniel Keith Conner, "The Law of the Pacific Salmon Fishery: Conservation and Allocation of a Transboundary Common Property Resource," *Kansas Law Review* 32 (1983): 17–109.

4. George Cameron Coggins, "Wildlife and the Constitution: The Walls Come Tumbling Down," *Washington Law Review* 55 (1980): 295–358; George C. Coggins, Charles F. Wilkinson, and John D. Leshy, eds., *Federal Public Lands and Resources Law*, 3d ed. (Mineola, N.Y.: Foundation Press, 1993), 412–14.

5. Timothy Egan, *The Good Rain: Across Time and Terrain in the Pacific Northwest* (New York: Vintage Books, 1991).

6. D. W. Meinig, *Great Columbia Plain: A Historical Geography, 1805–1910* (Seattle: University of Washington Press, 1968).

7. Gus Norwood, "Bonneville Power for Southern Idaho," *Public Power* 8 (October 1950): 9, 34.

8. Applicant's Opening Brief, 5 November 1954, p. 98, Formal File 100–2: Part 7, box 254, FPC Project No. 1971, FERC Accession No. 138–88–006.

9. North Pacific Division, Army Corps of Engineers, "Main Control Plan—Columbia Basin," Appendix H, par. 105, House of Representatives Document No. 531 (81st Cong., 2d sess. 1950).

10. Todd Shallat, ed., *Snake: The Plain and Its People* (Boise, Idaho: Boise State University Press, 1994).

11. Idaho Power's Opening Brief, 88–89.

12. Ibid., 87–88.

13. Meinig, *Great Columbia Plain.*

14. Shallat, *Snake,* chap. 5. Mark Fiege, "Creating a Hybrid Landscape: Irrigated Agriculture in Idaho," in Goble and Hirt, *Northwest Lands, Northwest Peoples,* 362–88.

15. Mark Fiege, *Irrigated Eden: The Making of an Agricultural Landscape in the American West* (Seattle: University of Washington Press, 2000), should be read in conjunction with Worster, *Rivers of Empire,* for valuable insights into the marriage between culture and capital that produced intensive irrigation regimes in the Snake Basin.

16. Secretary of State, *Idaho Blue Book: 1987–1988* (Boise, Idaho: Secretary of State, 1989), 277; Worster, *Rivers of Empire.*

17. Idaho Power's Opening Brief, 15–16; Stacy, *Legacy of Light,* chaps. 9, 11, 13.

18. Idaho Power's Opening Brief, 57, 98–100.

19. Ibid., 98, 16; Presiding Examiner's Decision, 6 May 1955, Finding of Fact 40,

Formal File 100–2: Part 9, FPC Project No. 1971, FERC Accession No. 138–88–006.

20. Fiege, "Creating a Hybrid Landscape"; Shallat, *Snake;* Stacy, *Legacy of Light.*

21. Arthur A. Hart, *Wings over Idaho: An Aviation History* (Boise, Idaho: Historic Boise, Inc., 1991), 101–18.

22. Merle W. Wells and Arthur Hart, *Idaho: Gem of the Mountains* (Northridge, Calif.: Windsor Publications, 1985); Carlos A. Schwantes, *In Mountain Shadows: A History of Idaho* (Lincoln: University of Nebraska Press, 1991); Randy Stapilus, *Paradox Politics: People and Power in Idaho* (Boise, Idaho: Ridenbaugh Press, 1988).

23. *Idaho Blue Book, 1987–88,* 277.

24. Application for License (Oxbow), 9 December 1950, Part 1: Formal File No. 100–2, FPC Project No. 1971, box 253, FERC Accession No. 138–88–006.

25. Nancy Langston, *Forest Dreams, Forest Nightmares: The Paradox of Old Growth in the Inland West* (Seattle: University of Washington Press, 1999).

26. Robbins, *Landscapes of Promise.*

27. Statistics about the New Deal dams are drawn from Paul B. McKee, "Power in the Pacific Northwest," *PUFN* 52 (27 August 1953): 291–97. National and regional fuel-source comparisons come from the Federal Power Commission, *Annual Report: 1947,* 15 (national electric generation by fuel supply); FPC, *Annual Report: 1949,* 9 (national and regional electric fuel sources); and FPC, *Annual Report: 1950,* 67 (water-power potential by geographical divisions). Consumption figures are from Alex Radin, "More Power for the People," *Public Power* 10 (May 1952): 16–22. White, *Organic Machine,* advances a provocative thesis about electrification's effects on riverine ecology and human society in the basin.

28. Presiding Examiner's Decision, 6 May 1955, 53–54.

29. Ibid.

30. Ibid., 26.

31. Idaho Power's Opening Brief, 6; Presiding Examiner's Decision, 26.

32. Price comparisons are drawn from David Cushman Coyle, *Conservation: An American Story of Conflict and Accomplishment* (New Brunswick, N.J.: Rutgers University Press, 1957), 186–89 (map).

33. Lowitt, *The New Deal in the West,* shows how smoothly New Deal hydroelectric policy in the Pacific Northwest during the prewar years meshed with mobilization. Gerald D. Nash's two companion studies of World War II in the West are indispensable: *The American West Transformed: The Impact of the Second World War* (Bloomington: Indiana University Press, 1985); and *World War II and the West: Reshaping the Economy* (Lincoln: University of Nebraska Press, 1990).

34. "Northwest Power Pool: A Lesson in Democracy," *Public Power* 8 (November

1950): 14–16; Springer, *Power and the Pacific Northwest,* chap. 4; Blumm, "Hydro-electric Heritage: Prologue," 203–4 (Power Pool).

35. Blumm, "Hydroelectric Heritage: Prologue," 195–202.

36. Application for License (Oxbow), 9 December 1950, Formal File No. 100–2: Part 1, FPC Project No. 1971, box 253, FERC Accession No. 138–88–006.

37. Rural electrification comparisons are in "Public Systems Pay More Taxes," *Public Power* 6 (November 1948): 21. John Gunther, a popular contemporary jour-nalist, acutely perceived how the Depression and World War II had transformed the Columbia Basin in *Inside U.S.A.,* chap. 6. Schwantes, *The Pacific Northwest,* chap. 16, assesses the war's impact on the region. Rodney P. Carlisle and Joan M. Zenzen, *Supplying the Nuclear Arsenal: American Production Reactors, 1942–1992* (Baltimore: Johns Hopkins University Press, 1996), shows how Columbia Basin electricity lured the Manhattan Project.

38. David Nye, *Consuming Power: A Social History of American Energies* (Cam-bridge, Mass.: MIT Press, 1998), 10–12, 184–91, charts electricity's unforeseen impacts on industrial organization and residential development.

39. Oregon and Washington growth figures from White, *"It's Your Misfortune and None of My Own,"* 515 (table 14); *Information Please Almanac: 1991* (Boston: Houghton Mifflin Co., 1991), 797. Eastern Oregon's decline comes from Hells Canyon Development Association, Informal Protest, 16 April 1951, p. 5, Formal File 100–2: Part 1, box 253, FPC Project 1971, FERC Accession No. 138–88–006.

40. Stephen E. Ambrose, *Undaunted Courage: Meriwether Lewis, Thomas Jefferson and the Opening of the American West* (New York: Simon and Schuster, 1996).

41. Netboy, *Columbia River Salmon and Steelhead*; Joseph E. Taylor III, "Burning the Candle at Both Ends: Historicizing Overfishing in Oregon's Nineteenth-Century Salmon Fisheries," *Environmental History* 4 (January 1999): 54–79.

42. *In re Pacific Northwest Power Co./Washington Public Power Supply System,* 31 F.P.C. 247 (1964), offers a thorough history of postwar dam-building plans for the entire Hells Canyon reach of the Snake River and the lower Salmon River.

43. Memorandum in Support of Summary Judgment (Nez Perce Tribe), *Nez Perce Tribe v. Idaho Power Co.,* CV 91–0517 (U.S. District Court for District of Idaho).

44. Wendell Smith, "Where Did All the Salmon and Steelhead Go?" [n.d., prob-ably 1980], Idaho Power Co., folders IIA/B (Hells Canyon Dams), Natural Resources Policy Bureau Archives, IDFG.

45. Ron Ross, "Hells Canyon Decision Faces Congress," *Public Power* 14 (Janu-ary 1956): 7–10; Congressional Quarterly, "The Hells Canyon Controversy," *Congress and the Nation,* 946–49.

1. Flood Control Act of 19 August 1944, ch. 665, 58 Stat. 887.

2. Blumm, "Hydroelectric Heritage: Prologue," 204–6.

3. "Attacks on Preferences," *Public Power* 9 (June 1950): 18.

4. Congressional Quarterly, "Natural Resources and Power . . . Developments before 1945," in *Congress and the Nation*, 772–76.

5. William Pearl to Governor Len B. Jordan, 13 July 1954, CBIAC Charter folder, box 1, CBIAC Papers, Accession No. 1659–3, University of Washington Archives.

6. Federal Power Commission, *Annual Report: 1947*, 111.

7. Resolution Adopted by the FIARBC—Establishment of the Columbia Basin Inter-Agency Committee, 5 February 1946, Pacific Northwest Governors' Power Policy Committee, July–August 1954 folder, container 17, Governor Paul L. Patterson Papers, Oregon State Archives; Charles McKinley, *Uncle Sam in the Northwest: Federal Management of Natural Resources in the Columbia River Valley* (Berkeley: University of California Press, 1952), 91–95.

8. FPC, *Annual Report: 1947*, 112.

9. Paul J. Raver to CBIAC, 6 May 1946, folder 14–2, box 14, CBIAC Papers, Accession No. 1659–2, University of Washington Archives.

10. FIARBC Resolution/ CBIAC, paras. 2–4.

11. CBIAC Minutes, 5 February 1946–10 December 1953, box 1, CBIAC Papers, Accession No. 1198, University of Washington Archives.

12. Congressional Quarterly, "1946: Federal Power Policy," in *Congress and the Nation*, 808–9; Watkins's fine Ickes biography, *Righteous Pilgrim*, never mentions this major policy statement.

13. Congressional Quarterly, "1946: Federal Power Policy"; Richardson, *Dams, Parks and Politics*, chap. 1.

14. Craig Wollner, *Electrifying Eden: Portland General Electric, 1889–1965* (Portland: Oregon Historical Society Press, 1990).

15. "More Public Power for Private Utility Distribution?" *PUFN* 39 (10 April 1947): 511–12.

16. Quoted in Nelson Lee Smith, "Wanted: A National Power Program," *PUFN* 39 (5 June 1947): 732–737. Smith was chairman of the Federal Power Commission.

17. Frank McLaughlin, "It Is Not in the Cards," *PUFN* 39 (5 June 1947): 738–45.

18. Ernest Clifford Potts, "Some Adverse Effects of a Federal Power Monopoly," *PUFN* 40 (18 December 1947): 811–17.

19. Ibid.

20. Raver to CBIAC, 6 May 1946, folder 14–2, box 14, CBIAC Papers, Accession No. 1659–2; Norwood, *Columbia River Power for the People*, 181–87.

21. Columbia Basin Inter-Agency Committee, *State and Inter-Agency Program Related to Conservation and Development of Land and Water Resources in the Pacific Northwest: 1950–1955* (1 December 1949), "Foreword and Basic Objective," Columbia Basin (Genl.)—1949/Part I folder, box 1, series I, Governor C. A. Robins Papers, Idaho State Historical Society (hereafter cited as ISHS).

22. Arthur Maas, *Muddy Waters: The Army Engineers and the Nation's Rivers* (Cambridge, Mass.: Harvard University Press, 1951), 123–24; McKinley's 1952 tome, *Uncle Sam in the Pacific Northwest*, 114–18, approvingly noted that former president Herbert Hoover's 1949 government-reform commission recommended abolishing both agencies.

23. Palmer, *Snake River,* 202.

24. *Public Papers of the President: Harry S. Truman, 1947* (Washington, D.C.: Government Printing Office, 1962–65), 1–9 (State of the Union), 55–82 (Budget); Clark, *Energy and the Federal Government*, 376–77 (Krug); Marc Reisner, *Cadillac Desert: The American West and Its Disappearing Water* (New York: Penguin, 1986), 142–46 (Straus); "Government Officials to Speak," *Public Power* 9 (March 1950): 9 (Davidson); Watkins, *Righteous Pilgrim*, 778–80 (Ickes' influence on Straus, Raver).

25. *Oregon Journal*, 10 December 1947, 1; Region 1 Director to Reclamation Commissioner, Supplemental Report on the Payette Unit/Mountain Home Project, 18 May 1949, Formal File 100–2: Part 1, box 253, FPC Project No. 1971.

26. H. T. Nelson (Reclamation Region 1) and Paul J. Raver, Columbia Basin Account, Exhibit O, CBIAC Minutes, 8 March 1950 (Spokane, Wash.), 76–80, CBIAC Meetings—March 1950/Part II folder, box 1, series I, Robins Papers, ISHS.

27. Region 1 Director to Reclamation Bureau Commissioner, 18 May 1949, Formal File 100–2: Part 2, FPC Project No. 1971.

28. Krug to Smith, 29 August 1947, Formal File 100–2: Part 1, FPC Project No. 1971.

29. *Hearing Transcript* 1:40–46 (14 July 1952), 885–87 (17 July 1952), FPC Project No. 1971, box 210, FERC Accession No. 58-A-161.

30. Straus to Idaho Governor C. A. Robins, 12 March 1947, CBIAC Meetings/Part IV folder, box 2, series I, Robins Papers, ISHS.

31. Krug to Federal Power Commission Chairman Nelson Lee Smith, 29 August 1947, Formal File 100–2: Part 1, FPC Project No. 1971.

32. Ibid.

33. *Idaho Daily Statesman*, 10 July 1947, 12.

34. This brief sketch of Kulp's career relies on the voluminous reclamation and

irrigation files maintained by successive Idaho governors, from 1947 through 1957: C. A. Robins, Len B. Jordan, and Robert E. Smylie. ISHS houses their official papers. No useful history apparently exists of Kulp, or of the State Reclamation engineer's office in the postwar era.

35. Lynn Crandall to Senator Glen H. Taylor, 19 May 1947, CBIAC Meetings/Part IV folder, box 2, series I, Robins Papers, ISHS.

36. Idaho State Chamber to Robins et al., 24 May 1947; and Robins to Krug, 31 May 1947, ibid.

37. Krug to Robins, 14 June 1947; "Suggested Comments to Secy. Krug," Kulp Memorandum, 5 August 1947; Robins to Krug, 6 August 1947; Robins to Krug, 27 September 1947, ibid.

38. Robins to Krug, 27 September 1947, ibid.

39. Krug to Robins, 24 October 1947, ibid.

40. Among the vast historical and legal literature on prior appropriation in the arid West, Donald Worster's and Donald J. Pisani's dialogues supply some of the most helpful introductions and interpretations. Worster, "Freedom and Want: The Western Paradox of Aridity" (17–35), and Pisani, "Water Law and Localism in the West" (36–55), both in *Halcyon,* vol. 14 (1992). Also invaluable are Charles F. Wilkinson, *Crossing the Next Meridian: Land, Water, and the Future of the West* (Washington, D.C.: Island Press, 1992), and Peter L. Reich, "Studies in Western Water Law: Historiographical Trends," *Western Legal History* 9 (1996): 1–7.

41. Stacy, *Legacy of Light,* 131, 142.

42. Potts, "Some Adverse Effects."

43. McLaughlin, "Not in the Cards."

44. J. H. Gutride (FPC acting secretary) to Army Engineers Chief, 14 July 1947, Formal File 100–2: Part 1, FPC Project No. 1971.

45. Leon M. Fuqua (FPC secretary) to Idaho Department of Fish and Game, 14 July 1947, ibid.

46. Krug to Smith (FPC chairman), 29 August 1947, ibid.

47. Taylor to Nelson Lee Smith, 16 August 1947, ibid. LeRoy Ashby and Rod Gramer, *Fighting the Odds: The Life of Senator Frank Church* (Pullman: Washington State University Press, 1994), 47–52, 57–61, offers a useful brief account of Taylor's Idaho liberalism.

48. CBIAC Minutes (14th Meeting—Baker, Ore.), 4 February–2 April 1948 Minutes folder, box 1, CBIAC Papers, Accession No. 1198, University of Washington Archives.

49. *Oregon Journal,* 10 December 1947, 1.

50. CBIAC Baker Minutes, 10–11 December 1947.

1. White, *Organic Machine*, 74–75.

2. [Corps of Engineers/North Pacific Division], Summary of . . . Columbia River Report, 10 November 1948, folder 14–3, box 14, Accession No. 1659–2, CBIAC Papers, University of Washington Archives.

3. *PUFN* 41 (15 January 1948): 36, and 41 (20 May 1948): 430–32; *Public Power* 6 (March 1948): 6.

4. "Stockman Urges Program," *Public Power* 6 (May 1948): 11, 19.

5. "Interior Dept. Appropriation," *Public Power* 6 (July 1948): 8.

6. McCullough, *Truman*, chap. 14; Samuel Lubell, *The Future of American Politics*, rev. 2d ed. (Garden City, N.J.: Doubleday and Co., 1956).

7. *Oregonian*, 8 June 1948, 1; 11 June 1948, 1.

8. Truman to Krug, 1 June 1948; Krug to Truman, 3 June 1948, McNeil 1948 folder, box 1, Accession No. 1659–3, CBIAC Papers; "Truman Mans Reclamation Pumps," *PUFN* 42 (1 July 1948): 37–38.

9. "Water-Power Development by Public Urged," *Public Power* 6 (May 1948): 8; *PUFN* 42 (3 June 1948): 11–13.

10. *Oregonian*, 1 October 1948, 6.

11. "NWPPA Discusses Power Shortage," *Public Power* 6 (September 1948): 4–5.

12. CBIAC Minutes (Portland, 20th meeting), CBIAC Papers.

13. House of Representatives Document No. 531 (81st Cong., 2d sess., 1950); CBIAC Minutes (Portland, 23d meeting), CBIAC Papers.

14. *Idaho Daily Statesman*, 9 December 1948, 9; 10 December 1948, 16.

15. *Oregonian*, 12 December 1948, 10.

16. Ibid., 18 December 1948, 9.

17. "Washington and the Utilities," *PUFN* 43 (3 March 1949): 303–4.

18. McCullough, *Truman*; Hamby, *Beyond the New Deal*; *Idaho Daily Statesman*, 20 April 1949, 1

19. McKinley, *Uncle Sam in the Pacific Northwest*, and Richardson, *Dams, Parks and Politics*, remain the most useful studies of the Columbia Valley Administration saga.

20. Commission on Organization of the Executive Branch of the Government, *The Hoover Commission Report* (New York: McGraw-Hill, 1949).

21. *Oregonian*, 25 January 1949, 1; 29 January 1949, 1; *Oregon Journal*, 12 April 1949, 6.

22. Summary of [Corps] . . . Columbia River Report, 10 November 1948, CBIAC Papers.

23. *Idaho Daily Statesman*, 4 February 1949, 9.

24. Ibid., 5 February 1949, 1–2.

25. Ibid. Idaho Power's opposition to the High Dam led the *Daily Statesman*'s story about the Army Engineers' hearing.

26. Statement of Idaho Power Company, Public Hearing on "308 Report," 4 February 1949, Formal File 100–2: Part 1, FPC Project No. 1971.

27. *Public Papers of the President: Harry S. Truman, 1949* (Washington, D.C.: Government Printing Office, 1964), 208–13; *Oregonian*, 29 January 1949, 11; 17 April 1949, 12.

28. *Oregonian*, 29 January 1949, 11; 17 April 1949, 12; *Idaho Daily Statesman*, 4 February 1949, 10.

29. *Oregon Journal*, 12 April 1949, 5.

30. *Idaho Daily Statesman*, 20 April 1949, 9.

31. Ibid., 21 April 1949, 12.

32. Ibid., 14 April 1949, 1; 21 April 1949, 4.

33. Ibid., 16 April 1949, 1; 23 April 1949, 5.

34. Ibid., 22 April 1949, 1, 6.

35. "Hoover Commission Urges Expansion," *Public Power* 7 (April 1949): 6; *Oregon Journal*, 10 April 1949, 6; "Hoover Commission Splits on Federal Power," *Public Power* 7 (May 1949): 23

36. *Idaho Daily Statesman*, 17 April 1949, 3; 21 April 1949, 4.

37. Ibid., 20 April 1949, 1–2.

38. "Congress Holds Hearings on CVA," *Public Power* 7 (July 1949): 7, 21; "Field Hearings Planned," ibid., 7 (September 1949): 14.

39. "Northwest Meetings Highlight CVA," ibid., 7 (October 1949): 9, 22; Congressional Quarterly, *Congress and the Nation*, 817–18.

40. BPA Summary, Exhibit A, CBIAC Minutes, 8 February 1950, Columbia Basin Inter-Agency Committee Meetings—February 1950/Part I folder, box 1, series I, Robins Papers, ISHS.

41. "NRECA's Biggest Convention," *Public Power* 8 (April 1950): 13–14.

42. "Record Crowd at APPA Convention," ibid., 10–11.

43. Clyde T. Ellis, A *Giant Step* (New York: Random House, 1966), 117–19.

44. CBIAC Minutes, 8 March 1950 (Spokane, Wash.), CBIAC Meetings—March 1950/Part II folder, box 1, series I, Robins Papers, ISHS.

45. For formation of the Water Resources Policy Commission, see "Group Has

First Meeting," *Public Power* 8 (February 1950): 7–8. For Olds's defeat, see "Senate Turns Down Olds," ibid., 7 (November 1949): 9, 25; and correspondence in folder 235-A (Endorsements A-B), box 841, Official File, Papers of Harry S. Truman, Truman Library.

46. "Senate Kills Columbia Basin Plan," *Public Power* 8 (May 1950): 7, 28.

47. Congressional Quarterly, *Congress and the Nation.*

5 / PLANNING FOR PERMANENT CONTROL

1. Fred C. Cleaver, ed., *Fisheries Statistics of Oregon*, Fish Commission of Oregon, contribution no. 16, September 1951, 33–42.

2. FCO Chairman to Ickes, 26 October 1938, Personnel File 1947–67 box, Barn anteroom, Oregon Department of Fish and Wildlife (ODFW) Clackamas Archives.

3. Clarke, *Roosevelt's Warrior*, 376–77, and Watkins, *Righteous Pilgrim*, 778–80, offer the best recent studies of Ickes' conservation philosophy. Neither, however, adequately explores his fascination with public power. William E. Leuchtenburg, *Franklin D. Roosevelt and the New Deal: 1932–1940* (New York: Harper and Row, 1963), 70–71 (Ickes' Progressive heritage), 133 (public works mission rivaled Cheops's legacy); Anthony J. Badger, *The New Deal: The Depression Years, 1933–1940* (New York: Hill and Wang, 1989), 82 (loyalty to New Deal, aggressive methods).

4. Through 1953, Title 83, Oregon Compiled Laws Annotated (OCLA), and after 1 January 1954, Title 42, Oregon Revised Statutes (ORS), governed the Fish Commission.

5. Jim Gladson, Randy Henry, and Pat Wray, "Fish and Wildlife Management, 1893–1993: The Past, the Present, the Future," *Oregon Wildlife* 49 (Spring 1993): 3–11; Clark Walsh, "'The Good Old Days': A Review of Game and Fish Administration in Oregon," *Oregon State Game Commission Bulletin*, vol. 14 (December 1959) and (February 1960).

6. This system accorded with management experts' prescriptions for an "ideal" state fish or wildlife regulatory agency. Reuben Edward Trippensee, *Wildlife Management: Upland Game and General Principles* (New York: McGraw-Hill, 1948), 1:434; Ira N. Gabrielson, *Wildlife Management* (New York: McMillan Co., 1951), 241–48. Both works praised Aldo Leopold's pioneering *Game Management* (New York: Chas. Scribner's Sons, 1933) for first describing the proper political and administrative arrangements.

7. Fish Commission of the State of Oregon: 1921–59, History of Fish Commission—Deloris Parson folder, Steve King History File, Annex, ODFW Clackamas Archives.

8. Notice of preliminary permit application to Federal Power Commission, George Otis Smith to Fish Commission of Oregon, 9 June 1933, Personnel File 1947–67 box, Barn anteroom, ODFW Clackamas Archives.

9. *Fisheries Statistics of Oregon*, tables 8, 9, and 16; James H. Cellars, "Hydro Kills the Fishing Industry," *PUFN* 41 (25 March 1948): 417–25.

10. FCO Chairman to Ickes, 26 October 1938.

11. Pitzer, *Grand Coulee*, chronicles the dam's varied rationales and boosters. John Fahey, *The Inland Empire: Unfolding Years, 1879–1929* (Seattle: University of Washington Press, 1986), traces the inland basin's emergence as a commercial and agricultural region.

12. Watkins, *Righteous Pilgrim*, 468–70.

13. Fish and Wildlife Coordination Act of 10 March 1934, ch. 55, 48 Stat. 401, sec. 1.

14. Rock Island's power and fisheries history can be gleaned from articles in *Public Power* 9 (June 1951): 25; 9 (September 1951): 5; and 10 (October 1952): 20. Charles P. Schwartz, Jr., "Federalism and Anadromous Fish: *FPC v. Oregon*," *George Washington Law Review* 23 (1955): 535–47, and "*Niagara Mohawk v. FPC*: Have Private Water Rights Been Destroyed by the Federal Power Act?" *University of Pennsylvania Law Review* 102 (1953): 31–79, thoroughly discuss the Federal Power Act's legislative history.

15. Federal Power Act of 26 August 1935, ch. 687, 49 Stat. 863, codified at 16 U.S.C.S. secs. 791a–825*l*.

16. Pitzer, *Grand Coulee*, 223, misses the irony here. Federal law imposed conservation duties on Puget Sound Power, but none on the Reclamation Bureau.

17. Pitzer, *Grand Coulee*, provides an excellent account of the New Dealers' hopes for the Columbia Basin Project, anchored by Coulee Dam. Ickes' passion for public power germinated during his Chicago days as a Progressive gadfly. Forrest McDonald, *Insull* (Chicago: University of Chicago Press, 1962), identifies Ickes as one of the most vigorous, and ineffectual, opponents of corporate utilities in the interwar years. Leuchtenburg, *Roosevelt and the New Deal*; Badger, *New Deal*; and William U. Chandler, *The Myth of TVA: Conservation and Development in the Tennessee Valley, 1933–1983* (Cambridge, Mass.: Ballinger Publishing Co. 1984), appraise the New Deal's efforts to use hydroelectricity to stimulate industrial recovery and agricultural reform. A New Deal public servant in the postwar Northwest, Charles McKinley offered a lavish tribute to federal leadership in natural-resources development in *Uncle Sam in the Pacific Northwest*.

18. Pitzer, *Grand Coulee*, 223.

19. Ibid., 224.

20. Ibid., 226.

21. Mitchell Act of 11 May 1938, ch. 502, 52 Stat. 345, codified as amended at 16 U.S.C.S. secs. 755–57.

22. Quotes from Columbia River Inter-Tribal Fish Commission, "The Mitchell Act: An Analysis by CRITFC" (Portland, Ore., June 1981), 1982 Legal Miscellaneous folder, Annex, ODFW Clackamas Archives.

23. Veatch to Ickes, 26 October 1938.

24. Veatch to Ickes, 8 February 1939, 1947–67 Personnel File box, Barn anteroom, ODFW Clackamas Archives.

25. This first Corps of Engineers "308 Report" on the Snake Basin was reprinted in House of Representatives Document No. 531 (81st Cong., 2d sess., 1950).

26. Jackson to Veatch, 17 March 1939, 1947–67 Personnel File box, Barn anteroom, ODFW Clackamas Archives.

27. Ibid.

28. Bureau of Fisheries Memorandum for the Commissioner of Reclamation, 15 March 1939, ibid.

29. Memorandum for the Press, U.S. Dept. of the Interior, 31 March 1939, ibid.

30. Veatch to Ickes, 17 April 1939, ibid.

31. Keith Petersen, *River of Life/Channel of Death* (Lewiston, Idaho: Confluence Press, 1995), 96, 101.

32. Netboy, *Columbia River Salmon and Steelhead.*

33. Leo L. Laythe, "The Fishery Development Program in the Lower Columbia River," *Transactions of the American Fisheries Society* 78 (1948): 42–55, 47.

34. Fish and Wildlife Coordination Act of 14 August 1946, ch. 965, 60 Stat. 1080, codified as amended at 16 U.S.C.S. secs. 666a–666c.

35. Excerpts from statements made by Senator Cordon before the Fish Commission at their meeting on December 11, 1945, regarding the Coordination Bill, OFC Meetings 1946–47 folder, Annex, ODFW Clackamas Archives.

36. *Oregon Journal,* 15 March 1947, 1.

6 / SACRIFICING HELLS CANYON'S FISH

1. Rivers and Harbors Act of 1945, ch. 19, 59 Stat. 10.

2. Petersen, *River of Life/Channel of Death,* chaps. 5–6, offers a superb account of the local and national pressures for immediate postwar public works in the basin.

3. "Damn Dams" meeting notes/Cox and McChesney—Army Engineers, [n.d.], OFC Meetings 1946–47 folder, Annex, ODFW Clackamas Archives.

4. Ibid.

5. McKinley, *Uncle Sam in the Pacific Northwest,* 385, 427–31; Netboy, *Columbia River Salmon and Steelhead,* 78–79.

6. "Report of the Master Fish Warden," *Oregon Fish Commission Biennial Report: 1947,* 3–4, 6.

7. *Oregonian,* 8 June 1947, 6.

8. Gunther, *Inside U.S.A.,* chap. 6; Resources for the Future, *The Nation Looks at Its Resources: Report of the Mid-Century Conference on Resources for the Future* (Washington, D.C.: Resources for the Future, 1954); David E. Nye, *Electrifying America: Social Meanings of a New Technology, 1880–1940* (Cambridge, Mass.: MIT Press, 1990).

9. *Oregon Journal,* 24 June 1947, 1.

10. Public Notice, Office of the Chairman, CBIAC, 13 June 1947, court files, *Nez Perce Tribe v. Idaho Power Company,* CV91–0517 (U.S. District Court for District of Idaho).

11. McKinley, *Uncle Sam in the Northwest,* 425–28; Norwood, *Power for the People,* 55–62; and Clark, *Energy and the Federal Government,* 290–302, all discuss phases of Bessey's career with federal agencies in the Columbia-Snake Basin.

12. CBIAC Minutes: 6th Meeting (Seattle, 8 January 1947), 7th Meeting (Lewiston, 12 February 1947), 8th Meeting (Boise, 2 April 1947), Minutes 12 February 47–5 February 46 folder, box 1, CBIAC Papers, Accession no. 1198, University of Washington Archives.

13. Public Notice, Office of the Chairman, CBIAC.

14. CBIAC Minutes (10th Meeting, Walla Walla, 25–26 June 1947), CBIAC Papers.

15. *Oregonian,* 26 June 1947, 1, 4.

16. *Oregon Journal,* 25 June 1947, 1; *Oregonian,* 26 June 1947, 1.

17. "The Effect of the Proposed River Development Program on the Columbia River Fisheries," 25 June 1947, *FCO Processed Reports: Administrative, 1947–49,* no. 7.

18. *Oregon Journal,* 25 June 1947, 1; *Oregonian,* 26 June 1947, 1.

19. Idaho's 1947 salmon angling regulations limited catch to two. *Commission Minutes,* 1:377 (13 January 1947), Director's Office files, IDFG.

20. *Oregon Journal,* 27 June 1947, 1.

21. *Oregonian,* 27 June 1947, 1.

22. Ibid., 10.

23. *Oregon Journal,* 26 June 1947, 4.

24. Ibid., 1.

25. CBIAC Minutes (11th Meeting, 23–24 July 1947; 12th Meeting, 8 October 1947), CBIAC Papers.

26. CBIAC's papers contain an untitled memo, dated "[23 June 1947]" and "7/23," that reflects Bessey's subcommittee's evaluation of the Walla Walla evidence. Internal evidence indicates this memorandum focused CBIAC's negotiations over a fish-conservation decision between July and October 1947. Box 1, CBIAC Papers.

27. Washington Department of Fisheries, Oregon Fish Commission, and U.S. Fish and Wildlife Service, *A Program of Rehabilitation of the Columbia River Fisheries* (1947).

28. "Columbia River Watershed Remaining Salmon Spawning Grounds" map, [n.d.], 1947 Lower Columbia River Fishery Development Program (LCRFDP) files, Annex: ODFW Clackamas Archives.

29. *A Program of Rehabilitation*, 3–4

30. Ibid., 14–17.

31. Ibid., 3 (emphasis added).

32. Ibid., 5.

33. Don Gooding and Les Hatch, eds., *The Salmon Crisis* (Seattle: Washington Department of Fisheries, 1949), 12, 6.

34. Ibid., 6, 15.

35. Herbert M. Peet to H. B. McCoy, 14 October 1949, "Columbia Basin (General)" file, box 1, series I, Governor C. A. Robins Papers, ISHS.

36. Region 1 of the U.S. Fish and Wildlife Service included Washington, Oregon, Idaho, Montana, Nevada, and California.

37. Laythe, "Fishery Development Program."

38. Ibid., 47–48.

39. Ibid., fig. 3, 47–49.

40. Mark R. Kulp to Governor Robins, 17 October 1949, "Columbia Basin (General)" file, box 1, series I, Robins Papers, ISHS.

41. Day to Veatch, 31 August 1948, 1948 LCRFDP files, Annex: ODFW Archives.

42. "Agreement Covering Participation of the States of Washington, Oregon, and Idaho in the Program for Conservation of the Fishery Resources of the Columbia River Basin," 23 June 1948, ibid.

43. Kemmerich to Newell, 5 September 1947, folders IIA/B (Hells Canyon Dams), Natural Resources Policy Bureau Archives, IDFG.

44. Herbert M. Peet to H. B. McCoy, 14 October 1949, "Columbia Basin (General)" file, box 1, series I, Robins Papers, ISHS.

45. Veatch to Delegation, 13 January 1948, 1948 LCRFDP files, Annex: ODFW Archives.

46. Cellars to Delegation, 15 January 1948; Sandoz to Delegation, 15 January 1948, ibid.

47. Suomela to Albert Day, 14 January 1948; Representative Harris Ellsworth to Suomela, 13 February 1948; Cordon to Suomela, 16 February 1948, ibid.

48. Suomela to Senator Chan Gurney, 3 March 1948; Suomela to Day, 3 March 1948, ibid.

49. "Funds Appropriated for Salmon Restoration on Lower Columbia River," Department of Interior Information Service, 9 July 1948 (P.N. 40561), ibid.

50. Suomela to Day, 4 August 1948, 1948 LCRFDP files, Annex: ODFW Archives.

51. M. C. James, Assistant Fish and Wildlife Service Director, to Suomela, 8 September 1948, ibid..

52. Laythe to Suomela, 6 October 1948, ibid.

53. U.S. Fish and Wildlife Service Project Agreement No. 0–2–1, 5 January 1949, ibid.

54. Day to Suomela, 11 January 1949, ibid.

7 / UNPLUGGING THE NEW DEAL

1. Griffith, "Eisenhower and the Corporate Commonwealth."

2. Julius A. Krug, "Benefits of Federal Public Power," *Public Power* 7 (June 1949): 19–20, 28–29, 20.

3. Douglas McKay, "Why Interior Dropped Hell's Canyon Project," *PUFN* 51 (4 June 1953): 734–39, 737.

4. Mason Drukman, *Wayne Morse: A Political Biography* (Portland: Oregon Historical Society Press, 1997), chap. 6; Arthur Robert Smith, *The Tiger in the Senate: The Biography of Wayne Morse* (Garden City, N.Y.: Doubleday and Co., 1962), 300–310.

5. Quoted in "Hell's Canyon Dam: Pro and Con," *PUFN* 49 (8 May 1952): 645–46.

6. Ibid., 645; White, *Organic Machine,* chap. 3, deftly sketches public power's early impacts on the Northwest.

7. Quoted in Ames, "Private Enterprise Builds a Hydro Dam in the Northwest," 21–29.

8. Fones-Wolf, *Selling Free Enterprise,* extends Griffith's pioneering work on postwar economic policy, "Forging America's Postwar Order."

9. Frank McLaughlin, "Pacific Northwest in the Big Squeeze of Big Government," *PUFN* 49 (22 May 1952): 663–75, 663. Bonneville Dam, completed in 1937, generated 518 megawatts; Grand Coulee, completed in 1940, generated 2,082 megawatts. These two dams alone generated more than half of the entire West's hydroelectricity. Federal Power Commission, *Annual Report: 1953,* 78; FPC, *Annual Report: 1952,* 66. By contrast, publicly owned generating facilities produced only 19 percent of all electricity nationwide. "What Others Think," *PUFN* 48 (30 August 1951): 315.

10. White, *Organic Machine*, 64–67, describes the function of BPA long-term supply contracts with private and public utilities.

11. David Nye, "Electrifying the West, 1880–1940," in *The American West, as Seen by Europeans and Americans,* ed. Rob Kroes (Amsterdam: Free University Press, 1989), 183–202, 188.

12. Ibid., 192–93. Nye argued that, on the eve of the Depression, low-cost electricity was becoming "a precondition for farming" with irrigation in the inland West.

13. The 1947 Edison Electric Institute convention discussed Roper Public Opinion polling showing broad enthusiasm for public power. *PUFN* 40 (3 July 1947): 45.

14. McDonald, *Insull*, chronicles the rise and fall of the interwar years' most flamboyant utility capitalist.

15. Electrical World, *The Electric Power Industry: Past, Present and Future*, 1st ed. (New York: McGraw-Hill, 1949), explains and defends the industry's revival after 1940.

16. Nye, "Electrifying the West," 187–88.

17. Owen Ely, "Proposed Merger of Puget Sound–Washington Water Power," *PUFN* 51 (9 April 1953): 507–12.

18. McLaughlin, "Not in the Cards," 740.

19. Ibid., 742.

20. Ibid., 744.

21. "Confident and Enterprising Spirit Features EEI Annual Meeting," *PUFN* 40 (3 July 1947): 44–45.

22. Richardson, *Dams, Parks and Politics,* chap. 1, offers a serviceable account of CVA.

23. "Move against the 'Preference Clause,'" *PUFN* 48 (22 November 1951): 725–26, reported state public-utility commissions were criticizing preference clauses as "an unfair discrimination against the customers of privately owned electric utilities."

24. "Edison Electric Institute Holds Annual Convention," *PUFN* 52 (2 July 1953): 49–50.

25. Ibid. Sammis was president of Ohio Edison Company.

26. W. C. Mullendore, "National Defense for American Industry," *PUFN* 39 (5 June 1947): 757–65, 758, 760.

27. John P. Callahan, "Steam v. Hydro Power," *PUFN* 39 (2 January 1947): 28–33.

28. "Federal Power and the 1952 Budget," *PUFN* 47 (7 June 1951): 802–3.

29. Humphrey, "Northwest Power Puzzle," 468–69.

30. Daniel B. Noble, "Why Not States' Rights for the Columbia Valley?" *PUFN* 43 (28 April 1949): 544–53, 546.

31. Ibid., 551.

32. Charles Tatham Jr., "The Great Public Power Myth," *PUFN* 48 (11 October 1951): 486–91, 490.

33. J. E. Corette, "Have the Private Power Companies Any Future?" *PUFN* 50 (31 July 1952): 143–52, 149–50, 151 (chart).

34. An example is "CVA Approved by Labor Federation," *PUFN* 42 (26 August 1948): 319–20, reporting the Idaho State Federation of Labor's annual convention action. Oregon's top union official addressed the Idaho convention, urging "construction of four new dams on the [Columbia] river, which he said would provide cheaper power and more industry in the Pacific Northwest."

35. "New Public Power Plans," *PUFN* 42 (2 December 1948): 808.

36. "Interior's United Western Plan," *PUFN* 49 (3 January 1952): 54.

37. Tatham, "Public Power Myth," 490.

38. White, "*It's Your Misfortune and None of My Own*," chap. 18, extends the analysis of western political strategies best described in Worster, *Rivers of Empire*.

39. Chan Gurney, "Grass-Root Sentiment Does Not Favor an MVA," *PUFN* 40 (23 October 1947): 547–55.

40. Humphrey, "Northwest Power Puzzle," 465–69.

41. Dr. Claude Robinson of Opinion Research Corporation, discussing popular approval of public power, advised the 1947 Edison Electric Institute annual convention that "it becomes urgently necessary for electric power managements to visualize the handling of public opinion as one of their primary jobs." *PUFN* 40 (3 July 1947): 45.

42. "Antiutility Lobby?" *PUFN* 40 (31 July 1947): 169–70.

43. Francis X. Welch, "Inside John Gunther," ibid., 179–81.

44. Mullendore, "National Defense," 757, 765.

45. Quoted in "Confident and Enterprising Spirit," 45–50.

46. "Retiring President Addresses EEI Meeting," *PUFN* 41 (17 June 1948): 874–77, 875. Oakes was president of Pennsylvania Light and Power Company.

47. George A. Dondero, "Wanted: A New Federal Power Policy," *PUFN* 42 (9 Sept. 1948): 333–42. During his brief chairmanship, in 1947–48, the House Public Works Committee, which oversaw federal dam construction, authorized no new Columbia and Snake dams.

48. Fones-Wolf, *Selling Free Enterprise*; Griffith, "Forging America's Postwar Order"; Chafe, "Postwar American Society."

49. Hays, *Beauty, Health and Permanence*; Robert Gottlieb, *Forcing the Spring: The Transformation of the American Environmental Movement* (Washington, D.C.: Island Press, 1993).

50. Paul Hirt, *A Conspiracy of Optimism: The United States Forest Service in the Inland Northwest, 1945–1975* (Lincoln: University of Nebraska Press, 1996).

51. Arthur F. McEvoy, *The Fisherman's Problem: Ecology and Law in the California Fisheries, 1850–1980* (New York: Cambridge University Press, 1986).

52. J. Willard Hurst, *Law and Economic Growth: The Legal History of the Lumber Industry in Wisconsin, 1836–1915* (Cambridge, Mass.: Belknap Press, 1964).

53. Donald E. Worster, *Dust Bowl: The Southern Plains in the 1930s* (New York: Oxford University Press, 1979).

54. Editor's note prefacing James H. Cellars, "Hydro Kills the Fishing Industry," *PUFN* 41 (25 March 1948): 417–25, 417 (note).

55. Gurney, "Grass-Root Sentiment," 547.

56. Ibid., 547–48.

57. "Power Plans Denounced," *PUFN* 44 (10 November 1949): 651; "Wild-Life Opposition to Present Water Planning," *PUFN* 47 (10 May 1951): 645.

58. Cellars, "Hydro Kills," 419, 420. In effect, combined losses by the time fish passed both dams would reach nearly one-quarter of the annual runs. Grand Coulee, of course, had extinguished upriver migrations after 1940 into the full extent of the Columbia Basin in northeast Washington and southern British Columbia. Ashworth, *Hells Canyon.*

59. Cellars, "Hydro Kills," 421, 423–24.

60. Potts, "Adverse Effects," 811–17.

61. John E. Thorson, *River of Promise, River of Peril: The Politics of Managing the Missouri River* (Lawrence: University Press of Kansas, 1994); Dale E. Nimz, "Rivers That Work" (PhD diss., University of Kansas, 2003).

62. Gurney, "Grass-Root Sentiment," 548.

63. Rothman, *Greening of a Nation?* chap. 2, offers one perspective on the post-war emergence of hydroelectric opposition in the Echo Park controversy of the 1950s.

64. Tom Knudson, "Looking at Dams in a New Way," *High Country News* 30 (2 February 1998): 1, 13; and "Dollars, Sense and Salmon," *Idaho Daily Statesman*, 20–22 July 1997 (reprinted 22 September 1997 as special supplement), provide two good overviews of the regional issue.

65. Ashworth, *Hells Canyon*, parts 2 and 3, chronicles Idaho Power's construction of the complex.

8 / CLAIMING THE PUBLIC INTEREST

1. "Comprehensive Plan for the Development of the Natural Resources of the Pacific Northwest" [draft], October 1951, Columbia Basin/Part XIV file, box 2, Governor Len B. Jordan Papers, ISHS.

2. *Public Papers of the President: Harry S. Truman, 1950,* Baker, Oregon, 10 May 1950, 351–52; Boise, Idaho, 10 May 1950, 344–46.

3. Ibid., Twin Falls, Idaho, 10 May 1950, 342–44.

4. Ibid., Boise, Idaho, 345–46.

5. Ibid., Baker, Oregon, 10 May 1950, 351–52; Pasco, Washington, 11 May 1950, 373.

6. "President Dedicates Grand Coulee," *Public Power* 8 (June 1950): 12.

7. Gunther, *Inside U.S.A.,* viii (election chart). Chapter 43 assesses southern conservatives' opposition to TVA, and chapter 8 discusses the politics of northwestern public power.

8. Congressional Quarterly, *Congress and the Nation,* 823.

9. Lubell, *Future of American Politics,* chaps. 2, 8; McCullough, *Truman,* chaps. 15, 16; Hamby, *Beyond the New Deal;* and Hamby, *Harry S. Truman and the Fair Deal* (Lexington, Mass.: D.C. Heath and Co., 1974).

10. 64 Stat. 163 (1950).

11. *Public Papers: Truman, 1950,* 22 May 1950, 427–30.

12. Quoted from CBIAC Minutes, 43d Meeting, 23–24 October 1950, CBIAC Meetings/Part V file, box 2, series I, Robins Papers, ISHS.

13. Ibid.

14. Schedule "T," U.S. Columbia River Power System, BPA Power Resources Branch, 7 December 1950, Department of Interior/Part IV file, box 4, Jordan Papers, ISHS.

15. McCullough, *Truman,* 813–14.

16. Drukman, *Wayne Morse.*

17. Stapilus, *Paradox Politics,* 81–85; Ashby and Gramer, *Fighting the Odds,* 50–61; *Idaho Blue Book: 1995–1996,* 241.

18. *Idaho Daily Statesman,* 5 August 1950, 6.

19. *Idaho Blue Book: 1995–1996,* 38.

20. Ashby and Gramer, *Fighting the Odds,* 349–53; Stapilus, *Paradox Politics,* 34–35, 104–6.

21. Chapman to Davidson, 19 December 1950, Reclamation/Part X file, box 6, Jordan Papers, ISHS.

22. Davidson to C. A. Robins, 28 December 1950, ibid.

23. Nye, *Consuming Power;* Ellis, *A Giant Step,* remains the best account of NRECA's penetration of the federal electrification effort.

24. "The Meaning of the Preference Clause in Hydroelectric Power Allocation," *Environmental Law* 9 (1979): 601–19.

25. Blumm, "Hydroelectric Heritage: Prologue," 194–95.

26. Coyle, *Conservation,* 165–69.

27. Ellis, *A Giant Step*, 122–23; Coyle, *Conservation*; Jay L. Brigham, *Empowering the West: Electrical Politics before* FDR (Lawrence: University Press of Kansas, 1998).

28. Ellis, *Giant Step*, 118–20, 121–22, 132.

29. Ibid., 125.

30. Ibid., 123, 132.

31. Ibid., 119.

32. Morris Llewellyn Cooke, "The Three Shell Game in World Power," *Public Power* 7 (December 1949): 14, 26.

33. Resources for the Future, "Water Resources Problems," in *The Nation Looks at Its Resources,* 173–74.

34. Gilbert F. White, "Broader Bases for Choice: The Next Key Move," in *Perspectives on Conservation: Essays on America's Natural Resources,* ed. Henry Jarrett (Baltimore: Johns Hopkins University Press, 1958), 207.

35. "New Commission Named," *Public Power* 8 (February 1950): 7, 30.

36. "News Grid," ibid. 8 (June 1950): 7.

37. F. J. Lawton (Budget Bureau director) to Chapman, 15 August 1951, FPC file. Chapman to Speaker of the House, 8 October 1951, Reclamation/Part XII file, box 6, Jordan Papers; H. T. Nelson to Gen. O. E. Walsh et al., 18 October 1951, ibid.

38. *Oregon Journal*, 10 August 1950, 11.

39. *Idaho Daily Statesman,* 15 August 1950, 6; ibid., 16 August 1950, 6.

40. Ibid., 15 August 1950, 6.

41. Stacy, *Legacy of Light,* offers a remarkably thorough, balanced study of the company's organization and aspirations.

42. Dennis C. Colson, *Idaho's Constitution: The Tie That Binds* (Moscow: University of Idaho Press, 1991), chap. 9, ably explains the origin and contemporary significance of Article 15, the Idaho Constitution's prior appropriation lodestone.

43. Kulp to Robins, 31 May 1950, President's Water Resources Policy file, box 4, series I, Robins Papers.

44. Murphy to Robins, 15 June 1950, ibid.

45. Joint and Combined Statements of the Governors, President's Water Resources Policy file, box 4, series I, Robins Papers.

46. E. W. Murphy to James H. Allen, 10 October 1951, Columbia Basin/Part XXVII file, box 2, Jordan Papers; Parry to Gov. Len B. Jordan, 15 October 1951, Reclamation/Part VI file, box 6, Jordan Papers; Jordan to John Spencer, 21 November 1951, Reclamation/Part XIII file, ibid.

47. Cooke to Robins, 27 July 1950; Robins to Kulp, 27 July 1950; Kulp to Cooke,

28 July 1950, ibid. Columbia River Compact, [10 July 1950], Columbia Basin Compact—1950/Part I file, box 1, series I, Robins Papers.

48. *Spokane Spokesman Review*, 30 November 1951, in Reclamation/Part VI file, box 6, Jordan Papers.

49. Inman to Federal Power Commission, 15 December 1950; Application for License, 15 December 1950, Formal File 100–2: Part 1, FPC Project No. 1971, box 253, FERC Accession No. 138–88–006.

50. Application for License, paras. 6 and 11.

51. Inman to FPC, 15 December 1950.

52. *Idaho Daily Statesman*, 18 December 1950, 6.

53. Ibid., 19 December 1950, 6.

54. McCullough, *Truman*, chap. 16.

55. *Public Papers of the President: Harry S. Truman, 1951* (Washington, D.C.: Government Printing Office, 1965), 15 January 1951, 84–87; Chapman to Speaker of the House, 8 October 1951, Reclamation/Part 12 file, box 6, Jordan Papers.

56. Donald L. McKernan, "Fisheries Problems Arising from the Construction of Ice Harbor Dam," *Fish Commission of Oregon Processed Reports: Administrative, 1951–53*, no. 8.

57. Notice of Application for License (Major), 1 March 1951, Formal File: Part 1, FPC Project No. 1971.

58. Veatch to J. H. Gutride (FPC secretary), 4 May 1951, *Nez Perce Tribe v. Idaho Power Co.*, CV 91–0517, court files, U.S. District Court for District of Idaho.

59. Forrest Hauck, "Chinook Arrive in Average Run," *Idaho Wildlife Review* 1 (October 1948): 6; "Steelhead Utilize Fish Ladder," ibid., 2 (June–July 1950): 11; "Spawning Operation Aids in Restoring Idaho Salmon Runs," ibid., 2 (August–September 1950): 15.

60. Murray to Gutride, 4 June 1951, folders IIA/B (Hells Canyon Dams), Natural Resources Policy Bureau Archives, IDFG.

61. O. E. Walsh, CBIAC Chairman, to Gov. Jordan et al., 14 December 1951, Columbia Basin/Part XIV file, box 2, Jordan Papers.

62. Jordan to John Spencer, 21 November 1951, Reclamation/Part XIII file, box 6, Jordan Papers.

63. Order Fixing Hearing, 13 May 1952; Designation of Presiding Officer, 28 May 1952, Formal File: Part 2, FPC Project No. 1971.

64. Chapman to FPC Chairman Monrad C. Wallgren, 21 May 1951, ibid.

65. Chapman to FPC Chairman Thomas C. Buchanan, 23 June 1952; Petition of Secretary of the Interior for Intervention, 27 June 1952, ibid.

66. Plaza, Washington, Grange Protest, 22 February 1951; Oregon State Grange Master Elmer McClure Protest, 20 March 1951, Formal File: Part 1; Petition of Washington State Grange to Intervene, 7 July 1952, Formal File: Part 3, FPC Project No. 1971.

67. Martin to FPC, 9 April 1951, Formal File: Part 1.

68. Petition to Intervene by NWPPA, 18 July 1952, Formal File: Part 3.

69. Petition of John Glasby for Intervention, 3 July 1952, Formal File: Part 2.

70. Petition [of Hells Canyon Development Association] to Intervene, 7 July 1952, Formal File: Part 3.

71. Statement of Idaho Power Company . . . in Opposition to the Petition of the Secretary of Interior for Intervention, 10 July 1952, ibid.

72. *Hearing Transcript*, 63–66, Formal File 100–2, FPC Project No. 1971, box 210, FERC Accession No. 58-A-161 [cited as *Hearing Transcript*].

73. *Hearing Transcript*, 40–46, 300–304.

74. Ibid., 436–37.

75. Ibid., 545–46, 253, 274–75.

76. Ibid., 613–14.

77. Ibid., 625–26.

78. Ibid., 664–65, 681, 701–2.

79. Ibid., 1021–24, 1060.

80. Ibid., 43, 47–48, 100.

81. Ibid., 58–59.

82. Ibid., 1104–8.

83. *Idaho Daily Statesman*, 20 August 1952, 1.

9 / PRIVATIZING HELLS CANYON

1. Stephen E. Ambrose, *Eisenhower*, vol. 1 (New York: Simon and Schuster, 1983), 460–61; Gunther, *Inside U.S.A.*, viii (chart); McCullough, *Truman*, chap. 14.

2. Robert E. Smylie, *Governor Smylie Remembers* (Moscow: University of Idaho Press, 1998), 60–62; Sherman Adams, *Firsthand Report: The Story of the Eisenhower Administration* (New York: Harper and Bros., 1961), 16; *Oregonian*, 21 August 1952, 8.

3. Dwight D. Eisenhower, *The White House Years: Mandate for Change, 1953–1956* (Garden City, N.Y.: Doubleday and Co., 1963), 377–78, 385–88.

4. *Oregonian*, 21 August 1952, 1.

5. *Idaho Daily Statesman*, 21 August 1952, 2.

6. Ibid.; Harvey, *A Symbol of Wilderness*; George Van Dusen, "Politics of 'Part-

nership': The Eisenhower Administration and Conservation, 1952–60" (PhD diss., Loyola University, 1974).

7. "The Power Issue—Up or Down," *PUFN* 50 (31 July 1952): 172; "Power Planks," ibid., 50 (11 September 1952): 367–68.

8. *Idaho Daily Statesman*, 4 October 1952, 1, and 2 October 1952, 1; *Oregonian*, 3 October 1952, 17.

9. "Consumers' Power Stake," *Public Power* 10 (July 1952): 10–11.

10. "Power Publications," *Public Power* 10 (September 1952): 5.

11. *Idaho Daily Statesman*, 26 October 1952, 6.

12. Ibid., 6 October 1952, 1, and 7 October 1952, 1; *Oregonian*, 7 October 1952, 1.

13. *Idaho Daily Statesman*, 8 October 1952, 4.

14. Ibid., 27 October 1952, 16.

15. Parry to Jordan, 23 October 1952; Jordan to Parry, 28 October 1952, Columbia Basin/Part XXVII file, box 2, Jordan Papers, ISHS.

16. *Idaho Daily Statesman*, 7 November 1952, 4.

17. Richardson, *Dams, Parks and Politics*, chap. 1, on Buchanan's handling of FPC in 1951–52.

18. McKinsey Company to Harold R. Talbott, 15 October 1952, enclosing *Restaffing the Executive Branch*, box 1, Charles F. Willis Papers, Eisenhower Library.

19. *Restaffing*, secs. I-5, I-8, I-13, IX-1, IX-8.

20. "FPC a Weather Vane?" *PUFN* 50 (20 November 1952): 789.

21. *New York Times*, 21 November 1952, 1, 8, 18; Gary W. Reichard, *Republicanism Reaffirmed: Eisenhower and the Eighty-third Congress* (Knoxville: University of Tennessee Press, 1975), 148–49; *Oregonian*, 5 April 1953, 8.

22. Reichard, *Reaffirmation*, 148–49; Adams, *Firsthand Report*, 61, 236; Elmo Richardson, *The Presidency of Dwight D. Eisenhower* (Lawrence: Regents Press of Kansas, 1979), 33; *Idaho Daily Statesman*, 21 November 1952, 2.

23. "Ore. Gov. McKay Heads Interior," *Public Power* 10 (December 1952): 10, 22; *Idaho Daily Statesman*, 21 November 1952, 2.

24. *Idaho Daily Statesman*, 21 November 1952, 2; *Oregonian*, 21 November 1952, 1; "Ore. Gov. McKay," 24.

25. Changing the Guard," *PUFN* 50 (18 December 1952): 917–18; Bayard L. England, "The Electric Light and Power Industry Looking Ahead," ibid., 50 (18 December 1952): 883–96.

26. "FPC Faces Far Reaching Decisions," *Public Power* 10 (December 1952): 20.

27. Idaho Power Motion for Continuance of Hearing, 10 November 1952, and attached Supplement to Application, 28 October 1952, Formal File 100–2: Part 3, FPC Project No. 1971, Box 253, FERC Accession No. 138–88–006.

28. *Idaho Daily Statesman*, 19 November 1952, 2.

29. *Oregonian*, 14 April 1953, 5.

30. *Idaho Daily Statesman*, 19 November 1952, 2; Motions of the Secretary of Interior in Opposition, 21 November 1952, FPC Formal File: Part 3.

31. [Staff] Answer to Motion for Continuance, 20 November 1952; Order on Motions, 3 December 1952, ibid.

32. [NFU] Petition to Intervene, 8 December 1952; Petition of . . . Secretary of Agriculture for Intervention, 30 December 1952, FPC Formal File: Part 4.

33. "1953: Expansion—More and More," *Public Power* 11 (January 1953): 7–8; "Regional Power Agency," ibid., 11 (January 1953): 10; "Truman Budget Asks More Power Funds," ibid., 11 (February 1953): 12

34. *Idaho Daily Statesman*, 18 January 1953, 1, 2.

35. Jordan to J. C. Jeppson, 15 January 1953, Reclamation/Part XIII file, box 6, Jordan Papers.

36. Columbia Interstate Compact Commission, 9 June 1953 Minutes; CRCC Bulletin no. 8, 30 June 1953, Columbia River Compact Commission folder, box 55, Idaho State Attorney General Records (Accession AR 4), ISHS.

37. "New Officials Named," *Public Power* 11 (March 1953): 18, 26; "Undersecretary," ibid., 12 (August 1954): 7.

38. "Kuykendall Named," ibid., 11 (May 1953): 20; "State Background for Federal Commissions," *PUFN* 51 (7 May 1953): 626.

39. *Facts on File: 1953*, 124; *New York Times*, 23 April 1953, 18; *Oregonian*, 23 April 1953, 6.

40. *Oregonian*, 18 May 1953, 8; "Tudor Will Speak," *Public Power* 12 (March 1954): 5; "Tudor Plans to Leave Interior," *Public Power* 12 (May 1954): 11; Tudor to McKay, 13 April 1953, Chronological Correspondence: April–August 1953 folder, box 1, Ralph Tudor Papers, Eisenhower Library.

41. "Undersecretary," *Public Power*.

42. Davis to Costello, 3 March 1953; Notice of Continuance of Hearing, 12 March 1953; Inman to Costello, 9 March 1953, FPC Formal File: Part 4.

43. Karl O. Loos to Costello, 11 February 1953, ibid.; *Idaho Daily Statesman*, 10 March 1953, 14.

44. Paul T. Quick (FWS) to Murray, 6 March 1953; Murray to Quick, 10 March 1953, folders IIA/B (Hells Canyon), Natural Resources Policy Bureau Archives, IDFG; Tudor to McKay, 6 May 1953, Correspondence: April–August 1953 file, Tudor Papers.

45. "Court Approves License on Roanoke," *Public Power* 11 (April 1953): 17, 52; *Oregonian*, 15 April 1953, 8; 11 April and 3 May 1953, "Ralph A. Tudor Notes Recorded

While Under Secretary Dept. of Interior: March 1953–September 1954," box 1, Tudor Papers, ["Tudor Diary"]; *Oregonian*, 14 April 1953, 5.

46. Davis to FPC, 24 April 1953; Notice of Continuance of Hearing, 27 April 1953; Notice of Continuance of Hearing, 30 April 1953, all in FPC Formal File: Part 4; 3 May 1953, Tudor Diary; *Oregonian*, 17 April 1953, 5; *Idaho Daily Statesman*, 2 May 1953, 2.

47. *Idaho Daily Statesman*, 6 May 1953, 1, 15; 10 May 1953, Tudor Diary.

48. 26 April and 10 May 1953, Tudor Diary; *Idaho Daily Statesman*, 5 May 1953, 11; *Oregonian*, 6 May 1953, 10; Davis to FPC Chairman, 5 May 1953, FPC Formal File: Part 4.

49. 10 May 1953, Tudor Diary; *Oregonian*, 6 May 1953, 10, and 19 May 1953, 3; *Idaho Daily Statesman*, 6 May 1953, 1, 15; *Oregon Journal*, 16 May 1953, 3; "Morse, Pfost Lash Power Company Plans," *Public Power* 11 (May 1953): 32.

50. "Secretary McKay Discusses Power Policies," and "Resolutions 5, 7," *Public Power* 11 (June 1953): 16, 32–34, 24–25.

51. M. O. Leighton to FPC Secretary, 6 May 1953, FPC Formal File: Part 4.

52. Order Rescinding Order Granting Intervention, 14 May 1953; Order Fixing Hearing . . . and Consolidating Proceedings, 26 May 1953, ibid.

53. Jordan and Kulp to FPC Secretary, 5 June 1953, ibid.; Inman to Jordan, 14 March 1952, and Application for Permit 22442 by Idaho Power, 24 March 1952, Idaho Power Company file, box 4, Jordan Papers; Jordan to Kulp, 22 March 1952, Reclamation/Part XII file, box 6, Jordan Papers.

54. 10 May 1953, Tudor Diary.

55. Masters to FPC, 12 June 1953, FPC Formal File: Part 4.

56. Redford, Mansell, Dianey to FPC, 22 June, 16 June, 25 June 1953, ibid.

57. Petition for Leave to Intervene (NHCA), 26 June 1953, ibid.

58. *Oregon Journal*, 4 June 1953, 12; Weston to Elmer McClure, 28 June 1953; J. T. Marr to NHCA, 23 June 1953; Washington Public Utilities District Association to Marr, 22 June 1953, FPC Formal File: Part 4.

59. Motion for Continuance of Hearing [HCDA, NRECA], 11 June 1953; Inman to FPC, 5 June 1953; Answer of Idaho Power to Motion for Continuance [I-OHCA], 12 June 1953; Order Denying Motions for Continuance, 17 June 1953, ibid.

60. *Oregonian*, 10 May 1953, 10; *Oregon Journal*, 9 June 1953, 1, 12; McKay to Pearson, 9 June 1953, Correspondence Folder, box 1, Tudor Papers; *Oregonian*, 11 June 1953, 1.

61. George R. Jones (Idaho Public Utilities Commission president) to FPC, 29 June 1953; Idaho Development Association to FPC, 2 July 1953, FPC Formal File: Part 5.

62. *Oregon Journal,* 3 July 1953, 1; *Oregonian,* 14 June 1953, 10.

63. *Idaho Daily Statesman,* 16 June 1953, 2; 17 June 1953, 6; 18 June 1953, 6.

64. *Oregonian,* 18 June 1953, 4; *Idaho Statesman,* 19 June 1953, 20; Answer of Idaho Power to Motion for Continuance, 12 June 1953, FPC Formal File: Part 4.

65. Federal Power Act, ch. 687, 49 Stat. 863 (1935), codified at 16 U.S.C.S. secs. 791a-825*l* (1997).

66. *In re City of Tacoma,* 10 F.P.C. 424 (1951); *In re Portland General Electric Company,* 10 F.P.C. 445 (1951).

67. *Idaho Daily Statesman,* 5 July 1953, 5; 7 July 1953, 2; 8 July 1953, 4. *Oregon Journal,* 7 July 1953, 1. The full FPC sustained Costello's rulings. [NHCA] Motions for Order Directing Revision and Completion of Applications, 14 July 1953; Order, 14 July 1953, FPC Formal File: Part 5.

68. "Hells Canyon Battle Blazing," *Public Power* 11 (August 1953): 7, 24; *Oregonian,* 8 July 1953, 4.

69. Opening Statement by R. P. Parry for Idaho Power, [7 July 1953], Idaho Power Company file, box 4, Jordan Papers.

70. *Idaho Daily Statesman,* 9 July 1953, 3; *Oregonian,* 11 July 1953, 4, and 14 July 1953, 8.

71. *Oregonian,* 10 July 1953, 2. *Idaho Daily Statesman,* 7 July 1953, 2; 13 July 1953, 2; 10 July 1953, 1, 5; 12 July 1953, 5. Tudor to Kuykendall and Tudor to Information Director, 16 July 1953, Correspondence File; 19 July 1953, Tudor Diary.

72. *Idaho Daily Statesman,* 15 July 1953, 2; 16 July 1953, 2; 17 July 1953, 6; 18 July 1953, 2. *Oregonian,* 15 July 1953, 6.

73. *Oregonian,* 15 July 1953, 6; *Idaho Daily Statesman,* 19 July 1953, 12; *Oregon Journal,* "Sunday Magazine," 19 July 1953.

74. *Idaho Daily Statesman,* 21 July 1953, 2.

75. Ibid., 22 July 1953, 2; 23 July 1953, 2.

76. Jordan to Col. E. C. Itschner (North Pacific Division commander), 5 June 1953, Reclamation/Part IV file, box 6, Jordan Papers; *Idaho Daily Statesman,* 3 July 1953, 4, and 7 August 1953, 12; Gen. C. H. Chorpening (Army Engineers) to FPC, 5 August 1953, FPC Formal File: Part 5.

77. *Idaho Daily Statesman,* 24 July 1953, 12; 25 July 1953, 2; 27 July 1953, 10.

78. *Oregonian,* 28 July 1953, 8; *Idaho Daily Statesman,* 29 July 1953, 2, and 30 July 1953, 12.

79. "Big Tax Benefits Seen for Companies," *Public Power* 11 (April 1953): 24; "Company Tax Aid Lashed," ibid. 11 (October 1953): 24; *Idaho Daily Statesman,* 21 June 1957, 1.

80. Statement of Applicant's Counsel, 9 March 1954, FPC Formal File: Part 5.

81. [NHCA] Motion . . . on Recess, 31 August 1953; Order Denying Motion . . . on Recess, 9 September 1953; Inman to Costello, 15 September 1953; Applicant's Objection to Intervenors' Motion for Stay, 9 October 1953; Order Denying Motions, 21 October 1953, ibid. *Idaho Daily Statesman*, 4 August 1953, 2; *Oregon Journal*, 1 September 1953, 3; *Oregonian*, 23 October 1953, 10. Tudor to Aandahl, 22 June 1953; to Dr. Gabriel Hauge (president's assistant), 10 July 1953; Notes on Power Policy Statement, 30 July 1953; to McKay, 13 August 1953; to Lee Kaiser, 24 August 1953, Tudor Correspondence, box 1, Tudor Papers. "New Interior Power Policy Unveiled," *Public Power* 11 (September 1953): 11–12, 32.

82. "No New Starts," *Public Power* 12 (February 1954): 12; "Tragedy of No New Starts," ibid., 20.

83. McKinley, *Uncle Sam in the Pacific Northwest*.

84. Applicant's Objection and Reply to Intervenors' Motion, 17 June 1954, FPC Formal File: Part 6.

85. "Northwest Posts Shifted," *Public Power* 12 (January 1954): 12; 11 April 1953, 19 April 1954, Tudor Diary.

86. "Hells Canyon Give-Away," *Public Power* 13 (October 1955): 23.

87. Murray to FPC, 23 June 1953, FPC File: Part 5. At Governor Jordan's instigation, the 1953 session of the Idaho legislature abolished the twenty-year-old Fish and Game Commission and vested appointment of new commissioners in the governor. Jordan quickly appointed three new commissioners and retained two from the abolished commission. After several stormy meetings with Murray, under fire all winter for his handling of big-game herds threatened by deep snows, the new commission requested his resignation. On the Friday before Costello convened the Idaho Power license hearing in Washington, Murray resigned.

State conservation managers in the Northwest have long believed Idaho Power orchestrated Murray's ouster, and Jordan and the Republican-controlled 1953 legislature did Tom Roach's bidding. No evidence reviewed to date supports this belief. Murray had alienated both hunters and department staff, as well as the first commission, well before Jordan's 1953 bid to exert more gubernatorial control over the agency. Some believed he had improperly profited from sales of department lands. In any event, after quitting Fish and Game Murray joined Idaho Power's staff in late 1953, where he worked on fish and habitat issues raised by the Hells Canyon Complex for a number of years. *Idaho Daily Statesman*, 18 January 1953, 5; 4 March 1953, 2; 31 March 1953, 8; 3 April 1953, 1; 4 June 1953, 1; 2 July 1953, 1; 28 July 1953, 9. Murray to Inman, 22 September 1953, folders IIA/B (Hells Canyon Dams), Natural Resources Policy Bureau Archives, IDFG.

88. Schoettler to FPC, 6 July 1953, FPC Formal File: Part 5.

89. Veatch to FPC, 3 July 1953; Arthur G. Higgs to FPC Secretary, 4 July 1953, ibid.

90. 28 June 1953, Tudor Diary; McKay to Kuykendall, 7 July 1953, FPC Formal File: Part 5.

91. McBroom testimony, *Transcript*: 12417–18, 10251–52 (10 February 1954, 14 January 1954), boxes 213 and 212, FPC Project No. 1971, FERC Accession No. 58–A-161.

92. Gale testimony, *Transcript*: 5419, 5421–22 (14 October 1953), box 211, ibid.

93. T. E. Roach Testimony, 4 August 1953 (*Transcript*, 4103–6), folders IIA/B (Hells Canyon Dams), Natural Resources Policy Bureau Archives, IDFG.

94. Findings 14, 27, 33, Decision, 6 May 1955, FPC Formal File: Part 9, FPC Project No. 1971, box 254, FERC Accession No. 138–88–006.

95. *In re Idaho Power Co.*, 14 F.P.C. 55 (1955), aff'd sub nom., *National Hells Canyon Assn. v. FPC*, 237 F.2d 777 (D.C. Cir. 1956), cert. denied, 353 U.S. 924 (1957).

96. Costello Decision, 5.

97. Ibid., 26–28.

98. Ibid., Finding 40.

10 / FROM ENERGY TO ENVIRONMENT

1. *In re Pacific Northwest Power Co./Washington Public Power Supply System*, 31 F.P.C. 247 (1964), had begun in 1955, even as the *Idaho Power* licensing case was reaching its crescendo.

2. Ross L. Leffler, "Program for Anadromous Fishes of the Columbia," in Cone and Ridlington, *The Northwest Salmon Crisis*, 335–37.

3. *Udall*, 387 U.S. 428, 436 (1967), quotes Interior's 21 November 1960 request that FPC defer licensing any new dams in its *In re Pacific Northwest Power Co.* proceeding.

4. Listed in Presiding Examiner's Initial Decision, app. A, *Pacific Northwest Power Co.*, 31 F.P.C. 307–379 (8 October 1962).

5. Administrative Procedure Act of 11 August 1946, ch. 324, 60 Stat. 237, codified at 5 U.S.C.S. secs. 551–59, 701–6 (1997).

6. Oregon Revised Statutes sec. 506.155 (effective 31 December 1953), formerly Oregon Compiled Laws Annotated sec. 83–216 (enacted 1921); Idaho Code sec. 36–104 (enacted 1939).

7. *Lott v. Guy F. Atkinson Co.*, No. 328, U.S. District Court for Eastern Districts of Washington (1948), from court files, *Nez Perce Tribe v. Idaho Power Co.*, CV 91–0517 (U.S. District Court for District of Idaho).

8. *Pacific Northwest Power Co./Washington Public Power Supply System*, 31 F.P.C. 247, reh'g denied, 31 F.P.C. 1051 (1964), aff'd sub nom. *Washington Public Power Supply*

System v. FPC, 358 F.2d 840 (D.C. Cir. 1966), rev'd sub nom. *Udall v. FPC*, 387 U.S. 428 (1967).

9. Ashworth, *Hells Canyon*, part 2, discusses regional reaction to the various administrative and judicial developments.

10. Coggins, Wilkinson, and Leshy, *Federal Public Lands and Resources Law*, 412–14.

11. In *Pacific Northwest Power Co./Washington Public Power Supply System*, the FPC's effort to consider more fully claims premised on biology consumed more than twenty pages of the licensing decision.

BIBLIOGRAPHY

MANUSCRIPT COLLECTIONS

Dwight D. Eisenhower Presidential Library, Abilene, Kansas
  Ralph A. Tudor Papers
  White House Central Files
  Charles F. Willis Jr. Papers
Federal Energy Regulatory Commission, Washington, D.C.
  Federal Power Commission, Project Nos. 1971, 2132, 2133 (FERC Accession
    Nos. 138–88–006 and 58–A-161)
Idaho Department of Fish and Game, Boise
  Fish and Game Commission Minutes, Director's Office
  Idaho Wildlife Review, vols. 1–10 (1948–58), Information and Education
    Bureau, Headquarters Building
  Natural Resources Policy Bureau Archives, Headquarters Building
Idaho State Historical Society, Library and Archives, Boise
  Attorney General's Office Papers (Accession No. AR 4)
    Robert Ailshie, 1947
    Robert E. Smylie, 1947–54
    Graydon W. Smith, 1955–58
  Governor's Office Papers
    C. A. Robins MD, 1947–50 (Accession No. AR 2/22)
    Len B. Jordan, 1951–54 (Accession No. AR 2/23)
    Robert E. Smylie, 1955–58 (Accession No. AR 2/24)
Oregon Department of Fish and Wildlife
  Hydroelectric Licensing Coordinator Archives, Portland
  Library, Clackamas
  Oregon Fish Commission Archives, Clackamas

Oregon Secretary of State, Archives Division, Salem
    Department of Justice/Attorney General Papers
        Robert Y. Thornton, 1950–58 (Accession No. 69A-073/002)
    Governor's Office Papers
        Douglas McKay, 1948–52
        Paul L. Patterson, 1952–56
        Elmo E. Smith, 1956
        Robert D. Holmes, 1956–58
Harry S. Truman Presidential Library, Independence, Missouri
    Official File, Truman Papers
United States District Court for the District of Idaho, Federal Building, Boise
    Nez Perce Tribe v. Idaho Power Company, CV 91–0517, court files
University of Washington Libraries, Manuscripts, Special Collections and
    University Archives, Seattle
    Columbia Basin Inter-Agency Committee Papers

NEWSPAPERS

High Country News, Paonia, Colorado
Idaho Daily Statesman, Boise
New York Times
Oregon Journal, Portland
Oregonian, Portland

GOVERNMENT DOCUMENTS

City of Tacoma, 10 FPC 424 (1951).
Cleaver, Fred. C., ed. *Fisheries Statistics of Oregon.* Contribution No. 16. Fish
    Commission of Oregon, 1951.
Columbia River Inter-Tribal Fish Commission. *The Mitchell Act: An Analysis
    by CRITFC.* Portland, Oregon (June 1981).
Federal Power Commission. *Annual Reports.* 1947–53.
Gladson, Jim, Randy Henry, and Pat Wray. "Fish and Wildlife Management,
    1893–1993: the Past, the Present, the Future." *Oregon Wildlife* 49 (Spring
    1993): 4–21.
Gooding, Don, and Les Hatch, eds. *The Salmon Crisis.* Washington Department
    of Fisheries, 1949.
Haas, James B. *Fishery Problems Associated with Brownlee, Oxbow, and Hells

Canyon Dams on the Middle Snake River. Investigational Report No. 4. Fish
Commission of Oregon (1965).

Hauck, Forrest. "Chinook Arrive in Average Run." *Idaho Wildlife Review* 1
(October 1948):6.

Idaho Power Company, 14 F.P.C. 55 (1955).

McKernan, Donald L. "Fisheries Problems Arising from the Construction of Ice
Harbor Dam." *Fish Commission of Oregon Processed Reports: Administrative,
1951–53*, no. 8, n.d.

National Hells Canyon Association v. Federal Power Commission, 237 F.2d 777
(D.C. Cir. 1956), cert. denied, 353 U.S. 924 (1957).

Norwood, Gus. *Columbia River Power for the People: A History of the Policies
of the Bonneville Power Administration*. Portland: Bonneville Power
Administration, 1980.

Oregon State University Extension Service. *A Snapshot of Salmon in Oregon*,
EM 8722 (1998).

Pacific Northwest Power Co./Washington Public Power Supply System, 31 F.P.C.
247 (1964).

Portland General Electric Company, 10 F.P.C. 445 (1951).

Public Papers of the President: Harry S. Truman, 1946–1951. Washington, D.C.:
Government Printing Office, 1962–65.

"Report of the Master Fish Warden." *Oregon Fish Commission Biennial Report:
1947*.

Secretary of State. *Idaho Blue Book: 1987–1988*. Boise: Secretary of State, 1989.

Secretary of State. *Idaho Blue Book: 1995–1996*. Boise: Secretary of State, 1996.

"Spawning Operation Aids in Restoring Idaho Salmon Runs." *Idaho Wildlife
Review* 2 (August–September 1950): 15.

Springer, Vera. *Power and the Pacific Northwest: A History of the Bonneville Power
Administration*. Portland, Ore.: Bonneville Power Administration, 1976.

"Steelhead Utilize Fish Ladder," *Idaho Wildlife Review* 2 (June–July 1950): 11.

Udall v. Federal Power Commission, 387 U.S. 428 (1967).

United States Congress. *Congressional Record*, vols. 95–96. 81st Congress, 2d
Session, 1950.

United States House of Representatives. *Army Corps of Engineers Review Report:
Columbia and Snake Rivers*. 81st Congress, 2d Session, 1950. House Doc. No.
531.

United States House of Representatives. *Bureau of Reclamation Comprehensive
Plan: Columbia and Snake River Basins*. 81st Congress, 2d Session, 1950. House
Doc. No. 473.

Walsh, Clark. "'The Good Old Days': A Review of Game and Fish Administration in Oregon." *Oregon State Game Commission Bulletin* 14 (December 1959): 3–8 and (February 1960): 3–7.

Washington Department of Fisheries, Oregon Fish Commission, and United States Fish and Wildlife Service. *A Program of Rehabilitation of the Columbia River Fisheries.* 1947.

Washington Public Power Supply System v. Federal Power Commission, 358 F.2d 840 (D.C. Cir. 1966).

BOOKS, ARTICLES, AND DISSERTATIONS

"1953: Expansion—More and More," *Public Power* 11 (January 1953): 7–8.

Adams, Sherman. *Firsthand Report: The Story of the Eisenhower Administration.* New York: Harper and Bros., 1961.

Ambrose, Stephen E. *Eisenhower.* Vol. 1, *Soldier, General of the Army, President-Elect, 1890–1952.* New York: Simon and Schuster, 1983.

————. *Eisenhower.* Vol. 2, *The President.* New York: Simon and Schuster, 1984.

————. *Undaunted Courage: Meriwether Lewis, Thomas Jefferson and the Opening of the American West.* New York: Simon and Schuster, 1996.

American Public Power Association. "Federal Power Policy." *Public Power* 7 (November 1949): 7–8, 24–25.

Ames, Roscoe. "Private Enterprise Builds a Hydro Dam in the Northwest." *Public Utilities Fortnightly* 49 (3 January 1952): 21–29.

"Antiutility Lobby?" *Public Utilities Fortnightly* 40 (31 July 1947): 169–70.

Ashby, LeRoy, and Rod Gramer. *Fighting the Odds: The Life of Senator Frank Church.* Pullman: Washington State University Press, 1994.

Ashworth, William. *Hells Canyon: The Deepest Gorge on Earth.* New York: Hawthorn Books, 1977.

"Attacks on Preferences." *Public Power* 9 (June 1950): 18.

Badger, Anthony J. *The New Deal: The Depression Years, 1933–1940.* New York: Hill and Wang, 1989.

Bessey, Roy F. "The Political Issues of the Hells Canyon Controversy." *Western Political Quarterly* 9 (September 1956): 676–90.

————. "Resource Conservation and Development Problems and Solutions in the Columbia Basin." *Journal of Politics* 13 (August 1951): 418–40.

"Big Tax Benefits Seen for Companies." *Public Power* 11 (April 1953): 24.

Blumm, Michael C. "The Northwest's Hydroelectric Heritage." In Goble and Hirt, *Northwest Lands, Northwest Peoples.*

————. "The Northwest's Hydroelectric Heritage: Prologue to the Pacific Northwest Power Planning and Conservation Act." *Washington Law Review* 58 (1983): 175–244.

Brigham, Jay L. *Empowering the West: Electrical Politics before FDR.* Lawrence: University Press of Kansas, 1998.

Callahan, John P. "Steam v. Hydro Power." *Public Utilities Fortnightly* 39 (2 January 1947): 28–33.

Carlisle, Rodney P., and Joan M. Zenzen. *Supplying the Nuclear Arsenal: American Production Reactors, 1942–1992.* Baltimore: Johns Hopkins University Press, 1996.

Cellars, James H. "Hydro Kills the Fishing Industry." *Public Utilities Fortnightly* 41 (25 March 1948): 417–25.

Chafe, William H. "Postwar American Society: Dissent and Social Reform." In Lacey, *The Truman Presidency.*

Chandler, William U. *The Myth of TVA: Conservation and Development in the Tennessee Valley, 1933–1983.* Cambridge, Mass.: Ballinger Publishing Co., 1984.

"Changing the Guard." *Public Utilities Fortnightly* 50 (18 December 1952): 917–18.

Clark, John G. *Energy and the Federal Government: Fossil Fuel Policies, 1900–1946.* Urbana: University of Illinois Press, 1987.

Clarke, Jeanne Nienaber. *Roosevelt's Warrior: Harold L. Ickes and the New Deal.* Baltimore: Johns Hopkins University Press, 1996.

Coggins, George Cameron. "Wildlife and the Constitution: The Walls Come Tumbling Down." *Washington Law Review* 55 (1980): 295–358.

Coggins, George, Charles F. Wilkinson, and John D. Leshy, eds. *Federal Public Lands and Resources Law.* 3d ed. Mineola, N.Y.: Foundation Press, 1993.

Collins, Robert M. "David Potter's *People of Plenty* and the Recycling of Consensus History." *Reviews in American History* 16 (June 1988): 321–35.

Colson, Dennis C. *Idaho's Constitution: The Tie That Binds.* Moscow: University of Idaho Press, 1991.

Commission on Organization of the Executive Branch of the Government. *The Hoover Commission Report.* New York: McGraw-Hill, 1949.

"Company Tax Aid Lashed." *Public Power* 11 (October 1953): 24.

Cone, Joseph, and Sandy Ridlington, eds. *The Northwest Salmon Crisis: A Documentary History.* Corvallis: Oregon State University Press, 1996.

"Confident and Enterprising Spirit Features EEI Annual Meeting." *Public Utilities Fortnightly* 40 (3 July 1947): 44–45.

"Congress Holds Hearings on CVA." *Public Power* 7 (July 1949): 7.

Congressional Quarterly. *Congress and the Nation: A Review of Government and Politics in the Postwar Years, 1945–1964*. Washington, D.C.: Congressional Quarterly Service, 1966.

"Consumers' Power Stake." *Public Power* 10 (July 1952): 10–11.

Cooke, Morris Llewellyn. "The Three Shell Game in World Power." *Public Power* 7 (December 1949): 14.

Corette, J. E. "Have the Private Power Companies Any Future?" *Public Utilities Fortnightly* 50 (31 July 1952): 143–52.

"Court Approves License on Roanoke." *Public Power* 11 (April 1953): 17.

Coyle, David Cushman. *Conservation: An American Story of Conflict and Accomplishment*. New Brunswick, N.J.: Rutgers University Press, 1957.

"CVA Approved by Labor Federation." *Public Utilities Fortnightly* 42 (26 August 1948): 319–20.

deLuna, Phyllis Komarek. *Public versus Private Power during the Truman Administration: A Study of Fair Deal Liberalism*. New York: Peter Lang Publishing, 1997.

Dondero, George A. "Wanted: A New Federal Power Policy." *Public Utilities Fortnightly* 42 (9 September 1948): 333–42.

Drukman, Mason. *Wayne Morse: A Political Biography*. Portland: Oregon Historical Society Press, 1997.

"Edison Electric Institute Holds Annual Convention." *Public Utilities Fortnightly* 52 (2 July 1953): 49–50.

Egan, Timothy. *The Good Rain: Across Time and Terrain in the Pacific Northwest*. New York: Vintage Books, 1991.

Eisenhower, Dwight D. *The White House Years: Mandate for Change, 1953–1956*. Garden City, N.Y.: Doubleday and Co., 1963.

Electrical World. *The Electric Power Industry: Past, Present and Future*. 1st ed. New York: McGraw-Hill, 1949.

Ellis, Clyde T. *A Giant Step*. New York: Random House, 1966.

Ely, Owen. "Proposed Merger of Puget Sound–Washington Water Power," *Public Utilities Fortnightly* 51 (9 April 1953): 507–12.

England, Bayard L. "The Electric Light and Power Industry Looking Ahead." *Public Utilities Fortnightly* 50 (18 December 1952): 883–896.

Facts on File: 1953. New York: Facts on File, 1953.

Fahey, John. *The Inland Empire: Unfolding Years, 1879–1929*. Seattle: University of Washington Press, 1986.

"Federal Power and the 1952 Budget." *Public Utilities Fortnightly* 47 (7 June 1951): 802–3.

Fernlund, Kevin J., ed. *The Cold War American West, 1945–1989.* Albuquerque: University of New Mexico Press, 1998.

Ficken, Robert E. "Grand Coulee and Hanford: The Atomic Bomb and the Development of the Columbia River." In *The Atomic West,* edited by Bruce Hevly and John M. Findlay. Seattle: University of Washington Press, 1998.

Fiege, Mark. "Creating a Hybrid Landscape: Irrigated Agriculture in Idaho." In Goble and Hirt, *Northwest Lands, Northwest Peoples.*

———. *Irrigated Eden: The Making of an Agricultural Landscape in the American West.* Seattle: University of Washington Press, 2000.

"Field Hearings Planned." *Public Power* 7 (September 1949): 14.

Fones-Wolf, Elizabeth A. *Selling Free Enterprise: The Business Assault on Labor and Liberalism, 1945–1960.* Urbana: University of Illinois Press, 1994.

Fox, Stephen. *The American Conservation Movement: John Muir and His Legacy.* Madison: University of Wisconsin Press, 1981.

"FPC a Weather Vane?" *Public Utilities Fortnightly* 50 (20 November 1952): 789

"FPC Faces Far Reaching Decisions." *Public Power* 10 (December 1952): 20.

Gabrielson, Ira N. *Wildlife Management.* New York: McMillan Co., 1951.

Goble, Dale D., and Paul W. Hirt, eds. *Northwest Lands, Northwest Peoples: Readings in Environmental* History. Seattle: University of Washington Press, 1999.

Goldman, Eric F. *The Crucial Decade, 1945–1955.* New York: Knopf, 1956.

Gottlieb, Robert. *Forcing the Spring: The Transformation of the American Environmental Movement.* Washington, D.C.: Island Press, 1993.

"Government Officials to Speak." *Public Power* 9 (March 1950): 9.

Griffith, Robert. "Dwight D. Eisenhower and the Corporate Commonwealth." *American Historical Review* 87 (February 1982): 87–122.

———. "Forging America's Postwar Order: Domestic Politics and Political Economy in the Age of Truman." In Lacey, *The Truman Presidency.*

"Group Has First Meeting." *Public Power* 8 (February 1950): 7–8.

Gunther, John. *Inside U.S.A.* New York: Harper Bros., 1947.

Gurney, Chan. "Grass-Root Sentiment Does Not Favor an MVA." *Public Utilities Fortnightly* 40 (23 October 1947): 547–55.

Halberstam, David. *The Fifties.* New York: Villard Books, 1993.

Hamby, Alonzo L. *Beyond the New Deal: Harry S. Truman and American Liberalism.* New York: Columbia University Press, 1973.

———. *Harry S. Truman and the Fair Deal.* Lexington, Mass.: D.C. Heath and Co., 1974.

Hart, Arthur A. *Wings over Idaho: An Aviation History.* Boise: Historic Boise, Inc., 1991.

Harvey, Mark W. T. *A Symbol of Wilderness: Echo Park and the American Conservation Movement.* Albuquerque: University of New Mexico Press, 1994.

Hays, Samuel P. *Beauty, Health and Permanence: Environmental Politics in the United States, 1955–1985.* New York: Cambridge University Press, 1987.

"Hell's Canyon Dam: Pro and Con." *Public Utilities Fortnightly* 49 (8 May 1952): 645–46.

"Hells Canyon Battle Blazing." *Public Power* 11 (August 1953): 7.

"Hells Canyon Give-Away." *Public Power* 13 (October 1955): 23.

Hevly, Bruce, and John M. Findlay, eds. *The Atomic West.* Seattle: University of Washington Press, 1998.

Hirt, Paul. *A Conspiracy of Optimism: The United States Forest Service in the Inland Northwest, 1945–1975.* Lincoln: University of Nebraska Press, 1996.

"Hoover Commission Splits on Federal Power." *Public Power* 7 (May 1949): 23.

"Hoover Commission Urges Expansion." *Public Power* 7 (April 1949): 6.

Horowitz, Daniel. *Vance Packard and American Social Criticism.* Chapel Hill: University of North Carolina Press, 1994.

Humphrey, Tom. "The Northwest Power Puzzle." *Public Utilities Fortnightly* 43 (14 April 1949): 465–69.

Hurst, J. Willard. *Law and Economic Growth: The Legal History of the Lumber Industry in Wisconsin, 1836–1915.* Cambridge, Mass.: Belknap Press, 1964.

Hutmacher, J. Joseph, ed. *The Truman Years: The Reconstruction of Postwar America.* Hinsdale, Ill.: Dryden Press, 1972.

Information Please Almanac: 1991. Boston: Houghton Mifflin Co., 1991.

"Interior Dept. Appropriation." *Public Power* 6 (July 1948): 8.

"Interior's United Western Plan." *Public Utilities Fortnightly* 49 (3 January 1952): 54.

Jarrett, Henry, ed. *Perspectives on Conservation: Essays on America's Natural Resources.* Baltimore: Johns Hopkins University Press, 1958.

Knudson, Tom. "Looking at Dams in a New Way." *High Country News* 30 (2 February 1998): 1.

Krug, Julius A. "Benefits of Public Power." *Public Power* 7 (June 1949): 19–20, 28–29.

"Kuykendall Named." *Public Power* 11 (May 1953): 20.

Lacey, Michael J., ed., *The Truman Presidency.* Cambridge: Cambridge University Press, 1989.

Langston, Nancy. *Forest Dreams, Forest Nightmares: The Paradox of Old Growth in the Inland Northwest.* Seattle: University of Washington Press, 1995.

Larmer, Paul. "Unleashing the Snake." *High Country News* 31 (20 December 1999): 1.

Laythe, Leo L. "The Fishery Development Program in the Lower Columbia River." *Transactions of the American Fisheries Society* 78 (1948): 42–55.

Leffler, Ross L. "Program for Anadromous Fishes of the Columbia." In *The Northwest Salmon Crisis: A Documentary History*, edited by Joseph Cone and Sandy Ridlington. Corvallis: Oregon State University Press, 1996.

Leopold, Aldo. *Game Management.* New York: Chas. Scribner's Sons, 1933.

Leuchtenburg, William E. *Franklin D. Roosevelt and the New Deal: 1932–1940.* New York: Harper and Row, 1963.

———. *A Troubled Feast: American Society since 1945.* Updated ed. Boston: Little, Brown, 1983.

Limerick, Patricia Nelson. *The Legacy of Conquest: The Unbroken Past of the American West.* New York: W. W. Norton, 1987.

Limerick, Patricia Nelson, Clyde A. Milner II, and Charles E. Rankin, eds. *Trails: Toward a New Western History.* Lawrence: University Press of Kansas, 1991.

Lowitt, Richard. *The New Deal in the West.* Bloomington: Indiana University Press, 1984.

Lubell, Samuel. *The Future of American Politics.* Rev. 2d ed. Garden City, N.J.: Doubleday and Co., 1956.

Maas, Arthur. *Muddy Waters: The Army Engineers and the Nation's Rivers.* Cambridge, Mass.: Harvard University Press, 1951.

May, Lary, ed. *Recasting America: Culture and Politics in the Age of Cold War.* Chicago: University of Chicago Press, 1989.

McCullough, David. *Truman.* New York: Simon and Schuster, 1992.

McDonald, Forrest. *Insull.* Chicago: University of Chicago Press, 1962.

McEvoy, Arthur F. *The Fisherman's Problem: Ecology and Law in the California Fisheries, 1850–1980.* New York: Cambridge University Press, 1986.

McKay, Douglas. "Why Interior Dropped Hell's Canyon Project." *Public Utilities Fortnightly* 51 (4 June 1953): 734–39.

McKee, Paul B. "Power in the Pacific Northwest." *Public Utilities Fortnightly* 52 (27 August 1953): 291–97.

McKinley, Charles. *Uncle Sam in the Pacific Northwest: Federal Management of Natural Resources in the Columbia River Valley.* Berkeley: University of California Press, 1952.

McLaughlin, Frank. "It Is Not in the Cards." *Public Utilities Fortnightly* 39 (5 June 1947): 738–45.

————. "Pacific Northwest in the Big Squeeze of Big Government." *Public Utilities Fortnightly* 49 (22 May 1952): 663–75.

"The Meaning of the Preference Clause in Hydroelectric Power Allocation." *Environmental Law* 9 (1979): 601–19.

Meinig, D. W. *Great Columbia Plain: A Historical Geography, 1805–1910.* Seattle: University of Washington Press, 1968.

Meyerowitz, Joanne J., ed. *Not June Cleaver: Women and Gender in Postwar America, 1945–1960.* Philadelphia: Temple University Press, 1994.

"More Public Power for Private Utility Distribution?" *Public Utilities Fortnightly* 39 (10 April 1947): 511–12.

"Morse, Pfost Lash Power Company Plans." *Public Power* 11 (May 1953): 32.

"Move against the 'Preference Clause.'" *Public Utilities Fortnightly* 48 (22 November 1951): 725–26.

Mullendore, W. C. "National Defense for American Industry." *Public Utilities Fortnightly* 39 (5 June 1947): 757–65.

Nash, Gerald D. *The American West Transformed: The Impact of the Second World War.* Bloomington: Indiana University Press, 1985.

————. *World War II and the West: Reshaping the Economy.* Lincoln: University of Nebraska Press, 1990.

Netboy, Anthony. *The Columbia River Salmon and Steelhead Trout: Their Fight for Survival.* Seattle: University of Washington Press, 1980.

"New Commission Named." *Public Power* 8 (February 1950): 7.

"New Interior Power Policy Unveiled." *Public Power* 11 (September 1953): 11.

"New Officials Named." *Public Power* 11 (March 1953): 18.

"New Public Power Plans." *Public Utilities Fortnightly* 42 (2 December 1948): 808.

Nimz, Dale E. "Rivers That Work." PhD diss., University of Kansas, 2003.

"No New Starts." *Public Power* 12 (February 1954): 12.

Noble, Daniel B. "Why Not States' Rights for the Columbia Valley?" *Public Utilities Fortnightly* 43 (28 April 1949): 544–53.

"Northwest Meetings Highlight CVA." *Public Power* 7 (October 1949): 9.

"Northwest Posts Shifted." *Public Power* 12 (January 1954): 12.

"Northwest Power Pool: A Lesson in Democracy." *Public Power* 8 (November 1950): 14–16.

Norton, Boyd. *Snake Wilderness.* San Francisco: Sierra Club, 1972.

Norwood, Gus. "Bonneville Power for Southern Idaho," *Public Power* 8 (October 1950): 9.

"NRECA's Biggest Convention." *Public Power* 8 (April 1950): 13–14.

"NWPPA Discusses Power Shortage." *Public Power* 6 (September 1948): 4–5.

Nye, David. *Consuming Power: A Social History of American Energies.* Cambridge, Mass.: MIT Press, 1998.

———. *Electrifying America: Social Meanings of a New Technology, 1880–1940.* Cambridge, Mass.: MIT Press, 1990.

———. "Electrifying the West, 1880–1940." In *The American West, as Seen by Europeans and Americans,* edited by Rob Kroes. Amsterdam: Free University Press, 1989.

"Ore. Gov. McKay Heads Interior." *Public Power* 10 (December 1952): 10.

Palmer, Tim. *The Snake River: Window to the West.* Washington, D.C.: Island Press, 1991.

Patterson, James T. *Grand Expectations: The United States, 1945–1974.* New York: Oxford University Press, 1996.

Petersen, Keith. *River of Life/Channel of Death.* Lewiston, Idaho: Confluence Press, 1995.

Pisani, Donald. "Water Law and Localism in the West." *Halcyon* 14 (1992): 36–55.

Pitzer, Paul C. *Grand Coulee: Harnessing a Dream.* Pullman: Washington State University Press, 1994.

Potts, Ernest Clifford. "Some Adverse Effects of a Federal Power Monopoly." *Public Utilities Fortnightly* 40 (18 December 1947): 811–17.

"The Power Issue—Up or Down." *Public Utilities Fortnightly* 50 (31 July 1952): 172.

"Power Planks." *Public Utilities Fortnightly* 50 (11 September 1952): 367–68.

"Power Plans Denounced." *Public Utilities Fortnightly* 44 (10 November 1949): 651.

"Power Publications." *Public Power* 10 (September 1952): 5.

"President Dedicates Grand Coulee." *Public Power* 8 (June 1950): 12.

"Public Systems Pay More Taxes." *Public Power* 6 (November 1948): 21.

Radin, Alex. "More Power for the People." *Public Power* 10 (May 1952): 16–22.

"Record Crowd at APPA Convention." *Public Power* 8 (April 1950): 10–11.

"Regional Power Agency." *Public Power* 11 (January 1953): 10.

Reich, Peter L. "Studies in Western Water Law: Historiographical Trends." *Western Legal History* 9 (1996): 1–7.

Reichard, Gary W. *Republicanism Reaffirmed: Eisenhower and the Eighty-third Congress.* Knoxville: University of Tennessee Press, 1975.

Reisner, Marc. *Cadillac Desert: The American West and Its Disappearing Water.* New York: Penguin, 1986.

Resources for the Future. *The Nation Looks at Its Resources: Report of the Mid-Century Conference on Resources for the Future.* Washington, D.C.: Resources for the Future, 1954.

"Retiring President Addresses EEI Meeting." *Public Utilities Fortnightly* 41 (17 June 1948): 874–77.

Richardson, Elmo. *Dams, Parks and Politics: Resource Development and Preservation in the Truman-Eisenhower Era.* Lexington: University Press of Kentucky, 1973.

———. *The Presidency of Dwight D. Eisenhower.* Lawrence: Regents Press of Kansas, 1979.

Robbins, William G. *Landscapes of Promise: The Oregon Story, 1800–1940.* Seattle: University of Washington Press, 1997.

Ross, Ron. "Hells Canyon Decision Faces Congress." *Public Power* 14 (January 1956): 7–10.

Rothman, Hal K. *The Greening of a Nation? Environmentalism in the United States since 1945.* Fort Worth, Tex.: Harcourt Brace, 1998.

Schwantes, Carlos A. *In Mountain Shadows: A History of Idaho.* Lincoln: University of Nebraska Press, 1991.

———. *The Pacific Northwest: An Interpretive History.* Lincoln: University of Nebraska Press, 1989.

Schwartz, Charles P. Jr. "Federalism and Anadromous Fish: *FPC v. Oregon.*" *George Washington Law Review* 23 (1955): 535–47.

———. "*Niagara Mohawk v. FPC*: Have Private Water Rights Been Destroyed by the Federal Power Act?" *University of Pennsylvania Law Review* 102 (1953): 31–79.

"Secretary McKay Discusses Power Policies." *Public Power* 11 (June 1953): 16.

"Senate Kills Columbia Basin Plan." *Public Power* 8 (May 1950): 7.

"Senate Turns Down Olds." *Public Power* 7 (November 1949): 9.

Shallat, Todd, ed. *Snake: The Plain and Its People.* Boise, Idaho: Boise State University, 1994.

Smith, Arthur Robert. *The Tiger in the Senate: The Biography of Wayne Morse.* Garden City, N.Y.: Doubleday and Co., 1962.

Smith, Nelson Lee. "Wanted: A National Power Program." *Public Utilities Fortnightly* 39 (5 June 1947): 732–37.

Smylie, Robert E. *Governor Smylie Remembers.* Moscow: University of Idaho Press, 1998.

Stacy, Susan M. *Legacy of Light: A History of Idaho Power Company.* Boise: Idaho Power Co., 1991.

———. *When the River Rises: Flood Control on the Boise River, 1943–1985.* Boulder: University of Colorado Institute of Behavioral Sciences, 1993.

Stapilus, Randy. *Paradox Politics: People and Power in Idaho*. Boise, Idaho: Ridenbaugh Press, 1988.

"State Background for Federal Commissions." *Public Utilities Fortnightly* 51 (7 May 1953): 626.

"Stockman Urges Program." *Public Power* 6 (May 1948): 11.

Sugrue, Thomas J. "Reassessing the History of Postwar America," *Prospects* 20 (1995): 493–510.

Tatham, Charles Jr. "The Great Public Power Myth." *Public Utilities Fortnightly* 48 (11 October 1951): 486–91.

Taylor, Joseph E., III. "Burning the Candle at Both Ends: Historicizing Overfishing in Oregon's Nineteenth-Century Salmon Fisheries." *Environmental History* 4 (January 1999): 54–79.

———. *Making Salmon: An Environmental History of the Northwest Fisheries Crisis*. Seattle: University of Washington Press, 2000.

Thorson, John E. *River of Promise, River of Peril: The Politics of Managing the Missouri River*. Lawrence: University Press of Kansas, 1994.

"Tragedy of No New Starts." *Public Power* 12 (February 1954): 20.

Trippensee, Reuben Edward. *Wildlife Management: Upland Game and General Principles*. Vol. 1. New York: McGraw-Hill, 1948.

"Truman Budget Asks More Power Funds." *Public Power* 11 (February 1953): 12.

"Truman Mans Reclamation Pumps." *Public Utilities Fortnightly* 42 (1 July 1948): 37–38.

"Tudor Plans to Leave Interior." *Public Power* 12 (May 1954): 11.

"Tudor Will Speak." *Public Power* 12 (March 1954): 5.

"Undersecretary." *Public Power* 12 (August 1954): 7.

Van Dusen, George. "Politics of 'Partnership': The Eisenhower Administration and Conservation, 1952–60." PhD diss., Loyola University, 1974.

"Washington and the Utilities." *Public Utilities Fortnightly* 43 (3 March 1949): 303–4.

"Water-Power Development by Public Urged." *Public Power* 6 (May 1948): 8.

Watkins, T. H. *Righteous Pilgrim: The Life and Times of Harold L. Ickes, 1874–1952*. New York: Henry Holt and Co., 1990.

Welch, Francis X. "Inside John Gunther," *Public Utilities Fortnightly* 40 (31 July 1947): 179–81.

Wells, Merle W., and Arthur Hart. *Idaho: Gem of the Mountains*. Northridge, Calif.: Windsor Publications, 1985.

"What Others Think." *Public Utilities Fortnightly* 48 (30 August 1951): 315.

White, Gilbert F. "Broader Bases for Choice: The Next Key Move." In *Perspectives on Conservation: Essays on America's Natural Resources,* edited by Henry Jarrett. Baltimore: Johns Hopkins University Press, 1958.

White, Richard. *"It's Your Misfortune and None of My Own:" A New History of the American West*. Norman: University of Oklahoma Press, 1991.

———. *The Organic Machine: The Remaking of the Columbia River*. New York: Hill and Wang, 1995.

"Wild-Life Opposition to Present Water Planning." *Public Utilities Fortnightly* 47 (10 May 1951): 645.

Wilkinson, Charles F. *Crossing the Next Meridian: Land, Water, and the Future of the West*. Washington, D.C.: Island Press, 1992.

Wilkinson, Charles F., and Daniel Keith Conner. "The Law of the Pacific Salmon Fishery: Conservation and Allocation of a Transboundary Common Property Resource." *Kansas Law Review* 32 (1983): 17–109.

Wollner, Craig. *Electrifying Eden: Portland General Electric, 1889–1965*. Portland: Oregon Historical Society Press, 1990.

Worster, Donald E. *Dust Bowl: The Southern Plains in the 1930s*. New York: Oxford University Press, 1979.

———. "Freedom and Want: The Western Paradox of Aridity." *Halcyon* 14 (1992): 17–35.

———. *Rivers of Empire: Water, Aridity and the Growth of the American West*. New York: Pantheon Press, 1985.

INDEX

Ada County Fish and Game League, 173
Administrative Procedure Act (1946), 220, 221
agriculture. *See* irrigation
Agriculture Department (U.S.), 29, 42, 43, 105, 187, 190
aluminum industry (Columbia Basin), 48, 58, 143
American Bankers Association, 120
American Fisheries Society, 109
American Public Power Association: Eisenhower administration's courting of, 93; High Dam supported by, 75, 119; membership in, 152; national allies of, 63; New Deal politics of, 222. *See also* public power
anadromous fish. *See* fish, anadromous
Angell, Homer, 61
Army Corps of Engineers: fish impacts caused by, 85, 91–96, 98–99, 100–106, 108, 111–12; Hells Canyon controversy provoked by, xii, 8–9, 39–40, 87, 156–58, 211; High Dam proposed by, 17, 24–25, 46–47, 53, 55, 57–59, 190; Idaho Power Company dams endorsed by, 187, 201, 204, 208–9; legal authorities of, 41–43, 76–79,

91–92, 151; Main Control Plan of, 64–65; and rivalry with Reclamation Bureau, 58–59, 61–65, 67–69, 72–75, 145. *See also* CBIAC; Federal Columbia River Power System; Weaver, Theron D.; Weaver-Newell Accord
Astoria (Oregon), 24, 60, 95, 135; and testimonies in "fish versus dams" hearing, 99–101

Baker (Oregon), 57, 58, 142, 143, 156, 182, 199, 205; FPC Hells Canyon hearing in, 167, 169, 171, 172–73
Barber, Lawrence, 100
Barnaby, J. T., 94, 96
Bell, Frank, 104
Bell, Roscoe E., 209
Bessey, Roy F., 191, 207; CBIAC work of, 57–58; Korean War and, 146–47; LCRFDP devised by, 96–99, 102–6
Big John Whiz, 100
Billington, Ken, 170
Bliss Dam, 163
Blue Mountains (Oregon), 32
Boise (Idaho), 12, 13, 14, 30, 31, 104, 167, 171, 198, 199, 202; Army Corps of Engineers 1949 hearings in, 67, 68;

Costello, William J., 190, 197, 211, 213; and FPC public hearings, 167–73; and Hells Canyon licensing hearing, 199–210; Idaho Power dam license decision by, 214–16; public power analysis by, 33–34

Coulee Dam. *See* Grand Coulee Dam

courts: and broadening of "public interest," 215, 218–19, 221, 222, 225; and consensus for dams upset by, 219–20, 220–21; and judicial review of agency action, 214–15, 219–20

Cowlitz River, 114

Coyle, Arthur Cushman, 151

Crandall, Lynn, 53, 208

Crookham, George, 160

Dalles, The, 99, 101, 104, 211

Davidson, C. Girard (Jebby): as advocate of CVA, 67, 70–72, 74–75; Hells Canyon licensing case handled by, 197, 199–201, 204–5, 206–7, 209–11; High Dam lobbying by, 149–50, 182; public-power philosophy of, 47, 80, 97, 196

Davidson, Clayton, 71, 173

Day, Albert M., 108–9, 110, 112–13, 114, 116

Defense Electric Power Agency, 146, 148, 150

Defense Mobilization, U. S. Office of, 34

Deschutes River, 114

Dondero, George A., 132

Duvall, Ralph, 152

Dworshak, Henry C., 149

Eaton, Orval, 101

Echo Canyon controversy, x, xi, 5–6, 19

Edison Electric Institute, 63, 120–21, 123, 125, 132, 185

Eisenhower, Dwight: conservative allies of, 176, 181, 197–98; and criticism of New Deal, xiii, 176, 181; and Interior Department, 183, 188–90, 217–18; and 1952 presidential campaign, 4–6, 150, 174, 176–82; "partnership policy" of, 177–78, 186–87; and postwar politics, 4–6, 182–83; public-power expansion opposed by, 42, 177, 183–85, 209–11

Ellis, Clyde T., 75, 151, 152–53, 154, 209

England, Bayard L., 125, 185

Entiat River, 85

Eugene (Oregon), 42

Fair Deal: High Hells Canyon as symbol of, 140–41, 144–45, 150, 159, 168, 174; and public-power expansion, 124, 144, 148, 154, 163–64, 177, 179–80, 188; and water projects, 67, 153, 181, 210–11. *See also* New Deal; Truman, Harry S.

Farewell Bend, 24

Federal Columbia River Power System: expansion strategy, 10, 19–21, 46–47, 49, 61, 74–75, 95, 98, 219, 224; member agencies, 9, 40, 90, 163

Federal Inter-Agency River Basin Committee, 42–43, 108

Federal Power Act (1935): and fish protection, 84; FPC Hells Canyon licensing under, 195, 199, 210; and "public interest" standard, 162, 166–67, 214–15

Federal Power Commission (FPC), 29, 33, 43, 105, 140; fish conservation

steps, 15, 84, 211–14, 217–19; handling
of Hells Canyon licensing case, 5, 13,
16, 18, 55–57, 150, 162–74, 182, 183–95,
197–214; judicial review of decisions
by, 214–16, 220–21; legal authority
for, 42, 84, 199; relations with Eisenhower, 177, 183–87, 184–90; relations
with Truman, 131–32, 154–55, 183.
See also Hells Canyon Complex
Federal Water Power Act (1920), 84, 221
Field and Stream, 173
Filer (Idaho), 70, 148
Finley, States R., 152
fish, anadromous, 6, 71; commercial
catch of, 92, 94–95, 98–103, 107, 111,
134–36, 219; federal management
over, 3–4, 42, 81, 85–86, 88–90, 91–
92, 96–98, 106–17, 212–13, 217–19,
223–24; and "fish versus dams" hearing, 98–105; Grand Coulee Dam's
impact on, 81–91; hatcheries for, 81,
85, 88, 90–92, 95, 102, 107–8, 111, 113,
115–17, 165, 212; Hells Canyon dams'
impact on, xv, xxi, 7, 15–19, 37, 65,
106–10, 147, 164–66, 172–73, 190–
91, 211–14; Native Americans and,
xvii–xviii, 15, 36, 90, 100, 107, 136,
220; public power's impacts on, 10,
17–19, 93–95, 107–8, 117, 134–37, 141,
199, 219, 221–25; state agencies' regulation of, 15–16, 82–83, 86–87, 98,
110–17, 165–66, 190–91, 211–12, 220.
See also salmon; steelhead trout
Fish and Wildlife Coordination Act
(1934 and 1946), 84, 91, 94, 97
Fish and Wildlife Service (U.S.), 135,
137, 190–91, 212–13, 217; Columbia
River conservation strategy of, 106,

108–9, 110–15; and "fish versus
dams" hearing, 97, 99, 116–17;
study of dams' ecological effects,
84, 94, 96, 102, 110–11. *See also* fish,
anadromous; "fish versus dams"
hearing; Pacific Northwest Field
Committee, Interior Department
Fish Commission of Oregon (FCO),
111, 113, 114, 165, 212; and Grand
Coulee Dam, 81–83, 87, 89–90; and
Hells Canyon dams, 15, 103–4, 117,
211, 213; and Lower Columbia River
Fishery Development Program,
105–7; postwar fish-conservation
policy of, 93–94, 98, 101–2; and state
regulation of anadromous fish, 83,
89, 91–92, 95, 223. *See also* fish,
anadromous; "fish versus dams"
hearing; Suomela, Arnie; J. Veatch,
John C.
Fisheries Bureau (U.S.), 85, 87, 88, 89.
See also Grand Coulee Dam
Fisherman's Cooperative Association,
219
fishing industry. *See* fish, anadromous
"fish versus dams" hearing (1947), 95–
105, 113–17, 136–38. *See also* CBIAC;
fish, anadromous; Pacific Northwest
Field Committee, Interior Department; Walla Walla
Flathead River, 128
Fleming, Lewis, 62
Flood Control Act (1944), 41–42, 73,
151

Glasby, John, 157, 168, 172, 182
Goslin, Ival, 164
Graham's Landing, 24

Grand Coulee Dam: fish migration blocked by, 15, 83–84, 94, 101–2, 136–37, 213; Hells Canyon High Dam compared to, 12–13, 18, 48–49, 111, 156, 165, 173, 211; New Deal symbolism of, ix, 16, 32, 39–40, 81, 134, 143–44; Northwest fish policy revolutionized by, 4, 81–91, 106–9, 112–13, 117; public-power significance of, 9–10, 31–34, 42, 95, 100, 120–21, 131, 211; Roosevelt and, 83, 140, 143; Truman and, 93, 140, 143–44

Grande Ronde River, 218

granges, 51–52, 73, 104, 168, 196, 209

Great Basin, 23

Great Depression, 127–28; and fish, 85, 87, 90–91, 109, 117; in the Northwest, 10, 12, 22, 30–31, 60, 109, 117, 158, 170; and public power, 45, 81, 224; and Roosevelt's New Deal, 82, 127–28

Great Falls (Montana), 42, 199

Gurney, "Chan," 112, 129–30, 134, 137–38

Hays, Samuel, 21

Hells Canyon (Snake River): geographic significance of, 3, 4, 11, 23–26, 32, 35, 37; location of, ii, ix, xv, xix, 23–24; and name's origin, 47. *See also* Snake River

Hells Canyon Complex (Idaho Power Company): Brownlee Dam of, xv, 17, 185–87, 194, 214; fish impacts of, 15, 165–66, 173; FPC license granted for, 55–56, 162–63, 174, 183, 185–87, 214; hydroelectric production by, 187; Low Hells Canyon Dam of, 185, 214; Oxbow Dam of, 15, 55, 56, 162–

63, 167–68, 170, 172, 175, 180, 182, 185–87, 195, 197, 202

Hells Canyon High Dam: conservative postwar critique of, 118–39; and controversy's impact on postwar Northwest, 3–20; Eisenhower's opposition to, 176–96; federal-state postwar fish policy shaped by, 98–117, 218–22; FPC and federal courts block building of, 197–216; historic significance of, ix–xiii, 222–25; Idaho Power Company's bid to block, 140–75; New Deal heritage of, 39–59; Truman's initial push to build, 60–80; and unexpected decision not to build, xix–xxi, 214–16

Hells Canyon High Dam controversy: and cold war political dissent, 19, 20, 22, 47, 150, 164, 166, 177, 182, 217–25; environmental significance of, 17, 20, 25–26, 37, 117, 138, 208–9, 211, 217–25; and federal upriver power expansion causes, 32, 37–38, 42–43, 60–80, 140–42, 147, 191–92, 209–11; legal consensus for new dams destabilized by, 22, 40, 52, 142, 201, 217–25; private power's role in, 19, 44, 59, 66–69, 118–19, 133, 141–42, 153–54, 156, 207; "public interest" in water at stake in, 18, 54, 158–59, 162, 169–74, 186–87, 197, 199–200, 215, 217–25; public power supporters' role in, 33–34, 39, 75–79, 122, 124, 145, 153–54

Hells Canyon Low Dam. *See* Hells Canyon Complex

Hemingway, Ernest, 71, 173

Herblock (Herbert Block), 69

High Dam. *See* Hells Canyon High Dam

High Hells Canyon Dam. *See* Hells Canyon High Dam

High Mountain Sheep Dam, 221

Hill, Lister, 75

Hillcrest and Long Tom Divisions (Snake Basin Plan), 50

Hirt, Paul, 133

Hoover, Herbert, 67

Hoover Commission on the Organization of the Executive Branch of the Government, 67, 72, 74, 77, 127

Hoy, M. T. (Mike), 83

Hudson, G. T., 105

Humphrey, Tom, 103, 127, 130–31

Hungry Horse Dam (Montana), 100, 128. *See also* Reclamation Bureau

Hurst, J. Willard, 133

Ickes, Harold, 47, 57; and Grand Coulee Dam, 81–84, 86–91, 106, 108, 112–13, 117; as Interior secretary, 16, 53, 98; public-power advocacy by, 44, 51, 156, 215

Idaho Daily Statesman, 71, 72, 73, 181, 203

Idaho Department of Fish and Game: assessment of Hells Canyon dams, 90, 165–66, 191, 211, 213; fish conservation position, 103, 110, 223. *See also* Murray, T. B.

Idaho Falls (Idaho), 52, 67

Idaho Fish and Game Commission, 102, 110

Idaho Power Company, ii; BPA expansion resisted by, 24–25, 33–35, 56–57, 59, 68–69, 118–19, 133, 174, 218, 219; and Eisenhower administration, xiii,

177, 192; fish impacts of dams by, 15–16, 17, 36–37, 117, 211–14, 220, 223; and FPC licensing case, xxi, 18, 162–63, 166–67, 169, 196, 198–216, 222; irrigation enabled by, 24–26, 28–29, 31, 52–55, 69–70, 158, 203–4; and opposition to High Dam, x, 4–6, 7, 8, 56–59, 80, 141–42, 221–22; and plan for Hells Canyon Low Dam, xvi, xviii–xix, 16–18, 55–57, 214–16, 224–25; political influence of, xviii, 52–54, 180. *See also* Hells Canyon Complex; Parry, R. P; private power; Roach, Thomas E.

Idaho State Chamber of Commerce, 53, 160

Idaho State Reclamation Association: Columbia Valley Administration, opposition to, 68, 71; High Dam, opposition to, 160, 172; Snake Basin Plan, opposition to, 52–54, 157–58

Idaho Wildlife Federation, 219

Imnaha River, 218

Indians. *See individual tribe names;* Native Americans

Inland Navigation Company, 104

Inland Waterways Association, 104

Inman, A. C. (Art): FPC High Dam license hearing, advocacy before, 159, 162–63, 185, 186, 188, 190; High Dam, opposition to, 8, 68–69, 141, 158, 169; as Idaho Power general counsel, 55, 150, 182, 195

In re Idaho Power Company, 199–216

Inside the U.S.A. (Gunther), 131

Insull, Samuel, 121

Interior Committee, Senate (U.S.), 188, 190

Lockwood, C. E., 93

Loos, Karl, 190

Lower Columbia River Fishery Development Program (LCRFDP), 91, 106, 109, 117, 165. *See also* CBIAC; fish, anadromous; "fish versus dams" hearing; Pacific Northwest Field Committee, Interior Department

Maas, Arthur, 46–47

Magnuson, Warren, 70, 189, 206–7; High Dam endorsed by, 16, 78–79, 180, 193

Main Control Plan, 64–65

Makah Indian Tribe, 219

Malheur River, 26

McEvoy, Arthur F., 133

McKay, Douglas, 6, 182; High Dam opposed by, 191–93, 197–98, 200–201; Idaho Power Company supported by, 69, 166, 190, 195–96, 212; as Interior secretary, 184–85, 187–89, 210, 217; public-power expansion opposed by, 69, 119, 148, 193–94, 202, 215

McKinley, Charles, 46–47, 209

McLaughlin, Frank, 55, 122–23

McNary Dam: construction of, 32, 73, 90, 111; fish, impact on, 90–91, 93–95, 98–99, 106–7, 109, 112, 114, 135, 137, 220; postwar significance of, 63, 98–99, 104, 211

Merchant Marine Committee, House of Representatives (U.S.), 86

Methow River, 85

migratory fish. *See* fish, anadromous

Miller, William J., 131

minerals industry. *See* phosphate fertilizer

Minidoka Relocation Center, 31. *See also* World War II

Missouri Basin, 124, 129, 137, 142

Mitchell Act (1938), 85–86, 87. *See also* fish, anadromous; Grand Coulee Dam

Mitchell, Hugh C., 70, 83

Molalla River, 114

Montana Power Company, 128

Moore, Carl, 74

Moore, Milo C., 103, 108, 110, 112, 115

Morris, Samuel, 75–76, 77, 152, 154

Morrison, Harry, 164, 190

Morse, Wayne, 6, 119–20, 130–31, 184–85, 193, 206–7

Mott, James, 86

Mountain Home (Idaho), 30, 156, 182, 195

Mountain Home Desert (Idaho), xvi, 13, 49, 50, 73, 76, 78, 174, 216. *See also* Snake Basin Plan

Mountain Home Project. *See* Snake Basin Plan

Mullendore, W. C., 125–26, 131

Murie, Olaus, 135

Murphy, Earl W., 160

Murray, T. B. (Tom): fish policy direction ceded to irrigators by, 110; as Idaho Fish and Game director, 102, 211; impact of dams on fish assessed by, 16, 102–3, 165–66, 191, 211

Nampa (Idaho), 173, 180

National Association of Electric Companies, 73, 121, 155–56. *See also* Idaho Power Company; private power

National Association of Manufacturers, 73, 120

Roosevelt, Eleanor, 63, 154–55

Roosevelt, Franklin D.: and New Deal, xiii, 67, 79, 83–84, 144, 154, 174, 182; and public power, 16, 33, 143, 176–77, 179, 215; Truman's emulation of, 66, 78, 80, 140. *See also* Bonneville Dam; Grand Coulee Dam; New Deal; public power; Truman, Harry S.

Royall, Kenneth, 62, 72–73

Rural Electrification Act, 151. *See also* public power

Rural Electrification Administration, 150–51, 154. *See also* Cooke, Morris; public power

Salem (Oregon), 70, 74, 184

salmon, xix, 4, 7, 10, 26, 86–87, 88, 92, 95, 96, 99, 134, 147, 172, 191, 220; biological qualities of, 23, 36–37, 81–83, 135–36, 173, 217–18, 223; chinook, 17, 36–37, 82–83, 88, 90–91, 101–3, 107, 109, 115, 218; chum, 82; dam passageways for, xvii, xxi, 14–17, 84–85, 93–94, 135–38, 164–65, 223; Lower Columbia River Program for, 90–91, 98, 105–17; Salmon River spawning of, 36–37, 102–3, 106–7, 211–12; silver, 115; sockeye (blueback), 82, 91, 102, 109, 115. *See also* fish, anadromous; steelhead trout

Salmon Basin, 17, 103, 211. *See also* Salmon River

The Salmon Crisis, 108

Salmon River, 7, 173; dams proposed for, 17, 36–37, 204, 224; fish dependent on, 3, 36–37, 103, 106–7, 109, 114, 218; flooding linked to, 17–18, 27

Salt Lake City (Utah), 27

Sammis, Walter H., 125

Sandoz, T. F. (Tom), 95, 98, 100, 101, 111–12, 219

Sandpoint (Idaho), 120, 142

Seaton, Fred A., 217–18

Selway River, 59

Seven Devils Mountains (Idaho): fish habitat influenced by, 35–37; Hells Canyon eastern wall formed by, xv, 23–24, 26, 32

Sharp, N. V. (Nick), 70–71, 148, 160

Simplot, Jack, 164

Snake Basin (Idaho), 5, 10, 21, 38, 60, 73, 95, 127, 128, 183, 225; and fish, 15–17, 35–37, 65, 81, 86–87, 90, 97–98, 101–11, 113, 117, 135–36, 164–66, 172–73, 190–91, 211–13, 218–20; FPC license hearings in, 167–72; irrigation in, 3, 13–14, 24–29, 49–50, 52–54, 69–70, 148, 157–62, 182, 195, 197–98; private power dominant in, 18–19, 29–30, 31, 35, 55–57, 68, 93, 124, 133–34, 138, 163–64, 174–75, 222–24; public-power expansion toward, 4, 8–9, 11–12, 22, 24, 32, 39–59, 63, 66, 76, 79, 119–20, 140–43, 146, 193, 202–3, 215, 222–24. *See also* Hells Canyon; Snake Basin Plan; Snake River

Snake Basin Plan: High Dam essential to, 48, 64, 69, 73, 79, 140, 143, 145–46, 157, 163, 172, 180, 192–93, 204; irrigated agriculture to be expanded by, 48–51, 58, 76, 141, 155, 161, 167–69, 174, 197, 215–16; Mountain Home Desert covered by, xvi, 13, 49–50, 73, 76, 78, 174, 216; phosphate fertilizer to be mined in, 12–13, 48, 51–52, 71–72, 143, 153, 180, 187, 209, 224; Senate

Teton Mountains, 27, 52

Thompson, Tommy (Wy-Um chief), 100. *See also* Native Americans

Torbert, E. N., 50

Trueblood, Ted, 173

Truman, Harry S.: and Columbia Valley Administration, 68–80, 124, 130; High Dam endorsed by, 61, 63–64, 74–77, 119, 140, 142–45, 149–50, 156–57, 159, 164, 174–75, 187, 201, 207–10; and New Deal public-power policy, 16, 77–80, 119, 122, 124, 140–45, 150, 152–56, 159, 162, 174–75, 196, 222; Northwest hydroelectric agencies prevail over, 63–66, 67–68, 72–73; postwar political campaigns, 64–66, 121, 132, 149, 166, 176–84; public-power expansion sought by, 47, 57, 93, 112, 116, 128, 135, 142–45, 146, 196, 215, 217; and Vanport flooding, 62–63, 70; Water Resources Policy Commission created by, 159–60, 163–64

Twin Falls (Idaho), 31, 143, 148, 157, 161, 188, 210

Udall v. Federal Power Commission, 221

Ullman, Albert C., 169, 182

Umatilla (Oregon), 60, 93

Umatilla Indians, 100

Umatilla River, 32

Union Pacific Railroad, 57, 143, 171

University of Idaho, 29, 52

urbanization: in Columbia Basin, 31–34, 41–42; fueled by low-cost electricity, xvi–xvii, 121, 215, 214–27; in Snake Basin, 35, 44, 48

Vancouver (Washington), 60

Vanport (Oregon): 1948 flood, 35, 60, 65, 189; as symbol of Truman's push for High Dam, 61–64, 70. *See also* Columbia River; Portland; Truman, Harry S.; World War II

Veatch, John C.: as chair of Fish Commission of Oregon, 81–82; and criticism of Grand Coulee impact on fish, 82–83, 86–89; Hells Canyon dams assessed by, 15–16, 111, 165, 212; postwar Northwest fish policy affected by, 98, 108, 113–14

Wallace (Idaho), 146

Wallace, Henry, 131, 148. *See also* Progressive Party

Wallace Miner, 69–70

Walla Walla (Washington), "fish versus dams" hearing in, 96–107, 108, 110, 113, 114, 116, 136

Wallowa Mountains, 32

Wallula (Washington), 24

Walsh, O. E., 58

Ward, J. Frank, 152

Warne, William, 97

Washington Department of Fisheries: and Grand Coulee Dam, 84, 85; and Lower Columbia River Fishery Development Program, 90, 103, 108, 115; and Snake Basin fish, 115, 165, 212, 223. *See also* fish, anadromous; Columbia River; Idaho Department of Fish and Game; Oregon Fish Commission

Washington Post, 69

Washington Sportsmen's Council, 100, 219

Washington Water Power Company, 120. *See also* Idaho Power Company; private power; Robinson, Kinsey M.

Water Resources Policy Commission (WRPC), 77, 152, 154, 155; planning and plans, 160–64. *See also* Cooke, Morris; Truman, Harry S.

Weaver, Theron D.: Army Corps of Engineers North Pacific Division led by, 43, 62; CBIAC chaired by, 43, 95–96, 99–100, 103–5; High Dam proposal directed by, 58, 64, 65, 75. *See also* Army Corps of Engineers; "fish versus dams" hearing; Newell, R. J.; Weaver-Newell Accord

Weaver-Newell Accord, 133–34; Army Corps of Engineers-Reclamation Bureau rivalry over High Dam resolved by, 64, 67, 73–74, 210; CVA impeded by, 76, 78–80. *See also* Army Corps of Engineers; CBIAC; Newell, R. J.; Reclamation Bureau; Weaver, Theron D.

Weiser (Idaho), 26–27, 156, 157, 158, 173

Weiser River, 16, 26, 59

Welch, Francis X., 131, 132, 185

Welker, Herman E., 149

Welsh, William, 68, 71

Welteroth, Charles, 148, 160, 172

Wenatchee River, 85

West, Herbert G., 104

Western Governors' Conference, 61

Wetherell, R. M. (Bob), 157

White, Gilbert, 155

White, Richard, 20

White Bird (Idaho), 36

Wickard, Claude, 151

Willamette Valley, 35, 44, 55, 184

Wing, Lesher S., 43, 105

World War II, xvii, 21, 22, 23; and economic change in the Northwest, xix, 4, 10, 25, 30–31, 37, 215, 224; hydroelectricity crucial to waging, 37, 39–40, 45, 62, 121, 156; Japanese Americans interned during, 31; population movements in Northwest during, 30–32, 60; public-power upriver expansion after, 63, 81, 90–91, 93, 120; and weapons production in the Northwest, 32, 34–35. *See also* Army Corps of Engineers; Bonneville Power Administration; irrigation; Northwest Power Pool; Vanport

Worster, Donald, 20, 28, 133

Wy-Um Indians, 100

Yakima Indians, 100

Yost, Harry, 160, 164

On the Road Again: Montana's Changing Landscape
by William Wyckoff

*Public Power, Private Dams: The Hells Canyon
High Dam Controversy* by Karl Boyd Brooks

WEYERHAEUSER ENVIRONMENTAL CLASSICS

*The Great Columbia Plain: A Historical Geography,
1805–1910* by D. W. Meinig

*Mountain Gloom and Mountain Glory: The
Development of the Aesthetics of the Infinite*
by Marjorie Hope Nicolson

Tutira: The Story of a New Zealand Sheep Station
by H. Guthrie-Smith

*A Symbol of Wilderness: Echo Park and the American
Conservation Movement* by Mark W. T. Harvey

*Man and Nature: Or, Physical Geography as Modified
by Human Action* by George Perkins Marsh; edited and
annotated by David Lowenthal

Conservation in the Progressive Era: Classic Texts
edited by David Stradling

CYCLE OF FIRE BY STEPHEN J. PYNE

Fire: A Brief History

World Fire: The Culture of Fire on Earth

*Vestal Fire: An Environmental History, Told through Fire,
of Europe and Europe's Encounter with the World*

*Fire in America: A Cultural History of Wildland
and Rural Fire*

Burning Bush: A Fire History of Australia

The Ice: A Journey to Antarctica